Acclaim for an extraordinary book:

"This is no glib, glossy pop psychology book. . . . It is a well-researched guidebook which gives specific and sympathetic advice on what to do if your husband dies or leaves you for a younger woman, how to handle sex, money and retirement, what to do about loneliness, health care, grown children and aged parents, and where to go for help. . . . Thanks for a good practical book, Adele Nudel. We needed that."

The Philadelphia Bulletin

"One hardly thinks of a book about women over 50 as being the kind one can't put down, but Mrs. Nudel has written such a book. It combines a wealth of information with a delightful style. . . . I recommend this book not only for every woman over 50 but for every woman who will be 50, and for every man who knows or will know a woman over 50."

Selma Gross, Executive Director,
Baltimore Commission on Aging and Retirement

"The author genuinely understands and *cares* about her intended readers. Understands so well that she has managed to consider every possible area of question, doubt, or concern. And cares enough to have gathered in highly readable form an invaluable array of information, insights, guidelines, and resource facts."

Leonard M. Rothstein, Instructor of Psychiatry,
Johns Hopkins S̶c̶h̶o̶o̶l̶ ̶o̶f̶ ̶M̶e̶d̶i̶c̶i̶n̶e̶

D0771423

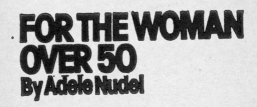

FOR THE WOMAN OVER 50
By Adele Nudel

 AVON
PUBLISHERS OF BARD, CAMELOT AND DISCUS BOOKS

AVON BOOKS
A division of
The Hearst Corporation
959 Eighth Avenue
New York, New York 10019

A hardcover edition was previously published
by Taplinger Publishing Co., Inc.

First Avon Printing, June, 1979

AVON TRADEMARK REG. U.S. PAT. OFF. AND IN
OTHER COUNTRIES, MARCA REGISTRADA, HECHO EN
U.S.A.

Printed in the U.S.A.

To my family:
my husband, David Nudel;
my children, Lisa and Marc Potash;
my daughter-in-law, Ellen Bortman Potash;
my sisters, Toby Rice Drews and Zenia Rice Scharlau

Acknowledgments

ᴖᴖᴖ

Some very generous people have given me information and shared resources (and this was quite important, since this book is a directory as well as a guidebook): Katie Riggs, M.S.W., group facilitator at the Woman's Growth Center in Baltimore; Leah Camp, M.D., and Master of Public Health; Marion Thomas, M.D., psychiatrist; Helen Padula, now retired and until recently Chief, Community Based Services for the Aged, Department of Health and Mental Hygiene, State of Maryland, and presently Consultant to the State; Irving H. Saxe, J.D., Supervisory Health Insurance Specialist at the Social Security National Headquarters; Donald Frank, Manpower Specialist; Selma Gross, Executive Director of the Commission on Aging and Retirement Education, Baltimore City; Dr. Jim Dasinger, clinical psychologist; Adele Wilzak, Assistant Commissioner of Health, Baltimore City; Robert E. Holt, J.D., host of *Outlook*, a weekly radio show dealing with aging; Roberta Scher, teacher of Adult Education classes in senior centers for the Way-Up Program of the Baltimore City Department of Education; Albert Barouh, legislative aide for the Commission on Aging and Retirement Education, Baltimore City; Dr. William Hall, gynecologist and member of the American Association of Sex Educators and Sex Therapists; David Schlein, a concerned pharmacist who gave me a wealth of information on how drugs can effect people; and Dr. John A. Harvey, Deputy Director, Consumer Programs, Food & Drug Administration, Rockville, Maryland, for providing some crucial material.

I particularly want to thank Ulysta Evans, Executive Director, Family & Children's Society, Project S.A.G.A., a multi-purpose senior center in Baltimore, and an Urban Services Program, for sharing important resource material on the middle-aged and older black woman, and for making available material from the National Black Caucus on Aging. And I want to express appreciation to the many members of these centers who helped me to understand better what it's like to be over-50 and black in our society. Their staff helped also.

Meyer Schlein, Director of Pre-Retirement Education, Commission on Aging and Retirement Education, Baltimore City, gave me a great deal of time over the last two years, sharing information on the problems of the pre-retiree and retiree.

And I am indebted to Leonard Rothstein, M.D., a psychiatrist who volunteers much of his time at the People's Free Medical Clinic, Baltimore, Md.; who is on the teaching staff of the Johns Hopkins Medical School. He patiently read my manuscript for errors, and gave me an abundance of time with suggestions and information.

Members of the Senior Adult Discussion Group at the Jewish Community Center in Baltimore, Maryland shared their opinions and feelings about aging with me over a number of years, and I want to thank these marvelous men and women. (Fannie Heine, Lillian and Hy Freedman, Ida Woolf, Joan Nathman, Abe Gallant, Anna Nathanson, Walter Silverberg, Edna Frank, Mitzi Stein, and so many others . . .)

I received support from other women while I was writing the book: Mae Gellman, who has the courage to take risks at any age; Ruth Meeron, who, in her mid-years, changed her work from social worker to construction worker and contractor; Shirley Auerbach, who taught me more than I knew about living and dying; Toby Rice Drews, my close friend and sister, who gave me constant encouragement; and Naomi Segal, who spent many hours giving me feedback.

I want to acknowledge especially my comrade, David Nudel, who helped make writing this book a joyous task—because, during the years I spent at my typewriter, while also working at a full-time job in aging, he had no role-expectations in our marriage.

Contents

❦ ❦

Acknowledgments   vii

Introduction   xii

CHAPTER I: The Silence About Our Changing
Bodies . . . and Feelings   1

Why Isn't Our Menopause Discussed by Anyone?   1

*"Exactly What Is Menopause—and How Will
It Affect Me?"*   3

The Estrogen Replacement Controversy   4
- Estrogen replacement—what is it?
- How it can relieve symptoms of
  menopause
- How to help yourself *without* estrogen
  replacement
- The maturation index test: How does it
  measure estrogen?
- Is it safe to take estrogen replacement?
- Keep up with new developments
- What, then, are women doing now?

Contents

Late Pregnancy   **8**
- Down's Syndrome
- The amniocentesis test
- Abortion's a very private matter
- The older man's sperm: defective?

Hysterectomies   **10**
- Why do doctors advise hysterectomies?
- Consult three doctors
- Your ovaries: To remove them or not?
- Symptoms of menopause right after the hysterectomy

Common Vaginal and Urinary Infections   **11**
- Should you douche for an infection?
- A homemade douche: safe and cheap.
- Do not douche every day
- How long should you take medication?
- Cystitis: what is it?
- Medication for cystitis
- To avoid cystitis

Breast Cancer   **13**
- Who's more prone to cancer of the breast?
- Learn how to examine your own breasts
- Special diagnostic tests for breast cancer

Depression in the Over-50 Woman   **14**
- What have you lost?
- How we need roles
- Coping with depression
- Medication: anti-depressants
- Can you talk about your feelings?
- Help from other women
- Choose a therapist who understands you
- Understanding yourself

Anxiety: What Is It? How Does It Feel?   **24**
- Getting relief from anxiety
- Can you change your life situation?
- Would you be comfortable making changes?

- Professional help
- Drugs to relieve your anxiety

You're Over 50—And It's Time to Stop Smoking!   26
- Join a group for support

You're Drinking Too Much   27
- It's a treatable illness

Your Eyes As You Get Older   27
- Cataracts
- Glaucoma
- Separation of the retina
- Who can treat your eyes?
- Eye tests; eye screening
- Continue to care for your eyes

The Changes in Your Skin   29
- Brown spots
- You shouldn't lie in the sun
- Your facial skin

Your Body and Senses: How They Change   30
- Your hearing
- Your energy level: chronic illnesses
- Your gums, teeth, and bridgework
- Is it harder to keep your weight down?

Older Can Mean Better!   32
- Live in the now!
- Begin new ventures!
- Use a strength to make up for a loss!
- Remain productive . . . Be useful . . . Feel joyful!

CHAPTER II: **Getting the Best Medical Care**   35

Be Particular about Your Medical Care   35
- What to look for

Your Family Doctor 36
  • The internist
  • The family practitioner
  • The general practitioner

Guides to Use in Choosing a Family Doctor 38
  • Be realistic in your expectations

Your Gynecologist: What to Look For 40
  • Does she treat you like a person?
  • Does she talk about menopause?
    Estrogen replacement?
  • Self-examinations; her examinations
  • Surgery
  • She isn't an authority on sex!

Your Mental Health Needs 42
  • Psychiatrists and psychoanalysts
  • How much do they charge?
  • Lay therapists: What are they?
    What do they do?
  • Using your clergy for help
  • What kind of treatment do you need?
  • How to choose a psychotherapist
  • Ask her questions on your first visit
  • Does she understand older women?
  • How to find a feminist therapist
    (one who DOES understand women)
  • Mental health directories

A Man for Your Doctor—or a Woman? 48
  • The younger female doctor: Often
    different from her older counterpart
  • Why a female physician might identify
    with you and understand you more than
    a male doctor
  • Why you might be a more intelligent
    health consumer with a woman as your
    doctor
  • How often *do* women use female
    physicians?

Choosing a hospital   50
- Private voluntary hospitals
- The teaching hospital
- Proprietary hospitals
- Government hospitals
- Single-specialty hospitals
- Choose a doctor who can practice at
  the hospital of your choice
- What to look for in a hospital

How to Buy Your Drugs and Save Money   52
- Discounts through a retirement
  organization
- Other money-saving tips
- Choosing a pharmacist
- Taking your medication with you on trips
- Purchase drugs by their generic names!

Getting Good Dental Care   54
- Use a dental school!
- A dental consumer directory

A Proposed National Health Insurance Program 54
- The Corman-Kennedy Bill (HR 21/S 3)
- How would the program be financed?
- What do other countries do about
  health care?
- Health consumers would be involved in
  policy-making
- What you can do to support this bill
- A long-term goal

Medicare   56
- Part A and Part B (You Pay for Part B)
- What Medicare doesn't cover
- How to reject or re-enroll in Part B
- Deductibles and limits in Part B
- How to apply for Medicare

Medicaid: What Is It?   59
- Applying for Medicaid

- Benefits—charges—limitations
- Special services

Health Insurance Plans Available through Retirement Organizations   60
- If you're between fifty and sixty-five years of age
- If you were a federal employee
- If you're sixty-five or older
- A plan to supplement Medicare

Group Health Insurance Plans through Your Job   64
- Get the facts!
- Major medical coverage
- Coverage of prescription drugs

Disability Income Insurance   65

Dental and Vision Care Insurance   66

Private Health Insurance Plans   66
- Coverage—kinds of policies
- Plans through special-interest groups
- The importance of health insurance—but be selective!

Health Maintenance Organizations (HMO's)   67
- What are they?
- Charges, limitations, advantages
- Medicare and Medicaid payment

Community No-Cost Health Services: Take Advantage of Them!   68
- Kinds of free health screening and examinations
- Free medical care is your RIGHT!

CHAPTER III: Forty-five Ways to Look and Feel Fantastic   70

1. *Get a Face Lift or an Eye Lift*
2. *Eat Anti-Aging Food*

Contents

3. Wear Clothes That Are Slimming
4. Wear Clothes That Make You Look Ageless
5. Try Cell Therapy
6. Learn to Relax (When You're Having an Anxiety Attack)
7. Use Herbs
8. Treat Yourself To Gerovital KH–3 Treatment
9. Gain Weight
10. Listen to Your Body
11. On a Diet?
12. More Clothing Tips If You're Overweight
13. Visit a Fat Farm
14. Join a Health Club
15. Buy a Postage Scale
16. Dress Breezy and Hip
17. Don't Take Sunbaths
18. Wear a Cape
19. Buy a Slant Board
20. Have Good Legs? Show Them Off
21. Change Your Eating Patterns
22. For Frizzy Hair
23. Make Your Own Wonder Shampoo
24. For Oily Hair
25. Make Your Hair Curly
26. A Home-Made Wonder Hair Conditioner
27. Invest In a Professional Makeup Job
28. Hang Your Full-Length Mirror Near a Window
29. Lose One Pound in Six Days
30. Keep Heavy Breasts Firm
31. Take Years Off
32. Minimize Bulging Eyelids
33. Avoid SEEMING Older
34. Look Good in Harsh Daylight
35. Change Your Hairdresser
36. If You Take a Size 3 or 5
37. If You Were Once a Terrific Jitterbug
38. To Look Heavier
39. Hire a Personal Shopper
40. Eat a Lot of Fish
41. Behavior Modification—For Fatties
42. Take a Belly-Dancing Class

43. *Flabby Thighs?*
44. *Very Thin Hair?*
45. *To Feel Refreshed after Your Bath*

CHAPTER IV: Sex, Relationships, Divorce and Remarriage   84

*It Is Different When You're Over-50 . . .
   Or Is It?*   84
   • What are the differences?
   • You have to make *three* decisions if you
     want a relationship

*Do You Really Want to Get Involved with
   a Man?*   88
   • What signals are you giving men?

Make Yourself Physically Accessible!   90
   • Where to meet men
   • Chance encounters
   • Meeting men through friends

Singles' Clubs: For You?   91
   • Why it works for certain women
   • And it might NOT work
   • Where are the clubs?

Singles' Bars: For You?   92
   • Be realistic as to how they're used
     (sometimes)
   • What kind is better for the over-50
     woman?

Get Out of Your Neighborhood!   93
   • The payoffs
   • What does your city have to offer YOU?

Ways to Get Involved   94
   • Cruises
   • Travel-study programs
   • Classes

Make Yourself Emotionally Accessible!   96
  • Are you avoiding intimacy?
  • The pitfall of the "Saturday Night Date"
  • How to be intimate
  • The risks and rewards of intimacy

"I'm Having an Affair with a Married Man—"   99
  • Three stories
  • Build a life outside the relationship
  • What are your expectations?
  • Be good to yourself

The Younger Man–Older Woman Relationship   101
  • Women who are in these relationships
  • Men were EXPECTED to be older (and
    taller and stronger)
  • The rewards

Do Widowers Want to Remarry?   103
  • Yes! (If they were happily married)
  • How to awaken his interest
  • Listen to what he says about his marriage

"He's Divorced"   105
  • There are more divorces—and more
    reasons for divorce
  • Listen to what he says, too (for your
    own good)

The Multiple-Marrier: Is He Worth Your Time?   106
  • Why have his marriages failed?

How About the Perennial Bachelor?   106
  • Be realistic about what he wants
  • Be realistic about what he'll give
  • The gay bachelor: How do you fit in?

*How to Handle the End of an Affair—When
   You Don't Want It to End*   108
  • You're asking, "What's wrong with ME?"
  • It *is* harder to cope with "endings"
    when you're older

- What can you do to feel better?
- Finding a replacement

Your Sex Life: Good, Bad, or Dead?   110
- How do you feel about your body?
- How men feel about their aging bodies
- Learn to please yourself sexually
- Where to make love
- Don't play "wifey"

Living Together—Without Marriage   113
- It's cheaper than living apart
- You have to decide for yourself

Taking Responsibility   114
- Your relationship with an ego-battered
  man
- Your relationship with a tradition-bound
  man!

Different Strokes for Different Folks   116
- The freedom to get involved or not
- Understand your feelings and act on them
- There is no "right" or "wrong"

"I've Never Wanted to Get Married!"   117
- Staying single is DELIBERATE

Divorce After 50: What to Expect   119
- Life may be BETTER after divorce!
- Concrete payoffs
- Forget the "shoulds"
- Sure, it's different when you're older

Remarriage: Is It for Every Woman?   121
- Two women reflect on their own
  situations
- Are your children objecting?

*Remarriage: A Long Time to Be with Someone—
from Breakfast through the Late Show!*   125
- Are the risks worth the rewards?
- Listen to your feelings

CHAPTER V: **Your Changing Marriage** 127

What's a GOOD Marriage? 127
  - The sharing of growth

*"What Sexual Changes Will My Husband Possibly
Go Through after the Age of Fifty?"* 128
  - Sexual potency—one man's problem
  - The doctor who is misinformed
  - The doctor who is more aware
  - The fear of impotence
  - Changes in sexual patterns
  - How can you help?
  - Understanding the changes
  - Together, create *new* sexual patterns

The Myths about Our Sexuality 132
  - The "experts" often believe the myths
  - Get the *facts*

*"But What Can I Do If My Husband IS
Impotent?"* 133
  - *Psychological* impotence
  - How to reassure him
  - Techniques to use
  - It takes patience—and love!
  - Sex educators and sex-therapy centers
  - You're NEVER too old to be helped!

*"What's This I Hear about Testosterone
Replacement for Men?"* 136
  - A hormone
  - How this treatment can help
  - Find a doctor who knows about it

*"What Sexual Changes Will I Go Through
after 50?"* 137
  - Our sexual lives go on and on
  - Older women's solutions when there are
    no men in their lives

- Differences in our sex organs and our sexual responses
- Estrogen replacement applied locally
- Experiment with sexual positions for comfort
- Alternatives if your husband is impotent or too ill for a sexual relationship
- Don't listen to the busybodies!

How to Turn Yourself On Sexually   **140**
- Payoffs to experimentation
- Be imaginative (no, you don't have to hang from the chandeliers)
- Unlearn the wrong things you were taught about sex
- Lust is GOOD!
- There's no CORRECT kind of orgasm
- We're not sexual performers with certain formulas
- Fake orgasms
- End role-definitions in bed

"My Husband's Depressed."   **143**
- The "Success Syndrome"
- He feels he can't buy extra time!
- Your own fear at this time
- The husband who can't verbalize his feelings
- Two women—how they felt (and what they did!)
- The psychological and physical adjustments he has to make
- Mutual support

"My Husband's Involved with a Younger Woman!"   **147**
- Of course it doesn't happen in all marriages
- Why does it happen?
- Do you still want him?
- Get support to help you through this
- Your priority: Build your own identity!

Contents

"My Husband Is a WOMANIZER!" — 151
- The typical pattern
- What are you going to do?
- Games that are destructive
- Build yourself up!

"What's Expected of Us As Grandparents?" — 153
- You both may be grandparents now. What's expected of you
- How grandparents roles were changed
- What *can* your role be?
- You're not doddering and useless!
- Share your life experience
- You really have a lot in common
- Your relationship with a very young grandchild
- Respect your children's limits on the relationship
- Is your husband a different kind of grandparent than you?

What about My Relationship with My Son-in-law? My Daughter-in-law?" — 157
- Feelings of competition
- "Letting go" of your children

"My Husband Is Ill" — 158
- Get "people" and "money" help
- It's important to make time for yourself
- Resources—health insurance coverage
- Resources for the cancer patient
- Don't have false pride when it comes to accepting help
- Drug discounts
- Help your husband organize his affairs
- Should you tell him if he's terminally ill?
- You are stronger than you think!

The Nice Things about a Long-term Marriage — 162
- A woman tells about her marriage
- There are many good marriages!

CHAPTER VI: **What to Do about Your Aged Parent**   164

"Now I'm the Mother and She's the Child!"   164
- How the roles reverse themselves
- Losses your parent may have faced
- The demands made on you
- And it's at such a bad time in YOUR life

"Why Am I the One Who Has All This Responsibility?"   167
- Women perceived as nurturers
- Insist on the family sharing responsibility

The Mother-Daughter Relationship   170
- Were you what your mother wanted herself to be?
- Does your mother live through you?
- Understand her fears . . . and her life

Is It Different Taking Care of Your Father or Father-in-law? .   172
- His rage at being dependent
- His feelings of depression
- What can you do for him?
- Maybe he's difficult to cope with
- When a grown child is demanding
- Aged parents of either sex may have problems
- —And it can be a great strain on the children

The Physical Changes of Aging   180
- Senescence: the process of aging
- The bodies of our parents: how they age
- How the aged's senses change
- How big—or small—is your parent's world?

How Does the Aged Person Learn?   182
- Learning goes on—at a slower rate

Impaired Hearing: What to Do About It   182
- People feel bad when they can't hear
- Your parent may not realize she's making too much noise!
- What about hearing aids?
- Special help to talk on the telephone
- Recognize signs of impaired hearing

Chronic Brain Syndrome: What Is It? What to Do about It?   184
- Does your parent act confused? Forgetful? Disoriented?
- The anguish a parent may feel at her behavior
- What can cause confusion? Forgetfulness?
- Brain damage in the aged
- How to reassure your parent
- What do you do if your parent hoards food?
- Does she accuse you of not feeding her?
- Help her remember to take her medication
- It's difficult—for everyone in the family
- Be sure your parent gets a medical checkup
- Make an appointment with a psychiatrist
- Have adult expectations of her
- TOUCH your parent!
- Help her regain a sense of identity

Help: What Kind to Get and Where to Find It   191
- Homemaker services
- Escort services
- Meals-on-wheels
- Chore services
- Social service agencies
- Information and referral help
- Instructive Visiting Nurse Association
- Special library services
- Telephone reassurance programs
- Funded free hot lunch programs
- Food stamps

Help Your Parent to Ask for Help!   194
- She's entitled to it! It's NOT charity!
- Her self-image

What Can a Senior Center Do for Your Parent?   194
- Programs offered
- What kinds of people are served?
- How to get your parent to join
- Make your parent part of the process
- Is she saying, "They're too old for me!"?
- Help her make contact with members she knows

Day Care: A Possible Answer for Your Parent   197
- Different kinds of day care centers
- What they offer
- How do they help? Who do they help?
- Eligibility requirements

"My Parent Wants to Stay in Her Own Home, But—"
                                                   198
- It may be very hard for your parent to move!
- Can she stay in her own home?
- Supportive home services
- Can someone live with her?
- Let your parent be part of the decision
- Are you being an unnecessary "rescuer"?

"My Parent Is Moving in with Me"   200
- How it used to be in the old days: The extended family
- But times have changed
- Make life easier for yourself and your parent if she moves in
- Encourage her to be independent
- Take vacations from each other

"How Will Having My Parent in My Home Affect My Marriage?"
                                                   204
- Your parent may or may not be sensitive to your marriage

- What does your husband want to do
  about her?
- Are there other alternatives?

*"Where Can My Parent Go If I Don't Take
  Her In? What Can She Do?"*   206
  - Possible solutions
  - Be honest about your feelings
  - If you have no other choices
  - Three women who coped

*If Your Parent Is Mentally Ill: The Community
  Mental Health Center*   208
  - The trend toward de-institutionalization
  - The need for community services
  - The need for advocacy to get these
    services
  - Using the community mental health center
  - Their structure . . . their fees
  - Finding a community mental health
    center

Protective Services for the Aged   210
  - State intervention

*Encouraging the Independent Parent to Stay
  Independent*   211
  - A seventy-four-year-old woman speaks

*The Parent Who Needs Help—and
  Hospitalization*   211
  - Getting pertinent information so you
    know what to do

Services for the Aged in a General Hospital   212
  - Who's in charge of these services?
    Find Out!

Nursing Homes: Sometimes a Necessity   212
  - When it becomes too hard to take care
    of your parent at home

- Get the help of a social worker (to help you work out your guilt feelings)
- Geriatric evaluation service

Nursing Homes, Rest Homes, Homes for the Aged, and Family Care Homes: the Differences   214
- Nursing homes
- Rest homes . . . family care homes . . . homes for the aged
- Which for your parent?

How to Choose a Nursing Home   214
- Will they accept Medicare and Medicaid Payments?
- Choose a nursing home near your home
- Choose a home that your parent will be comfortable in
- Visit!—ahead of time
- Notice the attitudes of the attendants
- An official view of nursing homes
- The plight of black aged
- You have to look hard for a good place

Your Feelings—and Your Parent's Feelings— During This Difficult Time   217
- You need relief from the stress
- Financial needs court worry
- Don't be ashamed of your feelings
- Be aware of your parent's feelings
- Find someone to confide in
- Don't deny your parent's need to talk about her anxieties

How You Can Grow Stronger from This Experience   218
- Learn from your parent's behavior— and self-image
- Death, dying, and old age—a silence
- Explore your feelings with other women: it's strengthening!

CHAPTER VII: What No One Ever Tells the Over-50 Widow   220

The Despair and the Anger: How to Cope with These Feelings   220
- Examine your feelings
- Talk to an understanding person

Grieving: How to Do It   223
- It's important to grieve!
- Let yourself cry and scream and talk out loud to your dead husband

Who Are You, Now That You're No Longer "Arthur's Wife"?   224
- Regain your own identity—or build a new one
- Why some women continue living through their dead husband
- Two women's stories
- Become your own person now!

Don't Move Right Away! Don't Sell Your Furniture Yet!   226
- Make big changes later
- Trust your own judgment

You Still Have to Eat!   227
- Take vitamins
- Eat healthy foods that help you cope with stress
- Eat foods the over-50 woman especially needs

The Loss of a Sexual Relationship   228
- You miss closeness, too (maybe more than sex)
- You have many options for your future
- Do what's comfortable for you
- Realize you may change your mind later

Loneliness and Aloneness (There's a Difference)   230
- Of course you miss the intimacy
- Coping with loneliness
- Bad Sundays
- Lonely dusks, lonely nightimes
- Holidays
- Plan ahead for Saturdays!
- What is creative aloneness?

Should You Move in with Your Children?   234
- No! No! No! (generally speaking)
- Why "No"?
- Try it first—on a trial basis
- It's their house!
- Be sensitive to their needs—if you do move in with them
- They didn't ask you?

See Your Children As PEOPLE!   237
- Don't be a critical parent
- Seek an open and equal relationship

The Car in Your Life   237
- Learn to drive!
- Are you too old to learn?
- Are you afraid to learn?
- Taking care of your car

Your Pocketbook: Shrunken with Widowhood?   239
- Learn how to budget
- Ask a woman to teach you how
- Get the financial facts
- Make records . . . Keep records
- Watch your spending
- Watch out for con men!
- Learn how to be an intelligent consumer
- If you've signed on the dotted line— and regret it
- More money tips
- A certified public accountant for help
- Help with investments and pension plans

- Insurance agents can assist you
- Ask other women for referrals

New Men in Your Life. When? Ever? 　243
- Are your friends pushing you to date?
- When to start dating (and your mixed feelings about it)
- It'll feel awkward at first
- The over-50 widow: A different story than when you were younger

Being Alone in a Couple-Oriented Society 　247
- When the dinner invitations slow down
- Three's a crowd. Sorry!
- You as the "other woman"—when it really isn't so

Great Expectations—from Relatives 　248
- Be intelligently selfish

You WILL Live and Laugh Again! 　250
- Treat yourself to goodies
- Get a physical checkup
- They're saying, "Pull yourself together"?
- Think about your future—when you're ready
- The new you—a challenge!

CHAPTER VIII: Working: Advice for the Non-Career Woman 　253

Telling It Like It Really Is 　253
- Three women speak up
- There's a whole army of us out there!
- Ageism . . . Sexism . . . Racism . . . Triple whammies.

Entering or Reentering the Work World— after Many Years 　256
- Steps to take
- Be realistic

Making a List — 258
- Strengths ... Talents
- Kinds of jobs to fit your strengths and talents
- Where are those jobs?

Contacting Employers — 261
- Speak directly to the boss

Using Contacts — 262
- How to be effective

Understanding the Want Ads — 262
- What do certain phrases mean?

Writing a Résumé — 263
- Get hold of a typewriter
- How to write a résumé—with no job experience
- Take a look at these résumés
- What's a résumé for?
- Keep copies

How to Write a Covering Letter — 269
- The purpose
- What to include in it
- A sample covering letter

Include Your Volunteer Work When You Sell Yourself — 270
The Follow-Up Interview Letter — 270
- When to send it
- Why are you writing this letter?
- Keep copies

Free Employment Agencies — 271
- Government agencies
- Agencies for the older worker

Private Employment Agencies — 272
- Understand their regulations
- Agencies specializing in temporary jobs

Employment Especially for the Older Worker   273
- The Senior Aides Program
- Operation Mainstream
- Green Thumb program
- Special handicraft programs
- Foster grandparents
- The Senior Companion program
- Can you teach arts-and-crafts?
- Federally-funded jobs

Programs That Will Also Hire the Older Worker   277
- Program for Local Service jobs
- Manpower jobs
- Remember the New Deal Days?

Vocational Rehabilitation   279
- Eligibility
- Services

Job Counseling for the Over-50 Woman   279
- Supportive, non-bureaucratic settings
- What kind of counseling?

The Household Worker—Strides She's Made   280
- Legislation . . . Advocacy Groups
- A proposed code of standards

Starting a Small Business from Your Home   283
- Kinds of home businesses
- Turn your hobbies into income
- Thrift shops do well in this economy
- Get advice

WHY Over-50 Women Work (And It's Not Always for the Money!)   286
- Why else besides the money?
- The work ethic
- Other incentives for working after 50
- Feeling part of the world out there

Promises You'll Make to Yourself before Your First Day at Work   288
- The work world is different today!

- Catch up with the changes
- Use the strengths you've gotten through getting older!

CHAPTER IX: **Strategies for the Career Woman**
(How to Get More Money and Power)   291

Making More Money   291
- Taking steps to get a raise
- A pitfall: identifying with the boss
- Learning to be assertive
- How much to ask for
- Using the "grapevine"
- Ask people what they're making
- Role-play approaching the boss
- What to do if you're turned down
- Bargaining
- A union can bargain for you
- Coalition of Labor Union Women

Reentering the Job Market As a Professional   297
- Adjusting to the economy

Checking the Job Out   298
- Ways to find facts about the place
- The value of contacting the umbrella funding agency
- How to use your information
- Payoffs to having the information

Using Your Strengths—and Weighing Advantages and Disadvantages   302
- Make a list!
- Be realistic about what you want

Free Yourself from Ageism!   303
- Internalizing society's attitudes
- How we're victimized by ageism
- Working together to make change
- Myths about the older worker

The Job Interview   306
- Show pride in YOUR accomplishments
- Sit closer to the interviewer
- How to dress
- Go easy on the perfume
- How do you look? Dated?
- Your cosmetics
- Disguise your figure faults
- Ask someone to look you over before the interview

Should You Lie About Your Age?   310
- A realistic view
- Age has nothing to do with your ability!
- Are there risks in lying?

Should You Lie about Your Education?   311
- Institutions that DO check

The Time to Bargain and Make Demands   311
- An approach to bargaining

Use Contacts   312
- What can your contact do for you?
- Who are your contacts?
- Be aware of the politics

Age Discrimination Legislation   313
- The Age-Discrimination in Employment Act
- When to use it
- Filing suit

Equal Pay Legislation   315
- The Equal Pay Act
- How to file a complaint

The Equal Rights Amendment: How Does It Affect You?   316
- How it affects your working life
- Who supports the ERA?

Knowing Your Job Rights—and Organizing   **318**
- Informing yourself
- Working collectively for benefits
- The common interests of older and younger women

Pension Plan Legislation   **321**
- The Employees Retirement Income Security Act
- How does this legislation affect you?
- Further pension reform is needed

Until You Retire—   **325**
- Your goals

CHAPTER X: Returning to School   **326**

Reasons for Going Back to School   **326**
- Every woman may have a different reason
- Feelings about it—and fears

Why Many Older Women Are Late Bloomers   **329**
- How we grew up: The material conditions
- The economics shaped the values
- And how times changed!
- What happens to women when they do return to school?
- Four women talk about themselves

And Some Women Are Afraid to Try   **332**

Be Realistic about Your Needs   **333**
- Look honestly at your motives

Budgeting Your Time   **333**
- Shortcuts

Adult Degree Programs   **334**
- What it is
- How it works
- Who offers adult degree programs?

The Weekend College 337
- Excellent for the working woman and the woman who lives alone

Residential Mini-Courses 338
- What they offer
- Be sure you're self-disciplined

The Non-Traditional School: Pitfalls . . .
Advantages 338
- A Loose Structure
- No Tests . . . No Grades
- Double check: Is the school accredited?
- Who benefits from the non-traditional school?

The Traditional Four-Year College 340
- Who's comfortable there?
- More rigid requirements

CLEP Tests—a Way to Get College Credits
Outside of Class 341
- It's based on how much you know
- Where can you take these tests?

Credits Through TV and Radio 342
- What your responsibilities are
- When are these programs scheduled?
- Who it can particularly help

Community Colleges—a Boon for the
Older Woman 343
- The community college may answer all your needs
- It can be the answer for the working woman

Scholarships and Grants and Loans for the
Older Woman 344
- Free tuition if you're sixty-plus
- A list of scholarships and grants and loans
- How to get more information

Vocational and Technical Training   346
- Be realistic about what you can physically do
- Where to get inexpensive training and apprenticeships
- Manpower on-the-job training programs

How to Graduate from High School with Other Adults   348
- If you want to finish ninth grade only
- Earning a high school diploma
- The public school system vs. private schools

Whatever We Do from Choice Is Usually Better Done   349

CHAPTER XI: Retirement: Make It the BEST Time   351

Retirement: A Nasty Word? A Good Feeling?   351
- It depends on your living situation

If Your Husband Retires While You're Still Working   352
- The wife who's a perfectionist
- The wife who resents her husband's freedom
- The couple who has to adjust its time clocks
- The role-defined couple
- The husband who becomes rigid
- Pre-retirement planning helps

When Your Husband Retires—While You've Always Been Home   356
- "I married him for better or worse— but not for lunch!"
- Help him plan his time
- Together, make a list
- One man's reacton
- Be willing to change YOUR routine

You're Alone—and You're Retiring 359
- What if you become ill?
- Where should you live?
- The advantages of being alone

*If YOU Retire While Your Husband Is
Still Working* 361
- Start new projects
- Don't expect more time from
  your children
- Pamper yourself
- You may have more energy than your
  working husband

*Money: Making It Work For Your Retirement
Years* 362
- Credit
- Assets
- Investments
- Earnings
- Mortgages

Make a Will 365
- "But I have nothing to leave!"
- Be aware of the laws
- Don't procrastinate
- Review your will periodically

Social Security Benefits 366
- Application procedure
- Facts
- Check your Social Security account
- Socal Security reform needed for women
- How to get your Social Security checks
  mailed directly to your bank
- Can you get other retirement benefits
  sent to your bank?

*Supplementary Security Income (SSI) At The
Age Of Sixty-five* 370
- What it is
- Are you eligible?

Thirty-eight Budget Tips   371

*When It's GOOD To Spend More Money
  On Food*   374
  • For convenience
  • For the personal touch—when you
    live alone
  • For fun!

Making A Budget   375
  • Get out your pencil and paper—to pin
    down your expenses

What Will Your Income Be?   377
  • Have you thought of all your sources?
  • Begin to live on your retirement income
    before retirement

*Should You Move To Another Part Of
  The Country?*   379
  • Southern California, coastal area
  • Southern California, interior areas
  • Central California, coastal region
  • Florida
  • The Southwest

Should You Sell Your Home?   382
  • Advantages
  • Turn your home into more income

A Retirement Community?   382
  • Some people love it
  • Others hate the idea
  • If you're left alone after the move

An Apartment House for Older People?   383
  • What kind of people live in them?
  • Be selective in your housing arrangements

A Mobile Home?   384
  • Mobile Home Living . . . the advantages
  • The problems

- Performance standards
- Get references about the dealer
- Is this the kind of home for you?
- Rent one first

Moving to Another Country   **387**
- Facts to consider
- Visit as many times as you can—
  before you move!
- A woman retires to Israel
- A woman retires to Mexico
- What about your health?
- How about costs?
- It is a big step

Your Relationship with Your Grandchildren   **390**
- What kind of a grandmother are you?
- The critical grandmother
- The grandmother with unrealistic
  expectations

Relationships with Grown Children   **392**
- Expectations
- Are you being sensitive about their
  need for privacy?
- The unrealistic adult child
- The overprotective grown child

Your Relationship with Your Ex-Daughter-In-Law
  (or Ex-Son-In-Law)   **395**
- Put your grandchild first
- Don't be critical or prying

Get Ready for the UNEXPECTED!   **396**
- Different times, different values
- Illness . . . How much do you tell a
  grandchild

Your New Leisure Time   **397**
- Work . . . How important is it to you?
- Leisure . . . attitudes towards it
- Some people continue with the same
  negative attitudes

- And some can adapt to leisure
- Playing without guilt
- A woman who's alone . . . How she
  uses her leisure
- A retired couple looks at leisure
- How do you feel about YOUR
  new free time?

Volunteer Work   402
- Different views
- Is it for you?
- The right kind of volunteer work . . .
  Questions to ask yourself
- How to *find* the right volunteer job
- Choose a meaningful task
- Government sponsored volunteer work
  . . . with a stipend
- Volunteer work to match your personality

Mandatory Retirement   406
- Retirement should not be mandatory
- What one firm does instead
- Do you have recourse if you're being
  forced to retire?

*Make the Rest of Your Years the Best of
  Your Years*   407

CHAPTER XII: "What Shall I Be?" "Where Shall
I Go?" "Who Shall I Be?"   409

Further Reading (Books, Newsletters, and
Pamphlets)   412

Directory: State Agencies on Aging and
Regional Offices   422

Introduction

❧ ❧

    This book is the outgrowth of my having been a "movement" person—spending years in the civil rights' movement and the against the war in Vietnam movement and the women's movement—of becoming aware, through these experiences, of who has power and who hasn't. And through this, learning that the middle-aged and the older woman needs every kind of support she can get. It's also an outgrowth of serving young-old and old-old people in institutional settings: the senior adult department of a community center and an inner city, multi-purpose senior center, where I discovered that the professional often unwittingly internalizes society's attitudes toward the older woman, and thus renders her more powerless. It's an outgrowth of my own development as an over-forty woman, and of many hours of listening to the questions of men and women at pre-retirement panels, where I struggled to give practical and honest answers. The book also grew from my experience as a member of an older-women's consciousness-raising group, where we shared our fears and found some solutions, and became close and gave each other comfort.

    I have written about YOUR problems and YOUR solutions, so that today is the day you are going to begin thinking differently about yourself . . . the day you are going to begin realizing how strong you are . . . the day you are going to begin knowing how you *really* feel (and stop worrying about how you *should* feel) . . . the day you will begin seeing yourself as you CAN and WILL be . . . as you WANT to be . . . because today is the day you are opening this book that can and will change your life.

As you read each page you will feel support. As you read a certain sentence you'll be startled into a "That's me!", and you'll feel a surge of recognition. As you're halfway through the book you'll begin to believe that you can be as excited about your future as you were when you were twenty. Because—in this book you'll discover how to be sexy at sixty; how to feel fulfilled at fifty; how to be magnificently serene at seventy. Eighty? That's the time to begin a new career, and that's the time to remarry, and that's the time to organize a sit-in at your legislator's doorstep so he (or she) will support a bill to eliminate bus fare for older people. Shall I go on and tell you about my seventy-two-year-old friend who wears dashing capes and who just opened her own plant and herb store? In this book you'll learn HOW to feel fine and HOW to be good to yourself without guilt and HOW to face each new life situation with courage and zest and a sense of reality. You will learn how to feel gusty and lusty and you will learn how to laugh at yourself. You will learn how to BE.

Am I ignoring the hardships of being an over-50 woman in a society that values youth and is afraid of aging? Open any page and you'll know I understand your occasional feelings of bleak despair (I never said it's *easy* to be an over-50 woman!) But I strongly believe that most of our profound growing can happen when we're over-50 (this is the growing that can change our lives), and that our sense of wonder can be keener at the age of fifty than it was when we were twenty or twenty-five (we were too busy, then, to feel much wonder; we were too harried running after crawling babies and trying to be "good wives"). I also believe we are more FREE to be whatever we choose when we are fifty and sixty and seventy and eighty (*and* older), because we're no longer afraid of becoming pregnant, because we're less consumed with "making it," and because we have the luxury of more time on our hands to do whatever we want to do.

I DO know that the middle-aged and older woman has problems and worries and anxieties. Here are some of them:

- you've just been widowed and you feel like you're falling apart
- you're terribly lonely but you want to live alone
- your newly-retired husband is underfoot all day and getting on your nerves
- you want to live with someone but you don't want to share your kitchen
- you hate quiet Sundays since you're divorced or separated or widowed
- you're furious at your kids because you feel they're neglecting you
- you want to get a face lift but you don't know whether you should
- you're depressed because you're chronically ill
- your husband left you for a younger woman
- you're responsible for your aging parent
- you hate getting old
- you're thinking of returning to school—and wondering if you'll make it
- you want to leave your husband but you're afraid to make the change
- your children don't want you to remarry
- your children disapprove of your boy friend
- you're taking care of a terminally ill husband
- you're being forced to retire from your job
- you can't find a job (and you suspect it's because of your age)
- you're bored
- your husband flirts with other women
- you're confused by the estrogen-replacement controversy: should you take it or shouldn't you?
- you're afraid of becoming sick and dependent when you're older
- you're attracted to a younger man
- your husband is frequently impotent
- your grown son keeps coming to you for financial help

- you want your husband to retire and he won't
- you want to meet a man and hate singles' clubs
- you don't know what's expected of you anymore
  —now that you're over-50

But—these problems and feelings don't have to immobilize you and keep you rigid with fear. Through this book you can learn *how* to take a long, hard, and honest look at each of your problems and learn, step by step, how to tackle and resolve the situation. You will learn *how* to accept what you can't change and *how* to change what CAN be changed. You will learn not to be afraid of your real feelings. You will discover more options than you knew you had in your work world, your marriage, your sex life, and your relationships. You will learn that the over-50 woman has *more* choices than the younger woman, but they're different choices.

I believe that a big hoax has been played on us. We grew up learning that if we acted certain ways we would get certain payoffs. We were taught that if we were good mothers and good wives, we would be honored and respected and loved in our middle and older years. Don't we all know a woman who was dumped in a nursing home in her last years and visited "dutifully" once a week for five minutes by her children—after she had spent forty-five years being a good wife and mother? Don't we all have a friend whose husband left her for a twenty-three-year-old woman after she had spent thirty-two years giving perfect dinner parties and taking the children to the dentist and putting her husband through graduate school? We have to relearn a lesson: we can't predict how our husbands and children will feel about us when we're older; that we can't depend on "bargains" we make in relationships. We must learn that if we expect "payoffs" from the people we took care of and loved, we might end up as bitter and angry middle-aged and old women. Life just doesn't hold guarantees. However—we can make bargains with OURSELVES. We can decide to forget about all the "shoulds" of how to act, and concentrate on making *ourselves* feel good. We can decide to be the best we can be—for ourselves. We can decide to depend on ourselves. And we can learn how.

Time is short, and the rambling, philosophical books on how-to-be-an-older-woman-in-our-society are nice (full of personal experiences), but I think you want straight, to-the-point answers: you need a book that gives you names and addresses of places that can help you when your mother is ill; a directory of places that hire the older-woman worker; you want solutions that *work*. You deserve a guidebook—and this is that guidebook. You'll never hear me saying, "Chin up!" and leave it at that; you'll get concrete solutions for your real problems . . . each time.

How should you use this guidebook? First select the chapter from which you need immediate help. Read that chapter carefully. Then read the rest of the book. Keep it on your night table so you can refer to it quickly, as problems arise. Re-read certain sections on the days you need comfort (and we all need comfort sometimes!). Mark the book. Underline the paragraphs you might want to come back to. Remember how you relied on your favorite cookbook during the early days of your marriage—how you turned pages back and left foodstains on certain, much-used pages, and marked other pages here and there? Well, don't be afraid to use this book the same way. These *are* recipes—for feeling better. For doing better. For making the successful transition from your youth to your middle years to your older years.

Tell your friends that finally there is a guidebook with real and honest answers for every over-50 woman. After they've read the book, suggest getting together once-a-week, to discuss various chapters and talk about how your own lives relate to what you've read and learned. Share your development and problems and concerns—and your answers. Send for the booklets I list. Use the social service agencies I write about, if you need help with your husband who is ill, or your granddaughter who lives with you, or your anxiety attacks. Read the tips on how to save money. Use the book as a directory, *and* a guidebook and a road map . . . to taking that unknown road toward middle age and your older years.

Let this book excite you and help you change your life. Because it can!

THROUGHOUT THIS BOOK I have mainly used third-person pronouns in the feminine gender. To those readers who may be confused or offended by this, I would like to explain this choice: At this point in the history of American women I feel female role-models are needed in "authority" positions (as doctors, for example). This is my conscious effort at meeting this need. Here's hoping that in the not too distant future, the need will no longer exist.

CHAPTER 1

The Silence About Our Changing Bodies . . . and Feelings

Why Isn't Our Menopause Discussed by Anyone?

When we were eleven years old we giggled with our girlfriends and speculated aloud about the mysteries of menstruation. During our teen years we talked about our periods and mourned our too-large or too-tiny breasts, staring at our bodies in the mirror.

Later, when we expected a baby, we spent hour after hour discussing our weight, our morning sickness, and how we felt the baby move. Doctors encouraged this. They showed us charts and explained what was happening to the fetus.

When our daughters became pregnant they attended natural childbirth classes with their husbands. They lay on the floor together in rows, learning how to relax. Their husbands took movies of them while they were in the delivery room! *Their* daughters learned how to say "vagina" at the age of three. And many young women are learning how to look at their own cervixes in a hand-held mirror at the age of nineteen.

When we approach menopause—silence. Absolute silence. How many of your friends told you they were skip-

ping their periods, once they reached their late forties or
early fifties? How many gynecologists said to you, "You're
probably going to notice some changes in your body
within the next few years"? *Why* this silence? Because
most of us have been brainwashed into feeling shame
about getting older. Gynecologists usually don't tell us
about menopause unless we ask, because they may feel it
marks "the end." Our family doctors don't tell us what to
expect from our changing bodies as we get older, because
they feel it may alarm us. Friends don't talk about their
own menopause because they don't want to be thought of
as old.

Let's all unite. Let's *insist* that our doctors tell us about
the changes in our bodies. Let's sit down together and talk
to *each other* about the changes in our bodies. THIS IS
THE *ONLY* WAY WE CAN REDUCE THE FEAR
EACH OF US FEELS AND LESSEN THE CHANCES
OF HEALTH HAZARDS—*we will know what to expect.*

How can we do this? Ask your gynecologist direct questions (write them down before you leave home so you
can read them off to her). If she hedges after hearing
your questions, and says something vague and indirect,
such as, "It's different for each woman," say, "All right,
but tell me more. Tell me generally what to expect during
menopause, as you would tell an eleven-year-old girl what
to expect during her next years as she goes into menstruation." Remind your gynecologist that she wouldn't say to
an eleven-year-old girl, "It's different for each young
girl," and leave it at that. If your gynecologist still hedges
—seriously consider changing your doctor.

Ask her to give you a mirror and show you how to look
at your cervix, as you lie on the examining table. This
way you can examine your own cervix at home at regular
intervals to see if there are any changes that you would
want to report to the doctor. Women in self-help medical
groups learn to do this.

Invite a few of your close women friends over, and take
turns reading parts of this chapter aloud and discussing
it. You might learn more about your changing body in
those few hours of discussion than you have in the past
ten years, and as you read and listen and talk, each of
your friends (once the ice is broken) is going to be eager
to tell what *she* has been experiencing and what's hap-

pening to *her* changing body. Why? Because this will probably be the first time she can get reassurances from other women who are going through the same physical developments and changes. This might be the first time she has felt free enough to tell anyone how frightened she's been, on occasion, and it might be the first time she's heard of estrogen replacement!

Let us take away the mystery from our changing bodies so we can take proper care of ourselves!

"Exactly What Is Menopause—And How Will It Affect Me?"

Menopause. The word means *cessation of periods.* Most women begin menopause around the age of forty-seven, and some women begin their menopause in their fifties. Others don't experience this phase of their life until they're close to sixty.

Is it true that the earlier you begin to menstruate, the later you will stop menstruating? Not always.

The pattern? When you begin menopause your menstrual bleeding may become shorter and scantier. Then you might experience some skipping or some lengthening of your periods. Some women just suddenly stop menstruating, without any variations in pattern. So you can see that menopause is as different for different women as menstruation was. The majority of women, however, just taper off, and have irregular periods for the last two to three years, which become more and more widely spaced.

Does it mean anything if you begin your menopause late, when you're sixty or close to sixty: Absolutely not. On the other hand, some women begin their menopause when they're only forty . . . and that, too, is "normal," even though unusual. The average age for the onset of menopause is the late forties.

A marvelous payoff to completion of menopause is knowing you won't get pregnant. This is the time of life, for many women, when sex is enjoyed fully for the first time; it is no longer tied in with worries of a late "period" and the need for contraceptives.

The Estrogen Replacement Controversy

One of the most significant changes that occurs during and after menopause is that the amount of an important hormone called estrogen produced by our endocrine system decreases.

Estrogen serves very important functions in our bodies. It may protect us against heart attacks; it can keep our bones from easily breaking; it can prevent hair from growing on our faces; and it can keep our vaginal tissues from thinning out (and thereby possibly decreasing our sexual pleasures).

• *Estrogen replacement—what is it?*

Since estrogen is so important, some gynecologists supplement the decreasing estrogen supply. This form of therapy is called estrogen replacement and the hormone can be given orally in the natural or the synthetic form. It can also come as a cream, to be applied locally in the vagina.

• *How it can relieve symptoms of menopause.*

Estrogen replacement may quickly relieve some of the unpleasant feelings we experience during menopause, such as hot flush (or hot flash). This is a sudden intense sensation of heat followed by sweating. It can prevent vaginal infections; feelings of numbness in our hands and feet and tingling feelings in our skin; a dry vagina that hurts when we have intercourse; backaches, headaches, and feelings that we have to urinate frequently after intercourse. Estrogen replacement can relieve anxiety and depression and fatigue—and reverse loss of interest in sex. It can prevent physical signs of aging. (A friend of mine ruefully pointed to the back of her neck and said, "See that hump? My dowager's hump. That developed when I went into menopause.") One woman might have trouble sleeping since her estrogen level decreased. Another woman might develop a fast heartbeat and palpitations. Diarrhea could be a reaction to a lowered estrogen level. So could constipation. Estrogen replacement can help *all* these ills.

• *How to help yourself without estrogen replacement.*

And if you decide *not* to take estrogen replacement,

there are other ways to alleviate the discomforts of menopause and to make up for the changes we may see because of a decrease in estrogen.

For one—exercise. Physical exercise can relieve the discomforts you may feel. Lead up to it slowly if you haven't been exercising. "Tell your readers," a physical education teacher said, "that it's cheaper to exercise in a community center or a 'Y' than a commercial health club—and they have just as many facilities."

Modified Yoga can help. Your Yoga teacher can give you specific exercises to take away your aches and pains.

(Of course, you should check with your doctor first before taking an extensive exercise program.)

Are you developing facial hair (due to a decrease in estrogen)? Bleach it. Or have it permanently removed with electrolysis.

Is your hairline receding? Is your hair thinning out? Are you actually losing hair? Fortunately, hairpieces are *in*. Buy one that looks natural. Shop around.

Some women, however, never experience *any* of these discomforts during menopause, and many women experience only the hot flush or one or two other symptoms. But I don't like to use the word "symptom" because that implies that menopause means illness. It doesn't. It is nothing more than a developmental change in our bodies, as menstruation was a developmental change.

- *The maturation index test: How does it measure estrogen?*

There's a simple test, administered by physicians, that tells the doctor what estrogen effect there is on your tissues and whether this is a normal level. It tells the doctor how much estrogen replacement you can take, or if you need any at all. After menopause, your adrenal and other glands produce some estrogen, and in your case, it may be enough. In some women, the body produces too much estrogen, so taking estrogen replacement may be unwise.

The test involves examining a sample of your vaginal secretions or cells. The physician takes a smear—a painless test—and this can be done when you get your semi-annual gynecological checkup.

Frequently, a doctor doesn't routinely administer the

Maturation Index Test, so you might want to ask for it
—and check up on the results.

• *Is it safe to take estrogen replacement?*

What if your estrogen level is too low, affecting your
body and feelings? Until recently, many gynecologists
would routinely go ahead and administer estrogen replacement. However, newly documented evidence shows that
women who have taken estrogen replacement orally have
a higher incidence of uterine cancer than women who did
not take estrogen replacement. Questions, such as the following, are being asked by women:

- Can adequate controls be maintained on the administration of estrogen replacement with each
  woman, to determine how much—if any—estrogen
  replacement she can safely take?
- Do these controls take the form of regularly administered tests? What do these tests consist of?
  Are the results conclusive?
- Are the risks of estrogen replacement worth it—
  since the risk of heart disease rises dramatically
  after menopause?

At this time everyone seems confused by the estrogen
replacement controversy. Some feminists feel that female
gynecologists would be more apt to be concerned, because
they would identify with the female patient's health needs.
Many male physicians are very cautious, however. One
told me he would never prescribe estrogen replacement
for the patient who has a history of breast cysts.

Meanwhile, gynecologists—both male and female—
take different positions. Many will only prescribe it in
carefully controlled dosages for a short time, when there
are uncomfortable menopausal symptoms. Some won't use
it at all. Others have their patients take it *before* menopause and continue throughout the rest of their lives
(although I suspect some of these same doctors are
reconsidering their position).

On September 27, 1976, the Food and Drug Administration announced two actions to better inform doctors
and the public about the risks of estrogens. They ordered
revisions of estrogen labeling for physicians, and ordered

estrogen manufacturers to print and distribute this revision within 60 days. They also proposed that a special lay-language brochure on the risks of estrogens be provided to women at the time they have prescriptions filled. The public was invited to comment on this proposed requirement, and given 60 days to do this, and FDA, in the *HEW News* of September 27, 1976, stated "FDA is encouraging manufacturers to print and distribute the brochure immediately, even while comment is being sought." The texts of the physician labeling was published in the *Federal Register* on September 29, 1976. However, by the middle of January, 1977, druggists reported no label warnings or package warning inserts for the estrogen replacement consumer. A call to a local FDA office brought forth the following information: "the FDA reviewed the public comment and scientific data, and decided that after September 21, 1977, package insert warnings are mandatory." It is interesting to note that birth control pills and DES (diethylstilbestrol, a highly suspect, possible cancer-producing drug, which is used as an emergency post-coital contraceptive) do already contain patient warnings in its packaging. Is this because older women haven't been as vocal and insistent as younger women about their needs? We need to be—to counteract the strong influence of drug manufacturers, who have a vested interest in fighting legislation regarding package insert warnings and label warnings.

• *Keep up with new developments.*

No matter what your doctor tells you, you should hesitate to take estrogen replacement if you have a history of cancer. And if you have a history of severe liver or kidney disease, tell your doctor before he prescribes estrogen. Keep up with the controversy—you should follow any new developments. If you do decide to take estrogen replacement, watch for any unusual bleeding patterns—and tell your doctor immediately, if this develops. If you bleed after your menopause is completed, call your doctor. Of course, unusual bleeding is something you'll want to report to your physician whether you're taking estrogen replacement or not.

Estrogen replacement, in the oral form, comes in both natural and synthetic form. There are usually no *minor*

side effects when you use it in the natural form. Some
women have an allergic reaction to estrogen taken in
synthetic form, such as nausea and vomiting. But the
synthetic form is usually less expensive, costing only
around ten cents a day.

While you're going through menopause it may hurt to
have intercourse. What has happened is that the decrease
in your estrogen level has thinned out your vaginal tissues
and/or decreased the amount of vaginal secretions that
keep your tissues moist. One solution is to apply estrogen
cream locally, in your vagina. This is *not* considered dangerous, and the cream can reverse this condition. The estrogen cream is *not* part of the estrogen replacement
controversy.

- *What, then, are women doing now?*

Are they listening to their doctors and continuing treatment? Are they discontinuing under their doctor's orders?
They're confused—just as many doctors are. One woman
who does have breast cysts frequently and who found that
estrogen replacement reversed her terrible feelings of
depression is *not* giving it up (and she told me that her
husband, a physician, really doesn't know what she should
do). A friend, who had cancer of the uterus and was
administered estrogen replacement immediately after her
hysterectomy (which was before estrogen replacement was
questioned as to its safety) immediately stopped taking
her daily dosage when she heard about the possible
dangers—even though her gynecologist disagreed with her.

We simply don't know enough yet, and extensive research is needed on this issue. You? You are an individual
with your own case history. Try to avail yourself of as
much current information as possible. And be aware that
it *has* been established that the risk of cancer is greater
if you continue with the estrogen replacement over a
longer period of time.

Late Pregnancy

What happens if you do become pregnant (your menopause wasn't completed)? Well, our ability to conceive
decreases as we get older, but to be really safe, continue

using contraceptives for at least one year after you've stopped having periods.

• *Down's Syndrome.*

You're pregnant and you want the baby. As we get older, there is a higher risk that our newly born child will suffer from a disorder called Down's Syndrome (that means the baby is a mongoloid). Fortunately, there is a test that can establish whether this is the case or not.

• *The amniocentesis test.*

Fluid is extracted from your womb by a needle, and an examination of this fluid tells the doctor whether or not your baby will be normal. *Ask* your doctor for this test— if she doesn't mention it herself. It is administered early in the pregnancy.

• *Abortion's a very private matter.*

No one should tell a woman whether or not to have an abortion: her body belongs to *her*. Remember, however, the earlier the pregnancy the safer and easier the abortion. Since abortion has been legal since the January, 1973 Supreme Court decision, if you have the money you no longer have to lie on a stranger's dirty kitchen table—risking infection and possible death. The surgery is done in a safe clean clinic or hospital. Many clinics have a female staff especially on hand to make you feel more comfortable. There is considerable pressure to reverse the decision which legalized abortions at this time of writing. On June 20, 1977, the Supreme Court ruled that medicaid funds cannot be used for abortions—and this means that poor women are often denied safe and legal abortions because of lack of funds. Thirty-eight and a half percent of black, Chicano and Puerto Rican women in our country rely on medicaid for health care.

• *The older man's sperm: defective?*

Recent research indicates that as men age, their sperm can play a role in the conception of an abnormal baby. We don't know very much about this yet, but it's something to think about, if you're welcoming the idea of a new child. All the more reason for the amniocentesis test.

Hysterectomies

Is a doctor advising you to have a hysterectomy? Consult two more doctors! Every year much unnecessary surgery is performed, and one of the most common unnecessary operations is the hysterectomy.

A hysterectomy is surgical removal, by abdominal incision or through the vagina, of your uterus—and *sometimes* removal of your ovaries and/or your cervix and fallopian tubes.

• *Why do doctors advise hysterectomies?*

A common reason is because a woman has developed uterine fibroids (these are benign tumors that are not dangerous if they remain small). A woman may chronically bleed from this condition and become anemic. Or a hysterectomy may be done because of a malignant tumor.

• *Consult three doctors.*

Why? Because you should have more than one or two opinions before undergoing any kind of major surgery. It can be emotionally and financially draining to undergo surgery, and why put yourself through this unless you *need* to? Also, *any* operation, no matter how minor, is a risk to the patient's life.

• *Your ovaries: To remove them or not?*

If you do decide to go ahead with a hysterectomy, realize that doctors sometimes disagree with each other on whether or not to remove the ovaries during the surgery.

Some surgeons and gynecologists believe that if at all possible, they should not be removed because they secrete small amounts of estrogen *after* menopause is completed —and we need estrogen. Other doctors are afraid to leave them in; afraid of the risk of ovarian cancer if they don't remove them. Ovarian cancer is a very sneaky kind of disease. It's difficult to detect because it doesn't show itself in a Pap smear.

So definitely consult at least three reputable physicians to decide: a.) whether to have a hysterectomy, and b.) whether your ovaries should be removed.

• *Symptoms of menopause right after the hysterectomy.*

After a complete hysterectomy (that's when your ovaries *have* been removed), you might immediately feel some symptoms of menopause. For this reason, to forestall these symptoms, some doctors administer estrogen replacement right after the surgery—while you're still in the hospital. Considering the estrogen replacement controversy, do you want it? It's *your* body and your decision. If you don't want it, tell the doctor emphatically so *before* the surgery.

Common Vaginal and Urinary Infections

Most women, at some time in their adult lives, experience a vaginal and/or urinary infection—and many over-50 women still don't know what to do about it.

A strong DON'T: don't use vaginal sprays. Not even once. Too many women have developed a mild but painful vaginal infection from their use. Throw yours away.

• *Should you douche for an infection?*

If you have any kind of vaginal discharge that smells bad or is discolored or is profuse, call your gynecologist. Ask her if a mild douche will help before you get to her office.

• *A homemade douche: safe and cheap.*

If your gynecologist says you should douche, try two quarts of warm water with two tablespoons of white vinegar *or* two quarts of warm water with two tablespoons of baking soda for a very effective douche—*much better* and much less expensive than commercial douche powders.

• *Do not douche every day.*

Under normal circumstances, when you do not have a vaginal infection, *do not* douche every day. If you have been taught that douching reduces the incidence of vaginal and uterine infection, that is not so. Too frequent douching disturbs the normal bacterial environment in your vagina that *protects* you from infection. Douching two to four times a month is sufficient. You hate vaginal odors?

Tub bathing instead of showers can help alleviate that. It may also help to remember that we've been brought up to believe that natural body odors are repulsive. This does not actually and objectively mean this is really so; in fact, they are now doing research that indicates that our natural vaginal odors make men sexually attracted to us!

• *How long should you take medication?*

When your doctor does give you medication for vaginal infections or bladder infections, take the medication as long as she tells you to—even if the symptoms disappear.

• *Cystitis: what is it?*

One of the most common bladder infections is cystitis. It is not serious but it can be very uncomfortable. You feel like you have to urinate every few minutes but you only void a very small amount of urine. It can also burn and bleed when you urinate. You may have cramps in your stomach and a dull pain in your bladder and your inner thighs and your back may ache.

• *Medication for cystitis.*

See your doctor right away, because she can relieve your discomfort through medication. This medication is taken orally and may discolor your urine, so wear a minipad for protection. Drink a large glass of water every hour while you have cystitis, and soak in a warm tub a couple of times a day to relieve discomfort. Take large doses of vitamin C, drink cranberry juice and stay away from coffee, tea and highly spiced foods. A urologist told me that cystitis is the middle-class woman's ulcer—a symptom of tension.

• *To avoid cystitis.*

During intercourse if you have been sitting on top of your partner, straddling him, pressure on your urethra might have stimulated cystitis. This does not mean you should not use this sexual technique; it just means that at that particular time your urethra was vulnerable to becoming irritated. Just stop temporarily.

Breast Cancer

Fortunately, breast cancer has been given a lot of attention in the press in the recent past, probably saving many women's lives.

• *Who's more prone to cancer of the breast?*

Studies have shown that certain kinds of women are more prone to cancer of the breast: women over thirty-five, women who have a family history of breast cancer, Jewish women, women who did not breast feed, urban women, women whose menstruation began early, and women who have cystic breasts. None of these factors are absolutes, so no matter what category you fall into, have your doctor examine your breasts regularly (at least twice a year), because, as women get older, the incidence of breast cancer increases.

• *Learn how to examine your own breasts.*

Examine your own breasts five days after your menstrual period has begun each month. If you are no longer menstruating, or if your periods are irregular due to menopause, pick a date in the month to examine your breasts (any date) and examine your breasts on that same date each month. Ask your gynecologist or your internist to show you, step by step, *how* to do it. It's very simple. Putting lotion on your fingers before your self-examination has been recommended by the American Cancer Society; this allows you to be more sensitive to any unusual thickening or lumps. The American Cancer Society has been presenting breast cancer teach-ins in many areas of the country, so call your local chapter if you want one presented to your group or if you want to attend a scheduled talk and demonstration. They tell and show how to examine your own breasts, using "Betty Breast" (a plastic model), and they give out brochures. They also arrange for free breast examinations.

• *Special diagnostic tests for breast cancer.*

Other diagnostic techniques for breast cancer are mammography (X-rays of the breast) and thermography (a diagnostic procedure that measures areas of heat in your breasts; the heat may indicate a benign or malignant tumor). A great deal of controversy exists at this time in the medical world about the value of mammography. Some doctors praise the procedure, especially recommending it for over-50 women, since the incidence of the disease increases with age. This test can frequently detect early pinpoint cancers not easily discovered through palpation. On the other hand, many doctors are wary of the procedure, afraid of the radiation exposure that could lead to cancer. A middle-ground for some medical experts is using the test very selectively.

At this time, thermography is not available in every community. Call your local American Cancer Society office for information on where to go for these tests in your area.

Planned Parenthood agencies also give breast examinations (*and* internal examinations), often at low cost to the woman who has a limited income. Your Planned Parenthood agency is listed in your phone book.

Depression in the Over-50 Woman

One of our developmental tasks, as middle-aged and older women, is listening to the changes in our feelings as well as the changes in our bodies. Our feelings can affect our bodies. Our feelings can affect our functioning. You're feeling blue? *Very* blue? You cry a lot? You awaken about three o'clock every morning and can't fall asleep again? You're feeling hopeless? Ask yourself this question: "What have I lost that is important to me?"

• *What have you lost?*
Your husband? Your children? Your youth? Your looks? Your health? Your job? Your role?

When you're left a widow, you haven't only lost a husband; you have lost the important role of *wife*.

When your children moved away from home and got involved with their own lives, you lost another important role: that of *mother*.

• *How we need roles.*
Roles prop us up. Roles make us feel wanted and

needed. If our roles are taken away, we can feel very
very let down—UNTIL WE REPLACE THE OLD
ROLES WITH NEW AND EQUALLY IMPORTANT
ROLES.

Blanche is a good example of a woman who lost her
role—and fell apart. She had been the head bookkeeper
in the same office for many years, and mandatory retirement demanded that she stop working at the age of sixty-
five. When her co-workers asked her what she was going
to do after she retired, she gaily retorted, "Don't worry
about me! I'll find plenty to do!" But Blanche had no
hobbies and her closest living relative was a cousin. She
had made work her life. Two months after her retirement
she developed diabetes, and right after that she had a car
accident. A woman she had worked with saw her at a
shopping center, and reported back to the women in the
office, "She's like a different person! She looks terrible,
and she kept repeating herself when she was talking to
me. I felt so sad!"

What had happened to Blanche? She had lost her role
as *worker*, and she hadn't replaced that role with any
other equally important role.

From childhood on we prepare for the role of worker:
We take certain courses in high school to prepare for
certain kinds of work; we pick a major in college according to the kind of job we want; and we're asked,
from the time we're little, "And what do *you* want to do
when you grow up?" No wonder Blanche felt she was
without an identity after she retired; she had lost that
important role of worker, and she had nothing to replace
it with that was meaningful to her. I understand that she's
now in a therapy group for newly retired workers, and
I'm hopeful that she'll find other equally important roles
to give her a feeling of self-esteem and status again.

Have you lost the role of *Beautiful Woman*? It is often
harder for a woman to face her own aging if she has been
a really beautiful woman all of her adult life, because she
has grown used to the payoffs: attention, adoration, even
good jobs and a "good" marriage. She now knows she is
losing the prime of her beauty, and this may be a terrible
loss to her; she knows she'll no longer get these payoffs.

I know a sixty-year-old woman who became depressed
when the role of *Child* was taken away from her. Yes—

child! She had never married, and had always lived with her mother who had perceived and treated her as a child ("my little girl"). When her mother died, my friend suddenly lost the role she had lived by . . . the role that had meant so much to her. She spent three months in a mental hospital. (Oh, she's all right now but it was rough for awhile!)

Another friend, Sylvia, who did *not* become widowed and who did *not* lose her job, became depressed and finally went for counseling. She discovered, after many sessions, that she was deeply mourning the loss of the role of the *Loved Wife*. You see, even though she and her husband Gary lived together, she knew he no longer loved her.

Henny became deeply depressed when her friend, Trish, died. She had lost the role of *Friend*, but she was made acutely aware through her friend's death that she was losing the role of *The Person Who Lives Forever* (yes, a fantasy role that we all indulge in and one that we must confront over and over again).

Rena became blue and despondent after she moved from her big old house into a small apartment. Why? She temporarily lost the role of *Secure Person*. She had changed the space and shapes around her, and this made her feel very uncomfortable. It also altered her perception of herself as *The Hostess* (another important role to her). She had played that role for over thirty years in the big old house (a perfect setting for the role of Hostess) and she didn't feel at ease in that role in a tiny, boxy apartment.

Belle suffered a profound depression after she had a breast removed. Of *course* she did. Belle had suffered a loss of an important part of her feeling of identity: part of her body. She also felt the loss of the role of the *Complete and Sexual Woman* because it was her *breast*.

This does not mean that these women did not replace these lost roles later and did not begin feeling better when their replacement roles became satisfying to them. Many of them did. But while they were losing their roles, and for a while *after* they lost their roles (before any satisfactory replacement) they felt great sadness, and they grieved their loss of role—which, to them, was partly a loss of *self*.

• *Coping with depression.*

How do you cope with this? By talking to people we know and trust can help. Joining a group of women who have experienced similar losses can really be helpful. I know of a group meeting right now, women who just retired (forced retirement) from their federal office jobs. They meet in a local social service agency, and they give each other great support during this critical time of their life. Groups can meet in homes rather than institutional settings. Living rooms are intimate, more so than impersonal offices, so how about starting your own group in *your* own living room?

Six women, all over 50, decided to do just this. It began when one of their social group, a dynamic energetic woman, looked at her own changing life and her own feelings of loss and decided that friends are for sharing anxious feelings and sharing problems and sharing *solutions.* She called five close friends and asked them to come over the following Saturday night—told them why, too—and there it started: once-a-week sessions; gratifying, soul-searching, honest sessions, where each woman could feel free to explore her real feelings and be vulnerable.

One very important fact became evident. They all felt the same way: *They didn't know what was expected of them anymore.* They no longer knew what their aging husbands expected, what their grown children expected, and what society expected. So they didn't know what they expected of *themselves* (most of their past behavior was based on what others had expected of them).

Jenifer was one of the members of the group. Her remarks on the "invisibility" of women over 50 were particularly apt: "Every young single girl knows what's expected of her. Every new mother knows what's expected of her. My goodness, there are child-study groups for young mothers and there are hundreds and hundreds of books written for the woman *under* 50 (about what to do in bed and what to do with your teen-age daughter and how to keep your husband interested), and the *advertisements*—just look at them! They're full of bride pictures and pictures of babies and photographs of young couples looking into each other's eyes. But—" she looked helplessly around the room at the other women, "we're invisible. Once we reach fifty we're ignored. We're *finished* being a mother. If our husbands have died, we're finished being wives. It's like we don't have a place anymore. We're an *embarrassment!*"

One of the women said bitterly to the unseen world out there, "Tell us! Tell us what to be and we'll *be* it."

There was silence. No one spoke for a while.

Then someone said, "What infuriates me are the younger people who are so patronizing. They act like we're so cute when we say something witty, and they're amazed when we do something really important or really creative. What do they think—that we're feeble, or like children? Just because we're middle-aged?"

But they kept on meeting. They decided that even though society had stopped telling them what to *be* and no one seemed to have any future expectations of them anymore—they *weren't* finished and they would decide on their own expectations of THEMSELVES. A big, tough job—but a necessary one if they didn't want to continue feeling depressed and useless and discarded.

In other words, they would depend on THEMSELVES to decide on their *OWN ROLES,* and they would stop worrying about what other people expected them to be, and they would start being what they ENJOYED being.

"Okay," one of the members, Emily, said, "I can't go back to my office. They gave me the farewell lunch and the retirement present, and after forty-one years I have nowhere to go at eight o'clock in the morning. So I'll enroll in an early morning art class three mornings a week to fill in that early morning void—and because I love to paint."

Clever Emily. She deliberately looked for a morning art class, instead of an afternoon class, because she knew that mornings—the time she got to work each day and enjoyed a cup of coffee and some chitchat with close office friends—was the time of the day she missed work the most.

Leona had always been a social activist. She was used to direct action—turning the world around—and she was *angry.* Why? Because society had decided that "old" means that people are no longer productive. One afternoon she received a call from another activist friend of hers (also in her sixties) who asked Leona, "Did you ever hear of the Grey Panthers?"

She explained that this is a national activist group of young *and* middle-aged and old people that organized to change the conditions of older people in our society, *and* to change the feelings that younger people have about old people (and the feelings that older people have about themselves). The group had been formed by a fantastic woman in her sixties, Maggie Kuhn, who had always been a muckraker and an activist.

"Maggie Kuhn," she said, "believes that if older people *gain* power—political and economic power—they'll feel more powerful and people will see them as more powerful, and this will help them gain even *more* power.

"Of course," she added, "it also means that gaining power will better our conditions."

Maggie Kuhn was scheduled to speak at a local church that week. Leona and her friend attended the meeting, and as Leona heard this articulate and passionate woman talk, she was immediately ready to organize a Grey Panther group in *her* city.

Maggie Kuhn is an inspiration, a model of what the older woman can be: a catalyst to change the lives of thousands and thousands of people over 50. (Perhaps there is a Grey Panther group in *your* city).

Today? Leona still meets with her group of friends each week to discuss feelings and problems and solutions (it gives her a shot in the arm) but she's mainly busy organizing, organizing, organizing. The local Grey Panthers group she formed (with other activist women and men she met) had just met with a local Disabled in Action group to get their local bus company to order buses that are accessible to people with physical limitations (after all, even having arthritis can make it hard to board a high bus step!). Their next project: investigating the reports they've heard that their state mental hospital has the geriatric patients herded together in a run-down building with few toilets and too few personnel. If they find the reports are true, then they'll swing into action.

Is Leona still depressed? She forgot what the word means. She has no time to be blue. Her phone rings day and night. She's constantly going to committee meetings. She's always meeting new and interesting and vital people from different groups that work in coalition with her Grey Panther group; people of *all* ages . . . and that includes some eighteen-year-olds who don't perceive Leona as *any* age because she is living so much in the *moment* and they have so much in common. Leona now has a PASSION. Passions take one outside of oneself. Passions are larger than the self. Passions make you exciting. Passions are possible at ANY AGE—and *EVERY* AGE.

Not all six women found their answers overnight. Some are still groping. But they're groping TOGETHER. They feel support from each other. They know that collectively, they can learn more about themselves and how they really feel and what they really want.

If reading this excites you, intrigues you, pick up the phone right away! Call three friends and ask them to come over TONIGHT. Start your own group. Don't wait. Your three friends NEED YOU. You NEED *THEM*. Four women's energy is a lot of energy. Use all of your crackling energy (which means shared ideas and shared solutions) to work out goals for yourselves. You'll find your new lives exciting and meaningful and creative and enriched!

• *Medication: anti-depressants.*

Medication? Yes, medication can often help us get through an uncomfortable period of depression—if your doctor advises it. Properly prescribed and properly used, it can do wonders. Some psychiatrists are reluctant to prescribe medication because they feel it *masks* symptoms —and keeps the patient from getting to the root of her problems.

Psychiatrists know more about anti-depressant drugs than other kinds of physicians, because their treatment often includes drug therapy, and they have made a special study of it; they have a chance to see the kinds of effects the drugs have on patients since they generally see the patient more frequently than the general practitioner; they're more in touch with which drugs are used in clinical settings with depressed patients; and—if the psychiatrist is responsible—she keeps up with the latest research in anti-depressant drugs. They're very familiar with drugs such as Tofranil and Elavil and Pertofrane and Sinequan and

Lithium (prescribed specifically for manic-depression). I think that if I needed medication to relieve depression, I would go out of my way to see that a *psychiatrist* prescribed it. I have known a couple of family doctors who are still prescribing medication that is hardly used anymore, and who prescribe the same medication for each depressed patient.

Get information on possible side effects of the drug you're taking. Some doctors may not tell patients about side effects because they feel the patient may *think* she's experiencing certain symptoms of feelings, but I feel this is a risk the doctor is obligated to take. She has a duty to inform the patient about her medicine and what it can and cannot do to her body. Let us take the mystery away from our medication *and* our bodies. This gives us more control over our bodies and ourselves.

It's important for you to know, for instance, that you can't eat certain aged cheeses or chocolate or pickled herring, or drink wine, while you're taking certain antidepressants. These combinations can make your blood pressure shoot up. If you feel you want to get as much information on each and every drug you're taking—go to your central library and look the drug up in the *Physician's Desk Reference*. This is a book that lists every drug and its functions and its possible side effects. If you want to purchase a good reference to keep at home, send for *The Medicine Show* (you can get it from Consumers Union, Orangeburg, N. Y. 10962; enclose a check or money order for $3.50).

I have found some pharmacists more knowledgeable about drugs than some physicians. Perhaps this is because many doctors get their drug information mainly (or only) from drug house salesmen and advertising literature. Of course, some very responsible physicians attend seminars and courses and workshops on pharmacology—and these are the doctors who do give you accurate up-to-date information. A very thorough health consumer may want to ask her doctor *and* her pharmacist about the drug she puts in her body—as well as look it up in the *Physician's Desk Reference*. An intelligent health consumer, if she is taking an anti-depressant drug, will also want to ask her pharmacist if it is compatible with any other drug she is taking.

And the conscientious health consumer, if she is taking Lithium (a drug that's often effective for a certain kind of depression) will want to know that she should be given blood tests while on the drug.

Do not take a drug for depression if you've stopped seeing your doctor. This can be dangerous. She has to know its effect on you.

• *Can you talk about your feelings?*

Thelma was going through a low period when she would awaken every morning with a sense of impending doom. She forced herself to jump out of bed and turn on the radio, and then she would dance to some jazzy music for at least fifteen minutes which would at least get her to the point where she could go into the kitchen, make herself some high-protein breakfast (for energy) and then face the day. She also started psychotherapy, because she wanted to *understand* the reasons for her feelings of depression—not just mask it every morning for a couple of hours.

When Thelma first began her psychotherapy sessions, she had a very difficult time talking about her feelings. She said to her psychotherapist, "I'm a very private person. I've *never* told anyone how bad I feel about myself—." This made it harder for Thelma to begin talking about herself and to begin facing herself, but she began to understand that she was not unique or alone; that most women over 50 find it hard to talk intimately about their feelings.

Perhaps this is because they grew up during the Depression, when it was a luxury to think about or talk about *feelings;* people were too busy trying to make a living, trying to survive. Because of the hard times, people became "achievement" conscious, not "feeling" conscious. It was a period when people felt it was important to keep their "chin up", when courage and a "stiff upper lip" were valued. Crying and allowing oneself to feel bad were considered self-indulgent, because all one's time and energy was needed to make a dollar. Together we remembered this time, Thelma and I, and we remembered our mothers who never talked about their feelings . . . but who had "headaches." We remembered our strong and stoic grandmothers who were silent. Did they suffer silently?

Many younger women, today, have had different kinds of lives. They've had more time and energy to think, to explore, to examine their feelings and their *changing* feelings (because feelings never stay the same). And women over 50 are learning that this is important . . . in order to know who we were and who we are and who we *can* be. It is sometimes frightening to begin exploring ourselves and our feelings. We're afraid of what we'll find out and we're afraid of feeling bad.

• *Help from other women.*

This is where other over-50 women can be of tremendous help. When you know that most older women have the same fears and the same conflicts you do, it helps put it all in proper perspective and you begin to realize that you're not alone; that you're not "crazy" or maladjusted or neurotic; that it is just plain hard, sometimes, to be an over-50 woman. And what's wrong with being scared? When you sit down together with other older women and find out you have the same feelings and the same problems, the next natural and logical step is to begin sharing solutions . . . and that is what gives you more power over your life.

• *Choose a therapist who understands you.*

If you do decide to seek the help of a psychotherapist (or psychologist or social worker), choose one who knows and understands the history of older women and the conditions in which women live; who understands that how you feel now and how you behave now has been shaped, to a large degree, by your material (economic and social) world as you were growing up. For instance, if you grew up the daughter of immigrant parents who sent their *son* to college, rather than the girls in the family, you might still feel resentful and cheated . . . especially if you were as smart as your brother.

• *Understanding yourself.*

Alone or with other women or with a psychotherapist (or both), we must struggle to understand how we feel, how our feelings are always changing, and how our feel-

ings can control our behavior . . . in our sex lives, our
work lives, and our social lives. Only then will we be
able to *FREE* ourselves from our bad feelings.

Anxiety: What Is It? How Does It Feel?

How to describe anxiety? Unbearable tension . . . the
feeling you get in your stomach when you're going down
in an elevator that lurches (and you're *not* in an elevator)
. . . a feeling of apprehension all over your body . . . a
dark feeling of impending doom . . . panic! "Free-floating
anxiety" is anxiety that you can't pinpoint; anxiety you
don't understand, and don't know what to do about it.
Anxiety can give you chest pains, stomach cramps, and
bad headaches. Anxiety can make you want to curl up in
a ball and not move. Anxiety attacks can make you want
to scream. An acute anxiety attack can force you to
pace up and down, back and forth . . . until the peak
simmers down. Anxiety cannot kill you but it can make
you extremely uncomfortable.

• *Getting relief from anxiety.*
There *is* relief from anxiety. The best kind of relief, the
kind that permanently erases the anxiety, is knowing *why*
you're feeling so bad and then finding out what to do
about it—and doing it.
Kaye found, after months of psychotherapy and a long
crippling period of anxiety when she couldn't even get
out of bed to do her housework, that she had been refusing to acknowledge to herself that she was unhappily married. She had been married in the 1950's, a decade when
great emphasis was put on being a "successful wife" (and
Kaye particularly wanted to be a "successful wife" because
she had married late). Almost everything went badly in
the marriage. It was a grim oppressive twenty-five years
with very little laughter, but Kaye insisted on putting her
head in the sand. She constantly pretended to herself—
for all those years—that everything was fine. But deep
down inside, she knew better, and this role-playing to herself and to others took its toll; it produced such inner
tension and conflict that the result was a constant feeling
of dreadful apprehension (anxiety). It was only when

Kaye began to allow herself to face her *real* and enormous anger that the anxiety gradually left her. She no longer needed to keep up the terrible strain of lying to herself.

- *Can you change your life situation?*

Sometimes people are in bad situations and *can't* change them—such as women who are taking care of terminally ill husbands. This can produce tremendous tension and feelings of grief and fear. Perhaps you can't change your situation, but you can try to find someone caring to talk to on a regular basis. Feeling free to face your fear and resentment about a situation you can't change and realizing it's acceptable to feel afraid can relieve your anxiety. But are you sure you *can't* change your situation? Have you taken a long look at all your possible choices?

- *Would you be comfortable making changes?*

Could it be that you just wouldn't be comfortable taking other choices? That you would be frightened changing your situation? Talking to someone can help you get *ready* to face other choices—and change a bad situation that *can* be changed, if this is what you decide to do.

- *Professional help.*

Choose a psychotherapist who understands how older women are perceived in our society . . . a psychotherapist who knows it to be *true* (and that you're not overreacting) when you say that your grandchildren act like you're not even in the room with them when they're talking to each other; who understands that sometimes younger people perceive older people as "invisible," and who understands that, of course, you feel bad about this.

- *Drugs to relieve your anxiety.*

There are drugs that can effectively relieve feelings of acute anxiety. Some psychotherapists will not prescribe tranquilizers because they feel the drug allows the patient to withdraw from confronting her anxiety and the reasons for the anxiety. There are other doctors who feel differently. Feel free to choose a doctor who shares *your* philosophy about this—and the degree of your anxiety feelings may affect your philosophy; if you're feeling terrible enough (so that you have trouble functioning) you may feel you have a right to a drug that will allow you to go out and earn a living and have a workable relationship with your husband. Not being able to function can hurt your pocketbook and make life a nightmare. (I'm all for any kind of relief.) And it does not mean you are weak or worthless or are going to become an addict if you see medication as an avenue to feeling better. At least talk to your doctor about it.

Of course you will only take tranquilizers under a doctor's direction. Why? Because even though a tranquilizer can change your days from hopeless to hopeful, there are possible side effects . . . and these might be injurious to your health. Valium and Librium sometimes (even though very infrequently) cause liver damage, lowered blood pressure, and blurred vision. These drugs can also cause nausea or skin eruptions or constipation. Tell your doctor if you're taking any other drugs while you're taking a tranquilizer, so she can tell you if they're compatible with each other. Don't be surprised if she tells you not to lie in the sun and not to drink liquor while you're taking a particular tranquilizer. Find out everything about the drug you're taking—preferably before you begin to use it. *Know* what you put into your body.

You're Over 50—And It's Time to Stop Smoking!

There are food-aholics and alcoholics and *smoke*-aholics. Did you begin smoking when you were in your teens so you could look sophisticated, and then found it was hard to stop—even if you wanted to? Smoking is bad for our lungs and our heart and, in our middle years, can cause all kinds of physical problems. But how to stop?

· *Join a group for support.*
Perhaps it would be easier for you if you join a group (yes, smokers can find groups just like alcoholics and overeaters). Smoking can be just as much an addiction as overeating and drinking too much. The support of a group can do wonders, and there are some excellent stop-smoking programs, like Smoke-Enders. You've heard that hypnosis can help? Well, why not try? And look at it this way:

The money you save by not smoking can pay for a trip to the Bahamas or a jaunt to London!

You're Drinking Too Much

Dr. Marvin Block, former chairman of the American Medical Association's Committee on Alcoholism, says that about 50 per cent of alcoholic people in our country are women. Are you one? (Many are older women.)

• *It's a treatable illness.*

Acute alcoholism may require hospitalization for detoxification. Psychotherapy can help. Joining Alcoholics Anonymous has saved many a life.

Al-Anon is an organization through which your husband can learn to understand your illness better, to live with you while you are ill and while you recover.

If you still have teenagers at home, Alateen is a group in which they also can learn how to cope—and not to be judgmental.

These groups exist throughout the nation. Each is listed in the phone book.

Get help. You would get help if you had diabetes, wouldn't you? There is no difference.

Your Eyes As You Get Older

Your eyes *do* change as you grow older. Most people find it harder to see great distances as they age, and they find it harder to focus their eyes on very near objects (like trying to read the names in the telephone book). Do you see dark spots moving in front of your eyes occasionally? Just harmless shadows behind your pupil! See that your glasses are checked regularly, and see that you get corrective lenses if you need them. You might want to buy a magnifier to make reading easier and invest in large-print books. The *New York Times* has a special large-print edition available that you can order and receive regularly by mail. A three-month subscription costs $11. To subscribe, send your name, address, and check to *The New York Times Large Type Weekly,* P.O. Box 2570, Boulder, Colorado 80302.

• *Cataracts.*

There are particular kinds of eye conditions that affect older people more often. Cataracts, for one. We all know at least one over-50 person who has had a cataract operation or who is waiting for her cataract to "ripen" before surgery is scheduled. Don't panic if you do develop the kind of cataract that needs surgery; the operation is much simpler than it used to be. It wasn't too long ago when cataract patients had to stay in bed after the surgery, their heads held very still (sometimes with the aid of sandbags). Today patients are out of bed two to four days after the operation, and the operation is quicker and easier than before. In fact, the operation is now so much easier that even ninety-year-olds are often operated on for cataract removal.

What *is* a cataract? Nothing more than a cloudiness in the lens of your eye. Physicians suggest removal when it gets to the point where it decreases vision. Some cataracts are so small that they don't impair vision and don't need to be removed.

• *Glaucoma.*

Another condition more common to people over 50 is glaucoma. Glaucoma patients have higher-than-normal pressure in the eyeball, and this causes damage to the optic nerve and in some cases can result in loss of vision. Acute glaucoma can produce severe pain in the eye, blurred vision, and rainbow halos which the patient sees around lights. There may also be redness of the eye. With acute glaucoma a patient usually gets to a doctor fast for diagnosis and treatment because the pain is so intense. Chronic glaucoma can creep up more slowly and a person may not even know she has glaucoma until her vision is seriously impaired. Symptoms could be blurred vision, occasional headaches on one side or another, and seeing rainbow halos around electric lights.

Glaucoma can run in a family, so if you have a history of glaucoma in your family, be checked regularly by your ophthalmologist. But even if no one in your family had had this eye disease, ask an ophthalmologist to check you every two years (never less) because it often does hit people over 50. Diagnostic tests are painless. And if you do develop this condition, surgery is only resorted to when medication does not satisfactorily control the pressure in the eyeball.

· *Separation of the retina.*

Sometimes an over-50 person develops a separation of the retina in her eye. If you see a sudden shower of shadows or a dark curtain in one side of your vision, or if you have a decrease in your vision a few hours or a few days after you experience a shower of spots in front of your eyes, call an ophthalmologist right away. Surgery can often correct this.

· *Who can treat your eyes?*

An ophthalmologist is an eye physician and surgeon. An optometrist can examine your eyes and prescribe lenses. An optician is qualified to fill the ophthalmologist's or optometrist's prescription for eyeglasses.

· *Eye tests; eye screening.*

In some communities, you can have your vision screened without charge to see if you need corrective lenses, through community services. For instance, in Maryland, the Maryland Society for The Prevention of Blindness occasionally conducts free acuity eye screening on a mass basis in the senior adult departments of community centers, and in senior centers throughout the state. Call organizations similiar to this in your area, and ask if you can be scheduled for a no-cost eye screening.

· *Continue to care for your eyes.*

Don't be vain about wearing glasses. Maybe you'd be comfortable wearing contact lenses. Don't be one of those women who lean forward and squint into people's faces (rather than wear glasses)—You'll look older!

"They" were right when they shook their finger at you, when you were ten, and said, "Take care of your eyes. They're the only ones you'll ever have!"

The Changes in Your Skin

Our skin becomes thinner and drier as we age. Have you noticed the skin on your hands looks older than on

any other part of your body? That's because there are
few oil glands to prevent the skin on your hands from
wrinkling and there's no underlying tissue to smooth the
hand skin out. Your hands may get a lot of rough wear
and tear, too . . . washing dishes and being exposed to
harsh detergents.

• *Brown spots.*

Have you noticed brown spots on your hands? This
comes with aging, and you can get rid of them (or try to)
by soaking your hands in a mixture of salt and lemon
juice.

• *You shouldn't lie in the sun.*

Don't lie in the sun for hours like you did when you
were eighteen. At the least, it will dry your skin even
more and give you more wrinkles; at the worst, you can
get skin cancer. *Pamper* your over-50 skin.

• *Your facial skin.*

How about your facial skin? You probably use more
makeup than when you were younger—heavier night
creams and a moisturizer under your makeup, too. This
means your face is harder to clean. Go to your cosmetic
counter and buy a good cleansing product, and use it
twice a day (morning and night). And do use moisturizer
under your makeup; the over-50 skin usually produces
less moisture, so your moisturizer is the most important
beauty aid you have. A dry skin ages faster!

Today it's easy to find cosmetics and cleansers made
with natural ingredients—I know of one cleanser made
with yogurt—and they're kinder to older skins. Particularly good for some of our skins are the hypoallergenic cosmetics and cleansers.

(A tip: Cleansers and cosmetics vary widely in price,
and often you'll find yourself paying mainly for the *container*. Bargain basements and five-and-dime stores are
excellent places to purchase cosmetics and creams!)

Your Body and Senses: How They Change

Some things are *known* to happen to our bodies when
we age; these things are part of the normal development

of aging. Other things are not yet known, and a lot of research is now being conducted to find out what happens to us after the age of 50: Gerontological studies are trying to discover just how our muscles shorten as we get older, and what chemical shifts occur in our bodies as we age, and how our heart and lung functions change with aging, and why some of us age well and some of us don't.

• *Your hearing.*

What is already known? Well, they know that our ears are usually less keen in our fifties than when we were younger. This is the time we want to be sure we have our hearing tested regularly. It's much better to wear a hearing aid than to wonder if people are talking about you; to wonder what the speaker said a minute ago; and to answer "Yes I did" to the question, "How do you feel?" If you've been saying "What?" when people talk to you, or "Pardon me?" a little too often—have your doctor check your hearing.

And *don't* buy a hearing aid without comparison shopping. There are a lot of sharp salesmen visiting women over 50 with a big con story and a big-priced hearing aid that doesn't work well. Ask your doctor to recommend a source for this kind of aid.

• *Your energy level; chronic illnesses.*

Gerontologists have also found that when we reach our sixties and seventies we may not have as much energy as we did before. But, of course, that is not true of everyone. Also, in our sixties and seventies, we may develop chronic health problems like arthritis and heart disease. It is known that black people over 50 have a higher incidence of hypertension. These conditions may mean that we have to somewhat limit our activities. But, you know, the woman who didn't sleep all night from her arthritic pain can *still* play cards with her friends the next afternoon; she can just go to bed early the next night. Right?

And in our seventies and eighties some of us may be full of energy, but others of us may be more frail than we were before. Again, we can adjust to the changes in our bodies. The seventy-year-old woman who tires easily can make it her business to take a nap every afternoon (or at least rest in bed with a book). This is one of the payoffs to being seventy in our society; there's *time* to take that nap. And that daily shut-eye will give her the energy to go to her daughter's house for supper that evening!

• *Your gums, teeth, and bridgework.*

Going regularly to your dentist for necessary gum treatment as well as teeth care is very important for the over-50 woman. Our gums are more vulnerable to disease when we're older, and the condition of our gums will affect the condition of our teeth, as well as what we can eat and how much we enjoy our food. If you have bridgework, wear it. If it sits in a glass in your bathroom, instead, eventually one side of your face can begin to look lopsided (caved in), and that isn't pretty. If you don't wear your bridgework, your teeth can shift position and affect your bite, and then, after a period of time, you may find your bridgework doesn't fit anymore. New bridgework can be very expensive! Also be sure you don't "click" when you talk—and we all know at least one older person who does, because her bridgework is loose.

Is it safe to use over-the-counter denture paste or powder to keep your bridgework from slipping? Yes, but be sure you take your dentures out daily to clean them, and also to clean your mouth. Bridgework that fits well should need no denture paste or powder. If your bridgework is bent, and really doesn't fit—don't try to wear it. You'll be inviting infections in your mouth.

• *Is it harder to keep your weight down?*

Extra weight is easy to put on and hard to take off when we're over 50. Have you noticed that when (and if) you do put on a lot of extra weight, it seems to settle in different areas of your body from when you were younger? Unsightly places—like around your waist, or your stomach or your thighs? What's the answer? Eat much less than you did when you were younger. You don't need as much food (and you'll look nicer, too).

Older Can Mean Better!

Do you catch yourself reading the obituaries now that you're over 50? Death *does* become more real to us now.

After all, our husband and some of our dear and close friends may have died. These losses have made us more conscious of our own impending deaths. Now that doesn't mean we think of death all the time (our healthy defenses don't allow this), but most over-50 women think of death more often than they did fifteen years ago. Naturally. This is realistic and this is normal.

· *Live in the now!*

You might find when you reach your sixties and seventies, that you really don't like to plan ahead too far in the future . . . or think too much about the future. Tillie, who is in her late sixties, told me, "My daughter-in-law invited me to join them for a trip to Europe that they're planning to take next summer. I told her I'll see, and she said, 'What do you mean you'll see.' She doesn't understand that I just can't make plans that far ahead."

If you're in your sixties or seventies, this can be good, because this can help you live in the *NOW*. For instance, one of the most exciting women I know just completed college at the age of sixty-eight. Someone asked her what she was going to do with her new degree. "Do with it?" she exclaimed, amused, "I have the luxury—at the age of sixty-eight—of not worrying about that. Who cares about five years from now? I had great fun *getting* it, and now I'll take one day at a time using it, as I took one day at a time getting it."

So our fear of death, or our horror of "the end," or our realism about life not being forever can play an ironic part in getting us to be NOW-oriented. It can push us to do exciting things NOW and to live NOW. And a marvelous payoff to this is that once you're busy doing exciting things NOW and living NOW—you stop worrying so much about your demise. Right?

· *Begin new ventures!*

Most of us, when we've reached our seventies and eighties, look back a lot and think of ourselves a great deal, and try to take stock and find meaning to our past lives. Isn't this also realistic? After all, we've lived a long life by then and we're trying to see if our life had value for us and for other people who were meaningful to us. That does *not* mean that women who have enough ego-strength won't begin exciting new ventures: There are women artists and women photographers and women writers who are productive and growing in their seventies and eighties. (Imogen Cunningham continued taking marvelous photographs through her early nineties!) There are women in their seventies and eighties living in communes with younger people; many older women who were political activists in the suffragist movement are still politically active. There are women in their seventies and eighties who still take in foster children. There are women in their seventies and eighties bringing up their grandchildren alone. And there are women in their seventies and eighties who still put up jars of fruits and vegetables and who still cook for hundreds of relatives at family gatherings. Are you one of them? Hurrah for you!

•   *Use a strength to make up for a loss!*

Of course your health will influence how much you do and what you do and how you do it—*and* also how you feel emotionally.

This is the secret: If you've lost a strength (perhaps you can't walk too well anymore, you can't see too well anymore, or you're in pain a great deal), *concentrate on a strength you have not lost.* Build up the strength you still have so it can make up for what you've lost. I think of Rosie, a seventy-year-old woman who lost her sight two years ago, but who comes everyday to a community center to sew with a group of women. She always did sew beautifully and enjoyed it, and she doesn't need her eyes to keep making lovely items to give to charity. I think of Gertrude, who had two major heart attacks in the past year, but who for a few hours a day works behind the boutique counter of the apartment-house-for-the-aged in which she lives. Gertrude can sell *anything,* and she gets a particular thrill when she sells several pieces of jewelry to a woman who didn't expect to buy anything.

•   *Remain productive . . . Be useful . . . Feel joyful.*

Replace a lost strength with a new found strength. Replace a lost strength with strengths you already had and used successfully. This is your key to remaining productive and feeling useful and being *joyful.*

CHAPTER 2

Getting the Best Medical Care

ح‍ۍ ۿ‍ۮ

Be Particular about Your Medical Care

As a woman over 50, be as selective in choosing your
doctor, hospital, dentist, and pharmacist as you possibly
can. Why? Because your life *and* the quality of your life
may depend on how well you choose. As we grow into
our fifties and beyond, we are more apt to develop a
chronic disease than when we were much younger (when
we were more prone to acute diseases), and if a chronic
disease has become part of your life, you want to be sure
that you've chosen the best medical care that is available
to you.

What to look for.
Medical care should be a total concept, involving the
right doctors, hospitals, group health insurance plans,
dentists, and pharmacists. You want to be sure that
you've chosen a doctor who knows as much as there is to
know about how to relieve any pain you may experience,
without endangering your health. She should know how to
arrest the disease, if possible, and the best treatments.
You want a doctor who keeps up with the latest medical
research that is being conducted throughout the *world,*
and who, if she feels it is applicable to your case and is

35

unable to provide it, will inform you about new kinds of treatment and where to get it. As an older woman, you know your body is more vulnerable than when you were twenty years old—at least in certain ways—and you'll want to choose a doctor who practices *preventive* medicine; one who is aware of how the environment affects your body. You will certainly want to choose a doctor who is interested in treating older patients, and one who is aware of the physical changes in our bodies as we grow older. Don't choose a doctor simply because her office is across the street from where you live. It's harder to get around than when you were twenty, but going to a doctor *only* because her office is nearby can possibly cost you your health.

Your Family Doctor

This is the doctor who will get to know you best. You will use her as the central physician in your life, who will examine you for any and all illnesses, and who will act as a referral service, if necessary—referring you to the proper specialist. This is the doctor who should know you intimately as a patient, because you're saying, "Here. This is my life," when you entrust your total health needs to her. This doctor should know about your emotional health as well as your physical condition—because she respects the fact that your feelings affect your body.

This means that you should carefully choose your family doctor—and select one whom you feel comfortable with and like and trust.

• The internist.

I have a bias. I believe that if you're over 50, you should, if possible, choose an internist for your family doctor. An internist is *not* an intern (a junior hospital doctor). An internist is a physician who has completed a residency in internal medicine. She is trained to treat you if you have heart, lung or kidney disease; if you have diabetes or arthritis; if you have disorders affecting your blood or your endocrine glands. These are disorders that frequently affect the older person—so you can see why I have this bias. If you do choose an internist for your family doctor, it might also save you time and money and energy, because the internist often has her office fully equipped for special diagnostic procedures, so you don't have to go to other specialists for tests. If your internist finds you need a chest x-ray, the diagnostic equipment might be right there in her office. If you need an electro-cardiogram, you might be able to have this done right there on the spot.

How will you know if a doctor is an internist? Call your library and ask the librarian to look up her name in *The Directory of Medical Specialties*. Look at the certi-ficates on her wall. Does it state that she is certified by the American Board of Internal Medicine? This means that she has successfully passed an examination in inter-nal medicine following a residency. Look up her name in *The American Medical Association Directory* (it's prob-ably in your library) and read about her credentials.

• *The family practitioner.*

I recently spoke to a medical director in a multipur-pose senior center who has another opinion: She feels the best source of primary care for the older patient is a family practitioner. Is she the same as a general practi-tioner? No. The general practitioner usually has had one or two years of rotating internship beyond her medical school training; the family practitioner goes through an internship *plus* three more years of training that is di-vided among the specialties. The family practitioner also goes through a residency, and must take examinations after the residency is completed. The American Board of Family Practice qualifies her, and a qualified family practitioner belongs to the *American Academy of Fam-ily Practice*. It is also required that the practicing family practitioner must do a certain amount of postgraduate work, and be reexamined every six years.

This did seem impressive, and I asked the medical director why she feels a family practitioner would be the best kind of family doctor for the older or middle-aged person. Aside from this thorough training, and the need to be reexamined at intervals, she said, the family prac-titioner sees the older patient's needs related to her *total* environment: Is a sixty-year-old woman suffering from depression because of her relationship with her children?

Is a fifty-five-year-old woman having stomach problems because of her relationship with her husband? The family practitioner uses para-professionals for outreach: An older woman may be suffering from a heart ailment and thereby require a different housing arrangement; the para-professional may contact the local housing department to arrange this. The family practitioner also uses the services of physician's assistants in the office, to take blood pressures and do a variety of other tasks, freeing the family practitioner to see more patients, and to spend more time with each patient.

When a patient has a particular need the family practitioner cannot meet, she refers the patient to a specialist, but the patient returns to the family practitioner after treatment: The family practitioner always knows what is happening to the patient.

However, this is a new concept (around five years old) and there aren't many family practitioners outside of urban areas. Your local medical society can refer you to one, if any exist in your area.

- *The general practitioner.*

There are no internists *or* family practitioners in your town? Well, why *not* a general practitioner? There are certainly many excellent ones. But choose a family practitioner or a general practitioner as carefully as you would a specialist. Use the same guides to determine whether she is a good family doctor.

Guides to Use in Choosing a Family Doctor

Some important criteria for evaluating a doctor are:

- Does she take at least an hour to complete a case history and examination during your first office visit?
- Does the doctor examine your breasts each time you come in for any kind of examination?
- Does she see you on appointment, and see you within a relatively short time after you've arrived in the office?
- Does the doctor schedule only one patient at a

time—or are there three or four patients being examined at the same time in various examining rooms (as the physician runs back and forth from one patient to another)?

- Is the doctor associated with a hospital that you would be willing to use?
- Does she make you wait more than two weeks for a non-emergency kind of appointment?
- Does she return your phone calls?
- Does she provide competent backup doctors when she is not available?
- Does she readily call in consultants?
- Will the doctor accept the Medicare fee (and you're covered by Medicare if you're sixty-five or over)?
- Does she charge an extra fee for completing insurance forms?
- Will this doctor work out a sliding fee, if you're on a low income or have high living expenses?
- Will she accept Medicaid (state medical aid for low-income people) if you have a Medicaid card?
- Does she charge a fee for telephone consultation?
- Does she tell you of possible side effects from medication *before* you take the medication?
- Will she let you see your medical records if you ask?
- Is she a member of the American Academy of Family Physicians (AAFP) or certified by the American Academy of Family Practice? If she's a specialist, an internist, is she certified by the American Board of Internal Medicine?

- *Be realistic in your expectations.*

It's unrealistic to expect your family doctor to be Marcus Welby. It's only on television that the family doctor gets so wrapped up in every patient that she lies in bed pondering the patient's private life, or dashes out of the house in the middle of the night to make a house call, or has heated discussions about her patients with her colleagues at a dinner party.

However, you can expect—and *should* expect—a family doctor who does not brush aside your aches and pains by saying, "What do you expect? You're no spring chicken!" People over 50 have as much right to proper medical care as the younger patient. Some doctors brush aside the complaints of older patients because they feel uncomfortable about their own aging. Many doctors feel so helpless about helping the older patient feel better (especially if there's an ongoing and painful chronic illness) that they'd rather not treat her. You should choose a family doctor who does *not* feel threatened by her own impending aging; who *is* willing and interested in treating older people. And you should select a doctor who understands that your aches and pains *may* be due to your fear about aging—but who also understands that your pain may be organic, and who insists on checking this out thoroughly for each complaint.

You should choose a family doctor who knows that sex life doesn't have to stop when one is fifty, and who isn't embarrassed about talking with the older patient about this.

Your Gynecologist: What to Look For

There are certain things you can and should expect from your gynecologist—and other services you shouldn't expect.

• *Does she treat you like a person?*

You *should* expect her to talk to you in the office before your pelvic examination, so she will have the necessary medical information to relate to the examination and to make you feel less like an object, once you're on the examining table. Talking to you ahead of time humanizes the situation. You will feel less vulnerable lying on the examining table with your feet and legs held apart. You can also expect her to *tell* you before she puts her finger up your rectum—before anything unexpected is introduced into your body. You should feel able to ask that the cold speculum be warmed before insertion. You should expect that the nurse be in the room with both of you, and that the door be closed for privacy. Did you grow up in a family where your parents and brothers and sisters were self-conscious about nudity and where no one talked about sex? You have a right to expect your gynecologist to understand this and be sensitive to this. Some of us are still self-conscious about our sexuality (again, this is how we were brought up) and having our sexual organs touched by a stranger can make us feel apprehensive, panic-stricken, ashamed. Your gynecologist should appreciate this, and should understand the collective social and sexual history of the woman over 50. She should act in a caring and perceptive way, part of which is making you feel at ease, as you lie on the table, legs apart and feet in stirrups, feeling awkward, during the examination.

· *Does she talk about menopause? Estrogen replacement?*
Expect your gynecologist to tell you everything you want to know about menopause. *Expect* your gynecologist to tell you about estrogen replacement therapy—and to be able to discuss the *New England Journal of Medicine*'s December, 1975, report, which linked this therapy to a substantially increased risk of uterine cancer. *Expect* her to be cautious in prescribing estrogen replacement for you. Choose a gynecologist who strongly feels that extensive, well-funded research should begin, so we eventually know the exact risks and benefits in estrogen replacement therapy.

· *Self examinations; her examinations.*
Expect your gynecologist to teach you how to examine your own breasts at home. Expect your gynecologist to examine you and give you a Pap test twice a year, now that you're over 50. *Expect* your gynecologist to give you an immediate appointment if you find a thickening or lump in your breast or if you experience irregular or unexpected vaginal bleeding. *Expect* your gynecologist to be concerned when you tell her of any extreme discomfort when you're menstruating or getting ready to menstruate, and not to tell you "It's all in your head" (or to imply it).

· *Surgery.*
Can your gynecologist perform surgery? Yes, for *particular* kinds of gynecological problems.

· *She isn't an authority on sex!*
What can't your gynecologist do? Well, you shouldn't

expect her to be your sexual authority. Frequently, women of all ages expect their gynecologists to be experts on sexual behavior and to have the right formulas for perfect orgasms, and to know what makes a "good" sexual relationship. Your gynecologist may know far less than you do about sex. She may have had very little training in medical school in this area (although some medical schools do include sex therapy or sex education, much more so than in former years, it is often still insufficient). Consider: Your gynecologist might be a *lousy* lover at home. But many gynecologists internalize this "sex expert" image society has given them and begin to believe it. Some are far too ready to give sexual advice —much of it sexist and misleading—to their floundering patients.

Make full use of your gynecologist in the many important areas for which she *is* trained. This is the way you will be good to your body.

Your Mental Health Needs:

You may be thinking, "Why is she bothering to write about this? Every woman goes to a family doctor—either one in private practice or one working in a clinic—and only a few go to psychotherapists." Wrong. That was perhaps once true, but today many people go for professional help when they're confused, or very angry, or depressed and anxious, or when they find they can't function on the level they want to. It's hard to be a woman over 50 in a society that values young, strong, energetic and productive people, and the most together older woman is going to feel bad about herself occasionally; useless, "invisible." It is at these times that women have found that they want to go for help. To whom should you turn for this type of help? Your choices are: a trained social worker, a clinical psychologist, a psychiatrist, or a psychoanalyst.

• *Psychiatrists and psychoanalysts.*
If you choose to be treated by a psychiatrist or psychoanalyst, you'll find these specialists are medical doctors who *can* prescribe medication. They specialize in the di-

agnosis, treatment, and prevention of mental and emotional disorders. Their training includes at least three years of residency training in psychiatry. Some psychiatrists are certified by the American Board of Psychiatry and Neurology, which means that they have passed a test (written and oral) that indicates a sound knowledge base. A psychiatrist may practice in a private setting or clinic setting, and psychotherapy can be conducted on a one-to-one basis or a group basis. Short or long term treatment is available. Most psychiatrists feel that psychoanalysis is not effective for the older patient—and one of the reasons is that treatment is long-term, sometimes lasting for years.

• *How much do they charge?*

Most psychiatrists are very expensive ($50 and up for fifty minutes of treatment), and some are low-cost or free. It is very hard to find a free psychiatrist in our society. However, community mental health clinics do exist all over the country, and it is in this setting that there is a sliding fee, according to income. Call your city or county health department to inquire about this service in your area.

If you want to look up the credentials of a psychiatrist, go to your library and find the *Biographical Directory of the American Psychiatric Association.*

• *Lay therapists: What are they? What do they do?*

Since it's often less expensive to use the services of a social worker than a psychiatrist, and for some patients, just as effective—what are her qualifications? She will have a master of social work degree or a doctor of social work degree. She may practice in a social work agency or a hospital or have a private practice or group practice. A social worker can't prescribe medication (although she may work under the close supervision of a medical doctor, who can).

Some patients use the services of a clinical psychologist. She has graduate training beyond a master's degree, and has taken an appreciable number of courses related to medicine (for instance, what drugs work for which disorders), even though she can't prescribe. A growing number of clinical psychologists prefer treating the older person.

If you've been going to a social worker or a clinical psychologist for a while and you feel you're not getting better, you might arrange for a consultation with a psychiatrist; your problem might need medication or further neurological checkup.

And if you're sixty-five or over, Medicare may pay for part of your treatment with a psychiatrist or a clinical psychologist.

• *Using your clergy for help.*

You might be more comfortable talking to your clergyperson about your feelings and your problems, rather than a psychiatrist or a social worker or a psychologist. Traditionally, the clergy is someone we can confide in; someone to give us support emotionally. Younger clergy, particularly, are learning how to counsel people as part of their training. Older clergypersons have their own life experience to draw on, years of listening to people in trouble, people who are hurting. And an advantage to talking to your religious leader is that she probably knows your entire family, and this allows her to see a larger picture. Competent and responsible clergy will refer you to a professional helper (a psychiatrist or social worker or psychologist) if she sees she does not have enough experience or knowledge to help you herself.

• *What kind of treatment do you need?*

There are "schools" of therapy—meaning there are different ways of treating a patient. Some psychiatrists adhere to one particular "school," but more and more have an eclectic approach; they attempt to use different methods of treatment at different times with the same patient, depending on the patient's needs at a given time. There is the kind of psychotherapy that focuses on your childhood and and kind that relates to the here-and-now. There is the kind of psychotherapy that stresses how our social conditioning has affected our feelings and behavior. There is also a movement in psychotherapy (Radical Therapy) that examines the political influences in our lives and how they affect us—such as realizing how powerless minority groups (blacks, women, Chicanos and Native Americans) begin *feeling* powerless and *acting* powerless.

• *How to choose a psychotherapist.*

Some people who have successfully terminated psychotherapy feel it is not the kind of therapy that made them feel and do better—it was the psychotherapist herself. They feel that if the psychotherapist was knowledgeable and warm and sharing and caring, this is what really mattered.

Choose a psychotherapist who does not stereotype women (and a female doctor may do this too!)! Especially older women. If the psychotherapist expects older women to behave a certain way, this will affect the way the patient will relate to her. More important, this will no doubt affect the way the older-woman patient will feel about herself.

I remember talking to a psychotherapist who strongly felt that women are happiest as wives and mothers; that they are "unfulfilled" if they have not "achieved" these roles. This is a doctor who would probably feel (at least subconsciously) that the over-50 widow, whose grown children had long left home, was *finished*. She would feel that her only real chance at happiness was in remarrying and again having the "important" role of wife. How would her sixty-year-old female patient feel about herself? Being sixty in our society, her chances at remarriage might be slim—and furthermore, she might not *want* to remarry. Would she feel there was something wrong with her because of this? I think so—because she would probably think the doctor was "right" (we grow up learning that our doctor is always "right"). She would probably feel like a failure.

Another common and potentially destructive stereotype is the psychotherapist who grows up being taught that women should always act demure and passive. She might have a hard time understanding the anger and deep bitterness of a sixty-five-year-old patient who finds that she's not getting the "payoff" society has cruelly promised her —love, honor, attention, and respect from her family, in return for years spent as a "good" mother and a "good" wife; recognition and respect from society in return for years spent as a "decent" citizen. It just isn't always that way, is it? Women over 50 don't inevitably get those payoffs. Grown children sometimes move far away and lose touch (after years of your having been a good mother) and aging husbands sometimes leave their wives for young women (after years of your having been a devoted wife). People over sixty-five find their Social Security benefits don't cover the bare necessities (after years of paying their taxes regularly) and aging women sometimes spend their last years in furnished rooms—isolated and frightened—after years of teaching their children that we live in the best country in the world that takes care of the needs of everyone. The young psychotherapist, often affluent and protected, lives in high-quality housing and still has the love and attention of her small children, and she may not yet be aware that we can't expect "payoffs" when we're older. She is often unaware of the realities of life for the aging woman. Her patient's anger and bitterness surprises her and she may feel it's "sick" behavior. But isn't it *society* that is "sick" for perpetuating the hoax of a "payoff" for certain behavior. Shouldn't the psychotherapist be examining this? Few do.

• *Ask her questions on your first visit.*

In choosing a psychotherapist, invest in an initial sum (if you can) for a consultation before you commit yourself to a particular doctor. Use the fifty minutes you have to ask *her* questions. Ask, "Do you know what the average income is for people over sixty-five?", "Do you feel that the same choices exist for people *over* fifty that exist for people *under* fifty?", "What do you think are the biggest reasons for depression in the older woman?", and "How do you feel many younger people feel about older people?"

• *Does she understand older women?*

You are a woman over 50; you *know* many of the answers to these questions. Does *she*? She must *want* to understand the material conditions of the older woman (how much money you get and how much money you have to spend), and the social conditions of the older woman (how younger people view you; how this affects your feelings about yourself) in order to understand *YOU.* Your material conditions and your social conditions have shaped your feelings and your fears and your self-image and your behavior. She should have the curiosity and the breadth and depth of vision and the political perspective to appreciate this.

• *How to find a feminist therapist (one who DOES understand women).*

Unfortunately, it's not always easy to find this kind of psychotherapist. Comparison-shop. Get referrals from women over 50 who are satisfied with their psychotherapist; call your local Women's Growth Center or Women's Liberation Center or People's Free Clinic (if these centers exist in your town) for referrals—these are the kinds of places where the staff values the kind of therapist I've described. Explain what you're looking for. You might find, in your local Woman's Growth Center, that group therapy sessions already exist for over-50 women.

And don't discount the idea of getting your own group of women together to meet in your living room to discuss problems and solutions. This is free and this is valuable and you can do this even while you're in psychotherapy.

• *Mental health directories.*

Some medical self-help women's groups are making up their own mental health directories, based on recommendations from satisfied women. A Ralph Nader research group recently has developed two consumer guides for would-be patients to find mental health consumer information. One guide lists psychologists, psychiatric social workers, and psychiatrists in the Washington, D. C. area. It lists their education and qualifications, as well as their fees and their specialties and the disorders they prefer to treat. It also tells the reader the percentage of patients that a listed doctor has on drug therapy. This directory, *Through The Mental Health Maze,* is available for $4.00 (prepaid). Their other guide, not a directory, but a general information book applicable to would-be patients all through the country, has the same title and is $2.50 (also prepaid). To order either, send your check or money order to Health Research Group, Department P, 2000 P St., N. W., Washington, D. C. 20036. Even though both publications have the same title, they'll know which one you want by the amount of money you send.

A Man for Your Doctor—or a Woman?

If you prefer relating to a woman as your doctor, seriously consider using the services of a woman doctor. However, do not assume that a woman is automatically more sensitive and caring than a man, as a doctor—it's not quite so simple. There are perhaps as many insensitive female doctors as there are insensitive male doctors.

- *The younger female doctor: Often different from her older counterpart.*

Whether a female doctor is sensitive depends largely on her age. Why do I say this? Well, the female doctor who is over forty-five started her career when it was *very* hard for a woman to become a doctor (it still isn't easy!) and because she had to be in constant competition in a male-dominated profession she might not have had too much time or energy left to become "sensitive" and to cultivate her capacity to be caring and to feel empathy. She may have even wanted to appear as businesslike as her male colleagues, so she would seem as competent as they appeared. Also, she grew up at a time when feelings weren't as openly explored as now, and the process of exploring feelings was less valued.

On the other hand, the younger female doctor was trained when more professional doors were open for women medical students and female doctors, and she didn't have to try as hard to compete with the men in her profession. She grew up in a feeling-oriented society. She was also trained at a time (perhaps in the 1960's) when it was appropriate (in some circles) for the young medical student and doctor to get involved with patients' rights. These were the young medical students and doctors who marched in civil rights' demonstrations and in peace demonstrations, medical bag in hand, ready to face Mace and tear gas, so they could protect the oppressed. These were the young doctors who volunteered their precious free time to work in storefront free medical clinics, helping patients get more personal treatment than they would in large hospital clinics. These were the kind of doctors who would be more apt to see the over-50 woman as having unique social problems, because these doctors would be more aware of who the "powerful" and "power-less" people are in our society—and how being "power-less" affects the older woman.

• *Why a female physician might identify with you and understand you more than a male doctor.*

Would the young male doctor who has developed this orientation be just as tuned-in to the older woman's needs as the young female doctor? Very possibly. However, I remember a female doctor bringing in another factor: "The older woman is possibly more aware of time slip-ping by than the older man . . . because she has been time-oriented all her life; she has measured time by very real biological occurrences she could not escape—her menstrual periods that went on for forty years or more!" Does this mean that the female doctor *must* be more aware of how the older woman feels—because she has the same built-in biological time clock that the older woman had? Perhaps.

• *Why you might be a more intelligent health consumer with a woman as your doctor.*

Maybe you don't want to use the services of a female doctor because she seems too much like yourself—a lit-tle insecure, somewhat vulnerable. Possibly you prefer a male doctor because you (at least unconsciously) want an authoritarian type of physician who will act like a father figure. But this has its pitfalls: You'll expect him to know "everything" (like all fathers) and never make a mistake . . . and there is no such doctor! If you enter into a patient-doctor relationship with this kind of expectation, you will find yourself behaving like a child instead of an adult consumer. Doctors who encourage the father-figure relationship frequently do not want their authority chal-lenged and do not want to be questioned too often or too closely and they let their patients know this (this is the kind of doctor who calls *you* by your first name, but expects you to call him Dr. ———). Of course you'll hesitate questioning a doctor like this because you won't want to "make him angry." On the other hand, women usually don't perceive other women as awesome authority figures, so if you use the services of a female doctor you may feel more free to *be* the intelligent health-services

consumer that you really are and ask questions when
you know you should.

• *How often do women use female physicians?*

But how often *does* the female patient use the services
of the female doctor? At this point in history (the history
of American women), I think women are caught in a
bind. Because the woman patient sees the woman doctor
as an equal, and not as a parent figure, she will use her
services in areas that do not involve life and death; she'll
use her as a psychotherapist but she won't use her as a
surgeon. She'll trust only a male doctor (the all-knowing
authority figure) to use a knife on her body. I see this attitude as a developmental step in our growth as women; I
foresee the day when we will comfortably use the services of female doctors for psychotherapy *and* for major
surgery. This will happen when women begin seeing
themselves as competent enough to be surgeons and
when the male-controlled medical profession, through the
pressure of confident women acting collectively, begin
admitting as many women to the specialization of surgery
as men (which is not the case now). Thus, it will be
through seeing large numbers of women successfully performing surgery that more women will begin *using* the
services of female surgeons—as in some other countries
throughout the world.

Choosing a Hospital

Even if you are healthy and over 50, it is good to
be informed about the *kind* of hospital you should choose
if and when you ever need this service. Different kinds of
hospitals offer different kinds of services and different
degrees of *quality* of services. There is the private voluntary hospital and the large teaching hospital; there is the
private proprietary hospital and government-supported
hospitals. Single-specialty hospitals exist, also.

• *Private voluntary hospitals.*

Private voluntary hospitals are non-profit community
institutions, where some patients pay more than others.
Their medical staff and facilities are usually good. The

small community hospital might be a very good place to go for simple procedures such as traction or diagnostic tests, because the nursing care may be warm and personal (because it *is* a smaller hospital).

• *The teaching hospital.*

The larger teaching hospital, which is a hospital connected with a medical school, is a good choice for major surgery. The atmosphere may be impersonal because of the size of the institution, but each doctor is watched by another doctor almost looking over her shoulder when it comes to patient treatment, and this makes for high-quality medical care.

• *Proprietary hospitals.*

Then there are the more fancy private proprietary hospitals, usually serving excellent food and looking very luxurious. But these hospitals are commercial establishments designed to make a profit, and they exert less control over the medical qualifications and activities of their affiliated physicians.

• *Government hospitals.*

Government-supported hospitals have many non-paying patients, and are usually spartan-looking and serve very plain but nutritious food—and give good care.

• *Single-specialty hospitals.*

Single-specialty hospitals exist to serve the patient with the unusual problem, as well as the patient who feels more taken care of in a hospital where everyone has the same kind of illness that she does.

• *Choose a doctor who can practice at the hospital of your choice.*

Your family doctor and your surgeon are affiliated with particular hospitals; they cannot send you to a hospital where they are not affiliated. If you need surgery, you might want to choose a surgeon who is affiliated with the hospital you would prefer to use. You can call her office and ask the nurse which hospital the doctor is affiliated with. For more consumer information on surgery and surgeons (plus health insurance information and a host of other things) send $3.50 to Consumer News, Inc., 813

National Press Building, Washington, D. C. 20045, for
The Shopping Guide Book written by Herbert Dennenberg.

• *What to look for in a hospital.*

Once you have chosen your hospital, find out before
your visit what all their fees are, item by item. Ask what
tests and procedures are covered and not covered by your
medical insurance. This is particularly important if you
are sixty-five or over, and have only coverage "A" in
your Medicare insurance and if you do *not* have supplemental commercial health insurance. Ask the purpose
and the nature and the possible risks of all procedures
practiced on you once you're in the hospital. Be sure the
hospital accepts the possibility that you may refuse to
sign permission forms. Find out if an anesthesiologist will
administer the anesthesia if you are going to undergo surgery (it *should* be an anesthesiologist). Tell them if you
are allergic to any drugs. Yes, as a consumer you are entitled to all of this information for life-saving and money-saving reasons. *Your* life and *your* money.

How to Buy Your Drugs and Save Money

• *Discounts through a retirement organization.*

If you're a member of the American Association of
Retired Persons (1909 K St., N.W., Washington, D. C.
20049), you can fill your prescriptions more cheaply by
using their AARP Pharmacy Service. There are, at this
time of writing, six regional centers where you can purchase your medications personally or by mail, and you can
ask your nearest center to send you a price list, giving
yourself an opportunity to save money through group-buying. Note the address nearest you:

1224 24th St., N.W., Washington, D. C. 20037
6500 34th St. N., P.O. Box 14417, St. Petersburg,
Fla. 33733
3823 Broadway, Kansas City, Mo. 64111
701 Main St., East Hartford, Conn. 06108
3557 LaFayette Rd., Indianapolis, Ind. 46222
201 Long Beach Blvd., Long Beach, Calif. 90801.

AARP membership is open to all men and women fifty-five years and older.

• *Other money-saving tips.*

Comparison-shop senior citizen discounts at pharmacies, get a union discount on drugs, buy your drugs in middle-class neighborhoods because the pharmacies in poor neighborhoods often charge more money; (residents in poor neighborhoods have no choice, they can't comparison-shop because they don't have a car and sometimes they don't have *carfare*).

• *Choosing a pharmacist.*

Use the pharmacist who demonstrates that she is careful and dedicated. Use the pharmacist who has begun the excellent practice of maintaining a personalized record of the drugs you purchase. This way, if you have changed your doctor and your new physician wants to know the name of a drug you took two years ago, and you simply can't remember—she can just call your pharmacist. Do you know that a growing number of pharmacists will now take your blood pressure upon request, and just for the small fee of about one dollar? Choose the pharmacist who WANTS you to know what you're putting into your body: It is estimated that 1.5 million hospital admissions a year are due to adverse drug effects. Choose the pharmacist who can tell you if the drug you are about to take is compatible with *all foods* . . . with *liquor* . . . who will tell you what the possible side effects of the drug are.

• *Taking your medication with you on trips.*

If you're going to be visiting your children in another city, pack two identical containers (labeled) of the drug you must take every day, and put each container in a separate place (one in your pocketbook and one in your suitcase); if you lose your suitcase—you can still take your medication each morning.

• *Purchase drugs by their generic names!*

See if it's possible to have your drugs prescribed by their generic (chemical) names rather than the brand names. Brand-name prescriptions often cost five to ten times more than their generic counterparts, and sometimes even up to *thirty* times more! And, in nearly all cases, you're not getting benefits from paying the name-brand prices.

Getting Good Dental Care

• *Use a dental school!*

If you have a dental school in your immediate area, you'll probably find that it offers excellent care—whether you need a tooth filled or more complicated work such as gum treatment, root canal work, an extraction, or dentures. The price is much lower than if you were to use the services of a dentist in private practice. Also, the advanced dental student working on you is under very close supervision; less prone to make mistakes than a dentist in private practice who has no one to check on her!

• *A dental consumer directory.*

A good consumer guide to dental care is *Taking The Pain Out Of Finding A Good Dentist*, researched and written by a Ralph Nader team. It tells you what to look for in choosing a dentist. It also includes a selective directory of dentists in the Washington, D. C. area, who completed and returned questionnaires sent to them by the investigators. Send $2.00 (prepaid) to Health Research Group, Department P, 2000 P St., Washington, N.W., D. C. 20036.

A Proposed National Health Insurance Program

At this time, we seem to be moving toward national health insurance. Since older people face the highest incidence of illness and disability, and are least able to pay for adequate health protection, it's about time! Medicare is not adequate. The coverage is only basic, and it doesn't provide for extended illnesses.

• *The Corman-Kennedy Bill (HR 21/S 3).*

The National Health Security Program seems to be the most comprehensive of the five major health insurance bills proposed. Everyone living in the United States would be covered. The $104 million that is presently spent on Medicare would be used for this plan; in fact, the plan would supplant Medicare. It would pay for nearly the entire range of personal health care services—and even for extensive illnesses. You'd get full physicians' services, inpatient and outpatient hospital services, home health services, optometry and podiatry services, and necessary devices and appliances.

The limitation on long-term nursing home care would be 120 days per benefit period, except when the home is hospital owned and operated and the care is covered by the hospital's budget. Psychiatric care would be limited to 45 consecutive days of hospitalization for active treatment during a benefit period, and psychiatric consultations would be limited to 20 visits. Prescribed medicines would not be covered unless provided through a hospital, an organized patient care program or for treatment of a long-term illness. But some Medicaid benefits would be retained in certain states to cover the limitations in the Health Security Program.

The program would eliminate deductibles and co-insurance. It would offer incentives to health professionals to serve in hardship areas and remote areas. It provides for *preventive* and health maintenance services by doctors and health maintenance organizations (HMO's).

• *How would the program be financed?*

The cost would be met by contributions—in the same way Social Security now operates—from your employer, from you, from the self-employed, and from the federal government.

Specifically, employees would pay 1 per cent on the first $15,000 a year in wages or non-earned income (employees presently pay about 1 per cent of their pay up to $10,800 in order to finance Medicare). An employer would pay 3.5 per cent of his payroll toward Health Security (the employer's payments and your payments toward private health insurance would stop). Self-employed people would pay 2.5 per cent of all their yearly income up to $15,000. The total amount paid by workers, employers, and the self-employed would be matched by the federal government as its contribution.

Since Health Security covers so many expenses that

aren't covered by private health insurance, new taxes would not mean new money, but a rechannelling of the present out-of-pocket payments into the Health Security Trust Fund.

• *What do other countries do about health care?*

Every industrialized country in the world has a national health insurance or national health service program. Although Germany started a national health care system in 1883, and some other European countries started before World War I, most of them began after World War II.

• *Health consumers would be involved in policy-making.*

There would be public control of the basic policies with the implementation of the National Health Security Program, as well as public accountability for its finances and operations. And there would be participation by the consumers in the development of the program and on councils that would help administer it.

• *What you can do to support this bill.*

Write to your member of Congress if you want to see the bill eventually go through. Make it a hand-written letter. This is the kind that will be taken more seriously when your representative is trying to determine how his or her constituents feel. You can also order a health security informational kit (free) from: Committee for National Health Insurance, 821 15th St., N.W., Washington, D. C. 20005.

• *A long-term goal.*

Eventually I would hope that emphasis would be put on *preventive* and all other health care, at *no* cost to the consumer; *no* limitations on services. Don't you agree?

Medicare

This is the present government health insurance available through your local Social Security office. Generally, to qualify, you must be a Social Security beneficiary, sixty-five or over and you must have registered at a Social

Security office. If you're an over-50 widow and have been severely disabled for at least two years but haven't filed a claim based on your disability because you were getting Social Security checks as a mother caring for young or disabled children, call your Social Security office to see if you're eligible for Medicare. Medicare for disabled people begins with the 25th month they've been entitled to monthly benefits. People who receive railroad disability annuities or retirement benefits because of a disability should contact a railroad retirement office about the special requirements they must meet to get Medicare.

The Medicare system came into existence in 1966, and since then the out-of-pocket health care costs for the person over sixty-five has risen dramatically. Presently, the older person has an average annual medical bill of $1,218 and Medicare pays only $463. Many doctors won't accept Medicare payment. Some who do, in order to make up for the low Medicare fee they receive, charge the patient for the paper work in filing the claim. Others simply bill an additional amount over what they get from Medicare.

• *Part A and Part B (You pay for Part B).*

There are two parts to the plan, Medicare Part A and Medicare Part B. You don't pay anything for Medicare Part A, but you might want to be part of the Medicare Part B, because in paying extra, you're going to get certain health services such as care in a skilled nursing facility or home health care when you leave the hospital.

At this time, the charge for participating in Medicare Part B is $7.70 a month, which is deducted from your monthly Social Security checks. This premium can be (and has been for the last two years) increased every July, but no increase may be larger than the percentage increase in Social Security cash benefits since the last premium adjustment. What, exactly, do you get that's extra when you enroll in Part B? Home health services *without* prior hospitalization for up to one hundred visits a year; certain services of dental surgeons, optometrists, chiropractors, podiatrists; and doctors of medicine or osteopathy. This includes surgery, consultation, diagnosis, home, office and institutional calls; and then some additional medical services such as certain ambulance services, diagnostic x-ray, laboratory and other tests; x-ray, radium and radioactive isotope therapy; surgical dressings and splints; casts, and certain other devices for reduction of fractures and dislocation; rental or purchase of durable medical equipment used in your home; prosthetic devices (but not dental)—braces, artificial eyes, legs, and arms; and blood transfusions after you pay the cost of the first three pints or provide replacement. You can go to a psychiatrist on an outpatient basis (for a limited time) and have it paid through your medical coverage, and you can get outpatient hospital diagnostic or treatment services of the type furnished inpatients.

• *What Medicare doesn't cover.*

It doesn't cover: eye examinations to determine if you need eyeglasses; the cost of eyeglasses or fitting expenses (except prosthetic lenses); cost of hearing aids or fitting expenses; routine foot care; orthopedic shoes; cosmetic surgery (unless you've been injured); dental service (except certain dental surgery); private-duty nurses; prescription drugs and biologics (immunizing vaccines, such as tetanus); routine physical examinations; injuries resulting from an act of war and injuries covered by workman's compensation law; payment for health services given you by a member of your family or household; and payment for any service outside of the United States and its territories (except in certain specified instances). If a medical service or health care item is not "reasonable and necessary" for diagnosis or treatment of an illness or injury, Medicare won't pay for it.

• *How to reject or re-enroll in Part B.*

If you don't want to be covered by Part B, you can reject this part of the coverage—which is implemented automatically once you apply for Social Security benefits —by filing notice that you do not want this part of the coverage and, thus, you do not want the money deducted from your monthly Social Security check. But if you change your mind later, you'll have to wait until the next general enrollment period, which is January 1 to March 31 of each year; also, your protection on Part B won't be effective until the following July 1. You can re-enroll in Part B only once, and rates are higher if you enroll after you have once rejected coverage.

• *Deductibles and limits in Part B.*

What do you pay besides the monthly $7.70 for Part B under Medicare?—the first $60 of covered medical expenses each year. Your Medical Insurance part of the plan pays 80 per cent of excess reasonable costs or charges (100 per cent in the case of in-hospital radiology or pathology services and home health services), but payment for treatment of mental illness is limited to $250 a year. Payment for physical therapy is limited to $80 a year. Many older people need to spend more than $250 a year because of mental illness, and physical therapy is a needed service for the many victims of stroke—a common disability of old age. It's hardly possible to get this service for just $80 a year.

As a result of this type of inadequate medical insurance, many over-sixty-five people just don't go to doctors or hospitals when they should. They neglect their health needs. They're living longer, their health needs increase, their expenses are higher in the medical realm, and their health services are fewer.

• *How to apply for Medicare.*

Are you going to be eligible for Medicare in the near future? Check with your local Social Security Office before you're sixty-five to understand the application process, and see if there are any changes in the charges and benefits since this writing.

Medicaid: What Is It?

Medicaid is a federally-subsidized, state-operated program, administered throughout the country. It gives no-cost and low-cost dental, pharmaceutical, and medical services to people of all ages—but the recipient must have a limited income and limited assets.

• *Applying for Medicaid.*

How do you apply? Contact your local Department of Social Services, the Medical Assistance Division. You'll need to document your income. Then, if you're found eligible, you'll be given a Medicaid card, to use in lieu of money. If there *is* a particular doctor or dentist you want to use, and you're on Medicaid, don't assume she will not accept the Medicaid payment. Pick up the phone. Call her to ask if your card will be accepted. Don't *assume* she'll turn you down.

• *Benefits—charges—limitations.*

Benefits do vary from state to state. For instance, in at least one state, there is a fifty-cent co-payment that has to be made by the user of prescription drugs. This can be a real hardship. Many older people take several kinds of medication daily, on an on-going basis, and that fifty cents adds up.

As I said, no particular doctor, nursing home, or dentist is legally obligated to accept a Medicaid payment, which is lower than their normal fee. This can create a hardship for the health consumer. It limits her choice of medical help.

• *Special services.*

Depending on the state, benefits *can* include doctor's care in a hospital or a clinic; home health services such as home nursing visits; eyeglasses; x-ray and lab services; and drugs and supplies. Your local city or county health department can give you specific information as to your benefits. Remember—each state designs its own Medicaid programs within federal guidelines.

Health Insurance Plans Available through Retirement Organizations

Meanwhile—if you're not old enough for Medicare (and remember, you have to be at least sixty-five) and/or you're not able to be covered by any group health insurance on a job, you might want to consider the various plans available through retirement organizations. This does not mean you have to be retired.

• *If you're between fifty and sixty-five years of age.*

Specifically, Action for Independent Maturity, the pre-retirement division of the American Association of Retired Persons (AARP), focuses on health insurance for people between the ages of fifty and sixty-five years of

Getting the Best Medical Care 61

age, who are still working. If you want particular information on the coverage and charges, write Action for Independent Maturity, P.O. Box 1007, Long Beach, California 90801.

• *If you were a federal employee.*

The National Association of Retired Federal Employees, with over forty-seven state federations and thirteen hundred chapters, provides a health insurance plan for its members. Their plan, rather than providing for direct payment of medical and hospital bills, pays cash to the insured and his survivor, and they pay the bills. NARFE calls itself the "Champion of Retired Federal Employees," and it might pay for you to look into what they offer if you're presently working for the federal government or if you've retired from government service.

• *If you're sixty-five or older.*

The American Association of Retired Persons uses a private insurance company as their insurer for their group medical insurance plan, and members are eligible for an in-hospital plan, which provides daily benefits for hospital confinement after the first seven days of eligible hospitalization. They also have available an In-Hospital Plan Plus, which features *extra* benefits after those first seven days, such as surgical benefits on a scheduled basis and allowances for private duty in-hospital nursing care.

The AARP Extended In-Hospital Plan covers you from the first day of hospitalization, and increases benefits after the 90th day of hospitalization. The AARP Skilled Nursing Facility and Home Nursing Plan pays benefits for eligible skilled nursing-facility confinements for up to 385 days per benefit period following a qualifying hospital confinement. The AARP Expanded Skilled-Nursing Facility and Home Nursing Plan pays the same benefits for the first 100 days of eligible skilled-nursing-facility confinement, and then pays higher benefits for up to 1,015 days per benefit period. Then there's the AARP Out-Of-Hospital Medical Plan, which offers payment for doctors' visits at the office, in a nursing home, or in your own home. It provides certain at-home nurses' visits; skilled-nursing facility confinements; a number of diagnostic studies and tests; consultations; blood transfusions and plasma; prescription medicines; and a range of medical supplies and equipment.

Some of AARP's plans are only available to members who are age sixty-five or over. The costs of each plan varies. Most members use these plans to supplement their Medicare coverage. For specific information on any of these plans, write to AARP Insurance Plans, 5 Penn Center Plaza, Philadelphia, Pa. 19103 (and by the time you read this, they may have changed some of their plans or added more).

• *A plan to supplement Medicare.*
The National Council of Senior Citizens has health insurance plans available for the older person, at amazingly low prices. All NCSC members—and it only costs a few dollars to become a member—are eligible for at least one of the plans, regardless of age, present health, or medical history. Your insurance will not be cancelled because of poor health. It terminates only if your premium isn't paid, or if you discontinue your NCSC membership. However, *you* may cancel at any time. Your coverage becomes effective on the first day of the month following the receipt of your enrollment form and check, unless you're hospitalized on that date. Pre-existing conditions (one for which you've received medical treatment or advice in the six months immediately preceding the effective date of your coverage) aren't covered until you've participated in the plan for six months. Conditions that develop after you enroll, however, are covered immediately.

For members under sixty-five and those over sixty-five who are ineligible for Part A Medicare, NCSC offers a $15-a-day in-hospital plan. You receive benefits from the very first day you go into the hospital, regardless of any other insurance you may have. For members under sixty-five, the cost is $15 per quarter, with automatic conversion to the Medicare Supplement plan of your choice when you reach age sixty-five. For those over sixty-five, it's $30 per quarter, with no upper age limit. Benefits will be provided for a maximum of 365 days per benefit period. But note—at this time this particular plan isn't available to California and Maryland residents, due to minimum standards of those states.

For members covered by Medicare Part A, there are two plans available. Plan 1, which costs $12.50 a quarter or $50 annually, provides you with the $26 a day not covered by Medicare Part A after you've been in the hospital 60 days. And you're provided that $26 a day up through the 90th day of hospitalization. Plan 1 also provides you with $52 a day for the 91st day of hospitalization through the 150th day of hospitalization.

Plan 3 (for members covered by Medicare Part A) has slightly higher premiums—$20 quarterly and $80 annually—but it gives you coverage for your first 60 days in the hospital, which Plan 1 does not. Specifically, it provides the entire $104 Medicare Part A deductible, and will increase benefits to cover any increase in this Medicare deductible any time in the future.

Medicare pays nothing for the 151st day of hospitalization through the 581st day of hospitalization, and both Plan 1 and 3 provide you with $52 for each of those days.

Both plans cover the 21st to the 100th day of a skilled nursing facility (Medicare covers up to the 20th day, provided you enter an approved facility within 14 days of a hospital stay of at least 3 days) with the $13 not covered by Medicare. Medicare pays nothing for the 101st day through the 280th day, and both plans provide you with $13.33 a day.

Both plans provide you with 20 per cent (Medicare pays 80 per cent) of allowable surgical charges, both in- and outpatient. Inpatient coverage includes x-rays, lab fees, and visits from one or more doctors during your hospital confinement. You do not have to satisfy the Medicare deductible to receive any of these benefits.

To obtain Plans 2 and 4, you must also be covered under Medicare Part B. Under Plan 2, you pay $22.50 quarterly and $90 annually; under Plan 4, you pay $30 quarterly and $120 annually. These plans are combination in- and outpatient Medicare supplements. Both plans provide you, as an outpatient, with the 20 per cent of Medicare-allowable outpatient expenses not covered by the Medicare Part B. You do pay the $60 Part B deductible for Medicare. Both plans cover the inpatient costs that you can get under Plan 1 and Plan 3. Plan 2 doesn't cover the $104 Part A Medicare deductible; Plan 4 does.

You don't have to be a member of a senior center to become a member of the National Council of Senior Citizens. If you aren't, individual membership is $4 and membership for a couple is $5 a year; if you *are* a member of a senior center *or* a union, it's $3.50 a year per person. For membership enrollment, write the National Council of Senior Citizens, Inc., 1511 K Street, N.W., Washington, D. C. 20006. If you are already a member, and want to investigate their insurance coverage further, or take out one of their plans, write The National Council of Senior Citizens, Insurance Administrators International Group Plan, 2100 M Street, N.W., Washington, D. C. 20037.

This is just a sampling of what's offered by retirement groups, and the premiums and coverage changes from time to time, so check these figures before you make any purchasing decisions. The dire need for free, comprehensive national health insurance still exists, because many people cannot afford even the lowest of these premiums, and the coverage of these policies often isn't enough for a major long-term illness.

Group Health Insurance Plans through Your Job

• *Get the facts!*

Your group health insurance plan usually cuts off automatically if you terminate your job. If you're changing jobs, call the insurance company that provides the service *before* you leave to find out the exact date your coverage stops. Then, if you wish, you can take steps to continue coverage for the in-between time (just in case you're not covered by any commercial private policy as well). Sometimes you may be lucky. Your coverage will take you to the end of the month after you've left the job two weeks previously, and you can arrange with the company you're starting with for their coverage to begin the beginning of the next month—so there will be no time in which you're not covered. If you can't arrange this, consider making plans to pay extra to have individual coverage with the group plan you're leaving until your new coverage begins at your new place of employment.

• *Major medical coverage.*

Most employee group medical plans include major medical insurance. Maximum benefits of such protection commonly range anywhere from $20,000 to $25,000 to even $100,000 or more, and help pay for almost every kind of major care and treatment prescribed, both at home and in the hospital. Generally, even with group major medical coverage available to you through your job, there is a "co-insurance" clause, meaning that the insurance company pays a specified percentage of your total medical expenses *after* the deductible (what you've initially put into your cost), and this usually means that after you've paid your share, the insurance company pays 75 per cent to 80 per cent of your major medical expenses. So you can see how important it is to have major medical coverage. If you already have it on your job, make yourself very familiar with your benefits. It will pay you to put a phone call through to the insurance representative for your policy at the insurance company and ask her exactly what the benefits are.

• *Coverage of prescription drugs.*

I have talked to many women who were not made aware, at their place of employment, of just how comprehensive *or* limited their coverage is. For instance, the employees in one company were not aware that a certain percentage of their prescription drugs were covered by the policy—and some of these employees had been under this coverage for five years and were still paying the total cost of their drugs. That adds up to a lot of money!

Disability Income Insurance

Disability income insurance is a good thing for you if you're still working, and especially if your only income is from your employment. This kind of insurance might be part of your group medical health insurance plan on the job, or it may not be. The main benefit of this kind of insurance is that it provides a continuing income if your salary ceases when you are too ill to return to work. As an older woman, possibly more prone to chronic illness, you need to know that you'll get a certain amount of money each week for a specific length of time, until you recover and can go back to work (and can perhaps continue getting benefits if you *can't* return to work).

Dental and Vision Care Insurance

If you have access to group dental expense health insurance—you might want to consider paying for this. As we grow older, we have more gum, denture, and teeth problems. Also, look into the availability of vision care health insurance in your group health insurance plan.

Private Health Insurance Plans

If you're not employed, you don't have access to a group medical plan on-the-job, and you might want to purchase an individual health insurance policy. Or you might want to supplement your group plan on the job.

• *Coverage—kinds of policies.*

A private plan may be either "optionally renewable" (that means you have the option to renew and the company can change the premium only if it is changed for everyone having that kind of policy) or "non-cancellable-guaranteed renewable" (you renew if you wish and the premium rate cannot be changed), or "guaranteed renewable" (you renew if you wish and the premium rate is adjustable for all policyholders or class of policyholders).

If you have more than one health insurance policy, find out exactly what each policy covers (in fact, do that before you spend any money buying a new policy). You'll want to be sure you're not paying for any duplicating plans. And periodically check the dollar benefits in your policies to see that they're in line with the rises in hospital and medical costs in your community—especially in this time of our changing economy.

• *Plans through special-interest groups.*

If you're not employed, you may still be eligible for group health insurance through the union you belonged to, through your professional organization, your fraternal organization, or any religious or alumni association to which you belong. Try each kind of source before spending the higher costs on individual coverage.

· *The importance of health insurance—but be selective!*

Invest in health insurance if you can (some companies won't give coverage to people sixty-five and over). Medicare coverage is limited, not everyone is eligible for Medicaid, health costs are extremely high, more illness takes place as we grow older, drugs are expensive. Particularly, as we grow older, our income often diminishes at the same time that medical costs become overwhelming. Be selective. A health insurance policy with breadth (few exclusions) but little depth (such as a quick cut-off date on hospital benefits) may sink you financially if major or long-term illness strikes. You have to take a careful look at balancing your pocketbook needs with your health needs in picking your plan.

Health Maintenance Organizations (HMO's)

· *What are they?*

HMO plans stress preventive medicine. You pay in a certain amount of money a month and in return you have access to every kind of medical coverage, such as regular checkups and in-hospital services, eyeglasses, psychiatric treatment, drugs.

· *Charges, limitations, advantages.*

Sometimes an HMO plan will charge around $50 a month, sometimes around $16 a month—depending largely on whether you're part of a group plan or not. You may use only certain hospitals and certain doctors, and a disadvantage may be that you find these doctor's offices too far away from your home or in a neighborhood where you're afraid to travel; you also may not like those doctors and that hospital. An advantage to belonging to an HMO plan is that the over-50 woman may find that she takes better care of her health; after all, if she puts out all that money each month she's probably going to find out right away what's causing those dizzy spells.

(Why spend that money for nothing?) And as we grow older and chronic ailments become more frequent, early treatment by looking into our uncomfortable symptoms right away can payoff. We'll go for frequent checkups if we have to pay anyway. You'll get your drug prescriptions filled immediately, instead of waiting until your monthly check comes, if your monthly HMO payments include prescription drugs payments.

• *Medicare and Medicaid payments.*

In order for HMO's to accept Medicare and Medicaid payments instead of money from the consumer's own pocketbook, they must conform to regulations of the HEW—the Health, Education and Welfare Department in Washington, D. C.

How can you find out *which* HMO's conform to HEW regulations? Call your state health department and ask which such ones exist in your community.

It has been found that HMO consumers spend one-third to one-half less time in hospitals than nonmembers; they undergo *40 per cent less surgery!*

Community No-Cost Health Services: Take Advantage of Them!

With health services as expensive as they are, take advantage of any free health screening that is offered from time to time in your community.

• *Kinds of free health screening and examinations.*

Eye screening, hearing screening, and diabetes testing are frequently offered at community centers and senior centers by health organizations. The American Cancer Society offers free breast examinations and pap smear tests at different sites throughout the country. Call your local community and senior centers, ask to talk to the director, and find out if there are any scheduled screenings within the next six months. Ask how you register for this. Free flu shots are given by city health departments to all older people who want them.

• *Free medical care is your RIGHT!*

You have paid your taxes all through your working life—maybe you still are paying taxes—and your taxes have helped *others* receive no-cost or low-cost health services. Now it's your turn. Good health care is a *right*.

CHAPTER 3

Forty-five Ways
To Look and Feel Fantastic

✺

1. Get a Face Lift or an Eye Lift:

Look in the mirror. Put your two hands, fingers slightly spread, just in front of your ears and pull lightly, upward and backward. Look hard—because that's how you will probably look after a face-lift.

Is it for you? Well, it won't glue together a bad marriage—but it might get you a certain job and it might keep you in the job market longer. It might allow you to continue your career, especially if you're in the public eye. If you're recently separated or divorced or widowed, it could give you the self-confidence to build a new and exciting life. "Isn't just wanting to feel younger a good enough reason?" a woman asked me. Yes, yes, yes!

A growing number of women are investing in plastic surgery, particularly face-lifts and eye lifts. You'll no doubt look ten years younger afterwards, and that's an exciting prospect. It is regrettable, however, that only high- and middle-income women, or women who have put every penny of their baby-sitting money in the bank can afford it. Your medical insurance probably won't pay for it. And it isn't cheap. It's major surgery—and you're putting out the kind of money major surgery requires.

The surgical fees are about the same whether you have

the operation in the doctor's office or the hospital. A full face-lift, including your eyelids, might be from about $2,500 to $6,600. The surgeon's fee is usually due ahead of time and includes a year or so of aftercare. Eyelid surgery only will run about $500 to $2,500. Cosmetic facial surgery can vary in price, depending on where you live: Small cities in the midwest may be less expensive than New York, for instance. Extra charges that will occur if the operation is done in the hospital: around $200 a day for the room (again, it may be less in certain geographical areas); $1,000 for the anesthesiologist, the special tests, and the operating and recovery room fees.

Some plastic surgeons are performing face-lifts and eye lifts in their offices, which is a way to save the money that you'd otherwise have to pay for hospital costs. Is it a good idea to have a face lift done in a surgeon's office? There are two schools of thought on this, and you'll really have to make up your own mind. You may not feel secure having major surgery done in a doctor's office, or you may not be able to because of your medical condition, or you may not be able to find a doctor in your area who will do it.

Plastic surgeons who prefer the out-patient procedure believe that a patient *feels* better when the operation is done *out* of a hospital. They believe that hospital environments—with nurses rushing back and forth, people in wheelchairs, the ring for the doctor—make you *feel* sick, even if you aren't. These surgeons also say that nurses give less attention to cosmetic surgery cases in the hospital, because their first priority is to the really ill patient. Finally, these doctors tell us that in instances of simple plastic surgery (an eye lift, for example) patients are back to normal more quickly if they haven't been hospitalized. If the operation is performed in the doctor's office it can be done on say, a Thursday. You can take Friday off, stay home and relax over the weekend, have the stitches removed Monday morning, and go back to work Monday afternoon—wearing dark glasses. A local anesthetic is used in office surgery, and there is oxygen and emergency medication available. When you go home, you can, of course, reach the doctor at any time, day or night, for comfort and medical help and reassurance.

Again, you'll probably find that office surgery for the

full face-lift is only available in certain geographic areas.

The strong arguments for having your face-lift done in the hospital are: more facilities for unexpected emergencies and closely surpervised aftercare (you're right in the hospital if you suddenly feel ill). The hospitalization period for plastic surgery is usually about three days. Some plastic surgeons will do only eye lifts, chemical peels, hair transplants, and ear and nasal surgery in their offices.

What are some of the things you should know if you're considering a face-lift or any kind of plastic surgery on your face? Dry, fine skin responds best to plastic surgery. On the other hand, that kind of skin will bruise more easily (take longer to heal) and look worse during the immediate recovery period. Expect to look pretty bad right after the surgery—and expect to look great six months later.

A face-lift remains effective for about ten years. Some women—even in their seventies and older—will repeatedly have face-lifts every ten years or so.

How is a face-lift done? The skin is separated from the muscle and then the skin is attached to a *new* area of muscle; a healing layer between the skin and facial muscles is created. The healing layer is actually composed of the scar tissue from this procedure. Some plastic surgeons use permanent sutures under the skin to keep the new tissues in place, as well as sutures that dissolve by themselves.

From a purely physical standpoint, the postoperative period will be unpleasant. Your hair and eyelashes will look faded for months after the operation. You're not allowed to cry for awhile after the surgery, and you can't drink alcohol for about ten days. And because you're trying to avoid bringing blood to your face, you can neither eat hot foods nor take hot baths. Your eye stitches will be removed about the fifth day after the operation. Until then you have no appetite, your eyes itch and water, and you may feel miserable. After that, you'll feel better, but you won't feel like yourself. For four to eight weeks you'll experience numbness and tightness and itching. Your face may still be swollen. In fact, swelling may last for many months. Expect to feel afraid to move your face and neck for several weeks after the operation. You may feel depressed for awhile. Remember, you've been through major surgery and if you've ever had major surgery, you know how you feel afterwards.

But—you'll look fantastic in the long run! If not gorgeous, at least glowing and younger and prettier.

Aftercare presents some problems, so if you live alone, get someone to stay with you for at least a week after you get home from the hospital. Or stay in a hotel that has good prompt room service. Why? To get you ice packs (which you'll be applying to take down the swelling); to bring you food (because you won't feel up to cooking).

People who have already had face-lifts will probably be the most sympathetic to you. Others may not consider your hospitalization an "illness" (which it isn't), so they may not appreciate your discomfort. Also, some of your friends may feel it's narcissistic of you to undergo this kind of surgery. They may think you're vain. Don't blame them—face-lifts aren't yet fully accepted by a lot of people. Just stay away from hostile or impatient friends, and seek out the supportive ones.

Husbands sometimes object to a wife having a face-lift; the money; the trauma of the hospital stay and the recovery; and the change (he may be afraid other men will become interested in her, now that she looks so good). It may be frightening to some men. I've read articles that recommend you don't tell your husband until after the surgery—and I find that distasteful. What kind of relationship is it where you can't share your fears and hopes and vulnerabilities? If you're a doll-wife, and your husband treats you like one (a doll that *belongs* to him), I can see why you might not tell him—but isn't that the kind of relationship we're trying to grow *out of?* A doll doesn't become a grown woman.

A major face-lift may seem excessive to you, but mini-face-lifts are looked at with skepticism by some plastic surgeons. They think the results aren't worth the money.

An eye lift is done via two incisions—one below the eye and the other in the fold of the upper lid. The excess fat is cut away. Some women only have to have surgery on the lower lid. The operation takes about an hour.

Reputable plastic surgeons will not perform plastic surgery on everyone. They will first interview the women to see if she has realistic expectations and to see if she's emotionally strong enough to go through the operation and the possible after-depression.

How do you find a good plastic surgeon? Ask around. Talk to women who have had it done. Then write to the Secretary, The American Academy of Facial, Plastic, and Reconstructive Surgery, 1110 North Main, Durham, North Carolina 27701 for information on the plastic surgeon's background and to find out what hospitals he's connected with.

Plastic cosmetic surgery is considered so desirable by a growing number of women that I wasn't surprised when a very attractive thirty-eight-year-old vice-principal of a school said to me, "I'm saving a certain amount of money each year for an eventual face-lift. A little bit in the bank for the next ten years should do it." Who would have said that fifteen years ago?

2. *Eat Anti-Aging Food:*

Some doctors believe that protein is essential in the production of new cells by the body. Eating foods with high protein content may help restore the balance of new with dying cells in our bodies. Recommended: proteins from plant and ocean foods that contain collagen (a substance that may smooth out wrinkles!) Which foods contain collagen? Brewers yeast, nuts, whole grain cereals, peanuts, sunflower seeds, dried peas, wheat germ, sesame seeds, avocados, and olives. Combine the protein foods with vitamin C. Vitamin C foods? Grapefruit, tomatoes, oranges, strawberries, green peppers, tangerines, broccoli, collards, kale, mustard greens, turnip greens, and sweet potatoes in their jackets.

3. *Wear Clothes That Are Slimming:*

Big caftans. Skirts that are fuller at the *bottom*—to make your legs look thinner. Dark colors. (It doesn't always have to be black. Try rich wines, deep blues, dark purples).

4. *Wear Clothes That Make You Look Ageless:*

Ethnic clothes. Long Greek skirts and Mexican ponchos and Indian saris make you look *interesting*, and interesting-looking women don't look a certain "age."

5.   *Try Cell Therapy:*

Although it's not available in this country, we're hearing a lot about cell therapy. What is it? Injections of specially prepared or freeze-dried or fresh cells from unborn lamb (or other animals) fetuses that are reputed to make you feel and look younger. There are basically two approaches to treatment: a massive series of injections given in the buttocks followed by rest in bed for several days, *or* lower dosages administered over a period of time. Some doctors eliminate all the components from the cellular formulations that cause discomfort and possible allergic reaction.

Revitalizing effects are expected after three and a half months, and arteriosclerosis, impotence, anemia, frigidity, ulcers, menopausal arthritis, eczema, asthma, and insomnia are some of the disorders that practitioners claim can be fully or partially corrected.

After the injections, you may not indulge in drugs, alcohol, hormones, sun baths, saunas, diathermy, or use hot hair dryers.

Even the most ardent believers in cell therapy do not claim to be able to improve or cure diabetes, cancer, or acute inflammation.

How does cell therapy work? Theory has it that the injected cells (composed, as are all cells, of the two basic protein molecules DNA and RNA) travel to the organ in the injected body that corresponds to the organ from which they derive in the donor animal's body. There the cells of that organ utilize the injected material to form antibodies; in turn, the antibodies recirculate in the system and gradually revitalize that organ. The stated purpose of cell therapy is to replace the cells we lose (and we lose cells more rapidly as we age), because cells are needed for life and health.

Cell therapy is taken very seriously in some parts of the world. There are five hundred cell therapy practitioners in Switzerland and about two hundred in France. One quarter of all the doctors in Germany use some kind of cell therapy. Dr. Peter Stephan in England has administered some fifty thousand cell injections and, at age thirty-one, has been receiving cell injections himself for a number of years. He's one of the youngest "youth doctors" (that's what they're called) around and he claims that older women will see improvement in muscle tone, skin, hair, fingernails—even sagging breasts.

But cell therapy is far from cheap. One particular clinic in Switzerland charges $2,800 to $3,500 (including room and board) for a thorough preliminary medical examination (blood and urine tests, stool tests, and urine-enzyme tests which supposedly show which of your organs and glands need cell therapy), and the injections. This clinic uses fresh cells from certain organs and glands of a lamb fetus, which was raised and slaughtered under sterile conditions. Dr. Peter Stephan's clinic in England is relatively inexpensive. The price for the treatment, including room and board, is about $800. He eliminates the allergy-producing protein and gives a series of injections with no bed rest. His degree is in homeopathic medicine (yes, he is an M.D.).

One of the most accessible places (in terms of travel time and money) where cell therapy is available is Nassau, the Bahamas. This island is the site for what is called "the world's first multi-therapeutic center of the revitalization sciences." Here doctors treat patients for loss of vigor, fatigue, frigidity, poor muscle tone, and premature aging. You stay at least ten days, and the price can vary ($300 to $2,000), depending on the kinds of treatment and the accommodations you choose. For $2,000 you can have cosmeticians, dieticians, kineso-therapists, lab technicians, masseurs, and doctors treating you. The price also includes examinations, tests, and personal consultations with the medical staff. Services include oral treatment with incubated chicken eggs, hormone therapy, external treatment with sea water, sea water inhalation treatments, sea-mud packs, seaweed baths, special diets, vitamin therapy, cosmetic therapy, topical application of oils and extracts and, of course, cell therapy.

Cell therapy is still highly controversial and experimental. Universal acceptance of these procedures is probably years away, but claims that low sex drive and menopausal symptoms can be reversed through cell therapy are being heeded, even in parts of the world where it is not currently practiced.

6. *Learn To Relax (When You're Having An Anxiety Attack):*

Breathe in and out of a paper bag for a few seconds (really!).

Drink a soothing cup of camomile herb tea.

Have a silent dialogue with yourself: "What am I really anxious about?"

7. *Use Herbs:*

Tired? Add a tablespoon of pine oil or a handful of lime flowers or peppermint leaves to your bath water.

A nasty pimple on your face? Apply a compress of witch hazel or valerian tea directly.

Dieting? Chew fennel leaves to depress your appetite.

Dull skin? Wash your face. Add a handful of sage, marigold, camomile, mint and tansy to very hot water in the washbowl. Tent a towel over your head *and* the bowl (leaning over the bowl), and breathe in and out for three minutes. Straighten up, swab your face with astringent-drenched cotton swabs or dash cold water on your face to close the pores.

Itchy skin? Try a cold compress of camomile.

Burning, tired eyes? Apply cold compresses of witch hazel, or elder or fennel or sassafras.

Feel neglected? Fill a discarded clean stocking with an ounce of lemon peel, rose petals, orange flowers, bay leaves, rosemary, pennyroyal, lavender, and common salt. Tie up the end of the stocking and place in a kettle filled with 2 pints of water. Boil with the top on. Cool. Strain the water, discard the stocking. Add the cooled scented water to your filled bathtub. Soak for a luxurious fifteen minutes (it'll take you so long to *make* the damned thing that you'll forget you ever felt bad).

8.   *Treat Yourself To Gerovital KH-3 Treatment:*

This is a fancy term for procaine, commonly called novocaine. KH-3 may be taken by injection, tablets, lotion, or face cream. In a fully supervised treatment, injections are given once a day for twelve to nineteen days, followed by an extended period during which tablets are taken orally.

The purpose? To reverse the signs of old age. Supposedly, patients grow new hair, find blotches disappearing from their skin, and discover their gray hair returning to its natural color. Memory and concentration improve, and people look ten years younger. It's claimed that symptoms are relieved in crippling arthritis, high blood pressure, angina pectoris, and depression associated with aging.

Where is KH-3 treatment being given? *Not* in our country. To name one place—Romania. In fact, the Romanian government fully backs this so-called anti-aging treatment, and over forty-five thousand patients have been treated at that country's Geriatrics Institute. Romanian physicians often recommend treatment starting at the age of thirty to forty-five. Medical treatment is no-cost and low-cost in communist Romania, so it's only $60 for the medical treatment and $15 to $25 a day for the spa accommodations. KH-3 treatment is now also given in Nassau, the Bahamas. Throughout Europe, pharmacies sell KH-3 face lotion and face cream, as well as the tablets.

Cynics have said that the novocaine (or procaine) treatment's real effect is to make one numb about one's aging—and we really don't have any conclusive evidence as to whether it works. Many medical people are listening and watching though. I've noticed ads in the travel section of the *New York Times* advertising package "spa" tours to Romania! But beware, even in Romania not everyone is eligible for Gerovital KH-3. Many people have allergic reactions.

9. Gain Weight:
Eat your meat before your vegetables. Drink milk shakes with an egg in them.

10. Listen To Your Body:
Rest when it tells you to.

11. On a Diet?
Mix soda water and plain water (half-and-half), lemon juice, three ice cubes, and a little liquid Sucaryl. Very, very low-calorie. Delicious.

12. More Clothing Tips If You're Overweight:
Buy a tent-dress pattern. Purchase some beautiful and varied upholstery material, enough for five dresses. Find a dressmaker (maybe you?) to make them up.

Shop at a store for large women. You'll find much

more variety than at a regular department store, and snappier-looking clothes.

13.   *Visit a Fat Farm:*

They come in cheapies—ones that are spartan, but where it's just as easy to lose weight (if you're serious) as it is at the very expensive ones. After all, how much more delicious can diet food be at an expensive one?

14.   *Join a Health Club:*

For exercise classes. To use a stationary bicycle. To have access to upright revolving bars and motorized tables. To swim. To sip carrot juice at a health-food bar. Some facilities offer a range of activities from tennis, saunas, gyms, massage rooms, steam baths, and whirlpools. Some health clubs even plan a nutrition program for you.

There are approximately two thousand health clubs in this country—from posh profit palaces to low-cost clubs in community centers and Y's.

Health clubs are a profitable industry, grossing over $100 million a year. Fees and payment arrangements vary. You may pay an initiation fee of $100 to $700, plus around $30 monthly dues; or $245 the first year (nothing more) and $120 every year after; or a $25 initiation (or "examining") fee, and $36 a month after. Some health clubs let you take out a three-month trial membership. Shop around.

Members are encouraged to use the club often—because the more you use it, the more money you'll spend. Because of much misrepresentation and misleading advertising, the Federal Trade Commission has set up regulations for your protection: Clubs cannot claim that participation will prolong your life; that advertised prices and specials exist when, actually, the same prices and services may always exist on an on-going basis anyway; that your weight reduction is guaranteed within a certain period of time. Beware of the health club that sends your contract to a finance company, or which legally charges you interest on arrears and penalties for default. If you are selective, however, a good health club *can* keep you motivated to get trim and stay trim.

15. Buy a Postage Scale:

To weigh your food if you're on a diet for medical reasons or for slimming. They're about $2.

16. Dress Breezy and Hip:

If you're thin (no more than a size 10).

17. Don't Take Sunbaths:

They're murder for over-50 skin. The sun wrinkles you, creases you. A come-on for skin cancer.

18. Wear a Cape:

Only if you're *thin*. If you're short and heavy, you'll look like a mushroom or a fat elf.

19. Buy a Slant Board:

An investment for staying young-looking! Lie with your head on the down side, and your feet pointing up. It'll reverse your circulation so your blood flows to your head. Do this for twenty minutes every morning, and see if you don't look better.

20. Have Good Legs? Show Them Off:

Legs are the last to go. A lot of eighty-year-old women have sexy legs. If you have good legs wear shoes that are young and show your legs off (you know, clogs and bare sandals). Cross your legs so your knee shows. Act like you *know* your legs are terrific!

21. Change Your Eating Patterns:

Eat six tiny meals a day instead of three large ones.

22. For Frizzy Hair:

Apply two tablespoons of wheat germ oil (from a health food store) to your hair and massage into your scalp. Comb through and brush. Repeat three times a week.

23. Make Your Own Wonder Shampoo:

Put an egg in your blender and beat. Pour one cup of baby shampoo (any kind) into the beaten egg, then add one package of unflavored gelatin powder. Mix very well. Use as you would any shampoo.

24. For Oily Hair:
Dissolve one tablespoon of salt in skim milk and rub into your scalp. Don't rinse. Let hair dry. Shampoo after one-half hour.

25. Make Your Hair Curly:
Use skim milk as a wave set. Don't rinse out.

26. A Home-Made Wonder Hair Conditioner:
Beat an egg yolk. Add one half cup of yogurt. Beat mixture until foamy. Comb it into your hair after your shampoo (and after you dry-towel your hair). Wait thirty minutes. Rinse in warm water. Rinse again with lemon juice added to the water.

27. Invest In a Professional Makeup Job:
So you can notice each trick the cosmetician uses—and write them down! Take your notes home and apply.

28. Hang Your Full-Length Mirror Near a Window:
So you can see all your flaws in harsh light—to do something about them.

29. Lose One Pound in Six Days:
By eating six hundred calories less a day.

30. Keep Heavy Breasts Firm:
By lying down, arms over your head, while holding something comfortably heavy in each hand. Slowly lower and raise your arms four times. Rest. Repeat.

31. Take Years Off:
By lightening the hair around your hairline. (But don't use a gray color for the lighter tone. Maybe light brown or ash blonde.)

32. Minimize Bulging Eyelids:
By applying creamy brown eye shadow.

33. Avoid SEEMING Older:
By never saying "dearie."

34. *Look Good in Harsh Daylight:*
By purchasing your daytime makeup in the *daytime*. By looking in a mirror near a window while you're applying it.

35. *Change Your Hairdresser:*
If she is still doing bouffant "hairdos."

36. *If You Take a Size 3 or 5:*
Don't buy your clothes in the teen or pre-teen department. You'll look like a ridiculous child.

37. *If You Were Once a Terrific Jitterbug:*
Jitterbug every morning to lose weight (it'll be fun dancing to those 1944 records).

38. *To Look Heavier:*
Wear clingy fabrics. Wear overblouses and vests. Wear wide belts and sashes. Wear cuffed pants.

39. *Hire a Personal Shopper:*
If you have the money. If you're unsure of what looks good on you. If you hate to shop for clothes. If you're hard to fit. If you're too thin or too fat. If you have the money.

40. *Eat a Lot of Fish:*
For weight loss. Try *sashimi,* a thinly sliced, marinated, raw fish available in Japanese restaurants. Eat fish seven times a week to lose weight *very* fast.

41. *Behavior Modification—for Fatties:*
Eat from a small plate only. Chew each mouthful seventeen times (don't cheat). Wait until you're finished swallowing before you put another spoonful in your mouth. Halfway through the meal, stop eating for five minutes. Eat the same thing every day.

42. *Take a Belly-Dancing Class:*
To get thin and to feel sexy.

43. *Flabby Thighs?*
Lie on one side, raise and lower your top leg as fast as

you can ten times. Rest. Repeat. Change sides. Repeat.
Rest.

44.   *Very Thin Hair?*

Mix dried skim milk powder with water to make a
paste. Apply to your hair as a pack for thirty minutes.
Wash out.

45.   *To Feel Refreshed after Your Bath:*

Mix hops and meadowsweet and pat it on your body.
Let it dry itself.

Now take a red pencil and circle each thing you try. If
it feels particularly good, or is *very* effective, call a friend
and share your find. And if it worked—try it again.

CHAPTER 4

Sex, Relationships, Divorce and Remarriage

৺৪ ৡৈ

It IS Different When You're Over-50 . . . Or Is It?

I find that women talk more openly to me than they did fifteen or twenty years ago. Maybe it's because many of us are learning to do this. I particularly wanted to find out what kind of relationships older women want with men. So I asked.

"I can't," said Elsie, a 50'ish-looking woman with short, curly hair and a Renoir-pretty face, sitting across from me at the department store restaurant table. "I just can't bring myself to go to bed with a man I don't trust. I have to know him well. I have to know he accepts me—my humor, the roll of fat above my waist, everything.

"But how will I know he accepts the roll of fat until I do go to bed with him. Oh, well."

She reached for a biscuit, broke it, buttered it.

"So I haven't been to bed with anyone for almost two years. I am an unwilling celibate. Sure, I've tried sex without a relationship—hasn't every woman at least once? —but it wasn't worth the bad feelings. I'd need reassurance and I'd need the man to tell me I was terribly important to him and that I wasn't just an object. I was even willing to believe him if he told me he loved me—even though I knew better. For those few minutes, after he rolled over, I'd believe anything, I was so desperate."

She wiped her fingers on the napkin. "But the last time . . . I had it. No more since. This was a man who had pursued me for weeks, and who had called me every day after we met at a party. He was good-looking and intelligent and politically active in just the way I like. He was so—persuasive!—that I really believed that this was the man I would spend the rest of my life with. I hadn't been so attracted to a man in years—. Well, we went to bed. And, afterwards—," there was a pause, "everything was immediately different. He suddenly turned off the charm, he didn't say more than two words to me from the time we got out of bed until the moment he left my front door, and I never heard from him again."

Elsie stared down at her plate. After awhile she said, "Do you know I'm still not completely over that? Oh, I don't mean I'm not over the man. What still hurts is the *rejection*. This was almost two years ago. I haven't been to bed with a man since."

Why did Elsie feel she couldn't develop a loving and lasting relationship with a man? She was attractive. She honestly liked men.

"I am divorced," she answered grimly, "and when the average man takes a divorcée out, he's sure she's dying to go to bed. He thinks that what she needs is a good— you know. The only men I've met who don't always make these assumptions are younger men. Maybe younger men aren't hung-up with the same stereotypes that men in their fifties are. Maybe men who are younger are more able to see women as *people*." She looked at me sharply, as though testing me. "I've been attracted to a couple of younger men."

"And?"

"And nothing. I've been too afraid to get involved, even though I knew they were interested. I didn't want anyone laughing at me behind my back. That's what people do when they find out you're dating a younger man. . . ."

Greta reminded me that some women *completely* avoid relationships.

It was obvious that she was a success at her job. Her office was decorated in muted shades of green. There was a Mexican tin mask on the burlap-covered wall. There were fresh flowers in a small ceramic jug on her desk.

"My job is my life, I'll admit it. Can you think of anything better? Why should I get in that rat race of trying to get a man? Here I am, fifty-seven. Why should I try competing with a bunch of younger women at a singles' party? Sure, I hate weekends, especially Sundays, and I've made work the focal point of my life. I can't begin to count the number of overtime hours I put in when I didn't have to—but it's better than desperately waiting for the phone to ring and feeling like a piece of meat on a rack on a singles' cruise. Just say that I've withdrawn from the race and that I've adjusted."

It was the biggest pear-shaped diamond I had ever seen. It was on the finger of a heavily made-up and good-looking woman in her fifties. She stared hard at the ring and then dropped her hand.

"Gorgeous. But I'll probably give it back."

"Why?"

"I don't know. I'm confused. He insists I love him, but I don't know. My husband's been dead for a year and a half. I hate this damned loneliness. I don't want to be alone. Maybe I will marry him."

She sat down and carefully crossed her legs. She lit a cigarette. "Maybe I'll get an eye lift instead, you know? I have a girl friend in Miami who got an eye lift and it took ten years off of her. She met someone she really likes—."

· *What are the differences?*

All three of these women are over 50, single, and lonely. Each of them has discovered that being alone when you're over 50 *is* different from when you're younger. Each has found that over-50 women *do* face special and unique problems. What are some of these problems?

   · older men often prefer much younger women
   · there's a shortage of personable men who are older (women frequently live longer than men)

- older women sometimes avoid intimate relationships because they're ashamed of their bodies
- grown children may become critical of their mother's relationships
- over-50 women usually are afraid they look too old to compete in the marketplace
- the older woman who is taking care of an aged parent in her home finds this gets in the way of intimate relationships
- the older man in a woman's life is sometimes impotent
- a man may be too interested in the older woman's financial affairs
- an over-50 woman may be afraid to marry a man because he has a heart condition
- the older woman's children may not want her to remarry—they're afraid she'll leave her money and property to her new husband and *his* children, instead of to them and *their* children
- the over-50 woman often doesn't know where to meet men (when she was younger she went to dances!)
- she doesn't want to lose her alimony check (which will happen if she remarries)
- the over-50 woman finds it too hard to begin sharing space and time and self all over again, after being alone for a number of years

And I could go on.

Don't you know an over-50 woman whose grown "problem" child still lives with her—and who feels that no man would want that problem?

How about the over-50 woman who has given up on relationships because she's consumed with the discomforts of a chronic illness?

And how about the over-50 woman who has climbed to the top of her profession, and guards her bank account and investments—letting no man near her, for fear he'll expect her to share?

And we all know a woman who feels she's "too old" for "that sort of thing" (meaning sex—and perhaps intimacy).

We all know women who will only consider a "professional" man; who feels she will lose status if she dates men who aren't doctors or lawyers or at least pharmacists or certified public accountants! (Yes, I think this is more often an attitude of older women than younger women.)

- *You have to make three decisions if you want a relationship*.

However, each year, in every city (*your* city), hundreds of over-50 women *do* enter relationships. This happens because they made three decisions:

- they wanted a relationship—*with no mixed feelings*
- they would make themselves physically accessible
- they would make themselves emotionally accessible

Have you made these decisions?

Do You Really Want to Get Involved with a Man?

I had gone to child study meetings with Holly when we were young-marrieds, and I remembered her as a reflective person . . . even open (for those days). Since then, we had occasionally met at parties and meetings.

She answered, "Of course!" when I asked her if she wanted a relationship. But after we talked for a couple of hours, she said, "I think I've been kidding myself. I think I really have very mixed feelings about this. You've known me for a long time, and you remember how I looked when my divorce came through. I was thirty pounds lighter then, remember? That was six years ago. Look at me. Why have I let myself go? I think I've deliberately put on that weight so I won't have to cope with a relationship. I'm lonely—but I'm also angry. Do you know, I still have bad dreams about Jim? I don't trust men. I don't know whether I want to start all over again at the age of fifty."

I then talked to a woman who did remarry very shortly after her husband died—a woman with no mixed feelings.

Joslyn spoke slowly, thoughtfully. "I want to be honest with you. Men are very important to me. I was my father's pet—I was the youngest—and I was my husband's pet for thirty-two years. I was always a pampered darling, I guess you could say. I admire strong women, but I know I do best when a man is taking care of me. After Fred died, and after I got on my feet, I knew I wanted to get married again, and I let all of my friends know it. They looked out for me. I went to a health spa and put myself in shape—although I had always taken care of myself—and I got a new wardrobe. I became very aggressive. When I met Paul I knew he was the kind of man who *wanted* to take care of a woman—and I grabbed him fast. I *like* men. I love being married again. There was never any doubt in my mind that I would get married again."

It was a sunny and cozy room—with plants hanging in front of windows and books strewn on tables. I was interviewing Ginger, a woman whose name had been given to me by a mutual friend.

"Do I want to get married again?" she answered in reply to my question, "No. Do I want relationships? Yes."

"In fact," she went on, hoisting her granddaughter up farther on her shoulder (she was baby-sitting for the day), "I'm presently involved with *two* men. Can you imagine? In my day, before I got married—that was in 1939—you didn't go all the way with even one man. I'm sexually involved with two men and it feels great and I feel absolutely no need to remarry. And I'll probably always be able to find a sexual relationship as long as I can hobble around."

She reached for the baby bottle on the table and shook a drop on the back of her hand, "I feel that if a woman really wants a relationship, she can get it. She gives special signals, whether she knows it or not, saying she's available and ready . . . and the law of averages says that a certain number of men are going to respond."

· *What signals are you giving men?*

I agree with Ginger. When a woman is absolutely sure she wants a relationship, she lets men know this in all kinds of direct and indirect ways. On the other hand, when a woman has mixed feelings about wanting a relationship, or doesn't want one, she also gives out signals: ones that say, "leave me alone" or "I don't trust you" or "I'm afraid of you" or "I can't handle this." *What signals are you giving out?*

Make Yourself Physically Accessible!

If you have been able to say, "Yes! I do want a relationship," ask yourself if you are putting yourself in situations where you will meet men.

• *Where to meet men.*
Do you have a passion? If it's politics, you'll meet men at political meetings. If it's painting, you'll meet men at your night art classes (men don't flock to weekday art classes unless they're retired). Is your passion hiking? Join a Sunday morning hiking group and you're sure to meet men there. Passions are for meeting people but they're also for *GROWING*, so if you don't meet a man at your painting class you will have developed something very precious anyway—the ability to get excited when you look at a particular work of art and the ability to lose your sense of time when you pick up a paintbrush; the ability to become CONSUMED. When you finally do meet someone exciting, you will have GROWN from your passion and you'll have more to give to a man. GROWING women settle for nothing less than growing men!

• *Chance encounters.*
Make yourself physically accessible through chance encounters. Talk to that man standing next to you at the art gallery. If he's looking at the Corot next to your Manet, and makes an "mmm" sound, he's obviously talking to you. He's saying only "mmm" because that gives you a choice of hearing or not hearing—and saves face for him if you choose not to hear. Hear. Especially if you haven't done this before. Take a risk—and it will be easier the second time. And talk to the man sitting next to you at the concert and at the lecture.

· *Meeting men through friends.*

Let your good friends know you want to meet men. Be direct with them. That's one of the things good friends are for. Does a friend's husband know an eligible man at his office? Does a friend know a man who has recently been widowed? Does a friend have a *brother?*

Singles' Clubs: For You?

They may very well be for you *if* you're feeling pretty good about yourself. Charlotte, who is fifty-eight and looks forty-five (and she knows it), objectively appraised her life situation and said to herself, "Okay, I'm divorced and I've met every eligible man in town and now it's time to branch out to Washington, D. C., which is only thirty miles away." Through the singles' grapevine, she discovered two singles' clubs in Washington that attract the kind of men she likes—urbane, sophisticated, over-50 and aggressive. Within six months Charlotte got involved with an economist who works for the federal government. She then decided to move to Washington because her experiment had obviously paid off; she knew that it would definitely be easier for her to meet this kind of man in Washington (there were several singles' clubs she hadn't explored yet), and why drive sixty miles each weekend when she could live there?

· *Why it works for certain women.*

Let's look at Charlotte more closely so we'll know why singles' clubs work for her. She's good-looking, and she feels self-confident. She does not find it uncomfortable to go by herself to a singles' party. (She knows it's better to go by yourself. Men can be very reluctant to approach a woman when she's with another female.) She is also not afraid of rejection. ("Look," she told me, "everyone is occasionally rejected. So what?")

· *And it might NOT work.*

But I advised Betty to think twice before trying that route. Why? Because she's depressed. She's been widowed less than a year and she feels bad about being overweight and she feels very awkward about beginning to date again. Betty is too vulnerable *at this time* to put herself in a situation where she might be looked at critically and found lacking. A woman needs a lot of ego strength to walk into a strange room and be looked over by a gaggle of strange men. Also, women can be very competitive with each other at singles' clubs' parties. Betty's ego is too weak at this time. Notice I say, *at this time.* Next year Betty might be feeling much stronger and better about herself, and a singles' club may fill her needs.

• *Where are the clubs?*

Be selective. In larger cities like New York and Los Angeles, you'll be able to find clubs that cater exclusively to over-50 (or over-40) men and women. This immediately eliminates a hurdle you don't need—the younger woman. She can be a real sister in a sympathetic setting, but that's one thing the singles' club isn't. It's a place where women are apt to view each other as competitors at the least, enemies at the worst. It's easy to feel overwhelmed and defeated when you walk into a singles' club and see a cluster of graying men circling a young and beautiful woman. Some singles' clubs attempt to give their group structure, so you won't feel so self-conscious when you walk in the door. A Unitarian church in one large city sponsors what they call a "Liberated Singles' Group," where a Saturday night may be devoted to buzz sessions around a particular topic that will interest everyone (like "How do you feel about getting involved with a married person?"). People are divided into small groups to exchange ideas on the subject. This is a great icebreaker for the shy person, and it allows a woman to feel like a person instead of like a piece of merchandise on sale.

Singles' Bars: For You?

• *Be realistic as to how they're used (sometimes).*

Accept the fact that many men look at singles' bars as ways of finding quick, no-strings sexual encounters and that you can feel pretty conspicuous sitting there trying to look inconspicuous. You will find a lot of younger men at singles' bars. Again, you need a strong sense of realism and a lot of ego strength to walk in and walk out of a singles' bar and still feel good about yourself.

· *What kind is better for the over-50 woman?*

If you're intent on trying it at least once, avoid the slick and plastic kinds that cater to the younger crowd and try to find the few that are reminiscent of the 1950's casual bohemian bar, where you can read your news-paper over a beer on a Saturday afternoon and where you might even find a couple of people playing chess. This is a more relaxed atmosphere, and you're more apt to meet older men there—but they may be anti-marriage or multiple-marriers, or men who work only three after-noons a week teaching sculpting. They can be stimulating and great fun for casual evenings and memorable affairs, but they rarely want to settle down.

Get Out of Your Neighborhood!

Leah, a very adventurous friend of mine, has a won-derful time about twice a month. She lives outside a large port city on the East Coast that has many old ethnic neighborhoods, and every other Saturday night she and her friend, Mae, get in Leah's car, leave the suburbs, and have supper at one of the Polish family cafés that dot the streets of the row-house Polish section of their city. These are warm and friendly working-class cafés and each one features an accordionist who plays Polish music all eve-ning. The clientele is mixed. There are married couples who frequent their favorite café every Saturday night, and there are older Polish women from the neighborhood who come in twos and threes, *and* there are the Polish seamen of all ages whose ships are docked at the port and who come in for a few hours of familiar atmosphere to assuage their homesick feelings. Leah and Mae, who have enjoyed folk dancing for many years, find ready part-ners to polka with.

· *The payoffs.*

Will they find a man they can have a lasting relation-ship with in one of these cafés? Maybe. Maybe not. But they are finding many hours of pleasure, and Leah said, "The extra padding around my hips is *appreciated* here. These men don't like thin women." A tip if you decide to try these neighborhood cafés: Be as friendly to the women who frequent them as you are to the men; otherwise you will be resented.

• *What does your city have to offer YOU?*

Does your city have an International Y? They're great places for meeting exotic and interesting men. Finnish and Lithuanian and Italian and German groups sponsor folk dances and potluck suppers, and they offer regular and structured activities for adventurous people of all ages. Try square dancing and folk dancing at local colleges and Y's in your area. Read the recreation section of your Sunday newspaper to see what neighborhood festivals are scheduled. These are the ways you can reach out into the larger community to find new men in your life. Don't fearfully huddle in your own neighborhood and refuse to explore the other parts of your city. If you do, you'll see the same people over and over again. Be curious, reach out, talk to strangers, poke your head into unusual places—and you will find your life changing.

Ways to Get Involved

• *Cruises.*

Are cruises always expensive? Not for occasional, short, weekend trips to nearby interesting places. Sadye met Ed, her present husband, on the mail boat (around $3.00 a round-trip ticket) to Smith Island, which is off the Eastern Shore of Maryland. They had each read about this intriguing little place where most of the residents speak English in the way it was spoken in the seventeenth and eighteenth centuries . . . where you can't spend a lot of money even if you want to . . . where you spend your time ambling along, people-watching and bird-watching, and meet some of the local residents across the groaning tables of the rooming houses where you stay for unbelievably low rates. A lovely piece of the past, intact in a small island on the Chesapeake Bay.

As soon as Sadye met Ed on that mail boat, she knew they were the same kind of people (it takes a certain kind of person to love Smith Island). Today? Today this couple in their early sixties are happily married, ready to celebrate their second anniversary.

I know another newly married couple, over-50, who met on a mini-mester cruise. What's that? A new trend where universities and colleges arrange cruises with non-credit and credit courses built into the fun, and *everyone* is invited to buy a ticket—college kids, high-school drop-outs, middle-aged intellectuals, and housewife oldsters. *Many* older men and women fill the ships. Teachers are recruited from universities and colleges, and artists and scholars and interesting lecturers are on hand to give your cruise the spark that the older woman who thrives on talking and learning loves. Who will you meet on these cruises? *Men* who get a kick out of this.

• *Travel-study programs.*

Then there's a growing number of travel-study programs abroad, offered by colleges. These programs combine travel and learning and a vacation in a foreign country, and range from one-week seminars to tours that last two or more months. People of all ages join up, and it's a great way to meet the intellectually curious man. For information on mini-mester cruises and travel-study programs, read the Sunday travel section of your newspaper, or call a travel agency and local colleges. Better still, contact the following associations that will gladly send you a directory of schools in your area offering travel-study programs:

Travel Division
National Education Association
1201 16th Street, N.W.
Washington, D. C. 20036

American Federation of Teachers (their service is
    not limited to active or retired teachers)
1901 Fort Myers Drive
Arlington, Virginia 22209

Institute of International Education
809 United Nations Plaza
New York, New York 10017

Travel-study programs and mini-mester cruises vary in
price and give you an opportunity to see new places
with an already-arranged group. When you join this kind
of adventure you don't look like a desperate manhunter
during your vacation. It gives you an image and a self-
image you can live with.

• *Classes.*
Enroll in classes that appeal to men as well as women.
Join an economics or geology or astronomy course. Take
a fun class on How to Make Your Own Wine. Enroll in
a real estate seminar. Call your city or state Commission
on Aging office (listed in your telephone book) and ask
where they're presently running a pre-retirement course.
These courses are free and you will learn from experts
who give you important information on such things as financial planning and Social Security benefits and suggest
creative ways to use your leisure time . . . and they are
chock-full of men.
   Particularly try to avoid spending all your free evenings
at meetings of women's auxiliary organizations. You can
do the same good philanthropic work in a mixed group,
sitting across the committee table from a friendly man.
   If you're over 60 and you want to combine a low-cost
summer vacation with classes, write Elderhostel, 15 Garri-
son Avenue, Durham, N. H. 03824 for information on
their exciting programs for older men and women. For
$100 a week (there are partial scholarships) you can
spend an enjoyable 1, 2, or 3 weeks on a college campus
(and participating colleges are throughout the country).
Room, board, tuition, and all leisure activities are included
in the fee—and the stimulating courses are informal: without grades or exams.

Make Yourself Emotionally Accessible!

You've decided you want a relationship (you have *NO*
mixed feelings) and you're looking in the right places—
so why have you had only two dates this year? Are you—

- allowing yourself to be *personal* with men?
- putting yourself in *intimate* situations with men?
- encouraging men to be personal with *you?*

- *Are you avoiding intimacy?*

April, who is fifty-eight and beautiful in an elfin way, is *not* personal. She prattles on and on when she's with Colin about the situation in the Middle East (important —but at three in the morning?) and the short stories of John Updike and the fine work Colin is doing as director of a social service agency, and she never stops talking about impersonal ideas long enough to ask him how he really feels, or *any* intensely personal questions. And she never tells him anything really personal about herself. Oh, he knows she has three grandchildren and he's had dinner at her son's house and he knows her favorite music, but he has no idea what her *inner* life is like. She has never dared say to him, "My most vulnerable time is the second I awaken—."

April is *afraid* to be that personal with a man. She puts up a thick wall between herself and men, taking refuge in no-risk conversation. She is afraid she'll be rejected if she "intrudes" on a man's inner world or exposes her own imperfect inner world. She simply doesn't realize that the impersonal wall she creates actually drives men away! She doesn't understand that men *want* to be discovered; that the woman who dares say, "Tell me how you *feel*" is going to find men telling her how they feel—and loving it. Men, like women, want to be probed and known. This tells them that they have worth; that someone values their friendship and shows it by asking about their real feelings. And when a woman also tells about herself and her feelings, she is saying, "I am willing to let you know about my imperfections because I trust you." There is no greater compliment. This creates intimacy. *ARE YOU DOING THIS?*

And are you allowing men (at least certain men) to see you in intimate settings? There's a great deal of difference between you, gussied up in your chiffon, hostessing a cocktail party in your living room—bowls of dips set out on the tables, the ice bucket ready—and you, sitting at your breakfast table, wearing a pair of pants and a Mexican shirt, pouring coffee for the man across the table, the morning newspaper on the floor and table. The cocktail party setting is formal and makes you seem—distant. The breakfast table? Ah, there you've created a feeling of closeness where the man sitting across from you feels you're *emotionally accessible.*

• *The pitfall of the "Saturday Night Date."*

How else and *where* else can you create that sense of intimacy? Did you ever stop to realize that the "Saturday Night Date" creates distance? It has a tight, structured, formal format. It's *planned.* It's not spontaneous. Women and men tend to worry ahead of time how they're going to act . . . and whether they'll be "successful" dates. It leads into an evening where a couple is likely to role-play instead of being really relaxed.

• *How to be intimate.*

Instead, arrange to see the man you're interested in at times of the day and evening that feel more cozy. How about 4:00 p.m. when you can take a walk together? Or how about an early supper at your house on Sunday evening? (He'll probably remember that time as a warm and nostalgic part of his own family history—the ritual Sunday night supper.) Do intimate things together. Shop with him for the things you'll need for supper. Invite him into your kitchen to help you cook—or, if you're having supper at *his* place, don't act like a guest; pitch in and make the salad, or set the table. Let him see you occasionally with your face scrubbed—with no makeup on—and keep the bathroom door open so he can talk to you while you're putting on your lipstick. These are the daily small but important moments he remembers from his past, and if they were good moments in his life, you will reawaken feelings of warmth, and he'll long to come back again and again to recapture and savor these feelings.

• *The risks and rewards of intimacy.*

Are there risks involved in trying to be intimate? Will some men draw back at your personal questions? And will some prefer the plastic nightclub setting rather than just the two of you taking a walk? Yes—but these are the men who are afraid of closeness, and do you really want a relationship with them anyway? These are the men whose ex-wives complained that they never really "talked" in all the years of their marriage. These are the men who feel threatened about their own frailties, and need to create emotional distances between themselves and other people so they won't be confronted by *themselves*. Dare to be intimate and the healthy, sharing man will respond . . . and isn't that who you're looking for? You really don't want the man who is afraid of closeness, do you? Dare to take the first step toward emotional accessibility!

"I'm Having an Affair with a Married Man—"

Choose men who are—*physically* accessible. Who isn't? The married man (and he's frequently not emotionally accessible, either).

• *Three stories.*
"The worst thing about having an affair with a married man," Julie said, "is that he can't sleep over."
Julie, fifty-four, has been involved with Don for three years, and she told me she still feels abandoned and angry every time he leaves her bed and house at twelve midnight.

Erica looks like a suburban housewife with nothing more on her mind than the dinner party she's planning —but her life is more complicated than that: "I feel such guilt sometimes," she said, "I didn't think too much about Marvin's wife when we first started seeing each other. Then I unexpectedly met her for the first time. Now, when he's still at my house at one in the morning, I can picture her waiting for him and eating her heart out. I wish I hadn't met her . . . I keep wondering what she's really like. I know there are a lot of things he really respects and likes about her. *I* get a piece of his time, and *she* gets a piece of his time—."

I still don't know Phyllis's last name. She had agreed to talk to me when she heard I was writing this book. Perhaps a need to talk to *someone* motivated her to let me into her private world: "I never thought I'd get involved with a married man," she said, speaking so softly I had to lean forward to hear her. "I was married for thirty-one years before my husband died and I was never unfaithful to him. I know he was true to *me*. I knew only one woman who went with a married man—a neighbor. I thought she was terrible. My husband and I used to talk about her. And then—" Phyllis was almost whispering. She fingered the doily on the arm of the sofa. "My husband died. He was sick for so long. I was so tired when he died. Cliff started to drop by. They had worked together at the plant for thirty years. He would just drop by to talk, to make me feel better. This went on, and one thing led to another. Yes, I'm still with him. In a way, I can't believe this is me, the way I've been. Another part of me feels it's right, like nothing's unusual or wrong."

There was a silence, then Phyllis said, "I know Cliff will never leave his wife and kids. I don't expect him to. It wouldn't be right if he did. I guess we'll go on like this. It'll go on as long as it's supposed to—"

Each of these women has gotten involved with a man who is not physically accessible . . . at times in their lives when they were very lonely. One of them told me she feels there aren't many more years left and that she better grab what happiness she can.

• *Build a life outside the relationship.*

If you're involved with a married man and have no intentions of breaking it off, at least care about yourself enough to build a life *outside* of the relationship. Honestly assess whether your expectations of the relationship are *realistic*. That means that you will find every day important, instead of living only for Thursday nights when he spends the evening with you . . . and you will not mope around the house waiting for your phone to ring . . . and you won't spend countless hours, each week, driving past his house to see if his car is there. You will *NOT* let yourself become a helpless puppet on strings, feeling great when he's with you and feeling tense and lonely when he's not. You may even want to consider seeing other men. You owe this man no total commitment . . . because he is not giving *you* a total commitment. Think about this point for five minutes.

· *What are your expectations?*

Are your expectations of the relationship built on realism? "I *am* going to leave her," the husband and lover
says, "but it's a bad time right now." Maybe that's true.
Perhaps he will leave her and marry you (it happens every day). However—has he said it frequently over the
years, and has something always come up that has stopped
him from leaving? The time she went into the hospital for
her hysterectomy? The time when their daughter was getting married? The time he had to get his son out of trouble? And now "business is bad and let's wait for just a
little while"?

· *Be good to yourself.*

Take an honest long look at the situation (and, yes, you
are strong enough to do that). The years can slip by . . .
and it may be harder to find another relationship in five
years. Is the constant anxiety and anger you feel worth
it? If you *still* feel you can't leave him, all right—as long
as you acknowledge to yourself that this is a high-risk
deal and you're knowingly taking the risk of later anguish
for the highs of right-now. Being this honest with yourself
is called *caring about yourself*.

The Younger Man–Older Woman Relationship

This is another high-risk relationship that can work
beautifully—or not work at all. It depends on how
reality-based you are, and what your expectations are,
and how much you need the approval of other people
(how autonomous you are).

· *Women who are in these relationships.*

"I've been involved with a man ten years younger than
I am," Frieda said, "but I don't look any older than he
does—or, at least, this is what I'm told." Frieda is tiny
(she must take a size 5) and she has wide blue eyes and
a blonde Dutch cut. She does look much younger than her
fifty-two years. "We both enjoy the same things. We have
a very good sex life. The only thing is—well, he's going
through stages of his life that I'm finished with. I watch

him struggle through certain things and I feel—removed.

"For one thing, he has teen-age kids. His wife has custody, but he has the children every weekend. If I had teenagers, that would be fine. We could all do things together. But my kids are grown—I'm a grandmother!— and frankly, I'm bored hearing about his son's grades at school. When he talks about his daughter's appointment with the orthodontist, I feel that's a part of my *past* life. I'm sometimes hit with a feeling of *what am I doing here*—?"

I feel Frieda has put her finger on one of the two really important risks in the younger man-older woman relationship: The man is experiencing what the woman has already gone through in her life (in situations *and* feelings) and she can feel a gulf between them—a distance; and the younger man may lose interest as the older woman visibly ages faster than he does, perhaps years after the relationship has begun.

Stephanie, over-50, has been married for eight years to a man fourteen years younger than she is, and she told me how she looks at this: "I knew when I married Richard that I might eventually lose him. After all, when I reach sixty, he'll only be a sexy forty-six. Well, I'm fifty-eight now, and I still haven't lost him, but I know there's still a way to go. There's even more of a risk—I'll now age faster than I did ten years ago. But I still look at it the same way I did when I married him. It's a great relationship for now. If and when I do lose him, I'll feel horrible—I'm not kidding myself about that—but I'll have had a wonderful ten or fifteen years. That makes it worth it."

Not every woman would be willing to live for the great moments in the "now" and risk the later abandonment. To Stephanie—it's worth it.

"Besides," she added, "*any* marriage could break up. Marriage is a risk in itself."

Other women have told me that they would never get involved with a younger man because people would laugh at them. I went back to Frieda and asked her about this.

"I just don't worry about that," she said, "I'm sure

some people do talk—or laugh. I know his mother thinks he's crazy, and she calls me 'that woman.' I just stay out of her way."

Frieda is an autonomous person.

- *Men were EXPECTED to be older (and taller and stronger).*

Why *is* a man expected to be older than a woman, after all? Only because women were once dependent on men for the roof over their heads and the food in their mouths, and the *older* husband was already established in the money-making world (he had had time to learn a skill and get a job). He was ready to support the many children that quickly came along.

- *The rewards.*

Today, it's a different story. Most women *can* and *do* take care of themselves, so this convention is obsolete and limiting when it comes to women's choices in selecting a mate. The next time you meet an attractive man who is ten or fifteen years younger than you are, and you hesitate—think about that. Another point to think twice about: Since women generally live longer than men, and many women are widowed by their mid-sixties, *you* won't be one of them if you marry a younger man. When you're sixty-five or seventy, your husband will probably still be around fifty, healthy and active, and still drawing a full-time hefty working salary. That means you'll have companionship *and* enough money in your later years.

Do Widowers Want to Remarry?

- *Yes! (If they were happily married.)*

Widowers are frequently more apt to marry than bachelors or divorced men—especially if they were happily married. After the initial shock of losing his wife, the widower often begins to miss keenly the many years he had of laughing and loving. If he's personable, this is the time women begin to converge on him in droves with invitations to the theater, to a dinner party, to a brunch.

• *How to awaken his interest.*

If you really want to awaken his interest, consider a different approach, because these women have become a blur of faces to him (there are so many of them and so many invitations). You're going to want to be creative as Irene was.

"Gordon's wife had died," she told me, "and after about a month women began calling him. I decided that *I* wasn't going to be one of those endless lines of women who just "happened to have two tickets" to something, anything. I couldn't live with that kind of desperate self-image. And from what I had heard of Gordon, he was too sensitive and selective to want that kind of over-eager woman. So I went to the neighborhood library to meet him.

"I'm a library browser on Saturday afternoons, and before Gordon's wife became ill, I used to see them there every Saturday. I figured that once he picked up the pieces of his life again, he would start going back—and he did. He didn't remember me, and I didn't feel strange introducing myself (maybe because library addicts feel comfortable with each other). It turned out to be a good and lazy afternoon. We even found out we're neighbors. That was six months ago. We see each other a couple of times a week now. We found out we have a lot of things in common."

Irene had let Gordon know she was someone he would find interesting because she let him meet her on turf *he* found interesting.

• *Listen to what he says about his marriage.*

Let the widower in your life know you had a good marriage—if you did. This will tell him you'll feel good to live with (after all, *you* contributed to your good marriage, too). Listen to how he talks about his marriage. Did he and his wife lead the kind of life you would enjoy? Were their values *your* values? What did he admire about his wife? Listen to him with your third ear (and that means listening to the silences and the tone of his voice when he talks about her), and you'll learn a lot about whether *you'd* like living with him. And if you wouldn't— well, he might make a good friend or lover anyway. He also might know a man you might want to marry.

"He's Divorced"

Men, like women, get divorced for all kinds of reasons, some of them very valid and healthy.

• *There are more divorces—and more reasons for divorce.*

Often the older couple find themselves divorced after many years of marriage because one of them has grown in ways the other one could not or would not tolerate. More frequently than before, women are leaving men, especially since they have discovered they can take pretty good care of themselves economically. (There are a growing number of desolate over-50 men who are being left behind by wives who wanted to get out of the relationship years ago, and finally, because it's more common now and they're working and making money, finally got up the nerve to do it.) We can no longer assume that the older man who's divorced is the guilty party and has left his aging wife for a younger woman. *She* may have left him for a younger man—or for any number of reasons. He may be depressed and feel deserted, and he may be seeking a lasting relationship for the years ahead.

• *Listen to what he says, too (for your own good).*

If you listen to the divorced man when he tells you about his marriage, he too will tell you a lot about himself and what he wants. Elizabeth, who had been seeing Tim until last month, told me:

"He was very bitter because his wife had started a career in her late forties. She had stayed home with their kids before that. After she got this great job, she stopped making the big dinners every night, and sometimes she wasn't even home for dinner because she had a meeting to attend. Tim got to the point where he hated to even hear about her career. That was the beginning of the end of their marriage. After the divorce, I'd listen to him complain about her—he was still angry, even though it was over—and I started to realize that I'd be absolutely miserable if I were married to him. *I* don't want to make the big dinners, either. I have my own dress shop, and I love it. There are many nights when I don't get out of the

shop till after nine. I just don't want to be tied down to a
man who has these expectations. When I realized he was
getting serious, I pulled out."

If Elizabeth hadn't encouraged Tim to talk about his
marriage and his feelings, she might never have realized
just what he did expect from a wife. She might have
blindly married him—and both of them would have been
unhappy. *Listen!* Listen to every word he tells you about
his ex-wife and his past marriage and himself!

The Multiple-Marrier: Is He Worth Your Time?

If you live in a reasonably large city and get around,
you'll no doubt eventually meet a man who's been married three or more times. He's usually charming, attractive—and a poor marriage risk. Chances are he'll get
married again—multiple marriers have great needs—but
ask yourself why all of his ex-wives left him, or agreed
that they should separate (and don't let him tell you
they were *all* bad).

- *Why have his marriages failed?*

If you have an opportunity to sit down and talk to
some of these women, you'll probably find that they each
have the same bitter complaints. The only multiple-
marrier I know who *did* finally settle down happily chose
a twenty-four-year-old girl for his fourth wife. She has
"daddy" needs—and he's happy to be her "daddy" (he's
fifty-five). So far it's working out well . . . or appears to
be.

How About the Perennial Bachelor?

If you're seeing an over-50 bachelor who is sweet and
wonderful and sexy, be satisfied to just be with him—
because this is a man who (and I'll bet on it) will probably never marry. Why has he avoided marriage all of
these years? For any number of reasons. He may not
want to share his time or money or life space (privacy).
He may be a loner. He has a mother? I knew it! They
spend endless hours on the phone and he takes her to

dinner once a week. Face it—he symbolically relates to her as a mother, wife, and girl friend. His father was most likely a quiet unassuming man who took a back seat while his mother made the decisions.

· *Be realistic about what he wants.*

Why am I down on bachelors? I'm not. But be realistic: The over-50 bachelor probably will never marry because he is getting concrete and gratifying payoffs by being a bachelor. He's been getting these payoffs for many years and he expects they'll continue for a long time. Either his mother will continue to hover over him and worry about his health and give him affection (so why does he need a wife?), or his routines and possessions will continue to give him feelings of permanence and security (not like relationships, which can be precarious). The antique vases on his mantelpiece never change— they've always been in the same spot, and they remind him of his childhood—and he likes knowing that at 7:30 every morning he will sit down, crack open his three-minute boiled egg, reach for his cup of Sanka, and open the morning newspaper. If he gets married, his wife might replace the antique vases with something of her own (displacing his familiar world) and want him to talk to her over the breakfast table, instead of reading the newspaper. Who knows, she might even insist that a daily egg is bad for his heart! Yes, a wife would definitely disrupt his routine (which he needs for his security). The bachelor fiercely defends and protects his daily outer world— because this protects his vulnerable *inner* world.

· *Be realistic about what he'll give.*

If you can accept your limited relationship with him, you will often find a good friend in the bachelor: reliable, dependable (as long as you're realistic in your demands), and considerate. Every over-50 woman should be lucky enough to have one bachelor on hand for Sunday afternoon rides in the country and lonely evenings. Fit into his structured routine, don't expect marriage, and you'll have a man in your life who will really be a good friend. Exceptions? Oh yes—they do happen. *Occasionally.* But don't count on it.

• *The gay bachelor. How do you fit in?*

"But what about the bachelor you've been interested in—and then found he's a homosexual?" one over-50 woman wailed. "I was married in a small midwestern town in the 1930's and before that, when I was dating, I had never even heard of homosexuality! Now that I'm widowed and circulating again after all these years, I'm finding it's a strange world! What's wrong with men today, that this is happening? I was seeing this man for six months before I found out what he was! I felt so helpless. I could compete against a *woman*, but—."

Why would a man date a woman for six months and hide the fact that he's a homosexual? Because of the pressures of society . . . or because he has mixed feelings about his sexuality . . . or because he liked her as a friend and never expected, as she did, that the relationship might go further.

"But I feel *used*," she said angrily. "I feel betrayed. Exploited!"

Did she have pleasant times with him? Did she laugh with him? Enjoy him? Then she wasn't used—any more than she was using him. They were using each other, as healthy people do, for mutual support and pleasure. It wasn't as though he had made any *promises*.

The important thing is not to personalize your gay friend's "rejection" of you; he is not rejecting *you*; he is rejecting a male-female relationship for himself. He *can* be a very good friend.

How to Handle the End of an Affair— When You Don't Want It to End

Knowing the following two facts (that very few people ever talk *or* know about) will help you get over an affair in *half the time:*

• *You're asking, "What's wrong with ME?"*

Women often go through a period of self-hatred and self-blame after men leave them, because we're trained, from childhood, to feel something is wrong with *us* if a man doesn't want us. Women are also conditioned to turn anger inwards, so the anger we feel toward the men who

reject us is frequently turned into anger at *ourselves*—
and this anger, because we don't know what to do with it,
turns into *DEPRESSION*.

• *It is harder to cope with "endings" when you're older.*

It often takes longer for older women to get over broken relationships because, as we get older it is harder for
us to cope with separations. You may have already lost
important people in your life—perhaps your parents,
brother or sister, or your husband. If your children have
left home you've experienced separation. If you're retired,
you're separated from your important work world. As
you've gotten older you may feel you've been separated
from the mainstream of life, especially if you've taken
more and more of a back seat in decision-making. And
now here's another separation, when you feel there's so little left—the separation from a man who made you feel
wanted and important. It *is* easier for the younger woman
to get over an affair that has broken-up. Men are more
easily accessible to her, and replacements can be instant
healers. Also, she doesn't feel as frightened about separation because she hasn't yet suffered that much loss in her
life. It's hard for her—but not *as* hard.

• *What can you do to feel better?*

Knowing all of this, what can you do? Keep busy during these bad months. Spend time with people who give
you love and support. Join a women's consciousness-
raising group where you'll quickly realize that all women,
no matter how attractive and smart they are, feel angry
at *themselves* after the affair is over. And learn from experience.

Don't do what Penny did. Manny left her and it took
her almost two years to get over it. She lost twenty
pounds during that time (and not on a diet). She told me
it was worse for her than when her husband died. Finally,
when she was back on her feet and feeling like a human
being again, Manny called and asked to see her. You
know the rest of the story. Penny got involved again . . .
and now she's going through the same anguish. Why does
Penny want to be a *victim?*

• *Finding a replacement.*

It may take longer to find a replacement now than when you were twenty, but if you make yourself emotionally and physically accessible, and encourage the men you're meeting to be emotionally accessible, you most likely *can* and *will* find companionship again. Meanwhile . . . GROW. Open and stretch your mind and your imagination and take a class or attend a workshop. Learn Yoga. Discover the art of Meditation. Join the local community center and sign up for swimming lessons. Grow—and growing men will be attracted to you!

Your Sex Life: Good, Bad, or Dead?

In talking to hundreds of older women about sex, here is what I hear most often:

"I want to go to bed with him, but I'm ashamed of my body."

"I haven't gone to bed with anyone since my husband died. How do I know I'll please a man?"

"How direct can I be? I could tell my husband what I wanted, but now I feel awkward—and I don't know how they'll take it if I say certain things in bed."

"Do I take a chance and have him sleep over? Suppose my children drop by unexpectedly the next morning?"

"I don't want to be just a lay! I don't want sex without love!"

• *How do you feel about your body?*

You're ashamed of your body? You're overweight? Your breasts and upper arms sag? You hate the stretch marks on your stomach and thighs? You detest the bulges on your thighs? Sure, you may have lost the supple lithe look you had when you were twenty—but so did the man you're interested in. Men have the same strong feelings about aging as women—the fears, the anxiety—and they're just as self-conscious about their potbellies as you may be about the bulge of fat on your thighs.

Our society teaches all of us to value youth, because youth is economically productive. It brings profit into the society. And until the magazine ads and our schools and all of our other institutions start teaching us that age is

as beautiful as youth; that the marks of *experience* on
our bodies are attractive—we *are* going to feel ashamed
of any visible signs of aging. You and I and every one of
us have been brought up with this ideology that makes us
feel bad about ourselves as we grow older, so look at
your feelings very realistically. We can't easily begin
feeling differently about our aging bodies—we've been
taught too long that aging is ugly—so live *with* your
feelings while you begin to take a critical look at how
your feelings began. Until you feel very secure with the
man you're sexually involved with, hide your sagging
arms with sleeves, and don't wear a shortie nightgown if
you have knotty legs. And then, later, when you're feeling very self-confident in the relationship and feeling better about being older, stride around your bedroom nude,
head high. The feeling of *SELF* that you'll project will be
STRONG and POWERFUL, and that's *really* sexual,
because it comes from within.

· *How men feel about their aging bodies.*

Beryl, a fifty-five-year-old friend, told me the same
thing is true of *men.* That when they feel all right about
their aging and secure about themselves, they come on as
sexier. I hadn't seen her for awhile and she brought me
up-to-date on what she had been doing—and with whom:

"I'm involved with this average-looking man who's
close to sixty," she said, "and when Raymond stalks
around my bedroom, no clothes on, cigar in mouth and
totally unselfconscious about his body, I swear that even
his bald head turns me on. It's like he's saying 'okay, so
this is my body so what. It's gone through many wars and
it did pretty well. Here it is, take it or leave it." We
both agreed that self-acceptance is SEXY.

· *Learn to please yourself sexually.*

If you haven't gone to bed with anyone since your divorce or since your husband died, and fear you won't
please a man, keep this in mind: Learn to please yourself sexually—and you'll please *him.* Discover, through
touching yourself, what makes your body feel sexually
good, and then tell him what you've learned. This will
turn him on sexually and he'll then feel free to tell you
what to do to him to make him feel sexually aroused.

But how do you become free enough to touch your body to explore your sexuality; to masturbate without feeling guilty? How do you show him what you want him to do to you without feeling embarrassed? Read! Get a copy of *Sex and The Over Fifties* by Robert Chartham (Brandon Books), and *Sex in Later Life* by Ivor Felstein (Penguin Books). Both are in paperback, and tell you, step-by-step, what to do and how to do it. The authors understand how over-50 women were brought up, and they know there's a lot of learning to be done and a lot of attitudes to unlearn. They can help you move into a freer way of sexually relating to yourself and your mate. Particularly, these books address the middle-aged and older person, taking changing bodies and changing health conditions into consideration (if these are your concerns, you'll appreciate this).

Definitely invest in a sex manual that has explicit informational drawings and written instructions. Looking at a picture can tell you immediately what to do and how to do it. I would recommend two books by Alex Comfort, *The Joy of Sex* and *More Joy of Sex*. They're also in paperback, published by Simon and Schuster. Be selective when you use these manuals—you'll know what appeals to you and what doesn't—and keep an open mind. Read them together with your mate!

• *Where to make love.*

Finding a place to make love can present problems. What if you're at your place and your children unexpectedly drop in the next morning while you're both in bed? Well, make sure that *won't* happen. Tell them ahead of time you're going to be busy from Saturday afternoon until Sunday night, and would they please hold off on any phone calls or visits during that time (phone calls can be very distracting). If they show any curiosity, and you don't want them to know about your relationship (of course, you may *want* to tell them), just refuse to discuss it, and remind them that you respect their privacy and you expect them to respect yours. This will help them see you as a *person,* not just their mother. You've never done this before? You feel uneasy? Well, time to start! No, you won't hurt their feelings (if they're reasonably mature) and it will help your relationship grow, because

you'll be relating to them as equals not expecting anything from them that you're not willing to give yourself.
Do it once, and it'll be easier to do the next time—and
maybe you won't have to do it at all the third time.

What do you do if you have a roommate? If she shares
your values about relationships and sex and you've had
an open and honest camaraderie, no problem. Just let
her know you're having a man stay over, so she can be
discreet enough (if necessary) to avoid bumping into him
in the hallway on the way to the bathroom in the middle
of the night. But if she's a very proper lady who is uptight about sex-without-marriage, go to his apartment.
Later, if your affair flourishes and you don't want to always spend the night at his place, consider changing
roommates or living alone.

• *Don't play "wifey."*

And if you do go to his place to spend the night, don't
play "wifey." That means don't fuss over him by straight-
ening his tie before he leaves for work in the morning and
don't reorganize his desk while he's out of the apartment.
Don't even bring him new kitchen curtains as a "surprise."
This is manipulative. (You're silently and indirectly saying, "Marry me! Marry me!") He'll feel pressured and
he'll feel like you're trying to control him (which you
are). No healthy man likes being manipulated (just as
you don't want to be manipulated) and you don't want to
spend all that time and energy being devious, because
healthy women feel better about themselves when
they're direct and honest.

Living Together—Without Marriage

Should you move in with him? Should he move into
your place? Do your grown children object?

There's a question of morals—or is there?—and there's
a question of economics. You may feel no qualms about
living together without marriage, but you might hesitate
because you have very conventional children. Grown
children sometimes have rigid ideas about how their
mothers should act, and you may feel it's not worth it to
embarrass them, since they live in the same city. Or you

might say, "Look, kids, this is *my* life. Your feelings are *your* problem." That choice is yours and I understand your possible conflicts in this area.

· *It's cheaper than living apart.*

Now money's another story. There are countless older couples who live together without marriage because it's cheaper (food is cheaper for two people; rent is less expensive when shared). Living on a fixed income is no fun; sharing expenses means more money for vacations and dinner out and an occasional movie. It can even mean being able to afford better medical care.

· *You have to decide for yourself.*

Countless numbers of over-50 couples live together without a marriage license, and at least they are getting human companionship and sexual fulfillment during middle and older years. Why not get *married?* One woman put it well: "What for? We're not going to have children, or buy a house . . ." There is no pat answer. You have to make up your own mind.

Taking Responsibility

When it comes to taking steps towards insuring your own sexual fulfillment, you can run into different (and opposite) problems. I think of two women, both in their fifties, who *are* facing very different kinds of situations.

· *Your relationship with an ego-battered man.*

Corinthia came to my office and when she started to talk I could feel her anxiety. "I was married for thirty-two years," she said, "and I was used to my husband. I could tell him what I wanted him to do to me in bed. But with Max—."

Max, the man she is seeing, is recently divorced, and his wife had left him after many years of marriage. He is still hurting. Corinthia wants to be sensitive to this, and knowing he feels weak and out of control of his life, she doesn't want to come on as the sexually agressive woman, a stance she felt would make him feel all the more powerless.

"I'm deliberately holding back, acting passive," she said.

"How does that make you feel?" I asked.

She was quiet for a few seconds. "Mixed feelings. I'm used to a full and satisfying sex life because I *could* be so open with my husband. I could say touch me here, touch me there. If I did this to Max, I'd be taking away even more of his manhood, he feels so bad right now. He feels so battered. But—what about me and *my* needs?"

I suggested she meet *both* their needs by being direct and aggressive *and* telling Max constantly how much she enjoyed his touch. And it works!

· *Your relationship with a tradition-bound man.*

Now Genevieve, an over-50 divorcée, has another question. She's seeing Gunther, who grew up in Poland sixty years ago and who is very traditional and conservative. After a courtship of several months, they are just beginning to be sexually intimate.

"I sense he's shocked at some of the things I say and do," she told me. "For instance, I rolled on top of him the other night in bed, and he froze. He stared at me like I was a stranger, and then he went limp. He wouldn't talk about it afterwards, either. Last week, on the way home from the movies, I asked him whether we should go to his place or mine for the night. He was driving, and I could see his body stiffen. After a very tense silence, he formally asked me if I didn't think this was a question *he* should be asking me."

I would never suggest that Genevieve approach Gunther in the same way that Max was approached. Max has no blocks against a woman being sexually aggressive. It just has to be done in a way that would enhance his ego rather than weaken it further. Gunther, however, comes from a cultural background where women were taught to be demure and passive, and where men called the sexual shots. He *was* genuinely shocked when Genevieve assumed what he considered to be *his* role. I seriously question whether he will ever be able to accept a reversal of roles. Is Genevieve willing and able to adapt to his sexual code without feeling cheated and angry? She's thinking very seriously about this question.

Different Strokes for Different Folks

There are countless men and women who don't enjoy sex. Some of them are widows and some are divorced women who are tremendously relieved because they no longer have to "put up with all that." They'll say, "I'm too old for that sort of thing," or, "Thank God that part of my life is over," or "I just want to be left alone." These are the women who gratefully swallow the myth that menopause means the end of sexuality.

We happen to be living at a time when society says that you are supposed to enjoy sex. One city has a lionized gynecologist whose specialty is talking to older-age groups about their sexuality. He tells them about vibrators and multiple orgasms and group sex. This is the day of sex manuals and sex clinics. We're taught that all women have a right to an exciting sex life and, yes, that all women owe it to themselves to learn to enjoy this part of their life.

• *The freedom to get involved or not.*

Where is the freedom of choice? The over-50 woman who doesn't like sex may find it very hard to change her feelings and may not want to. She should be given the sanction to do what she wants. On the other hand, she should definitely have access to information that could possibly change her attitudes—if she wants it. Let *her* make the choice. Our sexuality is very complex and tied up with feelings of guilt, anger, love, and nurturing. Therefore we should respect the feelings of men and women who withdraw from an active sex life and realize that digging up their feelings of guilt and anger may just be too anxiety-provoking for them. The deliberately celibate woman can have just as rich a life as the sexually active woman, by cultivating the wonderful sensations that come from experiences other than sex—learning to enjoy color and texture and shapes and sounds and people and *herself.*

• *Understand your feelings and act on them.*

I've heard countless indignant and irate women say, "I don't want to be just a lay! I don't want sex without love." If you feel this way, respect this need in yourself, and try not to feel guilty when your male friends, and sometimes even your female friends, accuse you of being rigid or sick or a Puritan.

· *There is no "right" or "wrong."*

Of course, you shouldn't become self-righteous and huffy, and tell your female friends who do go to bed that they're promiscuous, or don't let yourself judge them silently either. It's not that you're right and they're wrong or the other way around. There *is* no right or wrong. The important thing is what makes you feel good. And the important thing is to be in touch with your feelings— your real feelings—and to act on them, and to allow other people *their* feelings.

"I've Never Wanted to Get Married!"

Not too long ago women who never married were called "freaks" and "odd" and "spinsters" and "old maids." They're still called spinsters and old maids by some and if you're an older woman who has never married, you've probably hated this label, haven't you? But take heart —people are becoming aware that the unmarried woman has some special things going for her—like the independence to make her own decisions and have privacy when she wants it, and her own money.

· *Staying single is DELIBERATE.*

I feel it is deliberate when *any* woman is older and unmarried. Let's listen to Victoria:

"Everytime a relationship got serious," this good-looking, fifty-two-year-old woman told me, "I would destroy it. I would run out the door just as the man was ready to propose. And then I realized—I simply didn't want to get married! I'm a supervisor for a city agency, and I don't want to have to share my paycheck, or have anyone tell me how to spend my money. After all, I've been handling my own money since I was eighteen— thirty-four years! And I don't want to stop working because a husband tells me to. I have seniority in my job and I'm making as much as some men I know. I'll have a nice pension when I retire. Why should I share that? I worked plenty hard for it—."

Does this make Victoria sick or neurotic? I don't think so. More than most people, she recognizes her real feelings and her needs and she's honest about them. She *is* giving money top priority in her life, but she grew up during the Depression and she's afraid of *not* having money. She was a young working woman during a time when most women stayed home after they married and had children, and were dependent on their husbands to support them. She and her unmarried female friends took secretarial and sales jobs and made much less than the men they knew.

Victoria struggled to accomplish what she did, becoming a supervisor in a large office. The married women she knows who work, do hand over a large proportion of their paychecks to their husbands. So Victoria chose to adapt to a life alone, and has made what to her is a good life. She has friends. She is close to her sisters. She loves her two nieces as if they were her own children. She buys clothes whenever she wants to and she has a nicely furnished apartment. She has saved quite a lot of money. She fills her weekends doing all kinds of things with two or three women friends who also never married, and they know they can count on each other for comfort and support. Victoria occasionally gets involved with a man and enjoys the company of men, but there is no doubt that she has *deliberately* avoided marriage, because her relationships with men are usually short term. Many married women might envy her for the income she enjoys and the freedom she has.

Other older women who have never married may have chosen their life style because they're loners. They need privacy most of the time. They are *not* lonely—and we waste our time feeling sorry for them, because they *want* to be alone. Marriage would be devastating for them; they would feel smothered by the imposed intimacy. Let us finally acknowledge that the woman who decides to remain single is as complete a woman as the wife who is celebrating her thirty-fifth wedding anniversary and who is becoming a grandmother for the fourth time. They differ only in where they put their priorities.

Divorce After 50: What to Expect

It *is* often harder for the older woman to go through divorce. A group of older divorced women have been meeting once-a-week in a living room for several months now, and these are some of the things that have been said:

"I'm over fifty. Who would want me again?"

"I dread going through the Saturday-night dating game after all these years!"

"I'm bitter! He left me after thirty-three years."

"You bet I want alimony! He left me for a twenty-nine-year-old girl when I was fifty-three. I'm not trained for a job. I'm too old to begin a career. And to top it off, I put him through graduate school when we were first married so he could end up making fifty thousand dollars a year! After bringing up our kids and helping him become a big shot, I deserve every cent I can get!"

• *Life may be BETTER after divorce!*

Does all this mean divorce must be the end of your world? After you go through the terrible despair and the peak of the pain and self-hatred, you may find that life is *better* after the divorce. Margie, who has red hair and youthful freckles and whose husband left her last year, sat across from me in the crowded restaurant where we had arranged to meet during her lunch hour.

"First of all, I got my first full-time job after Dick left. I'm a secretary, and fortunately good secretaries are always in demand, despite the economy. I'm even called an administrative assistant! I did lie and take a couple of years off my age when I applied for the job—I said I was forty-eight. And this job has kept me from going out of my mind. Keeping busy is what can keep you out of the loony bin at a time like this."

We gave our orders to the waitress. Margie continued, "I started to date a few months ago. Would you imagine, here I am, fifty-one years old, and I'm just discovering sex? It's probably a familiar story to a lot of women my age. Sheltered, in a boxed-in world in a boxed-in suburb for years—and then let loose!

"I married Dick when I was eighteen. To Dick, women

were either good girls or bad girls—and I was a virgin, so I was a good girl. And all during those long years in the suburbs, my one sex teacher, my husband, taught me nothing. Good girls do it one way, with their husband on top of them, so that's all I knew. Enjoy? Who knew whether I enjoyed it? *I* didn't even know. I'd read about how great sex is and I'd think something was wrong with me, that I had a low sex drive. Dick and I never talked about it. Well, I'm seeing someone now who's just great. He's sensitive and caring and he takes a lot of time with me. He's really teaching me the things I should have known years ago, and I'm reborn.

"Sure, I feel cheated about all those years with Dick. I'm sure he was screwing around and having a great time with all those 'bad' girls. But I have a few years ahead of me, I figure. I'm at a good time in my life, you could say. I don't have to worry about becoming pregnant—I went through my change already. My kids are married. I don't have to worry about taking care of them, or cooking for anyone. I have a small efficiency apartment, which takes no time to clean. All I have to think about and worry about is myself. Like when I was a young girl! All I have to worry about is what I'm going to wear to-night—"

The waitress put our plates down and Margie picked up her fork.

"I figure my life's just beginning."

• *Concrete payoffs.*

Are *you* in the process of divorce? And afraid of an unknown future? Margie's right, there *are* pluses to being alone at the age of fifty or sixty, rather than twenty-five. Chances are you don't have to be responsible to anyone but yourself. Gone are the days when you had to worry about paying for the kids' braces. No worry about pregnancy. No one to keep you to a schedule. No baby-sitters to worry about. No child who suddenly comes down with the measles when you're ready to go out of town. You can now finally afford to *really* pamper yourself.

• *Forget the "shoulds."*

What can you do to make your life easier financially? What can you do to make your life richer emotionally?

Forget the "shoulds" in your life. ("I *should* put away more for my retirement and not spend so much." I *should* schedule my vacation so I spend the week at my daughter's, to make it easier for her after she has the baby.") Dare to take the vacation in Mexico that you've always wanted. Go back to school. Go skiing. Buy a sex manual with pictures. *ACT.* You'll then find yourself less afraid of the day-to-day questions and new situations the over-50 divorcée faces. You'll learn to take things as they come . . . like Marilyn does:

"I got a divorce, and then I remarried, so I gave up my house and gave all my furniture to my children for their homes. Then my second marriage didn't work out, so I left him and moved into a furnished apartment (remember, I didn't have any of my own furniture anymore). Then I realized I hated living in a furnished place . . . but I also knew I couldn't afford to go out and buy new things. I agonized over the question, 'should I ask my kids to return the furniture?' I didn't want to antagonize them. I finally did ask them—they're both in much better financial shape than I am—and it was okay. My daughter said, 'Why didn't you ask sooner, Mom.' It was fine."

• *Sure, it's different when you're older.*

The kind of situation you never would have had to face if you were a twenty-five-year-old divorcée? Yes—but so what? Life *is* different with different payoffs at *every* stage. Concentrate on the payoffs: The independence you'll have, the freedom of time, and, finally, the pampering you can give yourself to develop your sense of SELF.

Build a great new life for yourself around these payoffs!

Remarriage: Is It for Every Woman?

• *Two women reflect on their own situations.*

Bertha sat on the wing chair, part of the half-circle of women whose faces were turned toward her. Her eyes filled with tears as she talked.

"Harry keeps saying, it's *our* life. Am I marrying your son or your daughter? Do they have to live with me? He keeps telling me it's none of their business if we want to get married, that we should just go ahead and *do* it."

Bertha is a grandmotherly looking woman in her middle sixties. Her hair is gray and she has a soft, pretty face. She blew her nose.

"But I can't. I'm torn apart. They tell me that he's going to take advantage of me, that he wants my money. Heaven knows I don't have that much money, that they should think that. My husband left me a house that's paid for. After he died I got some money from the sale of our grocery store. I have my Social Security checks each month.

"What does he have? Well, he has *his* Social Security. He has a small house, and it's paid for."

She closed her eyes. There was silence. The women waited. Finally, "It's like I'm afraid of making my children angry. My daughter, particularly. She carries on about it. She can't stand even seeing Harry. The kids don't realize how lonely I was before I met him."

More silence. Then one of the women asked, "Do you think he's after your money?"

She opened her eyes. "No."

"I'm willing to go out with him," Goldye said, "and I'm willing to spend most of my time with him. But marry him—no."

She looked at me defiantly. "Do you know why?"

I waited.

"Because," she leaned toward me, her body urgent, "I'm tired of taking care of sick men who die on me!"

She straightened up and let out her breath. "Two husbands. The first one died of cancer, and the last one had a heart attack. Did you ever nurse anyone through cancer? I wouldn't wish that on my worst enemy. Karl, my second husband, I was with him when he died. I was alone with him. It hit him like a cyclone. It was five o'clock in the morning and by the time the ambulance came, he was gone. He had never been sick before, not even one day of his life."

We sat, not talking for a few minutes, engrossed in our own thoughts.

Then she said—and her tone was quieter, "He carries nitroglycerine with him, day and night. I should marry a man with such a heart condition? He shouldn't expect that of me. Let his children take care of him if he gets sick. He has good children. No woman should have to bury three husbands."

Her voice faded, "I can't take any of that anymore."

• *Are your children objecting?*

Bertha is not in an unusual situation. Many grown children do object to their parent remarrying. A social worker once bet me that more grown children object to their parent remarrying than parents object to their child's marriage. I didn't take that bet because I probably would have lost. *Why* do grown children object? Of the many possible reasons, these are the most common:

Your children may be saying the man is too interested in your money. Maybe it's true! What can you do? Any of the following things—

• Watch and listen closely and trust your feelings. If you're feeling resentful toward him, drop him.
• Marry him anyway, because you don't care. He can have all of your money if he makes you laugh and feel sexual and feel female. What's money for anyway but to be enjoyed.
• Insist that you both have an attorney draw up a prenuptial agreement, stating that neither of you will share your money and property with each other. Each of you will leave your money and property to your own children, respectively.

And then tell your children what you've decided to do and tell them you don't want to hear another word about it.

Your children feel you're being disloyal to their father by remarrying? There's probably a hidden message you're not hearing. They might be afraid they will lose their role as Mommy and Daddy's child, if you remarry. They might be feeling the threat of the loss of a part of themselves, even though they're grown with children of their own. As long as you do not remarry, your deceased husband is still intact as their father—symbolically. If you remarry, he's really buried. They've lost their father, and they've lost their role as *child* with both parents. This is hard to face in themselves, so they rationalize and say you're being disloyal to their father. Just tell them, firmly, that Dad would have wanted to see you happy again and you are going to marry this man. You cannot and should not build your life around their unrealistic and childlike fantasies and needs, and you know your deceased husband would have wanted you to keep living and loving. Time will help them grow to accept this.

They're jealous of the attention you give this man? Your family is upset because you're not spending as much time baby-sitting with your grandchildren, now that you have someone to be with again? Is your daughter used to a lot of attention from you (you bake for her, you call her every day) and now she's afraid she'll lose you? Sure, you'll have less time to give them when you remarry, but they'll find payoffs for themselves that they never imagined: You won't have to call them in the middle of the night when you're ill—you'll have your new husband to turn to; their children will have your new husband as an extra source of loving attention. They'll adapt quickly to these compensations for their losses, and little by little you'll find yourselves all a part of a family unit.

Now—if your children think it's disgusting that you want to get married again and have *sex* again at *your* age, *THIS IS THEIR PROBLEM AND NOT YOURS!* They're victims of the false ugly propaganda that says that over-50 people are "over the hill" and sexless; that the postmenopausal woman is no longer interested in sex; that lust is only for the young. No wonder your intelligent children have internalized these myths; even the "experts" have. I remember viewing a Planned Parenthood training session film, produced at a prestigious medical school, that dealt with sexuality in the aging. After the factual information was presented by the husband-and-wife team who were supposed to be experts in aging and sexuality, a nude couple was shown making love in various positions comfortable and effective for the changing bodies of the older man and woman—only the nude couple shown was in their twenties! Were the film producers afraid the public would find aging nude bodies too ludicrous to watch in the act of intercourse? Too inappropriate? A wry commentary, perhaps, on how the "experts" really feel about sexuality in the aging. And if the experts feel ashamed and turn their heads away—and they're the *teachers*—surely their students (the public) have learned their lessons well. If you've had an open relationship with your children, talk to them about this.

They may feel it's taboo of you to want sex because of the feelings that still linger from their fifteen-year-old days (the times they felt embarrassed when they heard intimate noises from your bedroom). Adolescents don't want to think of their parents as sexual beings. Again, you cannot build your life on their childlike fears. Your children may feel indignation and shame and disgust at your sexual desires—but you can't let them act their feelings out. You will feel reduced if you do. Stand up straight and tell your child who's saying to you, "Ma, you're making a fool of yourself!" that your life is *your* business. Tell your children if they interfere in your sexual and social life, you'll interfere in theirs. That'll stop them. Realize that no matter what your age, you have a *right* to a full and satisfying sex life.

Remarriage: A Long Time to be with Someone— from Breakfast through the Late Show!

If you're like Goldye, and you're hesitant to remarry because the man you're seeing has a serious or potentially serious disability, such as a severe case of diabetes or a heart condition or chronic high blood pressure, understand that it's all right not to want a sickbed and grief between you and your mate. However, realize that marrying an over-50 man who's *healthy* is risky, too; chronic illness is more apt to occur after the age of fifty. And even though you're healthy *now,* the older woman is also somewhat of a health risk.

• *Are the risks worth the rewards?*

The real question is—would the companionship of re-marriage be worth the risk of a later illness or death? Only you can decide this for yourself. Yes, separation is harder when you're older—and I'm talking about the loss and separation that occurs with death of a loved one —but again, there's a lot to be said for having someone to laugh with and to share life with each day.

Are you hesitating about remarriage because you don't want to lose your monthly alimony check? Because you don't want to share your assets? YOU know how secure or insecure you would feel if your income were reduced. YOU know how much (or how little) you really want to marry this man. Look at the kind of person you are, be honest with yourself, look at your feelings about the man in your life, and then make your decision.

"Should I remarry?"

• *Listen to your feelings.*

Answer this question knowing that if you *do* remarry, you'd better marry someone you like a lot, trust implic-itly, and are attracted to—because you're going to have to be with him an awful lot.

Because you *are* an over-50 couple it is probable that your new husband is getting ready to retire or is already semi-retired or fully retired. That means you're going to be thrown together more frequently than a younger couple. Be sure you're excited about this man (and don't let anyone tell you the older woman doesn't get excited just as much as the twenty-year-old!) and be sure you have fun with him. Being together *every day,* all-day, from breakfast through the late-show is a long, long time!

"Should I remarry?" No matter what your age is, the answer is—listen to your feelings and to your heart.

CHAPTER 5

Your Changing Marriage

⌘ ⌘

What's a GOOD Marriage?

What *is* a good marriage—how would you define it—
when you've been married for twenty-five years or more?
I think it means different things to different people. But
if we had ten married couples in the same room—all
over 50, each married a long time, each feeling they have
a good marriage—everyone might find they have certain
things in common. Support from each other, as a couple.
A sharing of value systems, between husband and wife.
Each wife feeling her husband is her best friend.

• *The sharing of growth.*
Particularly, I think that every woman in the room
would feel her husband is an enabler . . . helping her to
change and grow. (And, of course, she helps her husband
in his changing and growing.) That's one of the nicest
things in a successful, enduring marriage—the sharing
of growth. And growth means change. Men and women,
in successful marriages, do not resist change in their
partners. Oh, they may feel threatened for the moment,
because it shifts the equilibrium of their relationship, but

127

then they strike a balance again, as a couple. They're able to recognize the change, talk about it, and use it to enhance their marriage.

I think of one woman I know who became depressed after her last child left home, and decided to return to college as a way of redefining her identity. This meant a change of life style in her marriage. But her husband, recognizing her need, was able to accept this change. He pitched in to help make dinner every evening, so she'd have time to study; he helped rearrange their apartment so she'd have a place to study. He took pride in her growth, even though it meant a change in *his* life, too. The last I heard, he was using her as a role model for his own growth: *he* was returning to school!

A marriage that has successfully endured for many years means shared laughter . . . shared memories . . . someone to help quell your panics . . . someone to share your daily pleasures.

And the perceptive reflective couple will know that nothing ever stays the same; that there *are* going to be changes in their relationship in the next years, just as there were changes when they were younger . . . because they will *each* change. Understanding the changes helps them cope.

"What Sexual Changes Will My Husband Possibly Go Through after the Age of Fifty?"

Decreasing sexual potency as men age is not a problem in every marriage, but it can be very debilitating in cases where it does occur.

· *Sexual potency—one man's problem.*

Laura's story shows how an insensitive doctor can make this decline seem more of a problem than it needs to be.

Laura was normally a relaxed woman who laughed a lot, but as she sat there talking to me her eyes were tired and frightened, and there was a tight look around her mouth.

"The doctor told Bill that it's natural that a sixty-year-old man would no longer be able to have an erection. I'm horrified. I'm hearing that my sex life is over! I told Bill that maybe he should go to another doctor, but he's withdrawn and seems resigned. He doesn't even want to talk about it anymore."

• *The doctor who is misinformed.*

Bill's doctor had fallen into the socio-cultural trap of believing that it is normal for a man in his sixties (or even his fifties) to no longer be able to maintain erections —and because Bill (like so many of us) believes his doctor is always right, he now feels his sex life is over and finished. He doesn't want to talk about it to Laura because he's depressed and he feels like a failure.

• *The doctor who is more aware.*

What would another doctor possibly tell Bill? Well, if he goes to a doctor who has up-to-date information and who is thorough, she will first take a complete case history and then examine Bill to see if there is any physical reason why he is unable to attain erections. If he has had a non-cancerous prostate removed (a procedure not uncommon to men over fifty), and he found he couldn't attain an erection since the surgery, the doctor would explain that many men who were potent before this kind of surgery eventually regain their potency. The doctor would want to take time and talk to Bill to see how he felt about sex *before* his prostate was removed. Was Bill looking for an excuse to end his sex life?

If Bill has recently suffered a heart attack, she would want to examine him thoroughly to see what condition his heart is in now, and after the examination she might tell Bill, "You're fine. But you're terribly afraid you'll have another heart attack if you attempt intercourse, and your fear is preventing you from attaining an erection. This has happened to you several times now, Bill, so now you're afraid you're impotent."

And she'd go on to tell him, "Look, you're in good shape. We doctors now realize a normal sex life can *benefit* many men who have suffered heart attacks. Just use your common sense and observe one rule: Don't get overtired. That means that you might want to have intercourse in the mornings, right after a good night's sleep, when you're rested. You say you're used to having sex at night? But that's the time when you're really tired, aren't you? You're retired, Bill, and now you can stay in bed as late as you like. Take advantage of that fact. Tell your wife she doesn't have to jump out of bed at eight o'clock in the morning to clean the house. The house will wait. Use the mornings for sexual enjoyment. Consider this one of the great things about job retirement!"

She might also say (because she's thorough), "Lie next to each other on your sides, face-to-face, when you have intercourse. This is a more restful position. Or have your wife get on top of you. She can then do most of the moving, so you won't get over-tired. Find positions that avoid muscular cramping and tension. Experiment. And let your wife stimulate you orally, because that'll get you aroused more quickly (which will keep you from becoming over-tired). Stimulate her orally. You don't have to move around so much when you do this, and she'll get aroused more quickly. But be leisurely, and you needn't do it to each other at the same time. Do it separately. It'll take less energy."

If she finds Bill is suffering from emphysema, she'll give him pretty much the same kind of advice about sexual positions, because emphysema patients also have to conserve their energy.

• *The fear of impotence.*

Fear. This is what Bill's doctor would talk to him about if she finds Bill is physically healthy. She would explain that many men over fifty become terrified if they find they can't attain an erection as quickly as they did when they were younger, and this enormous fear is focused on one point: They're sure this change in their erection pattern means they are losing their potency. They become *so* afraid that the next time they attempt an erection their fear takes over—and they find they're limp. They don't realize that they're limp *because* of their fear. And some men become so afraid that they hesitate to try again, and when an uninformed doctor says to them, "What do you expect at your age?" they give up.

• *Changes in sexual patterns.*

Bill's doctor would carefully explain how erection patterns and ejaculation patterns change as a man ages. She would tell Bill that the man over fifty may take longer to attain an erection than a younger man (minutes instead of seconds); that the man over fifty may lose his erection faster than a younger man (he may find that his penis suddenly becomes limp immediately after his orgasm— and this can happen while his penis is still inserted in his wife's vagina); that it might take him longer to achieve a second erection than when he was younger (sometimes he has to wait a few hours or a few days); and that he often does not feel the need to ejaculate, even though he feels a high degree of sexual excitement. He may also find that he ejaculates less semen.

• *How can you help?*

Does any of this mean that his sex life is coming to an end? Absolutely not. The man over fifty who is in reasonably good health and who has a willing and interested partner can continue to attain erections and have intercourse into his sixties, his seventies, and beyond.

• *Understanding the changes.*

What *is* important is that he and his wife both thoroughly understand the changes that are normal in his sexual functioning—the changing patterns of erections and ejaculations—so that both of their expectations will be realistic and so they can both adjust their sexual behavior to these changes.

What does this mean in your life? When your husband takes longer to attain his erection you don't have to become frightened. If you sense *he* is apprehensive, you'll reassure him this change is normal, and just because he takes longer to attain an erection does not mean he *won't* have one. So what if it takes longer? When he does not ejaculate—yet seems sexually satisfied—you won't feel rejected and panic ("He's not attracted to me anymore!"), and when he can't immediately attain a second erection after you had intercourse together, you will not think it means the first sign of impotence.

• *Together, create new sexual patterns.*

Let his new and changing patterns teach both of you what you can expect. Together, create new ways of doing things sexually, so that the new ways fit his new needs. He hasn't been able to attain an erection at the time you felt an urgent sexual need? Why not let him excite and satisfy you orally? He has been able to attain a partial erection, and you want to help him attain a full one? Straddle him and insert his penis into your vagina. As you move up and down and sideways, and he sees your growing excitement (because he can see your face easily in this position), he'll develop a full erection pretty quickly because seeing your excitement will excite *him*. This is *creative* sexuality.

The Myths about Our Sexuality

And Bill's doctor would try to dispel some of the myths that society teaches us.

• *The "experts" often believe the myths.*

She would explain that many people (including authority figures such as ministers and doctors) believe that older people are not interested in sex. They believe this because they *want* to: They grew up learning the myth that it is "not quite nice" for older people to feel sexual yearnings and that sex is for "younger people." In rationalizing to themselves that older people are not interested in sex, they're able to avoid facing their own uncomfortable sexual conflicts. They don't have to confront the real fact that older people *do* have sexual yearnings and then confront their belief that this yearning is "dirty," "obscene," "unnatural," or "bad."

Most of us believe what the authority figures in our lives tell us, and when they teach us that we should be ashamed of sexual feelings after we're fifty and sixty and seventy, we *are* ashamed! The man over 50 is often all too ready to believe the doctor who may tell him, "You're not a spring chicken anymore. So your sex life *is* over—!" and the man over fifty may well believe that his wife's sexual yearnings are automatically over when she completes her menopause—simply because no one ever told him differently.

• *Get the facts.*

Fortunately, these myths are beginning to be confronted and for the man and woman who does want real facts, they are available. Sex manuals are easily accessible in most bookstores (no more plain paper covers!) and educational films are regularly produced on sexuality and aging. Sex-therapy centers give straight information. Some doctors are very well-informed. Agencies such as Planned Parenthood (an agency we associate with information on contraception and family planning) train their personnel to learn more about sexuality and aging. *Know* what changes take place in your husband as he ages. Help your husband learn about these changes. The couples who *do* understand the changes in a man's sexual patterns are the couples who will continue to have a rich and exciting sex life!

"But What Can I Do If My Husband IS Impotent?"

If your husband is impotent and the doctor has ruled out any physical causes and says it is psychological, you can play a very important role in helping him reverse the condition.

• *Psychological impotence.*

Does your husband find it hard to believe the reasons for his impotence are psychological? Tell him this *fact:* If he has erections during his sleep—as most men do every night—it clearly indicates he is absolutely capable of attaining an erection. *You* can tell him if he has nocturnal erections. If he has early-morning erections (the kind he awakens with and can *see*), it means he is definitely able to attain erections. He can literally use this evidence as concrete proof that he is capable of an erection, and that his problem is—fear. Fortunately, even though fear can be difficult to get rid of, it often can be overcome.

• *How to reassure him.*

Be supportive. You now know the reasons for impotence (if it is phsychological) and you'll want to discuss the changes in the patterns of sexual functioning with your husband, because he must thoroughly understand that these changes are common to men over 50, in order for him to even begin looking at his fear. Help him to realize how his fear began; that he feared failure after he found, the very first time, that he couldn't attain an erection immediately; that this fear of failure kept him from attaining an erection the *next* time he tried . . . *and* the next time he tried. By then, he was sure he was impotent and he took the display of his limp penis as *proof* that he was impotent. Add to this his *belief* that over-50 men do cease functioning sexually (the *myth!*) and it is easy to see why he's a pretty frightened man by this time (and depressed, as well).

Don't talk to him about this right after he's tried to attain an erection and couldn't. He feels bad enough and probably doesn't want to talk at all. Discuss it at the most relaxed time of his day and at the most intimate time for you, as a couple—whether it's over your second cup of coffee after a leisurely breakfast or while you're taking an after-supper walk through the neighborhood. You'll both be feeling more objective then, and when he sees you're not angry with him, he'll be able to begin *hearing*. He'll be able to absorb what you're saying. Is it easier for him to accept this information through a third impersonal channel—a book? A great deal has been researched and written about in recent years concerning psychological impotence. Buy a book that deals with this in the *older* man and simply give it to him. He'll give you a cue if he wants to discuss it after he's read it, or if he wants you to read it together.

· *Techniques to use.*

Masters and Johnson, the sex-therapist team, have some excellent suggestions in their various books that you might want to try: Lie in bed together and enjoy each other *sexually* without having intercourse. That means you will both do what is sexually pleasurable to you *without* expecting him to attain an erection. You will lie next to each other and stroke each other and kiss each other—*without* any goal. You will embrace each other and touch each other—*without* feeling he must "perform." And you won't step-up any feelings of sexual urgency or sexual expectancy. You will not touch his penis. What's the point of this? To help him begin to enjoy the sensations of the *moment*. To help him begin not to worry about whether he'll be able to "make it." To help him stop being a spectator at his own sexual performance (because that's what happens when a person worries about whether they're going to perform well). He *must* stop being a spectator in order to lose himself in the immediate pleasure of the moment . . . and he will eventually attain an erection *only* if he can lose himself in the immediate pleasure of the moment.

After lying in bed next to each other and "pleasuring" (Masters and Johnson's phrase) each other in this way over and over (through a period of weeks), your husband will gradually grow to trust the knowledge that you really *don't* expect him to perform, and if he has an erection— fine. If not, that's okay too. Once trust is established, you can both begin to caress each other's genitals—his penis and your vagina. However, still do not *expect* him to attain an erection. Just relax and enjoy each other. After repeating this "non-expectant" behavior over and over, time and time again, you'll find that you are both discovering new ways to sexually enjoy each other—because you have not been concentrating on a "goal"; the goal of erection and orgasm. By discovering new sexual enjoyment, by concentrating on the pleasure of the moment, by forgetting "goals"—you will possibly find that your husband *has* occasionally been able to attain an erection. *This* is what will teach him that he can attain an erection; that he is not impotent. This is what will take away his fear.

• *It takes patience—and love!*

However, you're going to need a lot of patience and a lot of *willingness* to do all this. If you've had a good relationship with your husband all these years, and you both really like and love each other, and you find it generally easy to communicate your real feelings to each other—it will be easier. If you know, in your gut, that he finds you attractive and that he is sexually attracted to you—it will be easier. If you feel good about *yourself*, it will be easier. But it won't be *easy*. It will be a struggle that will have its difficult times.

There may be times when your husband unfairly blames you for his impotence. You may often worry, "Does he find my body ugly, with its stretch marks and bulges? Do I look old to him?" Particularly, you may feel a helpless rage and frustration that this should happen to *you* when life is hard enough, getting older. It's *all right* to feel angry. It's *all right* to wish you didn't have to put up with all of this. When you realize that most women would find this a depressing and debilitating experience, you'll be able to take a deep breath, feel more objective, look at your husband with love, and get on with it.

• *Sex educators and sex-therapy centers.*

If the feelings you have of rejection are so overwhelming and the feelings you have of rage are too great, don't be afraid to seek professional help. More and more couples (of all ages) are using the services of sex educators and therapists at sex-therapy centers. Sex-therapy centers offer "crash" short-term programs—and the therapists, who have medical and psychiatric training, teach you and your husband how to change your ways of thinking (about your bodies and about sex), how to discover what you like sexually, and how to "pleasure" yourself and each other. It is a setting where psychological impotence is often successfully treated. For information-and-referral about your nearest sex-therapy center (they're scattered throughout the country), call the family-planning department of your local hospital or social service agency or call your local Planned Parenthood agency.

• *You're NEVER too old to be helped!*

Are you "too old" to seek treatment for sexual problems? As long as you feel sexual desire, you deserve the best treatment available for any sexual problems. Can an older person be successfully treated for sexual dysfunctioning? Successful treatment depends (in part) on how long the specific sexual inadequacy has existed, not on the age of the individual. No one is ever too old to feel better sexually!

"What's This I Hear about Testosterone Replacement for Men?"

• *A hormone.*

As women over 50 (or even younger) frequently experience emotional and physical discomforts because of a decrease of estrogen in their bodies, it has been found that some men have a similar hormonal need. As men age, their bodies produce less testosterone (as *our* bodies produce less estrogen), and this is a hormone that men need to function adequately in all areas, particularly sexually.

· *How this treatment can help.*

Testosterone replacement can make up for this bodily decrease. It is sometimes given to the man over 50 who might be suffering prostatic pain from spastic contractions in his penis during the time of ejaculation. It can reverse some of the physiological changes that affect his orgasm and ejaculation as he ages. It can help in other areas besides sexual functioning: It can relieve chronic fatigue; it can sometimes reverse some memory loss, and it can also occasionally relieve muscular weakness. However, at this time, testosterone replacement is not prescribed routinely, largely because little is known about the male climacteric (the so-called male menopause).

· *Find a doctor who knows about it.*

We should learn more and more during these next years, because there is a great deal of research being conducted. If your husband and you would like to know if testosterone replacement is indicated in his particular case, suggest that he ask his doctor about it. If his doctor doesn't know much about this procedure, find a doctor who does. Another term for testosterone replacement (*and* estrogen replacement) is sex-steroid replacement. Remember—the more you and your husband find out about your bodies and the way your bodies change and the *kind* of treatment that is available to reverse these changes, the more you will benefit and the richer your relationship will be. Constantly seek new information together!

"What Sexual Changes Will I Go Through after 50?"

"My children think I remarried just for companionship. They would be terribly embarrassed—no, ashamed is a better word—if they knew I wanted sex as much as companionship. It's been a lovely honeymoon!"

• *Our sexual lives go on and on.*

This was not a forty-year-old woman talking. She wore bifocals, her hair was white—and she was sixty-seven years old. Not typical? Wrong! This woman is no different from a lot of other women who are over-50, over-60, and *older* who have an active interest in sex and who are able to achieve orgasm. Many women are capable of achieving orgasm all their lives. The important difference between this woman and a lot of other sixty-seven-year-old females is that she's lucky: She has an interested partner available. There aren't enough men to go around for the over-sixty woman (and some women are sharing!).

• *Older women's solutions when there are no men in their lives.*

What can older women who can't find partners do? What *do* they do? Sometimes they masturbate to relieve their sexual tension (a legitimate and healthy release). Some of them use vibrators when they masturbate; I know a gynecologist who is also a sex educator, who *teaches* women to use vibrators. Frequently women employ fantasy to a large degree while they're masturbating (also very legitimate *and* very creative). Some women find female sexual partners who often provide emotional support as well as sexual relief (this is not to imply that a homosexual relationship is always a second-choice; many gay women would reject a male-female relationship even if it were available). So our sex lives may go on and on . . . sometimes more satisfactorily than other times . . . certainly in many ways we wouldn't and couldn't have predicted when we were twenty (but, then, did we *ever* wonder about what our sex lives would be like after the age of 50, when we were twenty?).

• *Differences in our sex organs and our sexual responses.*

Do our sexual organs change as we go into our sixties and beyond? In our post-menopausal years? We may develop a thinning of the mucosal lining of our vaginas. It may take longer for our bodies to produce sufficient lubrication during the foreplay period and during intercourse.

Our orgasms may become significantly shortened. The lips of our vulvas may become thinner (which means our clitoris is less protected against rough pressure). Intercourse *may* become painful, although this certainly doesn't always happen. We may feel bladder irritation after intercourse.

· *Estrogen replacement applied locally.*

What can you do if you're experiencing these difficulties? A gynecologist told me he has found estrogen replacement in the *cream* form, applied locally in the vagina, almost always alleviates any discomfort. As I've said previously, this type of estrogen replacement therapy *does not* present the same problems (the risk of uterine cancer) that estrogen therapy taken orally does. Your husband should be sure to wear a condom when you are using this cream. "And," he said, "tell your readers to have their sex partners apply the cream to their condoms and this way they'll be sure of having the cream reach all of the vagina." (The cream can be applied directly to your husband's condom, once he has an erection and the condom is on.)

· *Experiment with sexual positions for comfort.*

To prevent the feeling of needing to void and irritability of the bladder after intercourse, experiment with sexual positions that do not irritate your urethra. That's where a sex manual *with pictures* can help; it will show you the variety of positions.

· *Alternatives if your husband is impotent
or too ill for a sexual relationship.*

For the woman whose husband is impotent . . . or too ill to maintain a regular sex life or any sex life at all . . . or whose husband has lost his interest in sex, she can masturbate and find her orgasms just as richly textured and satisfying as with a partner; if her husband is willing, they can get sexual pleasure from oral sex.

· *Don't listen to the busybodies!*

And if your mate and you *can* continue an active sex life, don't listen to the people who say "Act your age!" and "Aren't you too old for this kind of foolishness!?" This is a time of your life when you may enjoy sex more than ever before—with no more worries about becoming pregnant; with more time on your hands; with no more worries about bringing up a family.

How to Turn Yourself On Sexually

Have you become sexually lazy? Are you and your husband doing things the same way you've been doing them for thirty years? Do you always have intercourse the same time each week? Does your foreplay always follow the same pattern? Old habits are hard to break. It takes *energy* to begin new ways. Why should you put out all the energy?

• *Payoffs to experimentation.*
Well, I can think of at least three payoffs immediately: you'll find that your husband will be more attracted to you (he may have been bored, too); you'll like sex more than you did before (because you'll discover new ways to become sexually excited); and you'll find that you both feel closer to each other—because this is what happens when two people *consciously* attempt to give each other more pleasure and different kinds of pleasure.

• *Be imaginative (no, you don't have to hang from the chandeliers).*
If you and your husband are no longer in the nine-to-five world, or are working just part-time, use the time of the day (or evening) when you feel the most energy to try new sexual positions and techniques with each other. You're probably living alone—your children have left home—so you're no longer confined to your bedroom when you want to make love. Why not use your living room sofa for a 4:00 p.m. sexual encounter? And won't having sex in the guest bedroom after breakfast one morning provide an element of excitement? If you and your husband are retired, you now have *any* part of the day for sexual pleasure; the great part about having no one else around is that you can walk around your apartment nude and make love in *any* room at any time.

• *Unlearn the wrong things you were taught about sex.*
Were you taught that women are supposed to be "passive" and wait for their husbands to make the first sexual

move? Were you taught that it isn't "feminine" to approach him first? As a woman over 50, you grew up during a period when most women were expected to act in certain role-defined ways (and so were men) and it is difficult to get to know what you really enjoy sexually when you are expected to act "feminine." For instance, how can you be "feminine" (passive) and tell your husband to press harder on your clitoris because it feels so good? And it *is* important that he knows this, because this is what will make you feel good sexually and telling him so is real SEXUAL COMMUNICATION—much more important than being "feminine." Another point in favor of sexual communication: If you feel able to tell your husband what you like and what feels good, it excites him sexually, and his excitement, in turn, can stimulate you.

Will he find you too aggressive? Realize that he watches television, and he goes to the movies, and he reads magazines, and he knows that it is not 1930 or 1940 and that women have changed. We are generally freer human beings who want to be equals in bed with our partners— equals who are not concerned with who acts "feminine" or "masculine" but who *are* concerned with getting and giving sexual pleasure, no matter who is the aggressor at a given moment.

You'll want to "unlearn" some of the things you were probably taught about love and life and sex and marriage during your teens and twenties . . . the *forms* of love-making rather than the content (because this is what women were generally taught in the 1930's and 1940's and 1950's). And the *forms* you were taught were based on the "etiquette" of love. For instance you may have been taught what kind of sheer and frilly nightgown to wear on your wedding night and how to make your body smell good and how to make your legs free of hair and how to make your bedroom look romantic—but were you taught about lust?

· *Lust is GOOD!*

Lust is our sexual appetite. The mechanics *of lust:* how to awaken your own sexual appetite and your husband's sexual appetite. You will want to start with your own body. How can you find out what excites you the most? Touch yourself. Explore your body. Stroke your clitoris and the surrounding area. You are your best teacher. *Ask* your husband to tell you what he likes . . . to take your hand and *show* you what to do and how to do it. This is how you will begin to know what excites you both. This is your first step toward learning about the lust mechanism.

Am I discounting the frilly nightgown and the romantic bedroom? Am I saying it isn't important? Am I suggesting that you should not be concerned as to whether your body smells delicious? No! Absolutely not! But I *am* suggesting that you consider the rest of it—what happens when you *get* in bed. And that's where the women who grew up in the 1930's and the 1940's were given the short end of the stick: Most probably you were not introduced to the human body and its erotic possibilities. You probably were not taught how to touch a man's toes (yes, toes!) in ways that would stimulate an erection. You probably were not taught how to teasingly rub your hair slowly over a man's penis. But you can still learn these things; *this* is what the newer sex manuals are all about. You can try all kinds of new things in bed without being a gymnast.

- *There's no CORRECT kind of orgasm.*

You'll want to "unlearn" the myths you were probably taught about orgasm. Were you taught that a "successful" wife always achieves orgasm, and is always able to bring her husband to orgasm? Were you taught that "successful" couples always attain their orgams at the same time? Were you taught that orgasms, in order to be perfect, must be explosive and earth-shattering?

- *We're not sexual performers with certain formulas.*

All of these myths assume that we are sexual performers, expected to "make it" in prescribed ways. Fortunately, we now know that we are human beings who find that each sexual experience we have is different. We may find that at one time we experience a quiet coitus that does not include orgasm, yet leaves us feeling happy. At other times we may experience a low-keyed orgasm. And at other times we may get carried away with one of those explosive and earth-shattering orgasms, or even multiple orgasms. Each experience, however different, has equal value.

• *Fake orgasms.*

Older men, too, have been taught these same myths. Males over 50 often feel they're a failure if they don't "give" their partner an orgasm. The age-old question, "Did you come?" whether asked anxiously ("Please reassure me that I'm a 'successful' man!") or critically ("It's your fault if you didn't come!") has led many a woman to fake an orgasm. Some women have gone through a large part of their adult life faking their orgasms. This can only lead to feelings of rage, of frustration, of alienation toward their partners.

• *End role-definitions in bed.*

The answer is to end the role-definitions. So you can be aggressive and feel free to tell him what pleases you sexually; so you *can* attain orgasms more frequently. The answer is to realize that you are not a sexual performer and that you do not have to have an orgasm, or a particular kind of orgasm, each time you have intercourse. And this freedom from role-definitions and this freedom from "a good performance" benefits your husband as well. Equals in bed, reality-based, you will then be able to move toward enriching sexual experimentation and sexual learning . . . giving your years together a texture and pleasure it may not have had before.

"My Husband's Depressed."

Many over-50 men have reached a point in their lives when they are feeling there is not that much time left to achieve the goals they had set for themselves when they were younger. They may look back and examine what they are presently doing, and ask themselves, "Have I been a success? Did I achieve what I set out to do? Did I 'become' what I felt was important?"

• *The "Success Syndrome."*

Of course, a man's idea of success may be very different at the age of sixty from what it was when he was twenty. Toby is married to John, who is a commercial artist. When Toby first met John he had just graduated from art school, and he was working on a local newspaper as an illustrator. It was in 1934, during the Depression, and that was a very good job during the Depression. John didn't think of changing his job (you clung to what you had during those terrible days) and when he did think of "goals," he thought of staying on the newspaper and eventually buying a small house in the suburbs, raising children, and building a "secure" life with his family. Modest goals. However, more than forty years later John is still an illustrator with the same newspaper while the men he graduated with from art school own advertising agencies and thriving art studios. He lives in the small house in the suburbs while the people he had been close to in his student days live in fancy split-levels and Tudor homes with swimming pools. John feels bad about himself. He looks at what they have achieved and he looks at his accomplishments and he feels like a failure.

Is *your* husband questioning his value as a person? Is he feeling like a failure? Is he feeling depressed? Let us begin to realize that men look in the mirror too, and anxiously look for signs of their aging. They see their balding heads and the sagging pouches under their eyes and this tells them there is not as much time left as they feel they need. If your husband has seen a younger man get the promotion *he* expected, if he has suffered a heart attack, if his company is making him retire—he may feel that his "last chance" to succeed has gone by. If he is closely questioning his identity through his work (and many men in our society see their identity closely tied up with how "successful" they've been in the work world), is it really surprising? Didn't your husband grow up at a time when men were supposed to "succeed" and do well as the "breadwinner" of the family? That means that even if you worked outside of the home, *he* was the one who was expected to bring home the bigger check; *he* was the one who was supposed to have the important career and climb in his career (you moved out of the city to another town for *his* job, not yours). Didn't your husband grow up at a time when a man's virility and eligibility were largely determined by how well he could make a living? Didn't your mother (who was also affected by these values) expect you to marry a good provider? And didn't your husband know, all these years, that *you* hoped he would be a good provider? Even if you never said so?

• *He feels he can't buy extra time!*

No wonder your husband may be terrified when he hears that his best friend died suddenly on the golf course. This means the same thing could happen to him. If he becomes ill, who will be the "breadwinner"? Death and illness are more of a reality than when he was thirty or forty. Time is more urgent. He can't buy extra time.

If this sounds stark, it is. If this sounds like the men in our society are burdened unfairly by imposed roles and expectations, many of them are. Your children and your grandchildren may have learned the valuable lesson that it is not *fair* to impose this "success" burden on the men in their lives, and they may be living their lives differently from you and your husband, so that both partners in the marriage share the "breadwinner" role. Many young people today consider a person successful if he or she *feels* good doing what they are doing, no matter how little money it brings in.

However, it is not so easy for your husband to shrug off his past learning. He is still a product of the time in which he grew, and he may feel bad if he is still struggling to make a living while his friends take annual trips to Europe. He may feel a failure if he has not achieved the status of the men he grew up with. He may be depressed because he's not considered a success by his friends and his coworkers and his neighbors.

• *Your own fear at this time.*

Of course you're frightened if your husband is suffering from depression and you feel terribly helpless. Perhaps you feel as though your marriage is falling apart. You feel particularly bad when your husband doesn't *tell* you what's wrong, when he shrugs and is silent when you plead, "What *is* it?" If he's depressed over a period of time, he may lose interest in sex. This often happens when people are anxious and depressed and it reverses itself when they feel better, but meanwhile you may wonder, "Does he mind that I'm getting older? Am I unattractive to him?"

• *The husband who can't verbalize his feelings.*

He may have difficulty telling you how he feels about himself at this time, because he feels he must continue to appear strong and adequate in your eyes. He may feel that

if he tells you he feels like a failure, he is *admitting* failure.
You can help him by telling him you understand how he's
feeling and you know it's a difficult time of change for *all*
men who are his age. Particularly, tell him, over and over,
that *YOU* consider him a huge success because he has
been such a good friend to you during these many years;
because he has been such a comfort when you needed
someone to comfort you; because he has been such a
strong support when you needed support. Let him know
what a good father he has been. Remind him of the time
he rushed to New York and took care of your son during a
crisis. Tell him your daughter still talks about the Saturday
mornings that he spent with her at the library, helping her
choose her children's books. She still remembers the times
he took her to lunch at the restaurant with the red carpet.
Tell him, in every way you know, that it is the care and
love and support that he gave you and the children that
made him the success that he really is.

· *Two women—how they felt (and what they did!)*

Sheila, whose husband was depressed, told him, "Look,
do we have to be millionaires? So the business is going
downhill! We can only eat one meal at a time and we can
only sleep in one bed at a time. This we can do on less
money. George—please!—let's just enjoy our years
ahead."

Marion, on the other hand, felt furious at her husband
because he wasn't a money-maker, because all of their
friends had been to Bermuda except them, and because all
of their friends were financially ready for retirement, except them. And here he was, almost sixty. She also loved
her husband, and she felt guilty because she was so angry.
(Hadn't she known, when she married him, that he was a
dreamer and that he'd never be a go-getter?) When his
depression didn't go away and when she realized that she
was too angry to comfort him, she decided that it was time
for both of them to go for professional help—separately.
They've each been going to their own social worker for
help for the past six months now, and they're just beginning to be able to talk to each other about how they feel. A
good start.

- *The psychological and physical adjustments
he has to make.*

If your husband has been depressed for more than two weeks, do not ignore it. Do not put your head in the sand, hoping the depression will go away. Don't turn away from him because you don't know what to do, and you're afraid to find out what to do. He needs your help desperately right now. These older years are difficult years for him, and he is at a turning point in his life. He is being required to make psychological and physical adjustments toward his own aging. Aside from his search for meaningful identity, he is finding that his metabolic processes have slowed and the sinews of his muscles do not respond as they once did. In other words, his sexual functioning may be changing; he can no longer eat big meals late at night and he gets tired after playing with your three-year-old grandson for more than two hours. *You're* going through difficult changes in your own life, also—physical and psychological and social—and why do you both have to go through these changes at the same time?! But there it is: you do. Hopefully, he will want to be as caring about your needs at this time as you hope to be about his.

- *Mutual support.*

This is a time when mutual support is very very important. But—to support each other you must both understand the process of aging for both men and women; you must both seek and have access to the information that will tell you about the changes you will experience. It is only by *KNOWING* what is happening to you (both of you) that you can confront it and talk about it and handle it. And, if necessary, do not hesitate to seek professional help for support and added insight in making these particular years of your changing relationship meaningful and rich. They can be . . . and they should be!

"My Husband's Involved with a Younger Woman!"

I recently talked to two women who are facing situations that are similar. Each of their husbands have been or are involved with younger women.

Anita sat, quietly shredding her paper tissue in pieces.
"Joe's teaching in a co-ed college. It's the perfect setup
for him. I can always tell when he's interested in one of
his students. He acts preoccupied and doesn't pay any attention to me. It's as though I stopped existing.

"He's still very attractive, you know. He has a beard
now, he wears tweed jackets with leather elbow patches,
he smokes a pipe. Joe knows all about how to project a
certain image."

Anita looked out of the window. She was still shredding
her tissue in little pieces. "They're all the same age as our
daughter."

When I spoke to Geraldine, it was on the run at the supermarket. She was pushing a shopping cart, and so was I.
We both stopped and started to talk at the same time. We
hadn't seen each other for years. I asked her what she had
been doing.

"Well," she said, "Floyd has just moved back into the
house. We were separated for a year. He was involved
with his secretary. I'll tell you the truth, I don't know
whether it's over or not! I tell him I believe him when he
says it is, but I just don't know. She's only thirty years old.
A good-looking, calculating home-wrecker. It's been a
nightmare of a year—."

• *Of course it doesn't happen in all marriages.*

Is the older-man, younger-woman syndrome *inevitably*
a part of the changing marriage, as a couple grow older?
Of course not. There are many married couples in their
50's, their sixties, and their seventies, who never experience this kind of situation. However, it does happen, and
it does happen frequently enough that it should be looked
at as a possible reality.

• *Why does it happen?*

Why are some men over 50 attracted to much younger
women? Well, for one thing, it is very flattering to a man
over 50 to suddenly find a young woman interested in *him*.
He finds it a sign that he is still attractive, still interesting,
and still sexy—at a time in his life when he may be doubt-
ing himself. Youth is given great value in our society, and
if a young woman pays attention to him, it must mean that

he has some value. The younger woman is also helping him kid himself into thinking that, with her, there are many, many years ahead—because *she* has so many years ahead. It is as though he is having a second chance at being twenty again, thirty again! It is indulging the fantasy of immortality! And for the man who needs to "possess" a woman, who sees women as sexual objects, he now owns the most desirable object of all: a straight young body, a young face, unlined and unmarked by age. How ego-boosting for him to walk into a restaurant with her and know that people are looking at them and thinking, "What a beautiful young girl—."

- *Do you still want him?*

Does all this mean that you should give up and walk away if your husband is interested in a younger woman? Being interested in another woman and being attracted to another woman is one thing—and doing something about it is another story. *Everyone* is attracted to people other than their spouses occasionally, and they can't help that. Is your husband *seeing* this other woman? If he is, you must ask yourself some straight questions and give yourself some straight answers (no matter how painful!), because you want to decide whether it's worth it to try to "keep" him.

Do you really like your husband? Do you love him? Do you enjoy being with him—or did you until this happened? Are you frightened that you'll be left alone in the years ahead? Are you terrified that, if he leaves you, you'll lose your financial security? Are you cringing because you feel people are laughing at you—the "neglected wife"? Are you feeling anguish about the *rejection* you feel, rather than anguish over losing the man himself? Are you enraged that he now considers you "obsolete"? Think all of this through, and take your time.

If you discover you are mourning the loss of the relationship and the *man*—hang on for awhile for further evaluation. If you find you're furious because you're losing the "symbols" of the relationship (the house in the country, the annual trip abroad, being part of a "couple" in a couple-oriented society) and the *man* is secondary to all of this (the man, your husband), is it really worth it?

You may find you have mixed reasons for wanting to

hold on to the relationship (most people have mixed reasons for everything), and that's all right. And in the process of thinking about these reasons, you will get to know yourself better, and you will find this is a growing period for you, however painful. Also, try to evaluate the situation as it really is between your husband and this woman. Has he been involved with her for a very long time? Have they become very close? Are they considering a more permanent relationship? Does he feel she is more a part of his life than you are? If you are answering "yes" to these questions, try to face the real possibility that you may not be able to keep your husband.

- *Get support to help you through this.*

If this is so, you're probably feeling terrible pain and you're going through a very bad time. Try to get some support *right away!* Make an appointment with a psychiatrist or a social worker, or join a group of women who are going through the same kind of thing at a local woman's growth center or a woman's liberation center (and no, you won't find those women different from you because of the setting; they, too, will be feeling the same pain and the same anguish—and it *does* help to share your pain with each other). Don't depend on just *one* close friend to help through this; your one close friend may feel threatened, or may get sick, or may move out of town, or may get plain tired of hearing about your pain. Get the support of a professional person or a group.

- *Your priority: Build your own identity!*

The really important move you must make at this time (and not wait till later) is building your own life and your own identity. You must, step by step, consciously organize and implement activities that will give you a sense of PERSONHOOD. If you were one of those women who did have a strong identity of your own *before* this happened, you'll walk away from this traumatic experience intact—because you were intact before. A good example of this is Esther. At the age of fifty-five, she walked out on Irwin one Saturday morning after eight months of bickering, anguish, and false promises from him that he would "stop seeing that woman." She went to her sister's apartment. She spent the day explaining, crying, unpacking her suitcase, and feeling a heavy sense of loss. Then, around eight o'clock that night, she stopped crying, stood very still for a moment, and thoughtfully said, "You know one of the things I'm really angry about? That my typewriter is at the house, my manuscript is at the house [Esther is a writer], and I can't get going on the chapter I'm working on to-morrow morning! I had planned to get up early and write all day!" Later, when she reflected on this, she realized that this was a sign that she has a strong sense of identity and that her career as a writer was as important to her as her relationship with her husband. This is what allowed Esther to get back on her feet again and to make a new life for herself . . . even though she never went back to her husband.

"My Husband Is a WOMANIZER!"

Suppose your husband is not interested in *one* younger woman: he's interested in *many* younger women.

• *The typical pattern.*
Suppose he has a predictable pattern: he meets an attractive younger woman, he woos her, wins her, and then loses interest in her after the conquest. After this had happened many times, you began to realize that he wasn't seriously interested in any of these women. Each one of them served a function: They provided *proof* that your husband was still desirable. Why does he need to continue proving this to himself? Why does he require fresh new proof, every few months? Because he feels so inadequate that he *never* can believe that he is desirable.

• *What are you going to do?*
Now you have to ask yourself if you really like him and love him enough to keep putting up with this teen-age behavior that has the power to make you feel constantly insecure, old, unattractive, and angry. Do you want the relationship enough to tolerate this indefinitely? (And "indefinitely" can be a pretty long time.) You may come up with the answer, "I want him on any terms," and that's all right. But realize the price you might have to pay (the bad feelings) and realize your strengths and vulnerabilities

(Can you tolerate these bad feelings over a period of time without suffering depression?) and realize that without some kind of counselling your husband will probably continue acting-out his excessive needs in this way.

• *Games that are destructive.*

And ask yourself—have you unwittingly been playing games with your husband.

Sick games between husband and wife are common, where they each feed the other's neurotic needs. I'm thinking of Irma, who would occasionally find scraps of paper around the house with women's names and phone numbers written on them. When she would confront Lou, her husband, he would first deny any relationship with the woman. After days of battling, he would finally "confess." What was happening in this household? Lou was setting-up the game, laying down the rules, and Irma was saying, "I'll play!"—and neither of them realized *this was a game.* Lou would stop seeing each of these women after his "confession." Why did he continuously set up this game? Because he wanted the reassurance from each of the younger women that he was desirable; because he wanted to be the bad boy and he wanted Irma to be the angry mommy; and because he wanted the fun of the extramarital relationships without the commitment and the responsibilities. I hear Irma is thinking of leaving Lou because the game has no payoffs for her: Lou keeps getting the payoffs (the brief, intense affairs; the reassurance that he's still attractive; the attention of mommy) but there's no prize in the popcorn box for her.

• *Build yourself up!*

Believe it or not (and this is a hard thing to believe), the really important thing is not whether you stay with your husband or not. The really important thing is that whatever decision you make, YOU MUST BUILD YOUR OWN FEELING OF SELF. To find out how *you* feel about life you must find out what *you* like and what your values are. You must develop *your* interests and *your* talents and *your* skills—and you must develop your own passions. Passions take you outside of yourself. Your passion can be painting or writing or politics. Passions are larger and more intense than "interests." Passions are as

large as—yourself. Passions build up feelings of self-worth
and self-esteem. How can you develop a passion? By trying *everything* you've ever been interested in, whether it's
writing poetry or running for public office or learning to
play the piano or taking a photography class. When you
find the one interest that becomes more important to you
each day, nurture it, encourage it, give it all the time it
needs—and it may become your passion. When you're a
woman with a passion, you have IDENTITY. You have
STRENGTH. You have feelings of SELF-WORTH. It
will help you walk out of the relationship intact, and work
through the pain, and survive. Or—it will help you choose
to stay in the relationship and perceive *yourself* as the central figure in your life (strong and not vulnerable to attack). You will no longer perceive yourself as passive, as
a person who someone can "do something to." You will no
longer be a victim. What is most important is what *you* are
doing for *yourself*—not what your husband is doing *to*
you!

"What's Expected of Us As Grandparents?"

- *You both may be grandparents now.*
  What's expected of you?
  In the old days, when grandparents and children and
grandchildren frequently lived in the same house, there
was an assumption that the elders were *authorities* on what
was right or wrong. Change was slow in those days, so
grandchildren *could* be guided by the experience of their
grandparents because their own experience wasn't very
different. But this changed.

- *How grandparents' roles were changed.*
  In the late 1800's and the early 1900's, when so many
families immigrated here from other countries, the grandchildren—indeed, the *children*—learned the new ways of
the new country and often the grandparents resisted or
found it too hard. This also happened when rural families
moved to cities. When people in families made some
money and their social class changed, frequently the
grandparents refused to become the consumers their

grandchildren and children had become, and the older people retained their old ways.

When separate households, consisting of the mother and father and children (the nuclear family) became the mode, the younger ones found it even easier to break away from the traditional ways of life. So the gap between the grandparents and the grandchildren became greater (and the physical distance between them, now that they were in separate households, increased the gap).

Technology, too, played a part. At one time a young woman went to her grandmother for advice when she was pregnant. Her grandmother may even have been the midwife during the delivery! But later the young woman in these families had their babies delivered in clinics and hospitals—and the doctor became the authority figure. Grandma had lost her role as an authority.

• *What can your role be?*

So now we're in the 1970's—and what *is* the role of the grandparent? If you can't (and maybe wouldn't want to) be your granddaughter's midwife; if you're not the expert cheese blintz maker *your* grandmother was (so you can't be an "authority" in this area); if your husband doesn't go hunting the way *his* grandfather did (so he can't show your grandson how to skin a rabbit)—what *can* you do? You can show them how to cope with change! You, more than they, have lived through the most rapid changes the world has known. You have lived longer, so you have had to cope with a swiftly changing society. Your granddaughter who can't find a job because of the economy is depressed and sure it's *her* fault? *You* remember the Great Depression, and you have an historical perspective on how unemployment demoralizes people. *You* can help her develop a healthy critical distance between the no's at the job interviews and her feelings about herself—by sharing with her what you remember: intelligent people selling apples; respected men and woman living in tarpaper shacks; thousands and thousands of citizens victimized by the economy through no fault of their own. You can teach her how to stop personalizing her turn-downs at employment offices . . . how to regain her feelings of self-esteem.

An older grandmother told me, "I think my grandson

started seeing me as a *person*—not just as a wrinkled, white-haired, old lady—when he heard how I had been part of a cadre of young revolutionaries in czarist Russia before the 1917 Revolution. Once he heard that—well, we haven't stopped talking about it since. I've told him how Stalin later betrayed the Revolution, and how I was put in jail years later, and we've been having serious talks on strategies to effect change. He's more conservative than I am, but at least he's realizing that *his* generation didn't invent reform and radicalism and idealism and activism! He's getting a sense of history!"

- *You're not doddering and useless.*

  Children's books often show grandparents as passive. Rocking on the porch. Trailing behind the small child who's discovering a flower. Television often does this too. Don't let the media mold your role as a grandparent! Be an active role model, an inspiring teacher. It can be one of the most profound experiences in your development!

- *Share your life experience.*

  Show your grandchildren the marks of your experiences . . . what you've learned. Share your mistakes with them. Don't expect them to take your advice. In fact, don't give advice. Just tell them what *your* life experience has been. And *LISTEN*. You have more time to listen than their parents. They don't have to struggle to become independent from you, as they do their own parents (as we all had to do with our own parents!).

- *You really have a lot in common.*

  You really have more in common with your teen-age grandchild than you might think: you're both searching for your changing identities; you're both asking yourselves the same questions: "Who am I?", "What do I really want to do?". Your introspection on these questions during a changing period of your life will give you more compassion for your grandson's introspection on these questions during a changing period in *his* life. I really believe a grandparent has far more in common with adolescent grandchildren than the grandchildren's own parents—who are still too busy "making it" to be introspective.

- *Your relationship with a very young grandchild.*

If your grandchildren are babies, or are very young, your relationship with them is also very special. A friend's daughter said to me, "I let my parents spoil my kids as much as they want to. It's a particular kind of nurturing—the attention, the gifts—that *can* come only from grandparents. My husband and I have to do the disciplining. *They* can be all-accepting. The kids adore them, and love knowing they're very special in their grandparents' eyes. Very good for their ego-strength!"

- *Respect your children's limits on the relationship.*

Not all grown children share this perspective, and some do put boundaries on how much they'll let the grandparents do with and for the children . . . and that's all right, too. You can adjust to the limits your children set. But isn't it marvelous knowing you *don't* have to discipline the kids, and that you *can* go home when you get tired of playing with them?

The role of grandparents. There is no formula. Just be yourself. Share yourself. Give as much nurturing as *you're* comfortable doing, and withdraw when you need time to yourself. And enjoy the very unique kinds of pleasures you can get from the relationship.

- *Is your husband a different kind of grandparent than you?*

And don't be surprised if it turns out that you and your husband are very different kinds of grandparents. Weren't you each different kinds of parents? Perhaps one of you was the disciplinarian and the other was the "permissive" one. Maybe your husband was strict with your daughter, and lets your granddaughter "get away with murder."

"Well," one grandfather said, when he was accused of just that, "Remember, it was the days before the Pill, and boys had double standards, and I felt I had to *protect* my daughter." He waved toward his son-in-law. "That's *his* problem, now. I'm just here to enjoy her." He smiled down at his five-year-old granddaughter.

Maybe the Pill is just a rationalization. Maybe this grandfather would be just as strict today, if he had a daughter growing up. Fathers often have all kinds of mixed feelings toward their daughters that can make them feel jealous and overprotective and—well, they sometimes feel no boy is good enough for their daughter. But there is more emotional distance between a grandfather and a granddaughter, even though there is love. No need to be "overprotective." Especially if the granddaughter lives with her *own* father.

"What about My Relationship with My Son-in-law? My Daughter-in-law?"

I remember sitting at an oilcloth-covered kitchen table as a child, hearing an older woman saying smugly to her sisters, "My daughter-in-law asked me what my son loves best to eat, so I gave her a recipe or two—and I left out a few things she should have put in!" The women got a big laugh out of that. Would this happen today? Maybe. Maybe not.

- *Feelings of competition.*

With "younger" grandmothers, who are in the work world and/or lead busy organizational lives or have time-consuming passions, there might be fewer feelings of competition with their daughters-in-law. Their own lives are too full. I know several over-50 women whose daughters-in-law call them by their first name; who talk to their son's wives about their feelings about themselves, and who perceive their daughters-in-law as "sisters" in the most real feminist sense. These women seem to get a great deal of satisfaction out of their relationship with their son's wives. I think it is easier for a woman to accept her daughter-in-law or her son-in-law as "a person," as an equal, rather than as threatening symbols, if she were able to "let go" of her son or daughter long before the marriage.

- *"Letting go" of your children.*

"Letting go" might be harder for the woman who brought up her child alone; for the woman who needs to control her environment (her family!); for the woman who wants her daughter and son to have "better lives" than she did (and that often means she wants them to "marry well"). Fathers often seem to be able to "let go" more than mothers. Is this because they have been part of an active work world all of their adult lives and they didn't need to put as much investment into "expectations" from their children? And if there were expectations, it was in other areas (not the marriage of their children)—finishing college, making a good living (especially with a son), not getting into trouble . . . .

Being a parent-in-law. Being a grandparent. It *is* part of your changing marriage. New situations occur that weren't part of your lives fifteen or twenty years ago.

"My Husband Is Ill"

Fortunately, many couples go through their older years in relatively good health. However, this doesn't always happen. A wife may find herself taking care of an ill husband, a husband who can no longer work. This can mean a sharp reduction in income . . . changes in the couple's life. Time may have to be arranged differently from before. Housing may have to be changed.

- *Get "people" and "money" help.*
  This is the time to use all the help you can get: "people" and "money" help. A long-term serious illness means you will need every bit of emotional strength you can get. Here are some tips: If you're taking care of him at home, arrange for a good friend or a relative to "sit" with your husband each day for a couple of hours so you can get out of the house. Organize a schedule so your son comes on Monday nights (so you can get out for a bridge game). Ask your daughter to come one afternoon a week (so you can get to the shopping center or to the library for a few quiet hours to yourself). Arrange for your daughter-in-law (she's part of the family, too) to visit another afternoon a week so you can go to the beauty salon. Perhaps two of your best friends will take turns relieving you another two afternoons a week. How about your husband's retired brother? Ask him to sit with your husband on Sunday afternoons so you can go antique-browsing with a friend, or visit your grandchildren. You MUST do this so you can recharge your batteries each time you get out of the house; otherwise you will be inviting physical and psychological trouble for yourself. "But I only need to get out of the

house once or twice a week!" you may be saying, "What's this about arranging for someone to come in and relieve me *every* day?"

. *It's important to make time for yourself.*

Once or twice a week is not enough. Taking care of a loved one who is seriously ill is an intense and emotionally exhausting experience. It can also be a physically exhausting experience. You may need to be a "nurse" for months, or even years. You may know the chances of recovery are low. If you can find two hours or three hours every day for yourself, you will be able to tolerate the tension and the demands more easily, and take the situation day-to-day with more resilience. Do not feel guilty about asking your children and friends or your in-laws to take on this responsibility; you have a RIGHT to ask them and you have a RIGHT to expect them to do what they can—because they love him too. Do not feel guilty about leaving your husband each day for a couple of hours. You'll be doing him a service by taking care of yourself. One woman, who is taking care of a terminally ill husband, told me, "I don't need any money; my husband owned a large plant and thank God we're doing beautifully—but I went out and got a part-time job anyway. To keep me from going crazy, being home all day!"

. *Resources—health insurance coverage.*

Not everyone is financially secure. Expenses can mount up quickly during a terminal illness. Watching one's retirement money ebb away can be terrifying. Check your husband's Medicare coverage, if he's sixty-five or over. Be sure you're taking advantage of all of the coverage (especially if you're paying for the "B" part of the coverage; the "A" part is no-cost). Call your nearest Social Security office to get all the details on his coverage. They administer the Medicare health insurance.

Also find out if your husband has any veteran's benefits coming to him that would help with medical expenses. Your local Veterans' Administration office can give you details on this. Do you have any commercial medical insurance policies? Investigate their coverage so you know you're taking full advantage of them.

If your income is very low and/or your expenses are

very high, call your local Department of Social Services to see if you're eligible for Medicaid, the federally subsidized program that's administered by states throughout the country. This medical help will allow you to purchase the drugs your husband needs at a very low cost or at no cost. It can pay for the hospital and doctor's expenses. It can help pay for a nursing home, if necessary. It's available to needy people of any age.

• *Resources for the cancer patient.*

The American Cancer Society helps out in different ways with needs of cancer patients (especially transportation to and from hospitals). Investigate this, if your husband is suffering from this disease.

• *Don't have false pride when it comes to accepting help.*

Above all, don't be ashamed and too "proud" at this time to apply for help. Shouldn't your primary goal be to keep your head above water—both psychologically and financially? If it upsets you to call a social agency for help, try to remember that your husband paid taxes all those long years of his working life that helped *other* people get the help they needed—and now you're simply asking for what you and he already paid for.

• *Drug discounts.*

Another money-saver during illness: Some pharmacies charge more (or less) than other pharmacies for prescriptions. Compare them. A long illness means a lot of money is needed for drugs each week, for perhaps months or years. If you (or your husband) are or were union members, see if you can get a union discount on the drugs you buy. Purchase his drugs through a retirement organization group buying plan (it's just a few dollars a year to join existing retirement organizations).

• *Help your husband organize his affairs.*

Try not to say, "No! I don't want to hear about it!" when your husband wants to tell you where all his important papers are. Yes, I realize that when you say "No!" and stalk out of the room, this is your way of denying the possibility or probability of his death. Perhaps you just don't feel able or ready to deal with it. A woman told me, "It'll

just depress him even more!" when we talked about this.
But her husband *wanted* to talk about it; *she* wasn't ready.
When your husband wants to go over these practical matters with you as he lies there, he is trying to give you the
best kind of gift he can possibly give you at this time: security and peace of mind in later months, when he may no
longer be with you. Let him give you this gift. Let him feel
he has at least this much control over his life; that he *can*
do this.

He'll probably want to tell you (if you don't already
know) where the bankbooks are, and where to find all the
insurance policies; where he keeps his will and his birth
certificate; where the deed and title guarantee to the house
are; where the deed is to the cemetery lot; where the stock
certificates are; where all the safe-deposit boxes are;
where he keeps income tax records from the past few
years. You'll possibly be upset when he tells you all of this.
Write the information down because if you try to remember all the details without recording it—you may not remember all the information and you are invalidating the
importance of his gift. If you find this too painful, ask your
son or your daughter to spend a quiet hour with him and
take down the information for you.

· *Should you tell him if he's terminally ill?*

If your husband is terminally ill, should you tell him?
He probably already knows. Exposure to media—especially television—has made everyone aware of the symptoms and treatment of terminal illnesses. You might find it
terribly difficult and painful to talk to your husband about
his impending death (and this is certainly understandable) and you might avoid it, saying, "He really doesn't
want to know!" However, if you can work your way
through some of the fear and the pain that you feel, and
listen to him when he directly and indirectly alludes to his
condition, it will be a great service to him.

Psychiatrists and doctors and social workers are exploring death and dying at great lengths these days, and they
have found that a patient who is dying goes through different stages: At times he or she doesn't want to think
about it (and doesn't) and at other times the ill person
feels a great need to talk about it and face it (even mo-
mentarily). It is at these times that you can fill your hus-

band's need by just listening—and not denying. Yes, this takes great strength, and maybe it is too much to ask of yourself; however, you might want to sit down with a psychiatrist or your religious leader at this crucial time in your life to work out your own painful feelings and try to deal with them. This can be an important support for you!

• *You are stronger than you think!*

Of course it is true that women who have been dependent on their husbands all through their married lives may have a more difficult time coping with the terrible demands of taking care of a terminally ill husband, but I have had the privilege of seeing some of these women change almost overnight when they had to. They coped and they made swift painful decisions and they showed great inner strength. *Do not doubt your own inner resources!* Some of our most profound growing takes place through necessity! Trust yourself. You're capable of more—much more—than you realize.

The Nice Things about a Long-term Marriage

I've talked about death and dying and illness and impotence, and depression and rejection, and married men who leave their wives for other women. I haven't talked very much about the good things, have I? But they exist —for countless older couples.

• *A woman tells about her marriage.*

"Nothing happened in our lives that hasn't happened to thousands of other couples," a woman told me, "but they've been sort of ordinary things, even if they were painful at the time. Our daughter had a nervous breakdown, and that was touch-and-go for a few years. My husband gets laid off from his factory job every so often, and that's always a strain on both of us. We fight sometimes. I'm not sure I like getting older. I wish my husband would talk to me more when he's worried. But we love each other, and we like each other. We like spending time together. It's been a good thirty years. We belong to a social club, and I daresay, most of the couples are like us . . . they have decent marriages and the women have good husbands. Are we unusual?" No!

· *There are many good marriages!*

Many many middle-aged and older couples respect and like and love each other. They have found that they've thrived and grown from their mutual support of each other. Many couples who have gone through some of the problems I've talked about have worked their way through these problems and feel they've learned and grown from them. Their marriages have flourished. A woman who just had breast surgery summed it up when she said to me, "He was like a brother and father and mother as well as a husband, helping me get through this. I can't imagine where else, except in our marriage, I could have had these supports!"

CHAPTER 6

What to Do about Your Aged Parent

❧ ❧

I think one of the first signs we see that makes us aware that we do have an *aged* parent is when our parents begin turning to *us* for their answers, and for the nurturing they used to supply to us. Our image of our mother as middle-aged is slowly replaced with the reality of the seventy-five-year-old face, the eighty-year-old body . . . the changes. And it *is* painful to face these realities.

"Now I'm the Mother and She's the Child!"

"You mean I'm not the only one who's going through this—?" an incredulous woman asked.

She had just finished telling me about her mother, recently widowed, who calls her at least fifteen times a day. She doesn't call "just to talk," she calls to ask questions: "Should I go to the shopping center today? It might rain," and, "What do you think I should wear this evening when I go to your aunt's for supper?" and, "Should I have the boy cut the grass this week, or should I wait until next week?"

Another woman told me a similar story. Her father, in his seventies, is bedridden, and her mother depends on her for every little thing. "I'm happy—*willing*—to

164

go over there every day and do what I can," she said, "but my mother acts so *helpless!* She just sits there and looks at me when I suggest we put Pa in a chair for a little while. She acts so *timid* when the doorbell rings, and it's like she can't speak up anymore! This is a woman who was the head of the household a few years ago— *she* was always the boss in the family, and *she* was always the one who made decisions—!"

• *How the roles reverse themselves.*

What's happening in these families? Is this typical? Well, this reversal of roles—when you become the mother and your parent becomes the child—doesn't always happen, but it certainly happens frequently. And if it has happened to you, it's troubling, isn't it? I'm sure it makes you feel uneasy . . . and sad . . . and perhaps angry. I'm sure it grieves you to know your parent is feeling helpless. One woman shuddered and said, "Is this what I'm going to be like twenty years from now?"

This shifting of roles can happen gradually. Many women have told me it began to occur when they were in their forties, and the reversal was so gradual they hardly noticed it at first. It happened abruptly in other families: when an aged parent lost a spouse; when a middle-aged woman took her seventy-year-old mother into her home to live; when an aged parent suddenly lost her health and seemed to fall apart. A fifty-five-year-old woman was bitter: "She always played my sister and me against each other. My sister was her favorite from the time we were little. And now—just because my sister lives across the country—she's depending on me. She leans on me constantly, she's like a child. But let my sister call from California—and her voice is chirpy and excited and she's full of life! She hangs up the phone, and I'm expected to wait on her again. She reverts right back to the helpless-old-woman act."

• *Losses your parent may have faced.*

Losses are hard to cope with at *any* age, and particularly difficult to handle when you're old. Loss of status and health and income and spouse . . . An eighty-four-year-old woman looks at herself and sees that she has no "role" left; she is no longer a wife (her husband has died); she is no longer a mother (her children no longer need her); she is no longer a worker (who would she cook for? Clean for?). Her friends are dying or dead. She can't hear very well anymore so she feels left out of things. She can't walk too easily because of her arthritis, so she stays in her apartment most of the time. Is it any wonder she acts helpless (like a child)? She *feels* helpless.

Or an older woman, always full of life and vitality, loses her husband. It was a very close relationship; they did everything together; they were dependent on each other. She *feels* like a lost child when he dies—and she acts like one. And she very naturally turns to her daughter for solace. She sees her daughter as powerful—which indeed she is, compared to her mother; she still is needed and she still has a *role*.

- *The demands made on you.*

Knowing why your mother is turning to you, as if you were *her* mother, doesn't always make it easier to handle, however. Perhaps you feel angry because you didn't expect all this extra responsibility. Acting the parent with your own parent is a great demand on your time and energy and maybe your pocketbook. It may take time away from your relationship with your husband. It may curtail your social and organizational life. I recently heard one woman say, "My daughter called me to baby-sit, and my mother called me because she had chest pains. For a minute I felt as though I was being torn in two pieces. Of course I went to my mother's, but I felt guilty because my daughter had counted on me."

- *And it's at such a bad time in YOUR life.*

I remember the woman who said, "My God, these are the years when I'm worried about my own retirement. Will I have enough money? Will I be well enough to keep working another ten years? And now—all of a sudden—I have a sick mother on my hands, and I'm *her* mother. I've taken money out of my retirement savings to keep her in a decent nursing home. What's going to happen to *me?*"

"Why Am I the One Who Has All This Responsibility?"

Most of the time it's the woman who is responsible for her parent and sometimes her husband's parent. Why is this? Why do men often feel it's the *woman's* responsibility?

• *Women perceived as nurturers.*

Perhaps because most men (most *people*) think of women as the nurturers, as the people who will "take care" of other people. A husband often provides the money to take care of an aged and dependent parent, and doesn't begrudge this, but he frequently thinks of his wife as the one who "mothers" the parent, who sees she gets to the doctor and eats properly and takes her medication on time. The husband may see his wife, who was a mother to his children, continue in the role of mother—going on to mother *her* mother and *her* father and *his* mother and *his* father—even if she resents this. Our role-definitions for people can go on through our entire lives. And yes, many women resent being pushed into this role, because it's an exhausting one, and they've had no choice in the role, and because they have dual feelings about their husbands sharing it.

Delores is a good example of a woman thrust into a nurturing role, and I could feel her rage as we talked.

Her eighty-year-old mother-in-law had just died a few weeks before. The house was finally quiet. The relatives had made their condolence calls, and we were in her kitchen. She was cooking, and I sat at the table, listening to her:

"Warren sat in his study every night for the four years that his mother lived with us. He would march right in there after supper and watch tv until it was time to go to bed—while his mother trailed after me and didn't let me alone until I went to bed!" She slammed the lid of a pot down on the counter, her face flushed. "And what could I do to change things? Nothing! I had set the stage long before that. *I* was the one who took his mother shopping for food every Saturday afternoon, years ago, when she had her own apartment after her husband died.

I never—not once—asked Warren to take her. And after she'd do her food shopping I'd take her out to lunch. I felt guilty if I didn't. After all, the woman didn't get out all week—. And she had no daughters!"

Delores went on to say it was too late to change things when her mother-in-law came to live with them. Warren had already settled into the convenient habit of expecting her to take care of his mother. But—didn't Delores *expect* to fill this role? Didn't she *see* herself as the nurturer? Hadn't she internalized the role that society and her husband and her family and friends expected her to play?

"For a long time," she told me, "I didn't even think of Warren taking some of the load off my shoulders. That's why I never asked him to help out. He went to work, and I was the one who cooked and cleaned and took care of everyone. I never worked. He didn't want me to work after we were married. Even after the children were grown. Well, I would have been too scared by then to try to get a job . . ."

She continued, "I guess I felt I was *meant* to take care of the house and the children, and then when his mother got sick—I guess I felt that naturally, it would be me. I would be the one to take care of her. After all, who else was there? But you know, it was my daughter who opened my eyes to sharing responsibility—that's what she calls it. She has a different kind of life than I do —oh, *does* she! She and her husband both teach college in Vermont, and they each take care of the children. Their hours are staggered—she's at school in the mornings and he teaches in the afternoons—and you should see him taking care of my two small grandchildren. He bathes them, he changes their diapers, he does the wash and the cooking—everything that my daughter does. They tell me they're deliberately sharing all the child care, so the children grow up learning that men and women can do a lot of different things. The children see my daughter plastering a wall—and they know that women do those things, too. When I asked my daughter why she feels it's important for them to see men doing the wash and the cooking—she said, 'Ma, what if I get sick? Shouldn't they know their father can take good care of them? What if I'm left alone with them? Shouldn't they

know their mother can do anything their father did?' "
Delores stopped stirring and wiped her hands on her apron
slowly, "Believe me, my eyes have opened. Was I a dope
when I was younger—!"

But Delores shouldn't be so hard on herself. She had
gotten married when women were taught that their place
was in the home. If a woman did go to work back then,
it was to supplement the family income at a time of
need, or it was because she was the occasional "professional" woman. Mainly, women were taught that their
role was to be the perfect hostess, the good wife and
the excellent mother. And now that Delores was beginning to feel trapped in this image of herself, she was
finding it very difficult to break away from the way she
had always done things. After all, twenty-five years of
taking care of other people! And was she absolutely sure
she wanted a shifting of roles? She *had* gotten payoffs
from her role all these years; she *was* valued as a good
mother, a fine wife and a perfect hostess. It was frightening for her to think of taking over any of Warren's
responsibilities—going out to look for a job, finding one,
keeping one. Could she do it . . . an over-50 woman who
had never worked?

But she was exhausted from the demands of the Wonderful Mother role. She had begun to be tired of it years
ago when she was playing the role to the hilt every Saturday with her mother-in-law, and by the time they moved
her into their house—. However, she had never allowed
herself to think of herself as exhausted or enraged. She
wanted to be what everyone else wanted her to be!

Ask yourself—are you clinging to the nurturer role?
Is your mother or father or either of your parents-in-
law living with you? Are you finding it draining? Are
you feeling resentful? Are you angry? Are you afraid
to ask anyone in the family to share the day-to-day
responsibilities?

• *Insist on the family sharing responsibility.*

Getting your family to share the responsibilities can
mean concrete payoffs for you. You won't always have
to be the one to get up in the middle of the night when
your mother has a gall bladder attack; your husband can

take turns with you. You won't always have to be the
one to give up your Sundays for your father; your brother
and his wife will take turns having him over for Sunday
dinner. Particularly, it means that your husband and sister
and brother will understand the limitations you've made
on how much time you'll put in, taking care of your aged
parent or parent-in-law, and they will be learning that
you will do no more than they will do. It will force
them into an adult role.

Sharing the nurturer role will be reassuring to your
parents, and they will be learning that there are different
kinds of support from different people in the family, and
they won't feel guilty about needing so much time and attention; they will know that no *one* person is being "used."
Also, it will be a secure feeling, realizing that they will not
have to be afraid of losing support. When the responsibility is spread out, they know that if you become ill or tired
or need to get away, there will always be someone else
ready to take over.

The Mother-Daughter Relationship:

The mother-daughter relationship has always been very
special—and unique. Mothers and daughters often have
ambivalent feelings toward each other. Sometimes they
are competitive. If you are now the "parent" to your
aging, dependent mother, old and unresolved angers may
flare up. Conflicts can become an everyday occurrence.
This is not to say many mothers and daughters do not
have adult relationships that are close and rewarding; it
is important to acknowledge, however, that frequently
the relationship can be difficult.

• *Were you what your mother wanted herself to be?*
When you were very little, your mother may have perceived you as an extension of herself, and this may have
continued through your childhood and teen years and
young womanhood. It may even exist now. Your mother
may project (act out) her hopes for herself on you—
hopes that didn't materialize in the ways she wanted.

Did she want you to "make" a better marriage than she had? A better life? Did she want you to have the career she never had? When you don't perform the way she wanted to perform herself, does it frustrate her? Does she feel you failed her? If this is the case, of course you feel frustrated and angry at times.

Mothers who were able to fulfill themselves when they were younger and are still fulfilling themselves tend not to project so much. However, your mother may have had few choices in life. Fulfill herself? She may have done well just to have come to this country alone, at the age of fourteen, and gotten a job in a garment factory while she slept on her sister's sofa on the lower East Side in New York! She may be acting out unrealized desires and unresolved conflicts and dreams through her mirror image —you. Perhaps she acts demanding and unreasonable. But how many of her demands are because she wants you to be what she couldn't or didn't become? And how many of her demands are because she's afraid of old age and sickness and dying?

"My daughter's husband is a very successful *doctor!*" we hear an eighty-year-old woman say to the women she plays bridge with. It's obvious she feels it's *her* achievement.

Or we hear an aging woman say bitterly, "My daughter's husband left her for his secretary!" Does she perhaps feel her daughter's failure as her own?

• *Does your mother live through you?*

People often live through other people's achievements when they have little of their own. You can't relive your mother's life for her and make her a famous opera singer or give her a rich husband. But you can realize that she may see herself losing the little power she once had through aging (losses of health, income, relationships, status), and she may be desperately trying to regain her feelings of power through your successes, and she identifies with your failures. When your husband leaves you, it's a stab to *her* heart. Of course, in reality, it's your heart and the blow has been dealt to you. But as her world grows smaller, as it does for an aging and dependent parent, you are her (in her perception) and she is you.

• *Understand her fears . . . and her life.*

You also *know* that she is afraid. When she demands immediate attention ("Joyce, come here right away!") she is really pleading, "Give me attention! Tell me I'm still important!" When she follows you around the house and complains, she is really telling you that she feels alone and that she needs reassurance. And when you answer her, it means that she is still *alive*.

Your anger and pain may ease if you try to get to know her as a *person*. Talk to her and ask her about her life. What was it like for her when she was a teen-ager? What was her mother like? Her father? Did she like him? What brought her to marriage? Was it a love match? Was it "arranged"? A way to get out of the house? As you listen to her answers, as you really *hear*—you may slowly begin to perceive her differently. She may begin to emerge with a younger face, with feelings that are familiar to you; she may become a multi-dimensional person who isn't "just a mother." She may begin to appear to you as a product of her times—which indeed she is—with all its limitations for women. You may then begin to understand, and maybe slowly to forgive. Even to like. And if you've liked her all along, your relationship will be even more enriched.

Is It Different Taking Care of Your Father or Father-in-law?

A father, living with a daughter who is still productive and active and healthy, can feel very angry. She still has visibility and status in the community while he, who formerly was the breadwinner, has been forced to retire and is no longer considered productive.

• *His rage at being dependent.*

Is he overreacting? Would *any* of us like to feel we've faded into the woodwork and are no longer important? He may feel rage that his daughter—whom he once took care of—is now taking care of *him*. He survived the system and took care of his family until they could take care of themselves. And now? Today he lives in your house and is taken care of by you and perhaps your husband. It can be a humiliating, degrading feeling—.

• *His feelings of depression.*

And yet his rage is impotent. It turns into depression and withdrawal. Feeling old and useless, he may become careless about the way he looks. He may not shave often enough. He may forget to zipper his fly. He may drink too much. He may sit around the house, staring into the television set and not seeing. When he watches you going to work in the morning, it may reinforce his feelings of uselessness. When he sees your husband pick up his briefcase or his lunchbox and go out the door at seven-thirty every morning, it reminds him of the strength he once had, and lost. Even if you're not working he sees you have purpose and order to your days. You're needed—and he knows he is not. He nods when you tell him you're going to a meeting, and he's acutely aware that he is not part of the community. Mandatory retirement may have done this to him. Illness or disability could have been the culprit. Being cut off from the mainstream of life could have been compounded by more depression brought about by the death of his wife. His world has shrunk, and his lifespace (his perception of the physical space around him—how much of it seems *real* to him) is now primarily his body and the immediate area around his body—the house, his room. The objects that give him momentary pleasure, like the television set, are important to him. He may not get pleasure from eating, the way he used to: his dentures hurt, there are many foods he can't chew, he can't digest everything—so mealtime is no longer an important part of his day.

• *What can you do for him?*

What can you do to give him back some feelings of self-esteem—to widen his world? Not as much as you'd like, possibly, but you *can* try certain things. Bring him into family discussions. Seek his advice on matters in which he used to show interest (what to do about the leaky roof; whether to buy stocks; where to get a good used car). Let him treat you and your husband to dinner at a restaurant occasionally, instead of you always treating him. Respect his privacy; always knock at his door and be sure you don't go into his room when he's not there (unless you have an arrangement to go in and clean). Did he like to play cards when he was more active? Are any of his cronies still living? Encourage him to invite them over. Put aside a space where he can entertain them. Buy the beer and salami he used to love to serve while the game's going on. Walk to the nearby senior center with him and introduce yourselves to the center director and see if you can get him involved. Get him to talk about old times to you (what was he doing during World War I?). Watch the six o'clock news with him. Discuss it with him afterwards. Help him feel visible again!

Sometimes we see older men and women hanging-out at shopping centers. They sit on benches during warm weather and talk and gossip and people-watch. This is legitimate. They're hanging-out for the same reasons teen-agers do, to socialize and to court and to feel a part of a *community*. Walk over to these places with your father. Does he see anyone he knows? Maybe he'll join them and make new friends. Perhaps he'll meet someone who likes to talk politics. Maybe he'll meet a woman who's lonely—.

• *Maybe he's difficult to cope with.*

Some parents make life difficult for their grown children. Their own excessive needs may be in conflict with their grown children's needs. This can work in reverse, as well. Some grown children have too rigid a concept of behavior they expect from their aged parent.

"Ha!" an indignant woman said. "That should be my only problem—getting my father-in-law involved again! That man moved into our house right after his wife died, and my life has been miserable ever since! He sits at the table and orders me around—serve me this, be sure the meat is lean, I can't eat brussels sprouts—and with never a 'thank you.' He expects me to do his laundry *and* in a certain way, mind you. 'Be sure my collars look right,' he says. He's on my telephone all the time—he's active in a German-American Society—and when I need to make a call and he's on the phone, he just waves me away and keeps talking. I don't feel like it's my house anymore!"

I asked, curious, "What does your husband say about all of this?"

She snorted, "My husband? He's as bad as his father. He feels the man should be the head of the house. He brags about his father's physical strength. 'I should be in that shape when I'm eighty-three,' he says. He's *proud* of the old man."

A few months later she walked over to the nearby thoroughfare where all the neighborhood stores are and got herself a job selling curtains in a dry-goods store. Her first job. She showed her reluctant father-in-law how to use the washing machine and the clothes dryer, and her husband, although uneasy with the change in their lives, doesn't say much because the extra money she brings in makes his life easier. They're paying for a new car with part of her salary. She worked out things so she cooks and her husband and his father do the dishes. "After all," she said, "I'm out all day and I'm tired when I get home—." They grumbled, but—well, her husband likes that paycheck she gets. She got his support when she insisted that her father-in-law make his telephone calls during the daytime, when she's at work, because her husband doesn't like the phone ringing all evening, either. Her husband is getting concrete payoffs from this new arrangement—so she was able to make him *part of the solution.*

Elsbeth had a very different kind of problem, when her father moved in with her and her husband. She had been a teen-ager in Europe, before the Second World War, when her mother had died. She had been brought up by her father, who had been an affluent doctor. He showered lavish attention on her (she was an only child) and they spent an inordinate amount of time together, even after she began college. He discouraged her dating, and he disapproved of every young man she brought home ("They're not good enough for you!"). Then the World War II began. The knock at the door in the middle of the night. Concentration camps. Years of separation. Elsbeth and her father weren't reunited until 1946 when she had already married and was living in the United States.

Her father, now in his early fifties, his life torn apart, tried picking up the pieces. He had been a specialist in

Europe, and he settled in New York City because he felt the small town Elsbeth lived in wouldn't be large enough to sustain a practice. Through the years he prospered again, while he kept in close touch with his daughter. He still considered her his *liebchen,* his little flower, his precious jewel. His son-in-law? He was disdainful. He never would have chosen this man. He visited the couple six times a year, carefully spacing each of the visits. He was formally correct with his son-in-law, and he often sat and stroked his daughter's hand. The years went by. Then unexpectedly he suffered a massive stroke. He spent months in the hospital, then in a nursing home. Elsbeth felt she had to bring him to her house, where he could live with them. And it was hell after that. . . .

"What can I do?" She cried, "I have to do something! He picks. He is—jealous. He acts like Luther took me away from him. He acts like *he* is my husband. He is jealous when I give Luther dinner, when I serve him first, when I talk to him alone. He is no longer the same father! We can't keep him here!"

He *was* the same father, only she had never before realized the kind of needs he had or the extent of his needs, and previous to his stroke he was able to fulfill those needs through the satisfactions of his work. He had nothing now but her . . . and the situation was impossible. Fortunately, Elsbeth's father had amassed a great deal of money. She arranged that he move into an apartment house nearby, and a companion-nurse— a man—was hired to live-in and attend to him. The apartment house had its own swimming pool and restaurant and sun deck and card lounge—and even a secretary to write letters for the geriatric residents. Her father is still feeling very bitter and hurt.

Elsbeth had been direct with him. "Papa," she had said, "this is not working out. You are not getting along with Luther. He is my husband—and I put him first, as is proper. I cannot live this way. We must find another way!"

Elsbeth is a traditionalist. She absolutely felt her husband came first. This made it easier for her to be direct and even blunt with her father. Her very definite value system—her rigid value system—made her feel less conflict about resolving the situation. She was able to bring the festering problem to a head quickly—and it is good that she did. It is good for her and her husband and even her father. He hadn't been able to cope with his sexual jealousy; he hadn't been able to even face the existence of his feelings.

· *When a grown child is demanding.*

Johanna, who silently and grimly watched her newly widowed father go off on two cruises this year, presented yet another kind of situation. Her expectations of her father were unreasonable. "Do you know who's paying for those cruises?" she asked, furious. "My dead mother. He goes so he can meet women. My mother worked alongside of him for forty years in their business, and he's spending every penny she left him in her will to go out and—betray her. There's no fool like an old fool!"

She sat at her dining room table, her arms folded tightly against her chest, and talked in tense, clipped, angry sentences. She told me about her father's life. He had been the son of a poor sharecropper in the South, and had packed up and come north when he was only sixteen, seeking a better life. He had struggled against terrible odds to build a small, successful business in the black ghetto of Philadelphia. He had married, and put his wife and children above everything else. Both he and his wife had worked long hours every day in their small grocery store to put all the children through college. We must have talked for nearly three hours. Gradually, as Johanna remembered her childhood, her voice softened and she spoke more lovingly, her eyes were remembering . . . "I was proud of my daddy. I still am—even though I'm angry. That was a *man!* If it hadn't been for him and my mother, I never would have become a high school principal. My two sisters wouldn't have made it as social workers. My parents saw to it that my youngest brother became one of the top surgeons in Boston! Even after my mother died, my father still worked ten hours a day in the store, until my husband and I put a stop to it and said 'now that's enough, you come and live with us, we're not going to see you drop dead in that store—' "

After a pause, I asked, "So what are you angry about?"

I could see the conflict in her face, the way she started to talk and then stopped, then started again.

"He seems like a stranger to me."

"How?"

"He wears color-coordinated clothes. Clothes never meant anything to him before. He gets a fashionable haircut—he spends over twelve dollars to get his hair cut!—and that wasn't my father. He *looks* different—"

I asked, "Do you want your father to be the same person he was when you were little?"

She nodded slowly. "I guess I do. I don't like change. I never did."

"You find change difficult to accept?"

"That's what I mean. It's not that I don't like change . . ."

"How would you feel if your father remarried?"

"Well, actually, once I got used to it, I'd probably be glad. He's lonely without my mother. My husband and I are at work all day, and there's no one in this big house with him. He misses working, and he's still healthy, you know. He probably has a few good years left. Why shouldn't he get married again? My mother wouldn't care —she'd want him to be happpy."

"You think he's going about it too aggressively—the way he tries to meet women?"

Johanna laughed uneasily. "All the more power to him. But if it had been my mother who had been left alone— *she* wouldn't have been able to get away with what he does!"

I asked, "What do you mean?"

"*She* wouldn't go to the Playboy Club every week and sit drinking—yes, *he* does—and she wouldn't have had the nerve to go off on cruises to meet someone to go to bed with or to marry! She'd have spent her time with the church, and her social life wouldn't be nightclubs and singles' clubs. She'd be going on bus tours to Niagara Falls or California with her church group, and she'd be keeping busy with her grandchildren—"

"Even if she wanted to get married again?"

"That's right! How many seventy-four-year-old women can run after men the way Daddy runs after women? How many seventy-four-year-old women are still considered sexy or attractive to men? Daddy is seventy-four and women call him on the phone all the time. They invite him to brunches, and cocktail parties, and banquets—"

Johanna strongly identified with her mother. She was right. Her father, being a man, "had it made," as she said. When we talked longer, Johanna admitted that it wasn't her father's fault that society has this double standard of aging; that if her mother had been widowed, and society had different expectations of aging women and their sexuality, *she* might be doing the same things her father was now doing. Johanna realized her father was very lonely. . . .

• *Aged parents of either sex may have problems.*

We see that problems *can* be different when fathers and fathers-in-law live with us—or they can be the same. Parents of *either* sex can grow very dependent and want you to make all their decisions. A father *or* a mother can become so ill or disabled that you're faced with the agonizing decision of whether to place him or her in an institution. Either of your parents, *or* your parents-in-law, can be stubborn and difficult to live with. Certainly, parents of both sexes are faced with the same dread of becoming dependent, and an aged wife *and* husband are devastated when it comes to the death of a spouse.

• *—And it can be a great strain on the children.*

Whether it's your father *or* mother *or* either of your in-laws who turn to your for support, it can be a strain. A woman turned to me and cried, "I just went through three years of taking care of my mother in my home— and now my father-in-law can't live by himself! I can't do it! I can't take him in and go through more years of this!"

What are the answers? *Are* there answers? If we understand what happens to our parents' bodies and feelings and health as they age, and if we understand what they want and what they need, and what *we* (as the grown children) want and need, it's a little easier to find the answers—and none of the answers are easy—to the question, "What can I do about my aged parent?"

The Physical Changes of Aging

• *Senescence: The process of aging.*

People age at different rates, and they age differently. "Look what good condition she's in!" we'll say about an active ninety-year-old woman. Then we'll say, "I never expected her to get old so fast!" about a sixty-three-year-old woman. Maybe the secret is to be able to pick and choose our grandparents—because scientists have found that we'll usually live at least as long as our grandparents have, and how well we age depends, to some degree, on our genes.

• *The bodies of our parents: how they age.*

What happens to some of the bodies of older people? Cardiovascular ailments are common, and this can limit the amount of walking a parent can do. Digestive problems are common, and this can affect what your parent eats and drinks. When loss of elasticity of the lung tissue occurs (emphysema), you might have to insist your father cut out his beloved cigars, even though they're one of his few pleasures left. Diabetes is a common chronic disease that affects the elderly, and if your mother is suffering from this ailment, she has to watch her diet carefully and perhaps take insulin daily. Bladder infections happen frequently—so you might often hear your afflicted father going to the bathroom in the middle of the night. Muscular-skeletal conditions can occur, commonly in the form of arthritis, and this can be very painful and limit activity. Weakness can occur on one side of the body following a stroke, and your parent may drag his leg when he walks.

• *How the aged's senses change.*

And the sensory organs experience change. Your mother might see warm colors more easily than cool ones. It'll take her longer to adapt to a room after the light is turned on. She may have trouble seeing out of the corners of her eyes. Glare might annoy her more than it did before. Contours between objects may be more difficult for her to perceive, and boundaries may seem to shift positions. But—distant vision can *improve* with old age!

Your parent's sense of smell may decrease as he or she grows older. There isn't as much loss in the sense of touch as there may be in the other senses—but it can become more difficult for an older person to detect textural changes in materials as they age. Tasting? Yes, food may not have the same joy as it once did, because taste can decrease.

But none of these sensory organ changes are absolute. An aged person may experience only a partial loss. We've all met an aged woman who can hear as sharply at the age of eighty as she did when she was twenty. Every individual experiences decreases in sensory organs differently—and some hardly at all.

· *How big—or small—is your parent's world?*

Lifespace perception changes. As infants, we perceive the space around us as limited to the area immediately around our bodies. As we grow older and our life experiences increase, so does our feeling about the space around us. This space widens and broadens and deepens. Then, as we age, and we experience losses, our lifespace shrinks. That means we only perceive as important the space around us that we can control—our room, our home, and perhaps our immediate neighborhood. The space we can no longer control—the larger community—is no longer as real to us.

Interestingly, senior centers have found that taking members on city bus tours sometimes helps broaden that lifespace again.

When an aging person experiences serious stress—illness, the death of a husband, hospitalization, a move from a home—the very familiar (the immediate room, her own bed) may seem like the only real parts of her life. She is experiencing this decrease in her perception of her lifespace. This may be why your seriously ill mother doesn't seem interested when her grown children tell her about their children. This is why some very old people seem self-centered. In fact, extreme old age can mean a return to the experience of infancy, where only the immediate body space matters.

But this process is often reversible. As one again gains

control over one's life and makes up for the losses, the world gets bigger again. This is encouraging, isn't it?

How Does the Aged Person Learn?

• *Learning goes on—at a slower rate.*

Intellectual functioning—learning—can go on indefinitely as people age! The only differences are that it can take longer to learn, and the responses may be slower. If teaching is geared to these changes, and the person *wants* to learn—exciting things can happen. Remember Grandma Moses—who started her painting career in her old age?

Impaired Hearing: What to Do About It

Most older people experience some hearing loss. This can affect you *and* your parent.

• *People feel bad when they can't hear.*

Often, the aged mother doesn't want others in the family to know she is having trouble hearing and she will try to hide it because it's hard for her to acknowledge the loss. It makes her feel powerless. She may get suspicious when she can't hear what you're saying to your husband. Or your parent may misunderstand what you're saying and might feel like you're talking about her. Not being able to hear properly makes people feel anxious and depressed and isolated and lonely.

• *Your parent may not realize she's making too much noise!*

And people who can't hear well don't realize when they're making irritating or loud noises. You might wince when your father, who has trouble hearing, pulls a chair noisily across the hardwood floor. Your mother may not realize she's whispering so loudly at the movies. She may not be aware that she is disturbing people when she noisily opens a paper bag of sourballs at the matinee, and then removes the cellophane wrappers.

When *you're* more conscious that your parent is unaware of the noise level she is making, you'll feel more understanding.

• *What about hearing aids?*

Hearing aids are not the answer for everyone with impaired hearing, although some salespeople would have you think so. As of August 15, 1977, regulations affecting over-the-counter sales of hearing aids went into effect. A person may now buy a hearing aid only by submitting a doctor's written statement that a hearing aid may be helpful, or by signing a statement waiving a medical examination. Salespeople are forbidden to encourage consumers to waive the examination. The waiver statement advises the potential buyer to seek out a doctor's opinion. Also, a provision requires dealers to allow buyers time to read the consumer information in a manufacturer's brochure (such as how the hearing aid works, and what it can and cannot do). The brochure must be given to every buyer.

• *Special help to talk on the telephone.*

What can help the parent whose hearing is impaired? A telephone might be his or her most important contact with the outside world, especially if he or she lives alone. Can a person wearing a hearing aid hear on the telephone? Depending on the degree of hearing loss, a phone switch built into the hearing aid can make this possible. Not every hearing aid comes with this built-in device. In comparison-shopping for a hearing aid (and you should comparison-shop), ask about this. It could open up a new world of communication and sociability for your parent —and, particularly, it can allow her to call you in an emergency.

When your parent orders a phone for her house, if she is living in an area of the country that uses the Bell system, tell her to avoid ordering the Trimline style or the "design line" phone. Both of these kinds of phones are constructed so the hearing-impaired person finds it difficult to hear, even with a hearing aid and a phone switch built into the aid. Any other kind of home phone is fine.

The telephone company makes available a bone conductor (for about 55 cents a month) for hearing-impaired people to use when speaking on the phone. This looks like a headset an operator may wear, but there is nothing to speak into. It fits behind the ear and is coupled with an amplifier that transmits sound vibrations to where they are picked up by the inner ear. Of course this would be used only in your parent's home, since it is so conspicuous—but it could be a link between your parent and the outside world, couldn't it?

If your parent needs to use a pay phone, tell her to use only those that have a light blue attachment on the mouthpiece (called a grommet)—or no attachment. She will have great difficulty hearing if she uses a pay phone with a black rubber attachment on the mouthpiece, even if she is wearing a hearing aid.

The telephone company, nationwide, sells a portable device with a phone switch that can be attached to a phone to amplify sound. *This can be used only by a person who wears a hearing aid.* It costs around $8. Some hearing-impaired people may find it embarrassing to use; they feel it makes their disability too obvious. And the aged parent, who may be forgetful at times, may not remember to take it along every time she leaves the house. But it might be an excellent device for some people.

- *Recognize signs of impaired hearing.*

Be on the alert to recognize signs of impaired hearing in your parent. Does she answer inappropriately when you ask a question? (*You:* "How are you feeling, Ma?" *She:* "It *is* cool, isn't it.") Does your parent seem to be ignoring people who are talking to her? Is she asking "What?" too often? Is she leaning forward toward the person who is speaking very attentively—and watching the person's face anxiously? If you feel your parent would reject seeing a doctor about her hearing, arrange with the physician ahead of time to have the hearing examination incorporated into a regular physical examination.

Chronic Brain Syndrome: What Is It? What to Do about It

Loss of brain cells and hardening of the arteries can occur which eventually can produce chronic brain syndrome—a disease that can change your parent's behavior. However, even if potentially usable parts of the brain cease to function, researchers are beginning to find new

ways to reawaken unused neurological pathways and stimulate the aged person to develop new ways of functioning, to compensate for the organic brain damage that has
resulted from what we commonly call progressive senility.

Also, it has been found that so-called senility is *sometimes* reversible—when the symptoms are not caused by
damage but by confusion.

- *Does your parent act confused? Forgetful? Disoriented?*

Does your parent wander aimlessly through the house?
Getting up while she is watching television, and walking to
another part of the room, and then walking back to the
chair—without any apparent reason? Is she tapping her
fingers on the arm of the sofa, over and over, or rubbing
the napkin back and forth on the table during dinner? In
some cases, an aged parent may even wander outside of
the house, sometimes inappropriately dressed, and have
to be brought home by a neighbor or a policeman. And it
can be very frightening, running down the street, looking
for your mother—.

- *The anguish a parent may feel at her behavior.*

Many times a parent isn't aware she is behaving like
this. But at times, when the symptom is very obvious (perhaps your parent has urinated on the living room floor or
defecated in the hallway) she may feel deeply ashamed
and afraid. Your parent then knows she has done this
terrible (and this is how she perceives it—terrible) thing.
I have also had aged people tell me they know they're
always forgetting where they are, and they're apologetic
and terrified. Of course they are! After a life time of control over their lives, they're suddenly finding they've *lost
control*. It *is* absolutely terrifying. And they *do* know
they're losing control!

- *What can cause confusion? Forgetfulness?*

A stroke, major surgery, hospitalization, or a major loss
in an aged person's life may be followed by confusion and
disorientation. A woman who has to be placed in a mental
hospital may suddenly become incontinent. A parent who
has just suffered a stroke may withdraw into herself and
not seem aware of what's going on around her. An aged
man whose wife has just died may have a very short atten-

tion span and not remember things. However, these people may be *acting out* symptoms of brain damage, when, in reality, there is no appreciable brain damage. They are acting confused because they're frightened. Your mother may forget "selectively." She may not remember what happened yesterday (after all, yesterday could have been pretty dreary for her, a day of physical pain), but she may remember happy things that happened forty years ago. She may forget her phone number (Who still calls her? Her friends are all dead.) But she might remember her wedding in great detail—even though that was fifty years ago. She remembers what it gives her pleasure to remember. We all occasionally block unpleasant things; she's doing it more frequently because life is now more unpleasant.

Your aged father may seem dazed and incoherent. He may wear dirty clothes. Your mother may repeatedly misplace her dentures and eyeglasses till you feel you could scream. Your mother may even start "hearing voices," especially if she lives by herself. These are their ways of acting-out their confusion, their hurt, their anger, their loneliness. The parent who "forgets" is telling us something: Memory-loss and the denial of reality is adaptive behavior—blocking out pain to make life bearable. When losses in relationships and bad health occur, withdrawal may be the ego defense that may be necessary for survival. The terrible alternative to some aged persons is monumental fear that would be overwhelming, and self-annihilating rage. *If* life can be made bearable once again —the symptoms may disappear. With replacements for lost relationships and a new-found meaningful life, defenses to protect themselves against inner conflicts no longer have to be used.

• *Brain damage in the aged.*

However, with the aged parent who has truly suffered brain damage, researchers are making slow headway about what to do. They're exploring avenues, using hormones and surgery to combat this disease. Meanwhile, medication is sometimes used to calm an agitated person suffering from chronic brain syndrome, and "reality orientation"—a kind of behavior modification—is used in some institutional settings where patients can be motivated to modify their behavior through rewards—the kind adults value, such as more space for valuables and more recognition and more responsibility. Victims of this disease are taught to make better use of their limited capacity through this kind of therapy.

• *How to reassure your parent.*

As the daughter of an aged parent who is suffering from chronic brain syndrome or "senility"—what can you do? Well, for one thing, realize that when your parent doesn't remember things, it *is* uncomfortable and embarrassing for her. You don't want to ask her to remember something when she's apparently having a hard time remembering—especially in front of other people. This can be shattering to her dignity. You want to avoid talking "for her." When you take your mother to visit relatives and they ask her something, and she appears confused—give her time. Sit back, relax and say, "That's all right, Mom, we have time." And then *give her that time.* When you answer for her, because you feel she's too confused, you make her feel even more powerless. What if she can't answer? Then casually reassure her that she'll remember later—and go on to something else. I remember, when I worked at a community center, having many men and women come in with their aged parents for registration, and the children would answer all my questions to the parent *for* the parent—and I remember the terrible helplessness in the parents' faces.

• *What do you do if your parent hoards food?*

One of the common things we find with some aging parents is the tendency to hide and hoard bits and pieces of food. Are you finding *your* parent is doing this? Do you suspect she feels you're not feeding her? Naturally you're hurt—and you're puzzled and confused. You may have tried to talk to your parent about this, and she just denies it, or openly accuses you of not feeding her. Why do some aged people do this? Are they really trying to save bits and pieces of their lives? Are they attempting to hold on to roles in their lives through the concrete symbol of food? Are they feeling desperate about food because it's one of the few things left in their lives that give them sensual pleasure? What can you do? Try leaving your parent's favorite snacks in bowls, easily accessible, and remind your parent to help herself. Verbally reassure your mother that the bowl of fruit is *hers*—and that she can take it to her room.

• *Does she accuse you of not feeding her?*

You might want to examine the possibility that your parent really feels you haven't given her dinner because she has forgotten—truly forgotten—that she has already eaten. As chronic brain syndrome progresses, some aged lose their sense of time. A parent might plead, "Why won't you feed me?" and this makes you, the daughter, feel anguished. A parent might become enraged and scream, "You are trying to starve me!" and you, the daughter, want to cry. It's very difficult.

Here are techniques which you might want to use, if your parent is very confused:

1. Have your parent eat near a large kitchen clock, within her eye level.
2. Place a sign next to her plate, which reads, in large letters, *LUNCH*.
3. Relate the clock and the sign together for her at mealtime by saying, "It's now twelve o'clock. It's time to eat lunch." Look at the clock, point to it, and have her repeat what you've said. Read the sign aloud.
4. Pick up the napkin and say, *"Feel* the napkin?" Encourage her to touch the napkin that she relates to eating.
5. Point to the plate and ask, *"See* your plate?" Suggest that she touch the plate and call it by its name.
6. And then say, *"Smell* the food, Mother. What does it smell like?" Take your time, suggest she put some food on her fork and smell it to identify it aloud. Help her out by reminding her what the food is.

After she eats, let the plate stay on the table for the next hour or so. Later, if she insists she didn't eat lunch, guide her to the table and show her the remains of the lunch on the table (her plate, crumpled napkin, and also point to the clock and the lunch sign). All of this takes *enormous* amounts of time and effort. You may not have the time—or the emotional strength—to do this, day after day. It's ALL RIGHT if you decide not to do this; you can do other helpful things, instead.

• *Help her remember to take her medication.*

If she takes daily medication in the way of a pill or capsule, put it in her spoon so she remembers to take it when she eats (if this is when she's supposed to take it). She will be helped by associating the medication with mealtimes.

• *It's difficult—for everyone in the family.*

Remembering. An aged father may not remember where his bedroom is . . . and then, ten minutes later, he remembers again. A sixty-year-old woman said to me, "The part that hurt the most was when my mother, who lived with us in her last years, didn't recognize me. My brother would come over, and she'd say to him, who is this woman in the room? It wouldn't last long, maybe a few minutes, but it happened a lot, and it hurt."

Yes, it hurts. I know it does. It deeply grieves you to see your parent, who was once the most powerful person in the world to you, act and feel helpless. However, your parent is fortunate because you *care*. It is difficult for you and you feel despair—but you care.

• *Be sure your parent gets a medical checkup.*

Perhaps the first thing you want to do, now that you're thinking what direction you can take with your parent, is make an appointment with a very good internist so the doctor can check out whether there is any unsuspected disease that is lurking and giving the symptoms of chronic brain syndrome.

• *Make an appointment with a psychiatrist.*

Then make an appointment with a psychiatrist—one who is particularly knowledgeable about the aging person and her developmental changes. Call your local health department and ask if there are *geriatric* psychiatrists in your particular area. The psychiatrist can determine the diagnosis and prescribe treatment. And do let the psychiatrist

know if your parent has suffered any severe losses in the
past few years. A loss of a sister? A husband? Or were
there any changes in your parent's life—a move from a
house to your home or the giving up of a business? A
knowledgeable psychiatrist (or social worker) can recommend supportive home services, such as day care for the
elderly. A day care center can mean hours of relief for
you, several days a week. If your parent is living with you
—you will need relief. A psychiatrist can prescribe medication to calm your parent.

• *Have adult expectations of her.*

If you have adult expectations, it is more likely your
parent will live up to these expectations. When you're
giving her instructions to sit down and eat lunch, or get
dressed, you can do this in the tone you would normally
use with any adult—even though you may have to repeat
your instructions over and over. Expect your parent to eat
at the same time as the rest of the family. Expect *normal adult* behavior and your parent will more frequently
try to live up to your expectations. The psychology behind your attitude is very simple: people often behave as
they are expected to behave.

• *TOUCH your parent!*

Try to touch your parent as often as possible. Stroke
your mother's arm. Hold her hand. Put your arm on the
back of her chair. Physical contact is particularly important to the aged person who feels isolated and alienated
and frightened. When you touch her it tells your parent
you love her. Touching is very hard for some people. It
may be hard for you. A woman told me, "We never
hugged or kissed in my family when I was growing up.
The only time my mother kissed me was when one of us
was leaving town." This woman found herself feeling
awkward and self-conscious the first few times she
reached out. When she found her mother gratefully re-
sponding, it made it easier to keep touching her.

• *Help her regain a sense of identity.*

You want to help your parent regain a sense of
identity. An eighty-five-year-old woman said poignantly,

What to Do about Your Aged Parent 191

"There's no one left in the whole world who calls me by my first name!"

Help: What Kind to Get and Where to Find It

Whether your parent lives alone or with you, you'll want to know where you can get supportive and community home services; and which agencies to contact for what kind of help. Don't try to find all the solutions to your problems and your parent's problems by yourself. The process and problems of aging and the aging parent are far too complex and overwhelming to try to solve them yourself.

• *Homemaker services.*

If your parent, because of disability or illness, needs housekeeping services to allow her to stay in her own home, get in touch with your local Department of Social Services Homemaker Service Department. Both private and public social service agencies provide light housekeeping and shopping services—and you might need this help if you live in another city. You might even need it if you're working during the day or have your own family to tend to, and your time with you parent is limited.

• *Escort services.*

A social service agency may also be able to provide escort service and transportation to the hospital or clinic for your parent.

• *Meals-on-Wheels.*

Meals-on-Wheels, in many cities, provides home-delivered hot meals to the homebound person (not only the aged) who can't cook for herself. Your social service agency can refer you to your local Meals-on-Wheels service. If your parent is leaving the hospital, the social worker at the hospital can arrange for this supportive home service at your request or your parent's request. The nice thing about Meals-on-Wheels (aside from the two important nutritious hot meals each day) is that a volunteer visits with the person who delivers the daily meals, to check and see that everything's all right.

• *Chore services.*

Some agencies offer the services of household handyman, geriatric aides, home aides, and outreach aides—all people who can go into your parent's home and help with the tasks that are now too hard for your parent. These aides can change window screens, give limited bedside care, do household repairs, run necessary errands to pay bills and help your parent dress.

Unfortunately, in our society, it's often only the aggressive person who seeks out these services (which are rarely advertised) and who finds help like this. You may have to be the advocate if your parent feels (or *is*) helpless.

• *Social service agencies.*

Look in your phone book to see if there is an Urban Service Agency. They specialize in services to people in the inner-city all through the country, but can refer you to other agencies if your parent's income is too high or if your parent lives in a geographic area outside their target areas of the inner-city.

If you're Catholic, call the Catholic Associated Charities. If you're Jewish, call the Associated Jewish Charities, or the Jewish Family and Children's Service. You may have a nonsectarian Family Children's Society in your city.

• *Information-and-referral help.*

The decade of the 1960's gave the aged more low-cost and no-cost supportive home services than our present decade. But the aged themselves are beginning to mobilize to demand more services. At the present, you can call your state health department for information-and-referral, and call your local Commission on Aging . . . and the senior adult department of your community center and the Young Women's Christian Association for help. Always ask to speak to the social worker on the staff, or the director of the department (they're more apt to give you the right information) and even if they, as an agency, don't have the right kind of help for your parent, ask them whom you *can* call.

• *Instructive Visiting Nurse Association.*

The Instructive Visiting Nurse Association (or Visiting

Nurse Association) in your town can provide bedside nursing and health instruction for short- and long-term illnesses, and provide other services such as physical therapy, surgical dressings, and health aides for the chronically ill. Some hospitals have a home care program for patients whose doctors are on that particular hospital staff. Call the social service department of the hospital and ask.

• *Special library service.*

There are services that are not only health related . . . but are very important to the emotional and mental well-being of the aged parent who can't get out easily. Does your parent love to read? Call your local library—the main branch—and ask if they have a book-by-mail service, where a borrower's card is not required.

• *Telephone reasurrance programs.*

Find out if your parent's city has a Telephone Reassurance program (sometimes call Ring-a-Day program or a similar name). The homebound are called daily, at the same time each day, by the same person. This can literally be a lifesaver, giving the aged homebound a bright moment in their day. Who would know about this service? The Red Cross, social service agencies, community centers, Commission on Aging offices, your state Office of Aging . . .

• *Funded free hot lunch programs.*

If your parent can get out of the house, encourage her to attend a multipurpose senior center for socialization purposes, and particularly for a free, daily, hot, nutritious meal that may be available. This meal is part of a federal program, and is offered in many cities throughout the nation. Contributions are accepted, but not required. If there is no multipurpose senior center near your parent, the meal might be available in a nearby church, or in a city housing project for the aged, or in a city bureau of recreation. This program is called Eating-Together or a similar kind of name. When you ask for information on this, just inquire about access to the free group meals that the federal Older Americans Act provides to the aged throughout the country. Your local Commission on Aging office can give you this information. Your local Information-and-

Referral Service for the Aging (whose number should be available from your local or state Office of Aging—see Appendix A—if you can't find a listing in your phone book) can also provide information on this.

- *Food stamps.*

Find out if your parent is eligible for food stamps. This is also a nationwide program. When the stamps are used at retail price, the dollar value is greater than the cost of the stamps. Call your local Department of Social Services, Food Stamp Division, for eligibility information.

Help Your Parent to Ask for Help!

Help your parent not to feel ashamed to apply for money help and subsidized social services.

- *She's entitled to it! It's NOT charity!*

Help her realize that the many years she paid taxes entitles her to a return. A social worker may be able to help your parent move toward accepting help more than a family member can. *Use* the social worker's services in this way, if you think it will make your parent accept help more easily.

- *Her self-image.*

It is sometimes very difficult for an old person to see herself as poor—when all her life she or her husband has been a wage-earner. And yet, on a fixed income, she may very well be poor! So it may be your parent's middle-class self-image that makes it hard for her to accept any kind of aid.

What Can a Senior Center Do for Your Parent?

Senior centers give the aged a place to go, to be with people their own age . . . and they offer opportunities for the senior adult to meet new people. The better the center, the more varied and sophisticated the programs they offer.

• *Programs offered.*

Modified Yoga classes, bridge lessons, flower-arranging classes and psychology of aging courses are becoming more and more common, and senior centers are moving toward the multipurpose center concept, giving multipurpose services—health, recreation, education, and social services.

• *What kinds of people are served?*

A good senior center, staffed by knowledgeable professionals, can give new life and hope to the man who has just retired and is depressed; the woman who is newly widowed, and lives alone; the couple who was frightened of retirement. Senior centers attract "young" oldsters and the older aged. As in any other setting, members find their "own kind" to relate to. Sometimes you find two generations in the same center—a fifty-five-year-old woman and her eighty-year-old mother—and they're both using the services of the center to meet their own needs. Door-to-door bus service is frequently offered the member, and you might want to ask the center's director about this if you're thinking of encouraging your parent to join.

Most activities are during the daytime—sometimes also on weekends—because most retired older people prefer going out during the daylight hours. Sometimes the services are free, and there is no membership fee, and sometimes there is a cost to the member to join (at times on a sliding scale). Some senior centers are run by the city, and some are sponsored by religious groups, while others are part of larger services—such as the Associated Jewish Charities and the Catholic Charities. Some are run by the city bureaus of recreation. More recently, some neighborhood associations are finding funds to run their own senior centers.

• *How to get your parent to join.*

How can you get your parent involved in a senior center? Perhaps a neighbor or friend who goes regularly can take your parent. Sometimes a parent resists. The reasons for this? Your parent may say she was never a joiner—and interestingly, most of the members of senior centers, contrary to what people think, were *not* joiners when they were younger. "Who would I know there?" your mother may ask, holding back. It probably would be a good idea for you to make the first visit yourself (and make a telephone appointment with the director ahead of time so you can tell her about your parent; why she doesn't want to come, what her interests were when she was younger, what her physical limitations are now—if any). Get an activity schedule—a copy for your parent and one for yourself—to take home. Take home any literature that describes each program offered. And then try to sell your parent on the one or two activities that once interested her. A music group? An art class? A discussion group?

• *Make your parent part of the process.*

Arrange, with the center's director, for her to meet your parent when you finally do go back. Sit down together, so the director can sell the idea of the center to your parent. When you hear the director asking questions, don't answer for your parent; if your parent is encouraged to answer for herself it will help her feel part of the process of joining.

• *Is she saying, "They're too old for me!"?*

And don't be discouraged if your parent says to you (after the first visit), *"I'm* not going back there! *Those* people are too old for me!" Senior centers enroll members aged fifty-five through ninety—and older. People of varying vigor and strengths. People who look younger, and some obviously aged men and women. Your mother is resisting being placed in an age-segregated situation, or she doesn't want to be identified as being "old"—which is really the same thing. If you can get her to make that second visit (and use a special activity as the lure), she will begin to sort out the individual faces and see for herself that there *are* people she can relate to.

• *Help her make contact with members she knows.*

It will also help if you can find out if your parent knows any of the members and then arrange for them to meet *at* the center, to talk about old times. This will be an important link to the new and strange setting.

Day Care: A Possible Answer for Your Parent

Day care centers can be a godsend for the aged parent *and* her children. They truly can keep some older people out of nursing homes and geriatric centers—which is a prime reason for their existence.

• *Different kinds of day care centers.*

A day care center may be connected with a medical facility (a hospital) and be on the same grounds, or it may be in a basement of a church. Some day care centers only take ambulatory people (people who can walk), and some are able to absorb patients who are in wheelchairs. This largely depends on what kind of pickup service they have. Yes, they usually do offer door-to-door van service, and some vans are equipped to handle wheelchairs and some are not. Some centers are called day treatment centers and some are called day care centers. Both serve the partially disabled older person. Some charge, and some are no-cost.

The day care patient lives at home, and is picked up every morning, on the average of two to three days a week, and is taken back home in the afternoon. While the person is at the center, she makes use of the varied services available—and this will differ, depending on the center.

• *What they offer.*

Well-funded centers staff social workers, doctors, occupational therapists, recreational therapists, and physical therapists. The patients use their strengths and skills in groups, making items with their hands that they can enjoy at home, sharing experiences and memories in oral history and discussion groups, and interacting with other patients. Eating together (there's a hot, free, nutritious lunch) gives them an opportunity to further socialize. Day care centers offer *structured* experiences, and help the disengaged elderly to reach out again, in meaningful activities and relationships. Medication is given to the patient (if she cannot take it herself) throughout the day, as she needs it, and one-to-one counseling is offered. Home visits are made so the staff can understand the needs of the patient better. Particularly, day care centers give the aged person a sense of anticipation and order to her days, knowing that she is getting dressed that morning to go to a place where she is *expected*. Birthday parties and sing-a-longs and occupational and recreational therapy enrich the daily activity.

• *How do they help? Who do they help?*

Certainly, the day care center can be the answer for the over-50, working woman who is taking care of her partially-disabled mother, afraid of what will happen while her mother is alone in the house. It can be the answer, possibly, for the woman whose mother is very depressed. It can be the answer for the woman whose mother is coming out of a nursing home and needs a transition from the nursing home to her own home. It can be the answer for the eighty-year-old man who is recovering from a stroke. It can fill the needs of the slightly confused man who lives by himself in a furnished room. It can prove to be the solution for the woman who finds she is *drained* from taking care of an aged parent!

• *Eligibility requirements.*

Your state health department can give you the names of state-approved day care centers. Your parent must be partially disabled to get into one. With the aged, partially disabled can mean many things: Your mother may suffer from severe arthritis and find it hard to move around; your father may find it hard to see (he has a progressive eye disease); your parent may be suffering from anxiety and depression; your mother may be disoriented. Don't take it for granted that your parent is *not* eligible for day care—find out first!

"My Parent Wants to Stay in Her Own Home, But—"

Does your aging parent live alone in a house that is in a dangerous or deteriorating neighborhood? And she refuses to move?

• *It may be very hard for your parent to move!*

It can be very difficult for an aging person to make that kind of move. It's hard enough for younger people to make major moves, and when a much older person, who has already suffered losses, loses yet another important part of her life—the home that belongs to her—it can be a great trauma. She is being forced to give up the home, the familiar space around each piece of furniture, the tree outside her bedroom window, the sound of the train that comes every night at the same time, and memories. If your mother had a happy marriage and she and her deceased husband lived in that house, she is giving up even more, for she is leaving the kitchen where she cooked the potato pancakes her husband loved and she is leaving the bedroom they shared for forty years. And what is she going *to*? She doesn't know. Even if it is your home, she does not know if it will feel all right, if it will *be* all right. She is going to the unknown—*and* as a *guest!*

• *Can she stay in her own home?*

Understand the stress factor. And you might want to consider if it is possible for her to stay where she is. Get her doctor's opinion on this.

• *Supportive home services.*

If she *can* stay in the same home, help her get supportive home services to meet needs that you (perhaps in a different geographic area) can't meet. For instance, she might need someone to help her with her weekly grocery shopping. Some community centers and senior centers have volunteers that take the aged shopping, on a weekly basis, with door-to-door service and help in taking heavy bags of groceries into the house. Other senior centers take their members shopping once a month in a van or bus, and they shop at a large shopping center where they take care of varied needs (clothes, food) under one roof. With some scouting around and detective work, you may find that in taking advantage of every appropriate and needed supportive home service in your parent's area, she *can* stay where she is. For a complete list of these services, call the Office on Aging or the Commission on Aging in your parent's area, or your local information-and-referral service for the aging.

• *Can someone live with her?*

Another answer is having someone move in and live with her. A student? Another older person? This may or may not work out. In our individualistic society, women and men are often reluctant to share their kitchen and living room. Sometimes a parent will accept a person coming in just to prepare dinner and eat with her—and that can be a first step toward acceptance of a full-time live-in companion.

• *Let your parent be part of the decision.*

If your parent agrees to move, be sure you encourage her to look for the new place and choose the new place *with* you. And if your parent has made it very clear that she does not want to move—I would try to respect that need. Let her stay in her own home as long as she can. The stress she may experience after moving may be worse for your parent than the dangerous neighborhood. The powerlessness your parent may feel when being forced out of the home she has lived in for so long may damage and age her far more than the conditions in the deteriorating house. What *we* feel is right for our aging parent is often a reflection of our own value system—and not hers. Your parent may not mind the roaches; your parent may not find her home depressing. And this is important for you, as her daughter, to appreciate.

• *Are you being an unnecessary "rescuer"?*

Ask yourself: Does my mother really need to move— or do I really need to be a *rescuer?* There is some evidence that the stress of moving from a loved home can hasten death—especially if the move is not the aged person's choice. Consider her other alternatives.

"My Parent Is Moving in with Me"

• *How it used to be in the old days: The extended family.*

Years ago houses were large and there was room and privacy for everyone when the aged parent came to live with her children and grandchildren. Families were so large that there were tasks for everyone all the time. The aging parent was needed to baby-sit and bake and sew— and sometimes give advice. She felt important because she was filling important and needed roles.

- *But times have changed.*

Today, with smaller families and modern applicances and easy-to-clean fabrics and smaller houses—in fact, often smaller *apartments*—there is little for the parent to do. She often feels she is getting in the way. And sometimes this is the case. Noise can be heard more easily in small living quarters, and it is harder to feel comfortable arguing when an aged parent is in the next room. It can be embarrassing to make love when you know your mother is sleeping (?) on the other side of the wall. It is easy for the daughter to feel intruded upon and resentful.

- *Make life easier for yourself and your parent
  if she moves in.*

How can you rearrange your life? Well, for one thing, if your parent lives with you, deliberately make time for *yourself* each day. If you work every day, come home and spend some time alone or with your husband. Go in your room, close the door, read the newspaper, turn on the television, and *DON'T FEEL GUILTY BECAUSE YOUR MOTHER IS ALONE IN THE LIVING ROOM.* Wave goodbye to your parent and take a bicycle ride or visit a friend. Taking care of an aging parent means that you will often feel pressure—and you *need* time alone.

Your parent and you will feel more privacy if her room is like her own living room, so she can entertain family or friends; so she can feel she's not trapped in a small bedroom when you want to be alone. She might want to place her bed against a wall, hiding it with a folding screen when she has company. Perhaps a sofa and a small cocktail table can be placed in a corner, making it a pleasure for her to entertain. How about a writing desk and chair, so she has a quiet place to write to her friends? A lamp with a light bulb of adequate strength?

Encourage your parent to bring some of the furniture she loved, from the old house, and put it in her room. It will feel more like *her* space. Don't decorate your parent's room for her—let the decision of where to hang the pictures be *hers*. And—never walk in on your parent without knocking and waiting for an answer (feel free to expect this kind of privacy for yourself, also. Discuss it with her, like two adults).

• *Encourage her to be independent.*

It is true that you like to clean in your own way, I'm sure, but don't fall into the habit of doing everything for your parent—making her bed, mopping the floor—because it's easier or quicker or you do a better job. Yes, your parent may be slow and not as thorough as you are; you may get impatient waiting for her to finish; you may not feel it's clean when she is finished—and you don't want to make her feel like a "maid" in your house. But your parent *needs* to feel she can do it, and if you do it instead, your parent will feel useless. Let your mother occasionally bake those cakes you loved. Don't take her role in the kitchen completely out of her life. It is a role she filled for many years, and it is a role that gave her a sense of importance throughout most of her adult life.

Your mother might seem less decisive than she used to. Dora, whose mother is living with her told me this story:

"I get so impatient with her! She used to be such a strong, independent woman, and now she won't make the smallest decision without asking me to tell her what to do! 'What should I wear to the store,' she asks me, 'who should I call, what should I do—.' She's driving me crazy—."

If your mother is doing this, return her questions: "What do *you* think you should wear?" "Whom do *you* want to call?" Give her the responsibility of making her own decisions by making her answer her own questions. She might not totally want that responsibility, and she might show you this by not answering, or by saying, "Tell me what to do." Repeat the questions. Force her to make her own decisions. This is the best thing you can do for her. By doing this, you are saying to her, "I will not let you be a child. You are a responsible adult. I will insist you use your strengths so they do not dry up and wither away."

Yes, this is tiring and irritating—but the payoff is that after you reply this way enough times (and don't ever give in!) she will eventually start making her own small decisions, as she used to . . . because there has been no payoff for *her*.

And an even bigger payoff (for both of you) is that

when your mother sees that she can still make small decisions adequately, she'll develop the courage to try making the big decisions for herself!

Don't say "yes" when she asks you to shop for her clothes, when she is physically able to do this for herself. And don't feel that her frail appearance means that she can't shop for her own clothes. Perhaps she does get tired more easily than she used to, but that means the simple adjustment of arranging for her to shop for only two hours instead of the entire afternoon. Have her arrange to shop for just one item that day instead of a dress *and* shoes. If she continues to do her own shopping, she will feel she has more control over her life. Her clothing is an extension of herself, and you take away that part of herself when you take the shopping out of her hands. If she does her own shopping, she will feel more like a responsible adult. *She* knows that parents shop for small *children*.

"But I have a time problem," you might be thinking, "I work every day. I don't have the time or the energy to take my mother to the shopping center every time she needs something. It's easier to buy *her* stockings when I buy mine."

Then ask other members of your family to take turns taking her shopping. Suggest your mother shop by mail-order. Get her the catalogues from different stores and let her leisurely pick out a dress, a robe. The once-utilitarian styles in catalogues have given way to much more sophisticated styles. Give it a try. Do anything to avoid shopping *FOR* her.

Why is she asking you to make decisions and shop for her and why is she acting like a child? Because she may be feeling like a child. She has lost some vital "grown-up" roles in her life: the role of wife and mother and housekeeper. Living with you, she is now in a dependent "child" role. She may also be testing you. She may be saying, "Do *you* think I'm a child? If you don't, prove it! Don't make decisions for me and don't buy my clothes for me. Let's see what you do." And—if she thinks you see her as a child, she will see *herself* as a child. But what she really wants is for you to say, "I *know* you can do it. I know you are a responsible adult." And the way for you to really say this is to act as though you know she can do all these things by *LETTING* her do them.

• *Take vacations from each other.*

Try to take short and long vacations away from your aged parent. If she is in reasonably good health, and can be left alone, do not be afraid to leave her alone. Appreciate that she is a person who has had a lot of living experience and she knows what to do if she hears a prowler lurking outside while you are away. If you feel there *is* a real problem—perhaps you are realistically apprehensive if she has a severe heart condition—arrange for her to stay with another member of the family, or (if you can afford it) hire a nurse or companion to stay with her. Arrange to have her stay at a nursing home while you're gone *only if there is absolutely no other alternative*, because this could be very frightening for her. Moving to a nursing home probably symbolizes sickness and death to her . . . and she may also fear being left there permanently. If you must choose a nursing home, select a good one and be sure that you tell your parent what date you'll return to get her. Repeat that information as often as she seems to need to hear it. *And keep your promise!*

"How Will Having My Parent in My Home Affect My Marriage?"

• *Your parent may or may not be sensitive to your marriage.*

Your parent may be very perceptive and caring and may be very sensitive to your husband's needs and the needs of your marriage. She may thoroughly accept the fact that you and your husband have a separate relationship from her. On the other hand, your parent may play games. Faye told me a story about the kinds of games her mother plays.

"Whenever my husband Gil isn't around," Faye told me, "my mother has to say *something* nasty about him. In her sweetest voice. 'He's very impatient with you, isn't he, Faye?' she'll say, or, 'He *does* like the girls, doesn't he Faye?' 'Did you notice the way he eyed that girl at the restaurant?' Or—'He didn't *hit* you in the bedroom, did he Faye? I heard all that hollering.' I end up screaming at her and then she gets that self-righteous look, that martyred air, and says 'I *won't* argue, I *refuse* to argue.'

"And do you know what?" Faye exclaimed, "she even denies having said any of those things! She's driving me up the wall!"

Faye's mother is acting-out the need to separate Faye and her husband, because she's afraid that Gil will eventually want her to leave (she's lived with them for two years). If she can drive a wedge between them, actually achieve a separation, she knows her daughter would never turn her out. However—she knows all of this on a subconscious level and would probably be honestly shocked if anyone suggested this is her motive. What should Faye and Gil do? Her mother would no doubt resist any kind of counseling or therapy—she's a woman who is not in touch with her real feelings most of the time and is not feeling-oriented. Perhaps Faye and Gil should begin to explore the possibility of her mother living elsewhere. She is too destructive to their relationship—and it probably won't stop. Sooner or later, the stress may seriously affect their lives. A social service agency could help them find an apartment for her, or even help them relocate her in one of the many apartment houses that are being constructed for older residents. Of course she will be very angry. She will feel terribly hurt. But Faye and Gil must preserve their relationship. That must be given priority . . . *without* feelings of guilt.

- *What does your husband want to do about her?*

Before you decide to bring your parent into your home, discuss the matter thoroughly with your husband. *Hear* what he says. Hear what he doesn't say! Listen with the third ear; the silences can tell you a lot about how he feels.

- *Are there other alternatives?*

Can your parent live by herself or himself? Can your parent be alone at night? Can she use the kitchen by herself? Can he use the bathroom by himself? Do you like your parent? Does your husband? Is there *another* alternative? Maybe you and your husband can think of *more* questions you should ask yourselves.

"Where Can My Parent Go If I Don't Take Her In? What Can She Do?"

* *Possible solutions.*

Seriously consider the alternatives. Can the family or your parent afford to hire a live-in companion, so she can stay in her own home? Might an apartment house for the elderly—with architecture designed for the handicapped, recreation programs and a restaurant or daily meal available—be the answer? Would your parent be willing to share an apartment with another older person?

* *Be honest about your feelings.*

Ask yourself the question: Do I want her? Don't feel ashamed to say no. Perhaps your parent is *difficult* (and maybe always was!). You may not have the stamina to take care of her . . . . You may feel her presence would threaten the equilibrium of your household. You may find your parent so boring that you feel like screaming after you've been with her for three hours—much less on a full-time basis. Your mother might play one grown *child* against the other.

* *If you have no other choices.*

You may feel you have no choice. If that is the case, try to work out a solution where you can stay sane.

* *Three women who coped.*

I talked to some women who had struggled with the question, "What should I do with my mother?" and although their lives were disrupted, once they took responsibility for their parent, they planned ahead so the disruption was minimal. They also chose solutions that worked reasonably well for their parent and themselves.

Audry, a tall, good-looking woman in her fifties, sat in her living room and told me what she had done:

"My mother is very hard to live with, but I felt I couldn't cope with my guilt feelings if I didn't take her in. Look, you can see I make a very good income. I'm chief copywriter with the largest advertising agency in the city. How could I have refused to share all this—" she waved her hand and motioned to the expensive furniture, the lush plants, the spacious sun porch.

"Especially," she said, "since I lived alone!"

It's easier for Audry to have her mother with her because Audry works all day—she doesn't have to be with her mother every minute. She sends her to Miami Beach for three months every winter, and pays for an arrangement where her mother stays with another widow in a condominium.

"It works out beautifully. My mother gets a great tan and I get a good rest."

But not everyone has the kind of income Audry has. Not every daughter can afford to send her mother to Miami Beach for three months every year. And it can be much harder to find solutions if you or your parent are on limited incomes.

Martha, an over-50 friend, told me that she felt guilty about not inviting her mother to live with her, but she knew she'd be inviting a breakdown if she did.

"Instead," she said, "I worked out a system where my mother stays in her small house (she wanted to stay there, anyway) and each of us takes turns visiting her—all my sisters—so there's someone stopping in each day to see if she needs anything and to talk to her for a half hour or so."

"We take turns taking her food shopping," she continued, "and this way each of us has the responsibility of looking after her just twice a week or so. This way no one feels too pressured."

Liz, also in her 50's, sat in her breakfast room with me over homemade cake.

"I get along fine with my mom," she said, "but my husband, even though he's a great guy, can't stand her for too long. They just get on each other's nerves. But when my father died, and mom got depressed, we knew we had to do *some*thing, so we agreed to this arrangement that we have now. So far," she crossed her fingers, "it's working out okay."

"How are you working it?"

'Well, mom came to live with us, and she stays with us

only during the week. Then, on Friday nights, after supper,
I take her back to her apartment—she never gave it up—
and she stays there until Sunday night. This gives Bob and
her a breather from each other. And we got her into a program where she volunteers every day in a hospital for retarded kids. She's fantastic at it! She even got one little
girl to talk—to say her first words at the age of five—just
because she gave her so much love. It's given her a new
life, working with those kids. She hardly ever gets
depressed now."

Liz reached over for the teapot, "It's good she kept her
own place. It was the best thing she could have done.
Sometimes she'll cook a big pot of soup, over the weekend, and bring it back to our house, then we'll have it
through the week. That's her gift to *us*. She wouldn't feel
as free in cooking if she were in my kitchen all weekend.
And she's just beginning to invite her old friends to her
apartment for Saturday night suppers—most of them are
widows, too. Maybe she'll be ready to move back to the
apartment later this year. I can see where she's moving
toward that."

If Your Parent Is Mentally Ill: The Community Mental Health Center

- *The trend toward de-institutionalization.*

The national trend today is toward keeping people of
all ages out of institutions, de-institutionalizing patients,
and protecting the legal rights of mental patients. How
does this affect the life of the aged person who is mentally
ill? Well, it has become more difficult to legally commit
the confused seventy-year-old-man who's wandering the
streets, and more aged persons are being released from
state mental institutions.

- *The need for community services.*

This is good—but, unfortunately, there aren't enough
community services to treat the mentally ill older person
who stays in the community, and the psychotic aged who
are released from hospitals frequently aren't treated
or followed-up, once they're back in the community. No
one sees that they continue on medication so they won't

"hear voices"; often there is no intervention from any agency or person to see that they have daily nutritious meals or adequate housing. They've been moved from invisible back wards of hospitals to invisible back alleys of cities. Perhaps if they lived in a society that valued old people—at least to the extent of seeing that they have enough to eat and are not lonely—many wouldn't have become mentally ill. But meanwhile there is a need, nationwide, for more community health services and supportive home services; for more and better foster-care homes and halfway houses.

• *The need for advocacy to get these services.*

This takes a lot of money, and getting the funds for these services takes a determined citizenry who demands that our country give priority to these health needs.

• *Using the community mental health center.*

Our society's emphasis on keeping people out of institutions is not wholly altruistic. It also saves money. Government money. And so government funds have been used to establish community mental health centers throughout the country where people of all ages can receive outpatient treatment. Some of these community mental health centers are programs within general hospitals, under the auspices of the hospitals. Others are in storefronts and new buildings and rented space in basements of churches that are under the control of nonprofit community organizations. All of these centers are largely government funded. What kind of services can *your* parent get for his or her mental or emotional problems? Many centers offer screening and evaluation to your aged parent, prior to being admitted to a state mental hospital (and, yes, sometimes our parent *needs* hospitalization, and how many of us can afford a private mental hospital?). The staff of a community mental health center can prescribe medication for your depressed father, and can follow up on his treatment. They can offer alcholism counseling to your parent who has a drinking problem. Centers offer crisis intervention—which means that you can call the center for quick help if your parent acts-out sudden, violent feelings. Use these community mental health centers to keep your upset parent *in* the community. The staff can refer you to the supportive home services your anxious mother needs; they can also help you find a nursing home for your father, who may be suffering from chronic brain syndrome.

- *Their structure . . . their fees.*

Community mental health centers are usually directed by psychiatrists or psychologists—although nurses can be directors (perhaps more nurses aren't in this role because they're women!). Mental health counselors and alcoholism counselors and social workers staff the centers. Sometimes a center—particularly one that is located within a general hospital—offers limited inpatient service. Patients usually pay a fee (which Medicare and Medicaid will cover), and the fees are considerably lower than what a psychiatrist in private practice charges.

- *Finding a community mental health center.*

How can you find a community mental health center in your area? Call your city or state health department and inquire. And then visit before you make any final arrangements to see what it's like.

Protective Services for the Aged

- *State intervention.*

There is a move, nationwide, to protect the aged from being exploited. States are examining legislation or passing legislation where, in selective cases, the state would act as legal guardian over the incompetent aged's financial assets. The issue is highly controversial, even among professionals who work with the aged. There *are* two sides to this issue. An adult child might think of a greedy sister who has her eye on their aged mother's funds and say, "Good!", and a civil libertarian might be wary of this move.

Your state health department can tell you if this kind of legislation has been passed in your state.

Encouraging the Independent Parent to Stay Independent!

Naturally, the aged parent who is still ambulatory and who is well enough to do things for herself, is easier to make arrangements with and for. In fact, some aging parents are *very* independent.

• *A seventy-four-year old woman speaks.*

A woman who went to live with her daughter and son-in-law in the suburbs, moved back to the inner-city recently, into an apartment of her own. "I couldn't stand it out there," she said, "they were good to me, but I had no one to talk to when they were at work all day. There was no one outside to pass the time of day with, to talk to over the clothesline! So I got myself a little place in the city, in the neighborhood where I had lived for thirty years, and now I sit out on my stoop in the warm evenings and talk to my next-door neighbor—who's also in her seventies! I can walk to the main street, just two blocks away, and shop. All the shopkeepers remember me. The suburbs are for younger folk—too quiet for me!" Good for her!

The Parent Who Needs Help—and Hospitalization

What if your parent is growing *more* dependent? . . . is now too ill or disabled or confused to make independent decisions and moves? And what if you're the one who has to decide what the next best step is? For instance, what if you have to hospitalize your parent?

• *Getting pertinent information so you know what to do.*

Many grown children know very little about geriatric institutions and nursing homes and even how (and if) general hospitals have special services for the elderly. Too often—suddenly—the grown child must get quick answers. And too often, grown children find that *good* institutions for an aged parent are few and far-between.

Services for the Aged in a General Hospital

There are special services for the aged in a growing number of general hospitals, and in many cases, one staff person coordinates all these services.

• *Who's in charge of these services? Find out!*
If your parent is being admitted to the hospital, find out who this staff person is. Get her name and contact her. When you make direct contact with that staff person, you can let your parent's needs be known, and you'll have someone to file complaints with (if necessary).

Nursing Homes: Sometimes a Necessity

What if your parent becomes so ill or disabled with a long-term illness that home care is no longer possible? You've probably asked yourself several questions: "Can I try to take care of her at home?" "How can I put my parent away—I have so many guilt feelings?" "*How* will I find the right place?"

• *When it becomes too hard to take care of*
  your parent at home.
Can you take care of your parent in your home? There are women who have attempted to do this—and the cost is great. You may need to rent or buy expensive large-scale hospital equipment. You may need to reorganize your entire house. You may need to turn your home into a miniature hospital . . . and find that you have to turn a dining room, living room, or a study into a "hospital room"—disrupting the function and rhythm of your household. You will find that you can no longer easily have friends over; a tremendous amount of your time and energy will be constantly needed. You and your immediate family may suffer enormous stress. It can certainly

cost a great deal of money that you may not have; money that you've put away for your own retirement years.

• *Get the help of a social worker (to help you work out your guilt feelings).*

But, you may say, "I can't do this to my mother." And here is where you will find talking to a social worker helpful; you are going through a very difficult period, and a worker can help you look at your conflicts. You may feel you're "pushing" your parent out of your life; that you're "putting Ma in to die at that place"; that you're "getting rid" of your parent in this way. *Should* you do it? Can you afford *not* to do it?! Are there other alternatives? Which place? Where do you find this compassionate, experienced social worker? Look for a private non-profit social service agency in your area, perhaps the local Family & Children's Society . . . and fees are on a sliding scale.

• *Geriatric evaluation services.*

And are there other alternatives? Some states offer a geriatric evaluation service program for the aged about to be admitted to an institution. Upon request a visiting evaluation team—a social worker, a nurse and a physician—comes to the home and recommends the program best adapted to the needs of the aged parent, and sees whether institutionalization is *really* necessary. Ideally, the aged parent should be able to request this service; it would certainly put more control of her own life into her hands. But often a parent is too ill or too confused to take this kind of action, and the request must be made by the family. Call your state health department to see if this service is available in your area, and ask how you go about requesting it. This evaluation should include tracking (another word for follow-up), and if the team recommends your parent *can* stay home, they can make referrals for supportive home services. Of course, if they feel institutionalization is the only answer, they'll be helpful in recommending the proper institution. And the decision for institutionalization is always the aged parents—unless he or she is incapable (and this should *help* resolve your guilt feelings).

**Nursing Homes, Rest Homes, Homes for the Aged,
and Family Care Homes: the Differences**

* *Nursing homes.*

A nursing home provides individualized skilled nursing
care to patients when the doctor has indicated this is
needed. Your parent must have a doctor who is able to
visit her in the nursing home, although at times your parent *may* go to an outpatient department of a hospital or
the doctor's office for some of the treatment.

* *Rest homes . . . family care homes . . . homes
for the aged.*

A home for the aged, sometimes called a rest home,
and a family care home (which doesn't accommodate
more than several patients) doesn't provide such nursing
care, or may not have a licensed practical nurse on the
staff.

* *Which for your parent?*

If your mother does not need skilled nursing care but
does need someone with her all day (you may be working
full-time), the rest home or the family care home or the
so-called home for the aged may be your answer. Supervision, personal care (someone to bathe and feed your
parent), and housekeeping services are provided in these
homes. There is someone available if your parent needs
help in transferring from the bed to the wheelchair.

How to Choose a Nursing Home

* *Will they accept Medicare and Medicaid payments?*

*Be sure the nursing home you choose will take Medi-
care and Medicaid.* Otherwise the medical bills will be
staggering.

* *Choose a nursing home near your home.*

Try to choose a nursing home that is close to your
home. This will allow you to have the time and energy to
dash over to the institution to visit your parent regularly
without major disruptions in your day-to-day living. One

woman told me, "I found I wanted to be with my mother during mealtimes, because she had lost some of her motor control and she couldn't feed herself properly. The place is short of staff—the attendants don't always have the time to sit with her and feed her—and they'd take her food away before she had a chance to eat everything. She lost a lot of weight and this worried me. So now I go over three times a day and feed her. I couldn't do this if I didn't live close to the place—."

• *Choose a home that your parent will be comfortable in.*

Choose a nursing home where the staff and residents have the same kind of background as your parent. Does your mother speak only Italian or Yiddish? Does your father speak only Greek? Do the nurses and residents understand and speak that language? Is there a chapel or synagogue on the premises for your parent who wants to attend religious services regularly? Does your parent eat only Kosher food?

• *Visit!—ahead of time.*

Visit the facility before deciding on it. Visit *several* times. Make each visit leisurely and try to talk to families of patients. Ask them what they think of the place —the care, the food, the medical attention. Does the institution offer occupational therapy? Physical therapy? Recreational therapy? Some of the families you talk to may be defensive; they may feel guilty about placing their parent in a facility; they may be afraid to criticize the place, thinking that if they're found out, the staff will punish their parent or kick her out. Some of the families will not have noticed the things you're asking about. However, if you talk to enough people, you'll get some consistent important information.

"Ha!" snorted one irate son, "recreational therapy? Yeah, they'll tell you they have it—but all they do is strap my mother in front of a television set all day—and that's recreational therapy!"

One woman confided, upon being questioned, "I thought it was a good place, until I visited my mother and went to get her hairbrush out of the bureau drawer—and found it full of roaches!"

- *Notice the attitudes of the attendants.*

It is likely the attendents will be key people in your parent's life. They'll be the ones to change your parent's clothing and move her from the chair to the bed, and turn her over so she doesn't get bedsores. Notice their attitudes when they're with patients. Do they seem involved? Do they seem to care? Do they smile at the patients? Talk to them? Are they impatient? Do they rush the old people? Distrust a facility when they won't allow you to see the kitchen, or discourage you from visiting and looking the place over.

- *An official view of nursing homes.*

Even our government reports that the majority of nursing homes in our country do not give proper services. The Senate Special Committee on Aging's subcommittee on long-term care, based on a fifteen-year study of conditions in the nation's nursing homes, put out a report called *Nursing Home Care in the United States: Failure in Public Policy.* The report tells a story of horror and neglect. Neglect in the enforcement of basic minimum standards for nursing homes set by state officials and the Department of Health, Education and Welfare. It reports case after case of inhumane and neglectful treatment of patients by nursing home personnel and operators. Physical abuse; untreated infections; over-tranquilization; frequent medication errors; deaths that could have been avoided. The study states, "Despite the sizable commitment in the federal funds, HEW has been reluctant to issue forthright standards to provide patients with minimum protection . . . enforcement is left almost entirely to the states . . . a few do a good job, but most do not. The enforcement system in many states can be characterized as scandalous, ineffective, and in some cases, almost non-existent."

- *The plight of black aged.*

To compound the problem, only about 3 per cent of nursing home aged patients are black. Why? According to Hobart Jackson, founder and past president of the National Caucus on the Black Aged, aged black people do not have easy access to nursing home care. He explains that black nursing homes "can't produce matching funds and are not usually in a position to amortize loans." He adds that the black aged are in their own homes—and often *without* essential services. Jackson proposes that black nursing homes become centers to provide both residential and non-residential services in black neighborhoods—and that our government make this possible by providing financial assistance to help minority nursing homes upgrade their operations.

• *You have to look hard for a good place.*

However, nursing homes are sometimes the only answer for our parent, and some good ones *do* exist. You just have to look *very* hard . . . and you may have to settle for less than you'd prefer.

Your Feelings—and Your Parent's Feelings —During This Difficult Time

• *You need relief from the stress*

Whether your parent is in your home, her home, or a facility—be sure to leave yourself time away from your responsibilities. It will no doubt be a time of great stress for you. You'll need daily respites so you won't court fatigue and depression and anxiety.

• *Financial needs court worry.*

Probably you will be greatly concerned about money. Tell your parent's doctors if you're having financial problems. Ask them to lower their fees. There are many humane physicians who *will* charge you less—but they're not aware you need them to do this unless you tell them.

• *Don't be ashamed of your feelings.*

If your parent is very ill—perhaps terminally ill—and you know there is little or no hope, you may secretly wish for her quick death. It's nothing to be ashamed of. It's a common kind of wish. You're weary—and you're frightened. Your parent may be experiencing pain. It *is* terrifying for you to see your money ooze away on medical treatment that perhaps does no good. You may picture yourself, in the years ahead, ill and alone, with no funds left. It *is* a very difficult time for you, and the more sup-

port you can get at this point—the better. Support? From
friends, family and perhaps a social worker to talk to—

• *Be aware of your parent's feelings.*

The aging parent who is ill or disabled and is dependent
on her children also feels bad. She feels worthless because
she *is* a burden. It is a lonely and terrifying time of her
life.

"I keep thinking of my impending death," a seventy-
nine-year-old woman told me with despair.

"Don't the children realize it's as hard for me as it is
for them?" asked an eighty-year-old woman.

"No one ever thinks they'll get like this," an aged
woman told me from her wheelchair. "I never thought
I would."

• *Find someone to confide in.*

Perhaps you can talk to each other about your feelings.
You and your parent. Perhaps you can't. Each of you
should have someone to confide in and to share your fears
with, and perhaps you can arrange this through an unusually perceptive person in the family or through a friend or
a professional helper.

• *Don't deny your parent's need to talk
about her anxieties.*

Possibly your parent needs to talk about her impending
death. Is this too hard for you? Can your sister do it more
easily? Can your minister? Don't ignore this need (and
your parent will let you know she needs to do this by
talking about it!). Confront it. If you can't, find someone
who can. Don't deny your parent's impending death; if
you do so, you will be invalidating her *life*. How do you
confront it? By just listening when your parent talks; by
not withdrawing; by not denying that she will die; by
sitting quietly and just listening; by taking her seriously.
However, leave her hope . . .

How You Can Grow Stronger from This Experience

Through your aging, dependent parent, you're being
confronted with your own aging. You're being forced to

look at the possible losses you may suffer: the loss of health and income and dignity and privacy and relationships and—vigor. Being confronted with our own impending aging is never easy.

• *Learn from your parent's behavior—and self-image.*

We can learn from the way our parents have aged. If we see our parent can't "let go" and insists on giving unwanted advice to her grown children, we can learn a lesson. If we watch our mother passively accept everyone's orders and suggestions we can learn from this. If we see a parent who had nothing left after the years of child-bearing and taking care of a husband, we can look at ourselves. And we can take lessons from our parent's *strengths,* as well. . . .

• *Death, dying, and old age—a silence.*

We seldom see articles that tell us what to do about our aged, dependent parent. It is a subject that is rarely dealt with in film and theater. Is this because old age and death are taboo subjects in our society—at odds with our values of productivity and profit?

• *Explore your feelings with other women;*
  it's strengthening!

All the more reason for women over 50 to sit down with friends to explore their feelings about their own aging and their parent's aging; to find solutions together; to grow *stronger* together. . . .

CHAPTER 7

What No One Ever Tells the Over-50 Widow

❦ ❧

The Despair and the Anger: How to Cope with These Feelings

Have you been widowed within the past few years? A high percentage of women are widowed by the time they're in their sixties. Or your husband may have died when you were in your fifties, or your seventies. Black women are—as a group—widowed relatively early; black men live to an average of 60.1 years, while white men have a life expectancy of 67 years.

Whether you were fifty-seven or seventy when you were left alone, you probably reacted (and may still be reacting) the same way: at first you felt numb (shock); then you felt so down you didn't want to get out of bed in the morning and sometimes when you sat down your mind drifted and you forgot what you had started out to do (depression); you also felt hopeless (despair).

But no one told you you'd also feel *rage*. Yes—rage. You feel angry because he left you—abandoned you—to take care of everything yourself. You feel furious because he left you at a time when you are feeling the terror of getting old and sick and dependent. You may be furious at your friends—the ones who still have their husbands. ("Why *me?* Why did *my* husband have to die—!"). And when you do feel angry at your husband, you ask yourself, with feelings of guilt and shame, how you can be angry at a dead man. Especially if he had been a good husband, a caring man.

Sit down, lean back, take a deep breath—and realize that you wouldn't be human if you didn't feel angry. Most women feel angry after their spouse dies—no matter how good their marriages were. This feeling stems from the child in us who still wants to be taken care of. . . . and we all have a child as well as an adult living inside of us. Subsequently, we feel guilty because we felt angry, and we concentrate on the guilty feelings instead of trying to understand our angry feelings. Why do we do this? Because it seems more acceptable to have guilt feelings after our husbands die than to have angry feelings. We even aggravate our guilt feelings, telling ourselves, "I should have made him go to a doctor sooner!" or, "I should have taken him seriously when he complained about the pain." Why does it seem more acceptable to feel guilty than to feel angry? Because we're taught, all of our lives, that it's wrong to feel angry. Because we have the mistaken notion that feeling guilty means we care about someone else and that feeling anger means we care only about *ourselves.*

• *Examine your feelings.*

Let's look at the guilt feelings you may feel toward your dead husband and let's look at the angry feelings you may feel toward him. Are you feeling guilty over the times you yelled, "Drop dead!" when he was alive? Or because you called him names only a few weeks before he died? Well, maybe he was rotten at times—like the time he might have had an affair with a neighbor of yours—and maybe you did store up a lot of anger during the years he was alive and maybe you never did really tell him about the rage you felt *at the times you felt it.* So you still feel angry and now it's too late to tell him and the anger is still there. Even if he was faithful to you all of those thirty-five years, you may have built up anger about other things: Perhaps he didn't take enough responsibility with decision-making in all the years of your mar-

riage (and now you're left with *all* the decisions); perhaps
he never really *talked* to you, listened to you, and wanted
to know how *you* felt in the many years of your marriage,
and now, at the age of sixty, what chance do you have to
find *anyone* who will!! So what's wrong with feeling angry about all of those bad things? (Even good marriages
have bad things in them.) And what's wrong with being
angry because he died and left you high and dry with no
one to love you and take care of you? Stop feeling guilty
about it. Start realizing that, of course, there were leftover love-hate feelings that you both had toward each
other when he died—that's a normal part of what happens when a spouse dies. FACE the angry feelings and
the reasons for them, because the sooner you're able to
face your real feelings AND the reasons for your feelings,
the better you will feel.

• *Talk to an understanding person.*
   You can't work out the leftover angry feelings with
your dead husband, but you can with someone else who
can really help. Who? Your minister, your rabbi, your
priest—or a social worker, a psychologist, a psychiatrist
or a very good friend. But be sure your good friend is
non-judgmental and is not concerned with who was
"right" or who was "wrong" in your marriage. Choose a
friend who tries to understand why you feel angry, who
understands that life is black and white *and* gray, and
who is not concerned with what people "should" feel, but
with what people *do* feel. I remember a widow telling
me, "I spent hours—literally hours—talking my head off
to Nora. Afterwards, when I felt so much better, I felt
really grateful to her. And then I realized: All she had
done was nod her head while I talked! She nodded her
head up and down, day after day, and that's what worked.
Can you imagine?"
   Yes, I can imagine. Nodding her head meant, "I understand," and "I know how you feel," and "It's okay
that you're angry." And that's exactly what you need
after you've been widowed—*someone* to reassure you that
all the extreme and strong feelings you're experiencing
that frighten you are normal and understandable.
   You *don't* need someone to tell you that Jack was right
in getting involved with someone else because you had be-

come fat and neglected yourself. You don't need someone to look at you with reproach and say, "How can you be angry with him? He was such a fine man!" You *do* need someone who does not keep a scoreboard on who hurt whom ten years ago; who does understand that anger is acceptable; who particularly knows and understands that you can love someone and still be very angry—and who can reassure you that once you vent and understand your anger, it will slowly disapppear.

Grieving: How to Do It

Grieving? That's another story. Grieving is mourning a loss. Like working out anger, it is legitimate and necessary. It's urgent you *LET* yourself grieve!

• *It's important to grieve!*
Don't let anyone tell you, "It's time you stopped grieving." YOU'LL know when it's time to stop grieving, because when it's time, you'll simply stop. Grieving is therapeutic. Grieving can take a very long time. As long as two or three years. There is no set limit. And the bad feelings don't go away suddenly. They go away very very slowly, so you hardly notice when you've begun to feel better. One day, however, you suddenly realize that you've lately had quite a few good days. Days without pain.

• *Let yourself cry and scream and talk out loud to your dead husband.*
There is a correct way to grieve. That means simply this: If you permit yourself to feel bad, you will feel better sooner! Cry as much as you need to, talk to people about your husband as much as you want to, and scream when you're alone if you feel like it. If it helps, pretend your husband is still alive and in the room with you, and talk to him. Ask him who you should call about the broken air conditioner. Complain about your son, who didn't call or visit you last week. Tell him how desperately lonely you are. And when you don't have to talk to him anymore—you won't. Many many women work their way through their grief by using this technique.

Who Are You, Now that You're No Longer "Arthur's Wife"?

You've been a widow for over a year and you still think of yourself as Arthur's wife . . . or Lou's wife . . . or Harold's wife. Okay, you're muttering angrily, so what if I do! You're feeling defiant, resentful, and you feel like yelling, "I *was* Arthur's wife—for thirty-four years!" That's true, you were, but you were also Marcia, or Ruth, or Claire—and you *still are*. A new man in your life is not going to be attracted to "Arthur's wife"; he'll be interested in you, Marcia. If you think of yourself as "Arthur's wife" you'll act like Arthur's wife, instead of acting like Marcia. That means you will think of yourself as an appendage of Arthur and you will act like an appendage of Arthur instead of Marcia, who has an identity of her own. That means that you will act as though you are still married, and you will act as *Arthur* expected you to do.

• *Regain your own identity—or build a new one.*

But—was that the complete you? When you were married did you stop wearing bright red because Arthur hated the color and said it made you look cheap? Did you slowly stop going to the ballet because Arthur was bored by the ballet? DARE to rediscover *Marcia*. Take the ceramics class you never found time for when you were married . . . join a rock-collecting group because you always wanted to but you didn't because you didn't want to leave Arthur alone . . . argue over politics at dinner parties even though Arthur hated it when you did. As you begin doing what *you*, Marcia, want to do, you will begin thinking of yourself as Marcia. You will stop thinking of yourself as "Arthur's wife." In beginning to think of yourself as an individual and not someone's wife, OTHER people will begin seeing you as an individual. And they'll begin to *treat* you as an individual.

• *Why some women continue living through their dead husband.*

There are some women who persist in being "Arthur's wife" because, essentially, that was a child's role and they still want to be a child. What do I mean by that? Well, living through someone else, being an appendage to someone else, means you're being propped up by someone else. You're not standing up straight by YOURSELF. That is satisfying to the child part of us because it means that someone is taking care of us. When we are used to having a husband make decisions for us and take care of us it is sometimes very hard to let go of this kind of dependency . . . even after our husbands die. So, as a consolation, we continue to think of ourselves as "Arthur's wife" and we continue to see ourselves as someone who will be taken care of. Thinking of ourselves in this way keeps us from acting as independent persons because we're always secretly hoping a rescuer will come to take care of us again. Of course, the trap in this is that if we *don't* find someone to take care of us—we might not grow up enough to take care of ourselves.

- *Two women's stories.*

Elayne was like that. You'd hardly believe it, to look at her. She's almost six feet tall, statuesque, and very self-confident looking. Her husband, Bernie, was a little shorter than she, and he was a quiet guy, almost placid. He adored Elayne. He waited on her hand and foot. He wouldn't allow her to change the light bulb in the kitchen herself because he didn't want her to climb on the step stool. He brought her breakfast in bed every morning. He took care of all the bills. Three years after Bernie's sudden death, Elayne still thought of herself as Bernie's wife. She still didn't want to let go of the "child" self-image she had. She was still looking for someone to take care of her.

"I don't get it," one of the men who had dated her told me, "she seems so capable, and then—when you get to know her—she seems to fall apart. She used to call me in the middle of the night if she couldn't sleep! She was like a child."

But people *are* able to change and grow, and it can be marvelous to watch. Denise is one of these people. She had been a quiet, timid girl and then a quiet, timid woman. She had married a European-born man, Sol, when she was very young, and Sol had the traditional view that a woman's place is in the home; that a woman should live solely through her husband and children. And that's how it went in their household for thirty-three years, until Sol became critically ill. Denise then nursed him for the next two years, and that's when I could see her personality change. As his condition deteriorated and he could no longer handle the family finances and the family business, it was Denise who took over the checkbook and who made the decisions about their property and their business. She hired a woman to come in every day to stay with Sol while she went down to run their hardware store. The business prospered; Denise discovered she had a real head for business. When Sol died, Denise was already seeing herself as an independent businesswoman; as an individual, and not as "Sol's wife." Denise married again last year, and the man she married considers her an absolute equal when it comes to running their real estate business.

"I didn't know who I really was during those thirty-three years," Denise told me thoughtfully, as I sat in her office talking to her one afternoon. "Lost years . . ."

° *Become your own person now!*
Start now to assert your own identity, to become your own person. When, months after your husband died, your sister still introduces you as "Joe's wife," take her aside later and gently tell her you prefer to be introduced by your own name. If she's open to it, tell her why. It could be a good learning experience for her—especially if she still has her husband!

Don't Move Right Away! Don't Sell Your Furniture Yet!

Expect to feel shaky when you finally begin to pick up all the pieces of your life. Make decisions slowly. Don't be in a hurry.

• *Make big changes later.*
Thinking of moving? Wait. Take your time. Why? Because leaving a familiar house or apartment is a strain on your emotions and your body. You're used to that familiar amount of space around you in each room; you're used to your favorite chair being in a particular place . . .

and all of this gives you a sense of security. Value feelings of security at this time in your life. It can make you feel more glued together right now. Don't move while you're feeling so rocky. And when you do feel more like yourself, sit down with a sheet of paper and a pencil and list exactly what you want in a place to live. For instance, are big old trees on the grounds important to you? Do you want a separate dining room instead of an L-shaped living room (which is a combination living-dining room)? Do you mind living in an apartment house where there are small children?

• *Trust your own judgment.*

Be wary of your children's advice, "Ma, sell everything. You don't need that big dining room table." "Ma, don't move downtown. It's dangerous." Your children love you and they're concerned about you, and they *think* they know what's good for you. YOU'RE the one who knows what's good for you. Trust your own feelings. *Listen* to your own feelings. The big dining room table they want you to sell might mean wonderful brunches on Sunday mornings for all the new friends you're going to meet later. Living downtown might mean you'll be able to walk to the central library for lectures and free films during lonely afternoons. You can always sell the big dining room table at a later time, and you can always move back to the suburbs if you find you don't like it downtown.

You Still Have to Eat!

• *Take vitamins.*

Experiment with health foods. Pay attention to nutrition. You're going to find that you're eating differently from when you cooked for your husband. Right now it might not seem worth it to cook two vegetables with fish or chicken or beef every evening. It might seem easier to throw a frozen dinner in the oven, or to simply make a quick sandwich. So take vitamins.

• *Eat healthy foods to help you cope with stress.*

Your energy level might be low for a long time. Keeping juice in the refrigerator (no preparation) will help

that. Also keep fresh fruit and yogurt in the house. You'll
feel better and your skin will look better if you nibble on
an apple, a pear . . . if you eat some yogurt for lunch
instead of a sandwich.

Later, when you feel better, you might want to start
cooking again—or you might not. If you don't feel like it,
don't feel guilty. You can eat those carefully balanced
nutritious meals in restaurants and at friend's dinner
parties. Eat cheese (quick and easy), and fresh fruit and
yogurt at home. Quick healthy foods, like nuts and raw
vegetables. Glasses of cold milk. One widow I know buys
already prepared dinners from a catering service. No
trouble—*and* nutritious.

• *Eat foods the over-50 woman especially needs.*

After menopause is completed, women have to think
about heart health as much as men do (we have less estrogen produced by our bodies, and it is thought estrogen protects us, to a large degree, from heart attacks), so
cut down on saturated fats. Eat less meat and more
chicken and veal and fish. A word of warning—a diet very
high in protein is unhealthy if you suffer from either gout
or kidney stones.

Fiber is essential for intestinal function, and helps prevent intestinal cancer, diverticular disease, and other disorders. Which foods have fiber? Whole grains, fruits, and
vegetables.

Cut down your calories, now that you're over 50. Staying slim is one way of guarding your health, and you've
possibly noticed that it's harder to take weight *off*, now
that you're in your mid-years or older.

Losing your husband means you're under stress. Your
resistance may be lower, making you more prone to illness. Fight back—with a balanced diet, vitamin supplements, and a carefully-watched calorie count.

The Loss of a Sexual Relationship

• *You miss closeness, too (maybe more than sex).*

You miss sex and you're glad I'm finally mentioning it
because how can you *tell* anyone this? In fact, you miss it
so much you almost ache . . . and, of course, it's not just

sex; it's mostly being close to a man, being held and being loved.

• *You have many options for your future.*

Fortunately, it is the 1970's instead of the 1930's or 1940's. Then no girl went "all the way" except a "bad girl." Now women have many more options in their sex lives and life styles. That means you have choices in how you will handle your growing sexual needs, and any way you choose is more or less acceptable to society. It means that many respectable older women are living with many respectable older men without being married. It means that the women over 50 who have deliberately chosen to be celibate are not considered "freaks" or "strange." It means that the older women who have chosen to have sexual relationships only with other women are at least silently tolerated in most communities. It certainly means that many older women do have men stay over in their apartments occasionally and if they're reasonably discreet, no one even seems to care. In the more urban and sophisticated neighborhoods, there is not even a *need* for discretion.

• *Do what's comfortable for you.*

The important question is how comfortable you would be with any of these options. Do only what is comfortable for you. If you still have feelings of wanting to be a "good girl" with all the implications of the phrase, fine. You may have had some pretty strong teaching and conditioning in the earlier years of your life about this.

• *Realize you may change your mind later.*

Just realize that what you're not comfortable doing now is something you may be comfortable doing two years from now. Don't tell yourself, "I'd *never* do that—." People change, and what you thought was right when you were twelve years old was not necessarily what you thought was right when you were thirty-five-years-old. If you *do* want to know more about the changing attitudes about sex, read and read some more; talk to some younger women about it. This does not mean that you are obligated to act in ways that are distasteful to you; it merely means that you are intelligently curious about a changing society, and you want to know about all of the options open to women that were not open before, so you *can* consciously pick and choose a way of life that is comfortable for you. And if you decide what you want for the moment, don't decide what you want five years from now, or even three years from now. Three years from now you will possibly be different . . . because you will have had three years of thinking and three years of experience that will shape you in ways that you simply cannot predict right now.

Loneliness and Aloneness (There's a Difference!)

Loneliness: Hundreds of widows have told me this is the feeling that causes them the most anguish. If you were fortunate during your marriage, your husband was your best friend, so you weren't lonely. And, if you weren't so fortunate, there was at least an animal comfort at times in just being together. . . .

• *Of course you miss the intimacy.*

If you had a good marriage, you miss the intimacy . . . someone to talk to . . . to take trips with . . . to share with and to be with. You might even miss these things more than sex. It's tough no longer having someone to share morning coffee with, not having someone to laugh with, not having someone as interested in your children as you are, and not having someone you like and love in bed with you every night with his familiar shape and voice. I share a moment of quiet grief with you. I know this is the most difficult part of your life as a widow.

• *Coping with loneliness.*

How can you cope? First, get your pencil out and a sheet of paper (it's marvelous what lists can do!) and write down the times of the day and night when you're feeling the lowest, the most lonely. Then set about making plans for just those times. You'll probably realize that your worst times are every evening from 5:00 p.m. on, and every Saturday night—*and* all day Sunday and special holidays.

• *Bad Sundays.*

Sundays can be devastating, can't they? You can't fill up time by shopping (but in some cities the stores *are* open now) and many of your friends are with their own families. Sundays are when you and your husband did things together—rides in the country, visits to relatives, cocktail parties, or just lazing around the house reading the Sunday papers. Now Sundays seem still and dead and you wish for Monday morning to come quickly.

There is no doubt that it will be easier for you to cope with Sundays if you live in a large city rather than in the country or in a small town. However, no matter where you live you can begin to start your own tradition of inviting friends and favorite relatives over for a leisurely Sunday breakfast or brunch. Make your house or apartment the place where they look forward to coming every Sunday from twelve noon till three. If you have a money problem, just have two or three people over at a time and serve simple inexpensive foods, like cheese omelettes or waffles, lots of hot coffee, and the least expensive fresh fruit in season.

People *love* being invited out for Sunday brunch—it's a cozy kind of social situation where no one has to get dressed up and where everyone *feels* casual. And don't have the same people over every Sunday. Vary your guest list. Ask a guest to bring a guest; this way you'll meet new people. By three o'clock, when your company slowly begins to think of leaving, you'll feel pleasantly tired, you *won't* feel lonely, and you'll be glad to have the rest of the day to yourself so you can read the Sunday paper, wash your hair, or spend an hour on the phone with your sister or daughter.

If you live in a larger town or city, look in the newspapers to see if there is a regular kind of lecture series that takes place every Sunday that you might enjoy. A friend of mine, who is not a churchgoer, saw a notice in her local paper advertising a Sunday lecture series sponsored by the Ethical Culture Society (you might have an Ethical Culture Society in your city). She went to the first of the series, enjoyed hearing a scientist speak on the relationship of science to ethics, shared refreshments afterwards with everyone and attended regularly thereafter every Sunday. Another friend discovered that her local

museum sponsors a concert every Sunday afternoon
through the winter months. She then found Sundays *important*. And another widow called a woman she had recently met and liked, who was also alone and asked her
if she wanted to go to dinner and a movie on a Sunday afternoon. It worked out so well that they go every
Sunday—*and* they've added two other widows to their
group.

"Until I found my own special way of handling Sundays," my friend Ruth told me, "I made it a habit to get
out of the apartment in the morning to buy my Sunday
newspaper. Just walking to the drugstore made me feel a
little more human. I'd have my first cup of coffee there.
Just getting out of the house—."

• *Lonely dusks, lonely nighttimes.*

How can you cope with the loneliness that comes at
dusk? Every night? If you're interested in what's going on
in the community and in the world, switch the television
on to the evening news at 6:00 p.m. Make it a habit to
slowly eat your dinner while you're watching the news. It
will be far better than eating in empty silence and you'll
be more interesting because you'll be learning about
what's happening in the world. And who said you have to
eat your dinner at the kitchen table or at the dining room
table? If your television set is in the living room, set up a
card table or a standing tray and eat in there. It will feel
luxurious and it will be a completely different eating pattern from what you had with your husband. Also, you
won't be staring at an empty chair across your kitchen
table.

After supper? If you've been working all day in the
business world you'll probably welcome the rest of the
evening to take a long relaxing bath, to write letters, to
read a book in bed. If you're not working and you've
been in the house all day, make it a point to get out in
the evening, even if it's only a short visit to a neighbor's
apartment. Later, as your energy level goes up, raise the
tempo of your weekday evening activities. Join an evening class in sewing, drama, or dancing. Get together
once a week and play cards with two or three of your
friends or neighbors. Take an auto mechanics course at
a local woman's college. Go square dancing. Join an or-

ganization. Do volunteer work at your local state mental hospital. But get out of the house at least two nights a week.

• *Holidays*

If you probably aren't going to spend Thanksgiving and Christmas (and other meaingful holidays) with your family, plan ahead—ask some other women who are alone to have a potluck dinner at your house. Or invite a couple of students who are away from home to share a gala dinner with you. (Just call your local college for referrals; foreign students who can't get home are usually very appreciative—and they can be very interesting guests.)

• *Plan ahead for Saturdays!*

Saturday nights? Plan an occasional dinner party (and it can be inexpensive—like spaghetti, salad, garlic bread, and sherbert). Look around and notice that women no longer need male escorts to go out on Saturday night. Call a friend to join you at a festive restaurant. Buy season tickets for the theater, making sure your tickets are scheduled for Saturday nights. If you have a car, plan an all-day Saturday trip to a nearby town where you can antique-browse, take snapshots, visit a museum, and eat at a country inn. By the time you get home, you'll be pleasantly exhausted and you'll look at the clock and realize Saturday evening is almost over.

Selma, who is in her sixties and widowed, discovered that there is a peninsula near her town that has clusters of small interesting villages on it. She spent the entire summer visiting a different village every Saturday, and fell in love with the fascinating area.

"What I would do," she told me, "is leave the house early Saturday morning with a map and a packed lunch. I'd arrive at the village about two hours later, stay there for the afternoon, walking and taking pictures—and, by the way, when you're photographing old houses all kinds of people come up to you and start conversations!—and then I'd ask about a local inn for supper (there's always an old country inn in these villages), and I'd relax over whatever kind of food the region was known for."

"Was it lonely, doing this by yourself?" I asked.

"As soon as I got my camera out, I stopped thinking about myself," Selma said. "In fact, I'm now thinking of putting the photographs together in some sort of book. I've really managed to get some great pictures of some beautiful old Federal houses."

Needless to say, Selma was so tired when she got home on Sautrday night that all she could do was take a bath and fall into bed. She didn't have the time or energy to feel lonely.

So perhaps the answer to loneliness—besides being with good friends—is to find something bigger than yourself to consume your time and your emotions. Which will it be for you—photography, painting, writing, hiking, birdwatching, politics, an organization? Turn your loneliness into CREATIVE ALONENESS!

• *What is creative aloneness?*

Creative aloneness is when you enjoy being by yourself; when you find *yourself* good company; when you are so involved in what you're doing that you don't *need* another person.

And when you reach the point of turning your loneliness into creative aloneness, you'll turn to other people out of desire—not *need*.

Should You Move in with Your Children?

• *No! No! No! (generally speaking).*

A general rule: Do not move in with your kids. Out of love for you, or because of guilt feeling or on impulse, they might beg you to, or at least ask you to. Don't.

• *Why "no"?*

Because if you do move in with them, they'll probably see you as MOTHER—and mothers do not have affairs and mothers do not let men sleep over (at least you should have a choice!) and mothers are expected to love baby-sitting regularly and cooking big meals on all holidays for the entire family. And do you really want to be tied down like that? If you're saying "Yes, yes I do, because I've always been a mother. It's the only role I know and the only role I'm used to!" then stop and consider the following problems which may arise:

Your children will probably expect you to take their advice on everything because they'll feel you *need* their advice. Unfortunately, they may have been brainwashed by society and they may tend to see every woman over 50 as a little feebleminded.

Your children will get huffy if you don't always heed the advice they cared enough to *give* you. Your children will probably act in ways that will get on your nerves. Chances are you will disapprove of at least some procedures they use in bringing up their children.

Finally, your feelings are bound to be hurt (no matter what your head says) when they plan social events for their peers and you're not included—when they don't invite you to the posh dinner party they planned for Saturday night.

· *Try it first—on a trial basis.*

If you still think you want to give it a try, then try it without giving up your apartment or house. Try it without selling your furniture. In other words, move in on a temporary basis (suggest to your children you want to try it on for two months as a trial) and leave yourself something to fall back on: your own place and your own furniture.

· *It's their house!*

Remember, it's their house, so they're the ones who really have the right to lay down the ground rules. Ask them to discuss these ground rules before you move in (they may call it "ideas" or "suggestions" instead of ground rules, but they're really ground rules) and if you find, in this initial talk, things sound too rigid to you, or even unfair, reconsider your position. It's not too late to change your mind. You don't HAVE to move in with them. But if you do move in, you still will have your apartment or house to go back to if it doesn't work out.

· *Be sensitive to their needs—if you do*
  move in with them.

If you do make this move, observe the following two rules (YOUR rules) all the time and no matter how much it hurts:

1. Never give them advice about anything.
2. Ask for as few favors as possible

To elaborate—it's very easy to tell your daughter-in-law unthinkingly that your son wouldn't be so grouchy in the morning if she fixed him a hot breakfast (like you used to). She doesn't want to hear that kind of interfering mother-in-law advice—and she's right. It's none of your business (no matter how sweet you sound when you suggest it). It's also unbelievably easy and tempting to suggest to your son-in-law that he count to ten so he won't lose his temper and spank your grandson for getting mud on the rug. That, too, is none of your business.

Favors? Oh, it's so easy to fall into the trap of asking for favors, especially if you have no car or don't drive. "Would you mind dropping me off?" is a dangerous question. Why? Because in a very short time your busy daughter and son-in-law and your eighteen-year-old grandson are going to get sick and tired of "dropping you off" and rather than tell you, they might seethe inside.

Are you feeling hurt already? Are you saying to yourself, "If they really loved me they'd *want* to take me places. They'd *welcome* my advice"? If you ARE feeling this way, you may feel even worse later. It is a perfect no-fail signal that you will be happier living apart from your children.

• *They didn't ask you?*

Maybe you're reading this and it suddenly occurs to you—"they *didn't* ask me to live with them!" You feel a lump in your throat, you feel like crying, and you feel it means they don't like you and they don't love you. But, no! Think about it from a positive point of view. Chances are you should feel flattered. Maybe they didn't ask you to live with them because they don't consider you old and feeble. Because they know you're still young and vital enough to want to make you *own* free life! And because the adult part of them realizes they don't want to share their vulnerabilities and their faults and their frailties on a day-by-day basis with *anyone;* they would feel too exposed. *And* because they realize that your move means a lot of stress for YOU. Don't feel hurt. Be glad you can have intimacy at a distance—it's easier.

See Your Children As PEOPLE!

It is most important to remember that you can have a wonderful relationship with your children *without* living with them. But you must first define how many of their demands you are willing to meet and vice versa. Be there if they need you (unless they make a habit of asking you to baby-sit and you don't want to). Don't be a martyr if they don't call every day (after all, their life is much busier than yours, especially if they have small children). Never pop in to visit without an invitation (they could be having an intimate moment together in the bedroom or your daughter might have a bad headache). And try looking upon every moment spent with them as moments spent with good friends, rather than moments spent with your *children*. This way you'll have a much better opportunity to get to know them as the people that they really are, and it'll be nice to have the chance to discover those interests you truly have in common—that you all love Bergman films, or playing scrabble.

- *Don't be a Critical Parent.*
You must not play the role of *Critical Parent*. If you look at them as close friends and not as your children, they'll *feel* more like your close friends, and they'll *act* more like your close friends. They will feel really good toward you and not *obligated* to you. This establishes a climate where they will feel able to share their real feelings with you and disagree with your political views and not role-play in certain ways they think you expect.

- *Seek an open and equal relationship.*
In other words, you can have an honest and open relationship with them . . . which is the only kind of relationship that leads to real intimacy and enjoyment.

The Car in Your Life

- *Learn to drive!*
If you're living anywhere but New York City, learn to drive if you don't already know how. Many a widow has

said, "My husband took me everywhere. I didn't know how to drive. So now I just don't go out as much, unless my friends pick me up." Depending on friends or relatives for transportation can mean many an evening spent at home. It'll make a world of difference in your life if you learn to drive. You'll feel independent because you'll *be* independent.

· *Are you too old to learn?*

Can an over-50 woman learn to drive? I asked a seasoned driving instructor, and he said that older people may tend to be more cautious than younger people—sometimes a little over-cautious—but that is the only difference. Countless over-50 women have learned to drive later in life. Many of them decided to learn when they were left with their husband's car after the death of their spouse.

· *Are you afraid to learn?*

Are you avoiding learning when you say, "I'm too nervous"? At least three women in their sixties have told me that driving soothes their nerves. And you're never too old to learn *anything*—it just might take a little longer to learn, that's all.

· *Taking care of your car.*

If your husband always took care of your car, and you look outside and see the big monster, realize it's freezing weather and wonder if it'll start—take an auto-mechanics course. Then, after the completion of this kind of course, you'll *know* what to do. And you'll feel more secure knowing that each strange sound you hear does not mean you have to take it to the garage. You'll also learn how to change a flat tire; knowledge that will come in very handy if and when you're stuck on a lonely road, miles from a telephone. You've heard all your life that women are not adept at learning mechanical things? A myth. We believe the myth because it's a lesson we were taught when we were little. Remember? You got the doll for Christmas while your brother got those mysterious-looking repair sets? But everyone is now realizing that women can and do learn how to do everything and anything. Have you seen the photographs of women climbing telephone poles to repair the wires, and have you noticed a lot more women working in gas stations (pumping gas!), and driving cabs?

Where do you go to find an auto-mechanics course? Call local colleges or your Y.W.C.A., or call the adult and community education department of your board of education. And remember—once you've completed the course, no car mechanic can present you with a big bill for an insignificant job, or tell you that you need a major kind of repair job when you don't. You'll know better.

Your Pocketbook: Shrunken with Widowhood?

Money. Finances. A big pain after you've been widowed. Perhaps you nursed an ill husband through a long debilitating sickness before he died—a terminal-illness that drained most of your financial resources. Perhaps your husband was not adequately insured, and you were left with little or no money after his death. This is terrifying isn't it?

• *Learn how to budget.*

If you were one of those wives who never handled the family finances, you may now feel panicky, helpless. But that does not mean you can't be as good as your husband was at counting . . . because that's all there is to it—counting and deciding, counting and deciding. There is nothing overwhelming about making out a budget and there is no mystique to it (although some people pretend there is).

• *Ask a woman to teach you how.*

Sit down with a woman you like and trust who is already handling her own finances and lay your cards on the table—tell her you know nothing about handling money, and you want her to please teach you what to do. Why go to a *woman* for help? Because if you see a *woman*, rather than a man, competently taking care of her own finances, you'll quickly begin to believe that women *can* do this, which means *you* can do it! And don't be afraid to ask for help: people are really flattered by this kind of request.

• *Get the financial facts.*

If you don't know already, find out from your lawyer or accountant where your husband's safe deposit box is; where the key is . . . where the bankbooks are. Get all the details from your insurance man about your husband's insurance policies. Find out from your stockbroker (if you have one) what you should know about each investment your husband has made. Get information about your mortgage and your house payments and the taxes on your house. Call your Social Security Administration office to find out what Social Security benefits you're entitled to and how to apply for them. If you're sixty-five, did you know that you get an additional personal exemption on your income tax? That you can get certain services at reduced costs, such as reduced bus fares (in some communities), discounts on drugs, and discounts on your movie theater tickets? Call your city or county commission on Aging for information on this (and ask them if your Social Security-Medicare card will suffice as proof that you *are* over sixty-five). Find out (if you're over sixty-five) if you can get a reduction in your real estate tax (your city municipal building office or county court house office can give you this information.) This is being done in various areas throughout the country.

• *Make records . . . Keep records.*

Keep a simple ledger and get in the habit of recording your income and expenses. This will help you become more conscious of how you spend your money and how you *should* spend your money. If you plan to work after your husband's death, call your Social Security Administration office and ask them how much you can earn before it reduces your benefit payments. Never discard your husband's birth certificate or his pension papers from his ex-employer or his military service record. You may need to refer to these important papers much later: it may mean extra money in your pocketbook. And keep *your* birth certificate in a safe place. Keep all your important papers in one place.

• *Watch your spending.*

If you find that you have to watch your spending, close your charge accounts. The interest is not worth it, and even if you arrange your account in a way in which you don't have to pay interest, merely having a charge account encourages impulse buying. Buy a used automobile. Buy used appliances. With prudent shopping you can do as well (if not better) as when you buy a new item, as far as the condition the car or appliance is in. Some of the best-dressed women I know buy most of their clothes in thrift shops. Most cities have at least one thrift shop where wealthy women sell their clothes after just a few wearings. Imagine getting a two-hundred dollar cotton dress for twenty dollars! Thrift shops are also great places for classic, timeless cashmere sweaters and tweed skirts.

· *Watch out for con men!*

Especially because you are handling your own finances, you'll want to be extra wary. Don't take anyone's advice when they tell you to buy stocks that will make you rich quickly . . . especially if you never bought stocks and bonds when your husband was alive. Immediately after your husband's death is not the time to start buying things you know nothing about. Don't let people talk you into giving more money to charity than you can afford. Realize that perhaps you can no longer afford to give at all to certain charities to which you always contributed as a couple (and don't feel guilty about this!). Be suspicious of surefire "cures" for any chronic ailment (expensive cures). Older people are approached frequently by high-pressure land salesmen. If a fast-talking, charming man tries to sell you land in Arizona or Florida or *any* state that you don't reside in and you're tempted to put your money into his hands, before buying check out his company with the Department of Housing and Urban Development, Office of Interstate Land Sales Registration, Washington, D. C. 20422 . . . and of course you'll want to visit the site. Beware of the person who wants you to put up a large investment or buy *anything,* or who wants you to risk your capital in any way, and realize that door-to-door salesmen usually are selling items where you make many installment payments at a high interest.

· *Learn how to be an intelligent consumer.*

You'll want to make sure that you are getting the most for your money in all areas. Make it a point to completely understand what kind of medical coverage you have, whether it's Medicare (and you get this information from your Social Security office) or whether it's a commercial insurance policy. If you're purchasing medical insurance (*or* car insurance), comparison-shop. Save money when you make purchases by sending away to Consumer Product Information, Washington, D. C. 20407, for their *Index of Federal Publications about Consumer Products. Planning for the Later Years* is one of their most informative pamphlets (catalog number 1770-003) and it's fifty cents. Call your central library for referrals to books on consumerism.

Take out a loan to convert your home into two apartments, and then you'll have property income. Rent out that extra bedroom to a foreign student at your local college (call the college's housing bureau and give them your name).

• *If you've signed on the dotted line—and regret it.*

If you have gotten into a situation where you've put your name on the dotted line to purchase something big and now you regret it and wonder if you can do anything about it, consult a lawyer. If you don't have an attorney, call the lawyer referral service of your local bar association and they'll give you the name of someone. If you have a very low income, call Legal Aid. They won't charge you.

• *More money tips.*

Save money by having your hair done in a beauty school instead of a commercial hair salon. Get your teeth fixed at your local dental school (if there is one in your community). It's cheaper, and they do excellent work. Consider living with another widow (you'll save money and have company when you're lonely.)

Widowhood very often does mean shrinking incomes, but with imagination, willingness, and a sense of adventure you can *still* enjoy the basic comforts in life (*and* some luxuries).

If it makes you feel more secure, it may well be worth the cost to use the services of experts who can tell you how to spend your money and how to invest your money; specialists who can help you prepare your income tax and plan your estate.

• *A certified public accountant for help.*

I would suggest consulting a certified public accountant if you find the preparation of your annual income tax too overwhelming. A certified public accountant is more authoritative and credible than an uncertified accountant, if you should have a tax department audit.

• *Help with investments and pension plans.*

There are specialists in your bank who can help you with planning your estate. A tax lawyer or expert can give you advice about investments, as can a stockbroker or an investment counselor. If you are working, consult the pension officer at your place of employment; you are entitled to a copy of your pension plan upon request (this is a *law*) and you can use the pension officer to explain the fine details. This service is free.

• *Insurance agents can assist you.*

Many women turn to an insurance agent for advice on insuring their car and their home and their personal possessions.

• *Ask other women for referrals.*

Get referrals from other women who are satisfied with their insurance agents and investment counselors and certified public accounts. You'll feel more comfortable and reassured about their competence.

New Men in Your Life. When? Ever?

You'll probably find, almost right after your husband's funeral, that your best friends will tell you not to worry, because you're so attractive you'll be married again soon.

• *Are your friends pushing you to date?*

You're going to hate them for this. You're going to feel alienated from them, angry at them, and betrayed by them. How dare they forget your husband so quickly! More to the point, how dare they think YOU will forget your husband so quickly! Of course you're upset, but try to understand that people just don't know what to say to a new widow. They feel awkward so they *say* awkward things.

Rhoda told me she experienced this situation. She had had a good marriage. Her husband and she had a very close relationship. They never had children, and they depended on each other for most of their needs. They spent practically all of their spare time together. They had been married thirty-six years when Bob died suddenly of a heart attack. Rhoda was devastated. Bob had considered her his best friend, his biggest booster, and his "baby doll" (Rhoda is tiny and very pretty). All of this was suddenly gone . . . and Rhoda had nothing with which to replace her wonderful life. She brooded and she remembered those marvelous thirty-six years . . . years when she had been waiting every evening for Bob to get home from work so she could serve him a hot dinner (Rhoda hadn't worked outside of the house, and on the afternoons she had played canasta with the girls, she made it a point to get home before Bob did); years when Bob had been the "man of the family" and kept everything in tip-top shape in the house; years when he had even planned every family vacation himself, not burdening her with any of the petty details. And Rhoda had loved being "just a housewife." She enjoyed being thought of as the perfect hostess, an excellent cook, a wonderful housekeeper. After Bob died, Rhoda was first numb, then depressed. Then—desperate. Crazy with grief, she stayed at home, hardly getting up to open the living room draperies until late afternoon. Later, urged by her friends, she ventured out a little. She became a tour guide at the local museum, even though she had no interest in art (a friend had pushed her into it). She shopped every day, bought things, and returned them, aimlessly—. She went on a cruise. She reluctantly joined a singles' group in her church. Men flirted, made passes. She was confused. She was frightened. She didn't know how she felt. Sometimes she responded, especially after a horribly lonely Sunday. She awkwardly flirted back. Then she would feel guilty and silently beg Bob to forgive her. When men would actually ask her out, she would refuse.

One night, just before she was ready to go to bed, all the lights went out in the house. She realized a fuse had blown and, panicked, she realized that Bob had never shown her how to fix it. She felt uneasy in the dark house, and she went to bed and her heart was beating fast. She could hear it pounding. The next morning, exhausted, she called a repairman. Sunday night, when she went to the singles-group supper, a short, heavy man (who had a nice face) told her how much he missed his wife, who had just died. He was an engineer. Thoughts raced wildly through Rhoda's mind. Engineers know how to fix fuses. Engineers can fix everything in a house. He looks kind, he *is* kind I can tell because of the way he talks about his wife, I need to be taken care of, I want to be taken care of. . . .

The next time she saw him he asked her out to dinner. She went—it was her first date since Bob had died—and he talked about his wife all through dinner. Rhoda felt left out and rejected and she started to feel guilty because she had accepted the date so soon after Bob had died. She made an excuse to go home early.

Her friends were worried about her. Three of them called her to have lunch with them, and they earnestly reassured her that she would meet someone very soon, that she shouldn't worry, that she was a beautiful woman and that she wouldn't be alone very long. They solemnly assured her that she would be married again in two years at the most. Not noticing her silence, they plotted as to how they would have a party in a couple of weeks and invite every eligible man they knew.

Rhoda felt heavy and depressed on the way home. Suddenly, curled up in bed tightly, she felt hot resentment. "How *dare* they assume I would forget Bob so soon! That I would betray him like this! They must think I am a shallow and desperate woman!" She sobbed in rage and grief.

· *When to start dating (and your mixed feelings about it).*

If Rhoda had understood her feelings better, if someone had told her what to expect to feel as a widow, she would have realized that she was feeling what *MOST* widows experience—uncertainty as to when to begin dating again, sexual yearnings, guilt feelings about being interested in other men, and anger toward well-meaning friends who seem to be betraying her dead husband and insulting her. She would have also felt more comfortable with her normal and growing need for male companionship and love, and if she had been very perceptive she would have recognized that she (the child part of her) wanted to be taken care of again.

If you've been feeling this way, try to separate yourself from your feelings for a minute and understand that it's all right to remember your husband and that it's all right to need to feel loyal to him. Also realize that it is just as normal and acceptable to want a man to hold you, to comfort you, and to make love to you. You have had these kind of experiences, and perhaps your marriage was good and you want those things again—they make you feel good. Doesn't that make sense? *And* it is just as acceptable to feel all of these things at one time: the loyalty toward your dead husband, the sexual yearnings, the need to be nurtured and cared about. When you realize that many widows feel these conflicting feelings at the same time, you will no longer feel so guilty. When you understand that it is OKAY to feel this way, you will relax more and not worry about it so much. Little by little, the feelings will fall into place and they won't conflict with each other anymore. Just give yourself time.

- *It'll feel awkward at first.*

Of course you'll feel awkward beginning to date again. And you'll possibly feel very awkward when you go to bed with someone for the first time.

"Bed?" laughed a friend of mine when we talked about this. "*I* felt awkward and self-conscious when a man *kissed* me for the first time after Ned died. I have bridgework in my mouth, and I was petrified that his tongue would hit that heavy band of steel at the roof of my mouth!"

- *The over-50 widow: a different story than when you were younger.*

We wryly agreed that being widowed at the age of fifty-five is simply not the same as being widowed at the age of thirty.

Being Alone in a Couple-Oriented Society

· *When the dinner invitations slow down*

You've been widowed now for over a year and at the beginning, after the funeral, your friends called you every day. They came over, dragged you out of the house, invited you over every weekend, and made sure you were still part of the crowd. And now—the dinner invitations have slackened and the daily phone calls have dwindled to a call about once a month. This is the first year you didn't get together with them New Year's Eve, and you were *sure* they would include you in those plans. After all, you and your husband celebrated New Year's Eve with them for twenty years! They were *your* crowd!

· *Three's a crowd. Sorry!*

You feel hurt and rejected and depressed, and you wonder whether you've become dull and uninteresting (after all, there must be *some* reason for their withdrawal). No, it is not that your personality has changed. If you have experienced this phenomenon it *is* probably because we live in a couple-oriented society where the "extra woman" becomes an embarrassment, even though the extra man is an enhancement. This is NOT YOUR FAULT. And, unfortunately, you can't change society's values overnight, even if you tried. A quick solution to this is to seek out other women who are alone—and when and if you are ready, men who are alone. This is the way you'll feel part of a group again, and this is the way you'll feel less alone and lonely.

· *You as the "other woman"—when it really isn't so.*

Yes, to answer that uncomfortable feeling you may have, some wives (who were your close friends) may begin to see you as a threat to their marriage—when of course, you're not.

Sandy, Norma's close friend for over thirty years, was waiting in the car while Marc, her husband, dashed up to Norma's apartment to get her. Norma, newly widowed, was joining them for dinner and a movie. Five minutes went by, ten——. Sandy felt herself getting tense. What were they doing up there? When Norma and Marc came down just a minute later (Norma had been held up, talking long-distance to her children on the phone) Norma could feel the tension and she could see the hostility on Sandy's face. She quickly figured it out—and she was badly shaken. How could Sandy think this of her? She felt so hurt that she didn't stop to think of *why* Sandy had reacted this way: Sandy was fifty-two and it is sometimes hard to be fifty-two in our youth-oriented society; Sandy felt she was getting old and that she was losing her attractiveness. Marc was sometimes impotent, and she worried about her marriage. *Any* woman who spent time alone with her husband was (she felt) a threat to her. Suddenly, after knowing Norma all these years, Norma had become a symbol; a symbol of the "other woman."

Sandy should have remembered that Norma was a caring and sensitive friend. She should have understood that she was going through a vulnerable period in her own life. But it was hard for her to be objective; because she was feeling too sorry for herself.

Does this sound familiar to you? Has this kind of thing happened to you since you've been widowed? Don't run in panic if it does. Try to reach out to your friend, who feels threatened by you, and give her "strokes." Reassure her when you're alone. Be open and verbalize what has happened in her feelings toward you. Don't attack. Tell her that you feel supportive and loving toward her and that you'd never hurt her like that. And be compassionate. She's more terrified than you are. She feels she might lose something (someone) very valuable to her. You understand how that feels because you *have* lost someone very valuable to you. Be courageous and reach out to her. She may be silent as she listens to you, but she will remember and treasure your gesture later.

Great Expectations—from Relatives

Many people, when thinking of the various members of their family who are living alone (and when trying to exonerate their own guilt about not doing more for them) try to indulge in a curious kind of "matchmaking." Perhaps one of these well-meaning meddlers has approached you with a plan like one of the following:

Miriam had only been widowed three weeks when a cousin approached her and told her that she should take in their Aunt Fannie, because that would cut down her expenses and neither of them would be lonely. Despite Miriam's numbness and feeling that her body was separate from herself; despite her intense and uncomfortable feeling that there was a pane of glass between her and everyone else (some very normal feelings for a new widow), she was able to immediately recognize that this was no time to make any major changes in her life. She said "no." And later, when she was able to really think about it, she decided that since she had never liked Aunt Fannie anyway, she wouldn't do it.

Jane's sister urged her to invite a cousin's daughter to live with her, now that Jane was widowed and the young girl was starting college in the town where Jane lived. "It'll be such nice company for you," Jane's sister repeated several times.

But Jane hadn't seen the girl since she was small, and she didn't know if she would have anything in common with an eighteen-year-old college girl. Besides, she didn't want the responsibility. She tried to explain this to her sister, and it was only when she said, "Why don't *you* take her in?" that her sister stopped pushing.

If your aging mother, who is also widowed, expects you to ask her to move in with you, now that *you're* widowed, do this: Look at your guilt feelings, step aside from them neatly, and say firmly to yourself, "I will wait until I am feeling like myself again, no matter how long it takes, before I make *any* decisions about major changes in my life."

· *Be intelligently selfish.*
This is the time to be intelligently selfish and to think of

your own needs. This is the best way to become whole and healed again, as quickly as possible.

You WILL Live and Laugh Again!

Now is the time to take especially good care of yourself in every way. Pamper yourself on little things, to start. Indulge yourself.

- *Treat yourself to goodies.*

Treat yourself to occasional short trips away from home. Go to New York for a weekend with a friend. Go to a beach resort to lie in the sun. Visit your cousin's home in Peoria, Illinois. These trips will distract you and give your life color and texture. At the same time these are not drastic and dramatic changes in your life. They're tiny new steps to take—safe ones. And get in the habit of planning these short vacations yourself, even if your husband had done all the vacation planning for the two of you. This will, painlessly and gradually, get you ready to plan bigger and more important decisions in your life *by yourself*. Be sure to do something for yourself every day that will make you feel pampered—like taking a long bath in expensive bath oil, or treating yourself to a leisurely lunch in a beautiful restaurant.

- *Get a physical checkup.*

Meanwhile, get a complete physical checkup after your husband dies. And get one regularly every year for the next few years. Why? Because after a severe emotional loss we are more susceptible to physical ailments. And it will be reassuring for you to know you're in the best of health. And keep in mind (but not to the point of actively worrying about it) that we can be more accident-prone after a severe loss. We're more apt to pay less attention when we cross a street, or we might not get out of the tub slowly enough. Just realize that you are likely to be somewhat distracted for a while and try to keep alert.

• *They're saying, "Pull yourself together"?*

Try to ignore the thoughtless but well-meaning people who tell you to "pull yourself together" and "keep your chin up" and "it's time to snap out of it." When you can do these things—you will. It's as simple as that.

Pick friends who have a zest for life, and who have a sense of humor. This will reawaken *your* zest for life and your sense of humor (which you may have temporarily lost).

• *Think about your future—when you're ready.*

Then there are more radical changes that you may want to consider (although you shouldn't allow yourself to be rushed in making these decisions). If you were already working at a job when your husband died, it probably will be easier to get through the next year or two . . . because you have less time to think and remember. This might be the time to think about going back to school, or changing your job, or beginning to take on volunteer work. You might want to go back into the job force if you haven't been working. These larger steps may be frightening to contemplate, but even thinking about them can help you realize your new identity.

• *The new you—a challenge!*

Nobody says it's easy. It's never easy to try to find a new identity. And, as a woman alone, you *do* have a new identity. But this search for the *new* you can be an exciting challenge. With each successful step you take toward personhood—no matter how small—you'll feel more powerful, more ready to take the next step. And if you make a mistake, ask yourself, "What's the worst that can happen?" Nine chances out of ten, you'll find the worst isn't so bad after all.

But no matter what your life situation (whether you're working or staying at home) remember that in time you *will* feel better. You *will* be all right. You *will* start functioning again. You have strengths you don't even know about! You are riper and smarter and wiser than a thirty-year-old woman because you have had more living experience . . . and these strengths are what will take you through the rest of these bad months, and help you sur-

vive the pain. Later, slowly but surely, there will be
fewer and fewer bad days . . . and then a couple of years
from now (or less!) you will feel *good* and realize you've
been feeling good for a while now—and that's when you'll
know the good life is beginning again.

CHAPTER 8

Working:
Advice for the Non-Career Woman

ᴇᴈ᛽ ᛘᴇ

Telling It Like It Really Is

You're an over-50 woman, you're looking for a job, and you have no job experience. Or you haven't worked since 1945 and you feel panic ("Who'd want me?"). Or you're tired of scrubbing people's floors and being called by your first name by sassy little kids in your employer's home. Or—you're feeling terrible because you've been a secretary for nineteen years and you're making the same money as your twenty-year-old niece who's only been working two years.

Do any of these shoes fit?

- *Three women speak up.*

Many older women who enter the job market for the first time, or reenter after a long time, have justifiable fears. Pearl, Marlene and Gwen tell their stories:

Here's Pearl: "I got married when I finished high school, and I didn't even bother looking for work. It was in 1934 and jobs were mighty scarce. We were lucky my husband could find work. Anyway, women weren't expected to look for jobs outside the home once they had

253

kids, and our children came along pretty fast. I was kept
busy cooking and cleaning and taking care of the kids,
and I never did like being away when the children got
home from school in the afternoons, not even when they
were bigger. So I never did go to work. My husband
wasn't too keen on my working anyway. He liked me
home." Pearl reached inside of her black plastic pocketbook and got out some wallet-sized snapshots of her
children and showed them to me. She showed me pictures
of her grandchildren, too.

"He retires next year, my husband, and our income is
going to be cut down a lot. He didn't have any choice in
the matter. He has to retire, his company makes them
quit at the age of sixty-five. I have to get a job—I need
to bring some money in, even if it's a little. We're going
to be really hurting for money, the way prices are today."

Marlene's story is different, but familiar: "My husband
passed away last year, and all year it's been a struggle
making ends meet. I know I have to go to work, but what
can I do? Who would hire me? The only time I worked
was during the Second World War. I was a 'Rosie the
Riveter.' I was good, mind you, but how's that going to
help me now? What do I say when they ask me what I've
been doing for the past thirty years—when I have to fill
out those applications—?"

Gwen sat in the corner of her maple, Early-American
sofa in a living-room full of matched furniture.

"Oh, I worked. Lord knows I worked most of my life,
and I worked hard and long—cleaning other people's
houses. I'm fifty-nine now and I've spent over thirty years
working for almost nothing, scrubbing other women's
floors while mine got scrubbed at midnight, when I'd be
so tired I could hardly hold up my head. I'd get up at
five-thirty every morning to take the bus to the suburbs—
in the cold, rain and snow—and I wouldn't get home till
after seven at night. Believe me, my kids had to fend for
themselves when they got home from school because their
mamma was busy taking care of someone else's children.
Do I sound bitter? You'd better believe it. And in those
days no one put in for your Social Security, none of those
madams did. Oh, they were supposed to, but no one *made*

them. We were all too scared to report them. My pay was so low, when I start getting my Social Security checks, my benefits are going to be next to nothing. I have to start saving for the days when I won't be able to work any more, while I still have some strength. My kids have finished college; they're working and they're married with kids of their own, and I don't want them to have to support me. But I won't clean anyone's house again! I refuse to. Who's gonna train an old horse for a new trade? *You* tell me. What else can I do besides be a damned maid again?"

Gwen said, "I'm in perfect health—and they tell me I'm too old to work. The last place I went was an advertising agency where I'd be a file clerk in a room where no one would see me—and the man told me he wanted a 'young image'!"

- *There's a whole army of us out there!*
  And there are the others:

  - women in their sixties who can only make a limited salary so they won't lose any of their inadequate Social Security benefits
  - over-50 women who are afraid to get sick (their paychecks are too low to pay for doctor bills, too high to qualify them for medical assistance—and they're not old enough for Medicare)
  - women who stay in jobs they hate because they can't transfer their pension benefits to another job (and they're just a few years away from retirement)
  - older women soaking their feet every night, from standing all day doing menial jobs, but who don't know how to do any other kind of work
  - women who've been "laid off" in their own homes as housekeepers and cooks and mothers (there's no one left at home) and they're ineligible for unemployment insurance because they worked for years as unpaid labor
  - women who can't afford decent housing because their paycheck's so low. They're ineligible for public assistance, since they're not physically disabled and since their children are already grown
  - women who can't get jobs because of their age

• *Ageism . . . Sexism . . . Racism . . . Triple Whammies.*
Taking job risks and trying to get a job without any work experience (hard even for a twenty-year-old) is is even more difficult when you're an over-50 woman. Ageism—discrimination against people because of their age—is often compounded by sexism. What's that? It's discrimination in terms of getting jobs or a raise or promotion opportunities because of your sex. It's when the man sitting across from your desk doing exactly the same work you do gets thirty dollars a week more in his paycheck—because he *is* a man. The reason given? "He has a family to support!" Ever hear of a woman getting an extra thirty dollars a week because *she* has a family to support? And if you're a Chicano or Chinese or Black or Asian or Native American (American Indian) or Japanese or Puerto Rican woman, you face ageism *and* sexism *and* racism.

Entering or Reentering the Work World
—after Many Years

Learn the *politics of work.* That's learning how the system works and then learning how to manipulate the system to your advantage. Maybe I should have called this chapter "The Politics of Work"—because that's what these pages are all about. And after you read this book, you might want to read Letty Cottin Pogrebin's book, *Getting Yours.* It's an Avon paperback, and it's $1.75. It's a whole book on the politics of work!

• *Steps to take.*
Are you one of the women who never worked—or who worked for only a short time? What do you do? You're going to make a special list (strengths). You're going to also make a list of people you know (contacts) that you'll later get in touch with for jobs. You'll learn how to write a resume. You'll learn how to write a covering letter. And you'll learn when and how to use your resume and covering letter. You'll learn how—and where—to apply for jobs *systematically.*
A different approach from looking in the want ads each Sunday and going to employment agencies? You *will* use

want ads and maybe employment agencies—but without any job experience, or with limited job experience gotten a long time ago, you're not going to leave it at that. You're going to be very clever and analytical in the way you look for work. You're going to use every one of your strengths and talents and contacts and resources to enter the job market. You're going to *need* all of this—because you are older and it may be harder to get work than when you were twenty. And when you do use all of your strengths and talents (and being older has given you *more* strengths and talents) you'll be equalizing the balance between yourself and the younger woman job seeker. You can make it—because you are willing to put in the extra time and energy to take every step outlined in this chapter.

• *Be realistic.*

You're also going to want to be very realistic. Here are some examples of how your age may affect your thinking about what type of job you are seeking.

A twenty-year-old woman may be willing to start out as a typist in an advertising agency so that, eventually, she stands a chance at becoming a copywriter. Can you afford the time to do this? Do you want to spend the next couple of years at a low-paying typing job in the *hopes* of becoming a copywriter? If you do decide to take this risk, at least realize that you may still be a low-paid typist when you're sixty—and sixty-two. Isn't it more realistic to give up the idea in the very beginning (especially if you need money), and shift gears so you start out looking for a higher-paying job than typing?

Or, the twenty-two-year-old woman may turn up her nose at being a live-in nursemaid because of the lack of job status, the confining hours, and the lack of privacy during her off-work hours. As an older woman, you may like it. Living-in might relieve the bleak loneliness you've felt since your husband died (there's always someone in the house) and living-in means less money that you'll have to spend on day-to-day living. This saving could translate into an annual vacation in Europe! It could be a *perfect* job for you, if you love children (and if you're not involved with a man, and don't expect to be, you may not mind the lack of privacy during your off-work hours).

Again, you can take that exciting part-time job in a bookstore (because you love books) where the younger woman, who's divorced with three children, can't even consider it. *You* can do it—because your earned income is limited to under $3,000 annually, in order not to have your Social Security checks reduced, and the salary *is* less than $3,000.

And another example: You can't make commitments because of disabling arthritis? You're afraid even to apply for a full-time job, where you may have to call in "sick" too often? For you, being realistic can mean opening a business at home, where you can change your hours at the last minute: offering a "wake-up" service (you can work from bed!); starting a "Find-a-roommate" business . . . making appointments for salesmen.

Now that you're beginning to think about your job needs realistically, you'll be more ready to approach your job-hunting realistically, and you'll be ready to take your first definite step. Time to get out your pencils and paper—.

Making a List

Choose a time of day or evening when you're most energetic. Are you an early morning person? Make your list at 6:00 or 7:00 a.m. Are you a night person? Make your list after supper. Be *ALONE* when you make your list. Choose a place to write where you'll be physically comfortable. Don't answer the phone while you're working. You'll need a pile of blank sheets of paper, a couple of sharpened pencils, and an eraser.

• *Strengths . . . Talents.*
Take a sheet of paper and list *Strengths and Talents* at the top. What are your strengths and talents? Are you a good listener? Are you self-disciplined? Are you a good organizer (remember, you were president of three organizations from the time you were sixteen)? One by one, list all of these strengths and talents under your heading. Now take a twenty-minute break. Watch TV for a couple of minutes. Feel more relaxed? Feel more self-confident because you're beginning to remember strengths and tal-

ents you haven't thought about in a long time? Good. Go
back to your list. Have you forgotten anything? You're an
excellent cook? List it. You write well (you were editor of
your school paper)? Write it down. You know a lot about
Yoga and could teach it informally? You crochet your
own dresses? You're a good bookkeeper (you kept the
books for your husband's business)? List them all! Look
at the clock. More time has gone by than you realized,
hasn't it? You've remembered strengths and talents you
haven't thought about in twenty years, haven't you?

Take a day-long break.

• *Kinds of jobs to fit your strengths and talents.*

Refreshed and ready, you're returning to your list.
What's the first strength and talent that you listed? Good
with old people? List that at the top of a separate sheet of
paper . . . and put that piece of paper aside. What's the
second strength and talent you listed? You're good on the
telephone (you've always been told what a nice telephone voice you have)? List that on the top of another
separate sheet of paper . . . and put that piece of paper
aside. Get the idea? When you've finished listing each of
your strengths and talents on separate sheets of paper,
you'll have a pile of papers with only a single listing at the
top of each sheet. Finished? Take your stretch break—and
then go back to your worktable. You're now going to take
each sheet, separately, and write, under the strengths and
talents you listed, the kinds of *jobs* that fit into these kinds
of strengths and talents. This is the part that will take a lot
of time, because you're going to list familiar kinds of jobs
(work) and jobs you'll make up. Expect this task to take
a couple of days, off and on.

Let's get started together. You're good with small children? Jobs that fit into that kind of strength and talent:
kindergarten aide; day care center assistant teacher; nurs-
ery school aide; live-in nursemaid; baby-sitter. Combine
two of your strengths and talents: you're good with children *and* a good organizer? Organize and run children's
birthday parties for busy parents (and you plan the refreshments, games, and fun). Organize children's tours
and trips to museums and farms and zoos and puppet
shows for parents who want their kids to have a good summer. Ask a local department store to hire you to organize

a children's corner (for parents who want time alone to shop while you keep the kids amused). Another combined talent and strength: You know how to crochet *and* you love to teach? Work in a yarn or craft or department store demonstrating and teaching crocheting. Teach crocheting in your home. Teach crocheting in a community or senior center or a bureau of recreation.

Do you know you've now taken the biggest step toward getting your first job?

You've methodically listed the kinds of work you can eventually apply for, those that match your particular strengths and talents. You've raised your own consciousness about how much talent you really have and what you *can* do, simply by writing it down.

Now reach for another pile of blank paper.

• *Where are those jobs?*

Take a "job" you listed under one of the strengths and talents (example: teaching crocheting in a community center or a senior center or a department store in their needlework department). List that job on the top of a blank sheet of paper. Get out your yellow-pages classified telephone book. Look up every department store, and under that job write the name of the store with address and phone number. Keep going. List the names of the department stores at the other end of town, too, especially if you have a car or a quick transportation system. Also list all community centers and senior centers. The yellow-pages classified telephone book will be on your worktable for a while, because you're going to refer to it for the names, addresses, and phone numbers of every place of work that relates to *any* and *every* listing of jobs you've jotted down. When you're finished, a sheet of paper might look like this:

Job: Needlework (crochet) Teacher.

Humbler's Department Store, 111 N. Howert St., tel. 555-3812
Jonathan's Department Store, 39 James St., tel. LK 5-7942
The County Senior Center, 1199 Courtley Dr., tel. JK 5-8855

Young Women's Community Center, 90 Delaware
St., tel. 555-3123
City Area Senior Center, 309 Belview St., tel.
LK 5-1813
The Needlework Nook, 675 Oldham Rd., tel. JL
5-2764
Blankard's Department Store, Blankard Place, tel.
KJ 5-2345

Notice that all these job listings are large department
stores and community centers and senior centers? That's
because the writer realized she'd have a better chance of
finding a job as a crochet teacher at a place where they
would obviously need one. Good thinking.

Now, take another blank sheet of paper and list every
social acquaintance, relative, friend, and casual acquaintance you know who works in a place where they may use
crochet teachers. Then head the sheet with the one word
CONTACTS. Attach this sheet of contacts to your completed
"crochet teacher" sheet with a paper clip. Do this to every completed job sheet. You'll end up with a list of contacts attached to each job sheet—to use later.

By this time you may be thinking: All this for a *job?*
Yes—because "all this" is what's going to get *you* the job
instead of the woman who limits herself to looking in the
Sunday want ads. "All this" is what is going to get *you*
the job when over a hundred applicants apply for each
good job these days.

Contacting Employers

Now you're ready to begin calling the places of employment you listed to see if there's an opening.

• *Speak directly to the boss.*
Ask to speak directly to the person in charge. That
could be the director of personnel, the owner, or the manager. You're calling a doctor's office to see if she needs a
receptionist? You do *not* want to ask the receptionist who
answers the phone if there's an opening—because she
may not realize her boss is thinking of replacing her; because she may not know she's considering hiring a second

receptionist for her other office; because she may have a friend in mind who would like the job. When you finally do talk to the doctor, she'll be impressed when she realizes you've called even though she hasn't advertised for help ("that woman has *initiative*") and even though she may not be looking for a receptionist, she may be happy to refer you to another doctor who is . . . if you say, before you hang up and after you've thanked her, "By the way, Dr. Smith, do you know any other physician in the area who may be thinking of hiring a receptionist?"

Using Contacts

You're going to call all of your "contacts," too. Who could be a contact and how do you use him or her?

• *How to be effective.*

Call the internist you've been using for five years and ask if she needs a receptionist. Ask your friend's sister, who's a pharmacist and owns a drugstore, if she needs a salesclerk. Ask the lawyer who's sitting next to you at the dinner party if she needs a typist. Call that woman who lives across the street from you and ask her—she's an advertising artist—if the agency she works for might need a bookkeeper. "I really don't know," she might murmur, but you could pursue it—and you *should* pursue it— by asking for the name of the director of the agency, and then calling her yourself.

That's using contacts.

Understanding the Want Ads

And you're going to examine each ad carefully, in the Sunday newspapers.

• *What do certain phrases mean?*

When you do see one that reads "experience preferred" or "a degree preferred" it usually means they'll hire you *without* experience and/or a degree—as cheap labor. That might be fine for your first job back in the job market, so don't skim so fast over these ads. When you see an ad that reads, "experience needed" and you have no *paid* experience, but you do have meaningful volunteer-work experience—answer the ad. Sure, you might be hired at much less money, but it's a chance to get your foot in the door, and who says you have to stay in that job forever?

"What nerve!" you might be groaning. "She thinks I have such nerve. How can I be so aggressive and nervy when all my life I was the quiet one. How can I do all that—?" Of *course* you have nerve. Because you have to have nerve when you're an over-50 woman who's looking for a job. All you need is to be told *how* . . .

And what's the worst that can happen if you're this aggressive? You'll feel uncomfortable. Now is that so terrible?

So here's *HOW*.

Writing a Résumé

You've made the phone calls. You've called and called and someone finally said, "Can you come in for an appointment Monday morning?" Forget your hair appointment. Forget the doctor's appointment (unless you're really sick). Say "Yes!" cheerfully, and either borrow or rent a typewriter if you don't have one. You're going to type a résumé and you *can't* write it in longhand.

• *Get hold of a typewriter.*

Where can you rent a typewriter? From a used-office-machine store or anyplace that sells typewriters and office machines. How much do they charge? They'll usually rent one by the month for under $20. A less expensive way of having your résumé typed is to take it to a stenographic service. Last I heard, the going rate is $2.50 a typed page . . . and stenographic services are listed in the classified section of the phone book.

Be sure you type (or have typed and Xeroxed) two identical copies (one to give to the interviewer and one to hold, so you won't forget a word you've written). You might be asked to *send* a résumé.

• *How to write a résumé—with no job experience.*

So how do you write a résumé? How do you write a résumé when you've had no job experience to write about? Your résumé won't try to sell job experience. It *will* sell your strengths and talents to match that job you're applying for—and you've already listed all of your wonderful strengths and talents on those sheets of paper, so you can quickly refer back to what you've written. Your résumé will be written in clever ways that will make the employer *assume* you can do the job.

• *Take a look at these résumés.*
  Examples:

> Name: Jane Doe
> Address: 100 Main Street, Anytown, Any State
> Telephone: 348-9675

Job Objective
Because of my skill and experience, I am interested in teaching crocheting. I have taught beginners, intermediate, and advanced level students in groups and on a one-to-one basis. I can teach people of any age and of both sexes.

Skill Background
I have crocheted 197 dresses (which I have designed myself), 68 hats, 26 lined coats, 57 baby layettes, 265 baby bonnets, and 180 sweaters for men women and children.

> Available: Immediately
> Health: Excellent

This résumé writer got a job demonstrating and teaching crocheting in a department store two weeks after presenting this résumé. Now let's analyze why this woman, who had only taught crocheting in her living room as a favor to friends and relatives, got a job so quickly:

1. She used numbers when she wrote *how many* crocheted items she had made. Numbers have power. Instead of saying she had crocheted many

dresses, she wrote she had crocheted *197* dresses. Feel that power?

2. She implied professional teaching experience, even though her teaching had been limited to informal sessions over homemade cakes, sometimes to enthusiastic twelve-year-old grandchildren and sometimes to earnest friends who wanted to make a dress just like hers. Why should she let the employer know she wasn't a "professional" teacher when she *knew* she could teach? Why not imply the "professionalism" when she knew she could do as good a job as any person with a Home Economics degree?

3. Why did she write she could teach people of "both sexes"? Once she had taught the bachelor brother of her neighbor's; a man who never smiled and never talked, but did find crocheting a passion!

4. She broke down, item by item, each crocheted piece she had ever made by *name* (layettes, bonnets, sweaters, etc.) to show the vast scope of her skill and experience.

She didn't mention her age. Why should she in an age-discriminatory society? So she played down a liability. Why did she mention her health is "excellent"? She knows she looks "over 50" and she knew the man who would be interviewing her might feel older women are more prone to mysterious illnesses and stretches of absence from work . . . so why not *stress* her good health?

And to show you how much nerve she had, she didn't back away when the manager of the store told her—when she first called her—that she didn't need anyone. She said, "let me bring a couple of my crocheted dresses in, anyway, so you can look at them. What is a convenient time for you?" She asked her, "This week or next week?" She didn't ask *if* she could come in, inviting a "no" answer; she asked which time was better—and either answer would have been affirmative. Jane *assumed* the manager would choose "this week or next week"—and she did. Assertive. Positive. The quality of Jane's crocheted dresses and the force of her résumé and the positiveness of her attitude got her the job.

Let's look at another résumé of an over-50 woman who had no job experience.

Name: Jane Doe
Address: 100 Main Street, Anytown, Anystate
Telephone: 658-7768

Job Objective

I am seeking a position as an aide in a mental hospital, working with men and/or women of any age, with any kind of disability.

Skill Background

I have been a volunteer for twenty-six years with the Golden Guild, a volunteer group that visits mental hospitals each week, arranging parties and outings for patients; giving one-to-one service to patients. Through this extensive on-going experience, I have learned how to work with the disturbed person; how to relate to the anxious and depressed patient; the acting-out hostile patient; the psychotic patient. I appreciate and understand their needs, and attempt to understand the dynamics of their behavior through courses I enrolled in at the University of Chicago.

Special Education

1975: 1-semester course at the University of Chicago, *Depression in the Middle Years*

1974: 1-semester course at the University of Chicago, *Institutionalization: When Is It Necessary?*

1973: 1-semester course at the University of Chicago, *The New Therapies*

Available: Immediately
Health: Excellent

You may ask why this résumé writer, intelligent and skilled in her area, would seek a low-level job as an *aide*. She is realistic. She knows that local hospital workers are unionized (so she'll never have to fight for a raise by herself); that they are paid decently, with a built-in six-year job ladder; and more importantly, she knew that she didn't have the formal academic credentials to seek a more prestigious job in the field. This Jane Doe is a down-to-earth woman. She doesn't need prestige, even though it would be nice. She needs money.

Why did she list the courses she had taken under *Special Education?* To give them a *special* look. A local state mental hospital hired her right away. They were glad to have her. Her résumé told them she is smart, that she understands the needs of their patients, and that she goes out of her way to give herself further training in the field. They liked the fact that she is older because it means that she will be responsible, won't quit to have a baby, and that she probably won't want to jump from job to job. To round off this success story, I think you should know that this woman was just made a supervisor. She now has two aides working under her.

Now let's look at a third résumé. This woman is a real go-getter. She worked with her husband in their dry-goods store for thirty-five years. She's now alone—he died and she sold the store—and she had no other job experience. She knew she didn't want to be a saleswoman. She was tired of selling. But why not use those thirty-five years of experience for something else? Why not try for a job as a *buyer?* After all, she had bought *and* sold the merchandise in their store—.

Her résumé looked like this:

Name: Jane Doe
Address: 100 Main Street, Anytown, Anystate
Phone: 578-0897

Job Objective
I am seeking a job as a buyer, having acquired the skill of buying merchandise in the ownership and operation of a dry-goods store for thirty-five years. I have expertise in increasing the sales volume of an established store or a department in a store.

Education
Graduated high school. Two years of business college, majoring in Accounting.

Skills

Buying; understanding the changing market and trends in marketing; pricing; supervising and training sales people; keeping accounts and records; understanding advertising techniques (graphic and copy).

Available: Immediately. Able to relocate. Ready to work irregular hours, and, if necessary, an over-40-hour workweek

Health: Excellent

What's different about this woman's résumé? She offered to work any hours—anywhere. In the world of merchandising, a buyer often has to work until 9:00 p.m. or later, and a chain store may need a buyer to relocate in one of their stores fifty miles away. She knew and took advantage of this. Not only did she get a job immediately as a buyer in the curtain department of a chain store, but after only two years (and she was almost sixty by then) she moved on to create and manage a totally new department featuring women's sportswear in a men's clothing store! Through her contacts (this woman is gregarious and made a lot of contacts in her buying job) she talked the owner of the store into this expansion— and she's now making a very handsome five-figure annual income.

• *What's a résumé for?*

Selling yourself in your résumé means selling what an employer *needs;* what you can give that most other applicants can't or won't give. That's why you'll want to refer to your list of *strengths and talents* when you write your résumé. You spent a lot of time developing that list of *strengths and talents;* you remembered things you had accomplished ten, fifteen and twenty years ago; you rediscovered skills you had forgotten you had (and still have). *Use* this information when you write a résumé. Ideally, each job requires a different résumé. But you can probably design several which will serve for all the different types of jobs for which you may apply.

• *Keep copies.*

Xerox or make a carbon copy of each résumé that you write, because you'll need to have one on hand *at* the job interview, so your information matches the information on your interviewer's desk . . . and because you might want to send out that same résumé again, for another job. Libraries usually have copy machines (at 10 cents a copy) or better yet, you may have a friend who has a xerox machine where she works.

How to Write a Covering Letter

What is a covering letter?

• *The purpose.*
It's the letter you're going to write to introduce yourself when you apply for a job. You'll slip it in the envelope with a copy of your résumé.

• *What to include in it.*
How do you write it? Start with a personal salutation. Write *Dear Mr. Jones* or *Dear Ms. Stauffer* (yes, *Ms.* It shows you're aware that many women prefer it). Do not write *Dear Sir,* or *To Whom It May Concern* (too impersonal). How do you know to whom to address a letter? Call the company's personnel office and ask who is in charge of the department to which you're applying. If there is no personnel department (and many small places don't have one), ask the receptionist who answers the phone for the information.

In your first paragraph, state that you're applying for the job, and be specific about *which* job—because they might have more than one job opening. Mention the source of your information about the job opening (An ad? Did a friend tell you about the position?). In your second paragraph, merely mention that you're enclosing your résumé. And in the third paragraph, briefly state why *you're* the person who could fill their needs. Your last paragraph should inform the person that you're looking forward to hearing from him/her for an interview. *End of letter.* Short—just a lead-in to your résumé and personal job interview. An introduction, not a chatty, personal history. And never be cutesy or clever.

• *A sample covering letter.*

Just a straightforward, positive introduction of yourself, as Wanda's letter was:

> Dear Mr. Feines,
>
> I would like to apply for the job as receptionist in the office of the Mass Transit Company, in reply to your advertisement in the Sunday *Post* of July 1.
>
> Enclosed you will find my résumé.
>
> Having had broad experience dealing with the public in various volunteer organizations, I feel I can fill your needs more than adequately.
>
> I am looking forward to hearing from you at your earliest convenience, so we can sit down and talk. Thank you very much.
>
> Sincerely,
Wanda Smith

Include Your Volunteer Work When You Sell Yourself

Wanda was selling her volunteer experiences—and why not? She had done important work at no pay for many years, and it had taught her a lot. In her twenty-five-year experience, the various directors of volunteers she had worked for were exacting and demanding people, asking as much from her as she would give a paid job. They expected and received a high-level performance and Wanda did well to turn those years into meaningful, important work.

How about you? What kind of volunteer work have *you* done? What did it teach you?

The Follow-Up Interview Letter

• *When to send it.*

After your job interview, send a "thank you" letter to your interviewer no later than two days after the interview.

Thank her for the time given you, and end your letter on the high note of telling the interviewer *why* you will be an asset to the company.

• *Why are you writing this letter?*

It's amazing how many people do not send these follow-up letters, when it's such an impressive gesture. It says you care about getting the job; that you'll put in extra effort to get the job and that you know how to handle yourself in the job world.

• *Keep copies.*

Keep copies of all covering letters and follow-up interview letters, as well as résumés. Separate them by job. You might have a manila envelope marked *Union Bank Job Interview. April 1.* Every piece of written material you've given the interviewer at that bank should be in that envelope—in the form of Xeroxed copies. This means that if there's more follow-up, you'll be consistent in the information you give about yourself (you won't accidentally stress something not relevent or give them a negative piece of information at the next interview . . . or skip an important item you had on your original résumé, because you'll *know* what you wrote in any previous correspondence).

Free Employment Agencies

Explore the services of the *free* employment agencies. Why spend money if you don't have to?

• *Government agencies.*

You probably already know that your city and state government offers you a free employment service, and that the federal government gives free employment services. But do you know that there are free employment services for *older* people in many cities?

• *Agencies for the older worker.*

In Baltimore, Md., for instance, there is the Over-60 Employment Counseling Service, which is a private, tax-exempt organization operated by people who have passed their sixtieth birthday. They place job applicants who themselves are over sixty. Each new applicant is registered, then referred to a job counselor who spends almost an hour interviewing the applicant and helping that person

assess her capabilities. Businesses with rigid retirement
regulations don't use the service of the Over-60 Employment Counseling Service, but many other kinds of
businesses do. Jobs secured for clients have been in a variety of fields—from domestic, sales, child care, and factory work, to executive-level positions. A married couple,
in their sixties, told me the agency has been using their
services for three years. The husband is called on during
the peak seasons in shoe stores—he's a crackerjack sales-
man—and the wife fills in for bookkeepers on vacation.
"The money," they said, "gives us the little luxuries our
Social Security checks don't cover."

Another free, valuable employment agency service for
older people is Mature Temps Inc. As you can tell from
the name, it focuses on temporary jobs. Mature Temps is
located in many cities and it could be the answer for you.
It's listed in your telephone book. And another source of
job information for the older worker is the Information-
and-Referral Service for the Aging centers located
throughout the country. It's a free service funded under
Title III of the Older Americans Act, and they can inform you about *special* employment programs for older
people in your area. Call them. They're in your telephone
directory. If you can't find it listed, call your local commission on aging office for the number.

Private Employment Agencies

If you use the services of a private employment agency,
find out whether *you* have to pay the agency's commission. Sometimes—but usually only in middle- and high-
level positions—the employer pays the agency's finder's
fee. Sometimes fees are split between you and the employer (if you're hired) while other jobs require that you
pay the full commission.

• *Understand their regulations.*

If you do use the services of a private employment
agency, be sure you understand their rules and regulations. And if they don't keep their promises, complain to
the Department of Labor, your state's human rights commission, or to the National Employment Association.

Does all this indicate that private employment agencies will do you no good? No—they might be very helpful. If you're reentering the work force or just beginning to be a worker, they *can* be discouraging if they insist you take a typing test (and some agencies automatically give all female applicants a typing test). However, every year about four million people are placed in new jobs by agencies—and that's impressive.

• *Agencies specializing in temporary jobs.*

Private employment agencies can be particularly helpful in placing an older female worker in a *temporary* job. And there are agencies that specialize in placing applicants in temporary positions. This can be advantageous to the older woman who has very basic office skills and to older women who seek jobs as nurse-companions, companions, or housekeepers.

Employment Especially for the Older Worker

Many people do not know that there are jobs designed *only* for the older worker. They're low-paying, but they can often be used as a transition for reentry back into the competitive labor market or they can be used to gain new job skills. Deliberately taking one of these jobs so you'll be able to say that you have had job experience and that you *do* have a particular skill can mean larger paychecks later.

• *The Senior Aides Program.*

The Senior Aides Program, originally administered by the National Council of Senior Citizens, has offices in many cities throughout the nation, and they hire men and women who are fifty-five and older and on limited incomes. This program has placed applicants (*and* trained them!) as outreach aides, home health aides, library aides, bilingual aides, sanitation aides, child-care aides, protective services aides, senior center aides, day-care center aides, medical clinic aides, social service aides, legal services aides, information/referral aides, teacher aides, arts/crafts aides, receptionist-typists, clerical aides, public safety aides, geriatric ward aides, research aides, home repair supervisors, nutrition education aides, consumer education aides, casework aides, juvenile detention center counselor aides, and administration aides. Call your local county or state or city commission on aging, or your local Information-and-Referral Service for the Aging, or your local Office on Aging, for more information on this program. They'll be able to tell you if the program is available in your area, and refer you to the proper persons for application. If you are placed, it will be with a public or private nonprofit community service agency where you'll work an average of twenty hours weekly, and your hourly salary (at this time of writing) will be $2.10 to $3.00 an hour.

Then there's the Senior Community Service Aides Program—also located throughout the country—sponsored by the National Council on the Aging. The work is part-time, and if you are placed you'll work in Social Security and state employment service offices, public housing, libraries, hospitals, schools, and other institutions. Aides provide escort services, and do a lot of the same kind of work as in the Senior Aides Program. For information on applying and eligibility, write National Council on the Aging 1828 L Street, N.W., Washington, D. C. 20036.

The National Retired Teachers Association and the American Association of Retired Persons sponsor a Senior Community Aide Program in over thirty-one cities, and they recruit, train, and find part-time work for aides in public or private service programs. Write NRTA/AARP, 1909 K Street, N.W., Washington, D. C. 20006 for more information.

• *Operation Mainstream.*

The Operation Mainstream program, administered by the Forest Service of the U.S. Department of Agriculture in about twenty states under an agreement with the U.S. Department of Labor, offers employment to older persons on an average of three days a week, in beautification and conservation projects. Write USDA Forest Service, Room 3243 South, Agriculture Building, 12th and Independence Avenue, S.W., Washington, D. C. 20250, for all the information.

• *Green Thumb program.*

Green Thumb, sponsored by the National Farmers Union in twenty-four states, provides part-time work for older people in community improvement, conservation, and beautification in rural areas or in existing community service agencies. Applicants should have a farming background and take a physical examination. Where do you get more information? Write Green Thumb, Inc., 1012 14th St., N.W., Washington, D. C. 20005.

• *Special handicraft programs.*

Some over-50 women reenter the work world by using their handicraft skills for professional business ventures that are designed especially and only for older workers. Washington, D. C. is the site for the nonprofit Handicrafts Marketing Sales, Inc., where around seven hundred fifty older people (mainly women) in Maryland, West Virginia, Virginia, and the District of Columbia sew place mats and napkins and ruffled hostess aprons and stuffed toys, right in their hometowns. The items are then sent to department stores such as Woodward and Lothrop, Lord and Taylor and Hutzler's. These workers do their sewing at home and at senior centers and sewing centers, and no one pushes them to work fast or to meet a certain production quota. They work at their own speed—so important with arthritic fingers. They might make $40 a month or $2 a month or *$200* a month. One of the women reports, "I don't do it only for the money—it's only pin money with me—I like getting together each week to sew." Another woman who *is* very self-disciplined about putting in a certain number of hours a week, said, "My daughter used to send me a check each month to supplement my Social Security check, so I could buy a little extra. After I started doing this, I told her to stop. It made me feel real good, being able to tell her I didn't need the money any longer. I feel independent."

Payments are made quickly after completion of each item. If you want to get involved, and live in that area, write Handicrafts Marketing Sales, Inc., 1001 Connecticut Ave., N.W., Washington, D. C. 20036. Their telephone number is (202) 293-5541.

The Mayor's Office for Senior Citizens in Chicago, Illinois, has a similar enterprise, a nonprofit corporation called Elder Artisans. Most of the women who crochet items for money are making handmade mice and ducks and monkeys and roosters, and these wares sell for $2.50 to $22, depending on the size. The women also knit wool coats, which wholesale for over a hundred dollars. High-quality stores, such as Neiman-Marcus, Bergdorf-Goodman, Marshall Field, I. Magnin, and Garfinkle's buy the completed articles. The business began when people who worked with programs for the older person saw the beautiful items in the gift cases of public housing projects for the aged in Chicago, and thought this would be a great money-making project for the talented older people who do the work. In 1972, the city began to fund Elder Artisans. As with the Handicrafts Marketing Sales, Inc., no one is pushed to produce. The women are given the raw materials free, and are paid most of the wholesale price for their work. If a woman makes a small animal that wholesales for $2.50, she gets $1.90 and this work represents about forty-five minutes of her time. Right now more women are being recruited for the project. Most older women have been brought up to do some kind of needlework—how about you? If you live in the Chicago area, and want to explore becoming involved in Elder Artisans, write the Mayor's Office for Senior Citizens, 330 S. Wells St., Chicago, Illinois 60606.

· *Foster grandparents.*

Have you heard of the nationwide Foster Grandparent program? Foster Grandparents serve children in institutions on a one-to-one basis, four hours a day, five days a week. These kids desperately need someone to give them affection and attention. To be eligible, you have to be sixty years old. You receive a small amount of money from ACTION, the government agency that sponsors the program. They see it more as a volunteer program than a work program, so they call the money you get a "stipend" instead of a salary. In addition to the personal satisfaction from this kind of work, it can possibly be a springboard for a better-paying job in a similar kind of institution. It can also serve as experience, if you're thinking of applying for a job as a nursemaid in a private home.

• *The Senior Companion program.*
ACTION also sponsors the Senior Companion program, where you serve adults with special needs in nursing homes and in other kinds of institutions, as well as in their own homes. Here, too, you make a small "stipend." And why can't being part of Senior Companion also give you job experience to go on to something that pays more? You can talk to an ACTION representative about these programs by calling (800) 424-8580, toll free.

• *Can you teach arts-and-crafts?*
If you can teach arts-and-crafts, call your local bureau of recreation and talk directly to the director of the senior citizens programs; ask if the agency has received any funds to hire older people to *teach* older people.

• *Federally funded jobs.*
There are Title III funds under the Comprehensive Employment and Training Act to employ and train forty-five- to fifty-four-year-old workers, and there are Title IX Funds under the Older Americans Act to employ persons aged fifty-five and over. Telephone your local Office on Aging or Commission On Aging to investigate older worker programs in *your* area.

Programs That Will Also Hire the Older Worker

• *Program for Local Service jobs.*
ACTION also sponsors a Program for Local Service (PLS), where ACTION and a cosponsor (a place of employment) work together to create jobs. The cosponsor actually does the hiring, but both ACTION and the cosponsor contribute toward your paychecks. You get about three thousand dollars a year—a low wage, but this could be just right for you if you're already receiving a monthly social security check and can't earn over a certain amount. The cosponsor might be a public or private, non-profit agency, and your boss would be the cosponsor. PLS places people of all ages, and they have potential for providing many more of these jobs for the over-50 worker.

For more information, write Program for Local Service, P. O. Box 996, Washington, D. C. 20525.

• *Manpower jobs.*

Call your mayor's office to ask if there are any Public Service Employment program jobs available. These are manpower programs that hire people of all ages. The deputy commissioner of health in one city reports that older workers have been hired under this kind of program to be health advocacy aides. They assist older patients in finding alternatives to institutionalization and work to remove barriers such as transportation and bureaucratic procedures, which can prevent the patient from receiving necessary out-patient services. For instance, one health advocacy aide was assigned to a patient who had missed several important medical appointments. The aide was able to arrange for transportation to the hospital and to provide Meals-on-Wheels in the home. Another aide arranged for a home care aide to visit a patient until she recuperated from her illness. In many states, the age cutoff of Public Service Employment program jobs is seventy —so if you've been forced to resign from your job at the age of sixty-five and need extra income, this might be for you. These jobs range from the arts to administrative work to social service work. Salaries can range from $6,000 a year to $9,000 annually. Usually, you are guaranteed that the job lasts a year. The usual requirement for eligibility is that the applicant has been out of work for a certain length of time prior to hiring.

• *Remember the New Deal Days?*

If you or your husband were involved in the work world during the 1930's, you've noticed that many of these jobs are similar to the kinds of work programs that existed in the New Deal days. Because of the high rate of unemployment then, they were created with funding made available through the government, as are *these* programs. However, funded programs can quickly come and go; check to see if there's a *new* work program in your area that I haven't mentioned. Call your mayor's office and inquire.

Vocational Rehabilitation

• *Eligibility.*

If you have any kind of psychological or physical handi-
cap which keeps you from gainful employment, you may
be eligible for help from Vocational Rehabilitation (VR),
a government-funded program with offices throughout the
nation (mostly in urban areas). First, you have to make
an appointment with a Vocational Rehabilitation counselor. You will be required to provide medical documentation that you are disabled and that your disability can be
remedied to the point where you will be able to work.

• *Services.*

Vocational Rehabilitation provides its clients with these
rehabilitation services that will put them back into the
work force: medical examination, corrective medical intervention, vocational assessment, testing, counseling, education that will lead to employment, and job placement
—as well as a follow-up service after placement. This is
a free service, and it is available to the over-50 woman.

However, priority is given to the *younger* older woman
—because they feel their investment in her is more likely
to pay off.

Job Counseling for the Over-50 Woman

• *Supportive, non-bureaucratic settings.*

You're no doubt feeling shaky about knocking on those
doors, and want all the help you can get. Job counseling
for the older woman is now available in some areas of
the country. These are self-help groups, funded by the
government and foundations. They offer warm, supportive, non-bureaucratic settings where women can learn
how to write a résumé, how to be assertive in an interview and how to complete a job application. If you live
in the Berkeley, California, area—stop in at the Jobs for
Older Women office at 3102 Telegraph Ave., or call
(415) 849-0332. Tish Summers, an over-50 woman, has
gotten this group going, and it's part of the National Alliance For Displaced Homemakers movement that she

has organized. Advocates for Women, another self-help employment group in the same area, aids women in starting their own businesses and offers job workshops. Their address is 256 Sutter St., San Francisco, Calif., telephone (415) 391-4870. New Directions for Women exists in Baltimore, Md., and like the other self-help employment groups, it's staffed by women. Their address is 2515 N. Charles St., Baltimore, Md. 21218. Call them at (301) 366-8570.

• *What kind of counseling?*

Group and one-to-one counseling is offered in these self-help employment settings, and often the staff will go out into the community to offer workshops. The services are often free. Call your state employment office to see if they fund such a group, or call your local woman's liberation center or National Organization for Women office to find out whether groups like this exist in *your* area.

The Household Worker—Strides She's Made

Ninety-seven to ninety-eight per cent of all household workers are women. Approximately two-thirds are black. The remaining third includes whites, American Indians, Chicanos, and other minorities. The median age is 50. Fourteen per cent of these workers are sixty-five or older. One and a half million Americans are employed as household workers. Are you one?

• *Legislation . . . Advocacy Groups.*

If so, do you know that you're now covered by the minimum wage law? That your employer has to pay Social Security taxes for you? That you can join organizations *for* household workers that are run *by* household workers (organizations like the National Committee on Household Employment and the Progressive Household Technicians of New York, that fight for better pay and humane working conditions)? Household workers are organizing all over the country. How is this different from the situation that existed ten or twenty years ago? Well, for one thing the 1974 amendments to the Fair Labor Standards Act (effective May 1, 1974) extended the act's provisions to domestic service workers employed in private households. That means you're covered by the minimum wage law if you receive wages from one employer in excess of $50 in one calendar quarter or if you work more than eight hours a week in one or more households. You can't make less than $2.20 an hour beginning January 1, 1976, and not less than $2.30 an hour after December 31, 1976. If you work in a household for more than 40 hours in a work week, the employer has to pay you time-and-a-half for the time you put in *after* the 40 hours, unless you live-in (you're *not* covered by the minimum wage law if you're a casual baby-sitter or a companion for old people or sick people). In states where the minimum wage is higher than that of the federal law, the state minimum wage must be paid. And your employer cannot pay a male household worker more than a female household worker. If you are covered by the minimum wage law, your employer pays a share of your Social Security tax, and the remainder is taken out of your paycheck—just like it would be if you worked in a factory or in an office. However, some employers will agree to pay the entire tax as a fringe benefit.

You can also recover unpaid minimum and/or overtime back wages. That means you can go back as far as two years (and in some cases, three years) to the date the law was made effective to get any wages you were entitled to and *didn't* get. If you're bristling, "She didn't pay me the minimum wage *all that time!*" look in the telephone book for U.S. Government, Department of Labor, Wage and Hour Division, or write the U.S. Department of Labor, Employment Standards Administration, Wage and Hour Division, Washington, D. C. 20210, and present your case.

· *A proposed code of standards.*

The struggle for better working conditions has just begun. The National Committee on Household Employment, 7705 Georgia Ave., N.W., Suite 208, Washington, D. C., telephone (202) 291-2422, organizes chapters all over the country, and they've drawn up a code of standards—demands that are in keeping with the kind of benefits given workers in other industries. They ask that wages be paid according to the cost of living of a particular area; higher wages should be paid for jobs requiring special training or skills; pay periods should be agreed upon in advance; clothing or food shouldn't be considered part of payment; and workers get sick leave, vacation leave, and legal holidays off. They're asking that a *written* agreement between the employer and employee be drawn up, and that this agreement clearly define the duties of the position, including specific tasks. Rest periods, meal-times, and hours should be specified. Work and work relationships should be periodically evaluated, with the intent of improving efficiency and understanding. Pleasant, private quarters should be provided for live-in employees, and telephone privileges and time off for private activities (such as church attendance) should be agreed upon in advance of employment and written into the "contract." Efficient and safe and workable appliances and cleaning aids should be provided. Actually, is this kind of "contract" so unreasonable? Professional workers in agencies have contracts. Job specifications exist for all kinds of workers in private and public agencies. It's time household workers have the same kinds of rights and benefits as other workers. It's been a long hard pull for the domestic worker to even reach this point of progress. Two black women in their seventies were telling me how they worked for three and four dollars a week many years ago, and how they were expected to do a week's work in one day. Well, they're making more now, but many household workers are still expected to do a week's work in one day. Fringe benefits are still the cast-off clothes, the leftover food, and the ride to the bus line after working hours; a poor substitute for paid vacations and sick leave with pay. I heard another household worker say that household work with its present conditions is probably the only antebellum occupation remaining in this country—and I believe it. Many women still call their household worker "my girl" (her "girl" may be sixty years old!), and the small children in the family often call the household worker by her first name. It's not unusual for an employer to call the household worker early in the morning and tell her not to come in that day —without offering to pay for the missed day.

At this point some states have unemployment compensation for household workers and some states have work-

33333333333333

er's compensation—but the National Committee on Household Employment relies on the goodwill of employers to implement the code of standards. They are not, at this time, working toward legislation of the code of standards, because they feel implementation of any legislation is an unrealistic goal. However, the very existence of the committee serves to raise the consciousness of household workers, and as their membership grows, it *is* possible that they will later press for legislation.

So write the Progressive Household Technicians of New York, Room 601, 370 Lexington Ave., New York, N. Y. 10017, and find out how they've developed into a social action group, and ask if they've done any organizing in *your* area. Organize—don't agonize!

Starting a Small Business from Your Home

How about opening your own business? Running your own business gives you independence. No one asks you if you have a college degree (or a high school diploma). No one asks you what your work experience has been. No one asks your *age!* You won't have to quit working when you're sixty-five—because no one can hit you with mandatory retirement.

• *Kinds of home businesses.*

What kind of home business? Do you know how to type? Rent or buy a secondhand typewriter and let students and writers know you're available to type their papers and manuscripts. To attract students, put an ad in college newspapers. Advertise by posting notices on bulletin boards in laundromats, bookstores, and drugstores near campuses. To let writers know you're in business, buy advertisements in the monthly writing magazines that have national circulations, *Writer's Digest* and *The Writer*. Both magazines hit the newsstands each month, and are read by countless aspiring and professional writers. Here's a typical ad you could run, for about $25:

Jane Doe Typing Service
P.O. Box 999 Los Angeles, Ca 90033
Phone: (415) 367-9786
Rates: 50¢ per page, plus postage

Includes: Minor corrections, one c.c.
Typewriters: Pica and Elite
Neat and Experienced.

Are you a superb cook? An excellent baker? Start a
small-scale home catering service. You can advertise that
you specialize in three gourmet entrees (accompanied
by a salad and an elegant dessert *and* homemade rolls).
You want to attract the woman who's busy with a demanding career and doesn't have time to cook—and yet
needs to entertain occasionally. And you can offer your
services to the man who lives alone and wants to give an
intimate dinner party, but doesn't have the time to fuss.
Choose affluent neighborhoods in which to advertise.
Get flyers printed (and that's not an expensive process)
that list what you offer; your name, address, and phone
number—and the fact that you deliver. It's a safe bet
that people who don't have time to cook don't have time
to pick up their orders. Even if you don't have a car,
invest money in taxi fare for deliveries—you'll attract
much more business. Breeze into expensive high rises
where singles live, take the elevator to each floor, and slip
a flyer under each apartment door. Hire schoolchildren to
put your flyers under the doors of restored townhouses
in your downtown area. You can keep this kind of business as small or as large as you wish. One woman who
placed a newspaper ad telling of her home-catering service got responses from *corporations!* She now has a large-
scale business with several people working for her.

Do you like working with people? Do you have a car?
You might want to be self-employed in the way Dee is:

"I'm a daytime companion for older women who live
alone. I drive them to the shopping center for lunch, I do
their shopping for them, I take them to lectures, I take
them to afternoon matinees. These are women in their
seventies and eighties, and they're usually sick or lonely
or frail or just afraid to be alone. They depend on me for
companionship and transportation. I enjoy it, too, and I
make a very good income. The kind of older woman
who can afford this type of help usually has money. She's
the widow of a doctor or a big lawyer, or her children
are paying for my services because they don't want their
mother to be alone all day. In a way, it's sort of a lark

for me. I don't do any cleaning or heavy cooking—oh, I'll make an egg or a cup of tea for them—and I get out to all the latest plays and movies with my ticket paid for, of course. And I didn't need any experience when I started. How do I get my jobs? Mainly through word-of-mouth. The first job I got was through a free ad I placed in a senior center newsletter."

I asked, "Are the women demanding?"

"Some of them are, sure," she said, "but isn't every job demanding in its own way? And some of the women are great. I think I'm pretty lucky. I have a new career after not having ever worked—and I'm sixty-two!"

Dee had created her own kind of unique service. "Companions are a dime a dozen," she told me, "but how many of them come with a car as part of their services? Last summer I chauffered and accompanied an eighty-year-old woman around Nova Scotia. She said she had always wanted to go—."

• *Turn your hobbies into income.*

Do you have a hobby you're very good at? . . . that you could turn into a business, working from home? One over-50 woman I met paints china exquisitely, and she accidently stumbled upon the fact that she could turn her hobby into income. She had her china plates on display at an arts and crafts show at a senior center, and a passerby asked if she could paint her an entire set of china —at an unbelievably high price. She got her next commission through a friend of this customer, who admired the china on the dinner table. Where does she do her painting? In an extra bedroom in her house. She put up a worktable, and pushed the bed against the wall. No overhead!

• *Thrift shops do well in this economy.*

"I was going to move anyway," a vibrant sixty-year-old woman told me, "so I moved into a row house that has a storefront. A perfect place for my thrift shop! Why did I open a thrift shop? The economy, my dear. . . . Any time we're going through a recession or a depression, people are going to buy second-hand clothes. This is one of the businesses that *thrive* on poverty.

"So you're doing well?" I asked.

"I just had to take in a partner, I'm doing so beauti-fully! I started out by keeping the shop open only on weekends, so I could keep my job in an office. I didn't want to give up the security of that job until I knew whether I could make it with the shop. And, then, when the shop was *packed* with people every weekend, and when they started to ask me when I was going to start being open during the week, I knew I had a regular trade, and I asked my sister, who's retiring this year from her job, if she wanted to come in with me. I love it—and I'm making better money than I did working in that job for fifteen years. No bosses, no worry about extra income after the age of sixty-five, no worry about whether I look too old to get work!"

• *Get advice.*

If *you're* considering opening your own business, get advice and information from the regional or national office of the Small Business Administration (Small Busi-ness Administration, Washington, D. C. 20416). They'll be very helpful with information about your competi-tion, your chances of success, the pitfalls of the kind of business you're considering, and how much capital you'll need. ACTION, the same federal agency that administers several national volunteer programs, also provides advice to the person opening a new business with the services of SCORE (Service Corps of Retired Executives). Older retired middle- and upper-management people, as well as executives and people who once owned businesses, are available, to give you all kinds of advice. Write ACTION, 1900 Connecticut Avenue, N.W., Washington, D. C. 20525, for more information. ACTION is a wonderful way for the over-50 person to use the *services* of the over-50 person; using the business expertise of the retired executive who now has the time to share his or her know-how.

WHY Over-50 Women Work (and It's Not Always for the Money!)

I was sitting in a cafeteria with two women. One was a young sixty-two, bouncy-looking with white hair, and the other woman was apparently older.

"I sold ten coats today!" the older woman announced proudly. It was Saturday evening and both women had just finished a grueling work week, selling in a downtown department store.

"Aren't you exhausted?" I asked.

"I'm never tired!" the older woman replied, "Listen, I'm seventy-three, and I work five days a week. If I stopped—*then* I'd go to pieces. I've always been in business. What would I do if I stayed home? Listen to my sister complain all day? I just thank God that the store lets us stay on after we're sixty. I've been there twenty-five years."

"Do you wish you could quit?" I asked the younger woman.

She was reflective for a moment. "No, not really. Two of my girlfriends work there—we have lunch together every day. I guess I'd miss it if I quit. Once I start on Social Security, I might cut it down to part-time."

· *Why else besides the money?*

Neither of these women mentioned money as a prime factor in their desire to continue working. Sure, money is important and necessary to them, but it was obvious they were getting other satisfactions from their jobs: the opportunity to perform; the sense of order they have in their everyday life (knowing they have to be at a certain place at a certain time); and, particularly, the opportunity to socialize with the same people every day on the job. Working is as much a social experience as a job to them. And the seventy-three-year-old woman is *proud* that she can sell ten coats in one day; she is fiercely glad that she can still be productive in a society that devalues the older person.

· *The work ethic.*

This is not to say that income is *not* important. For many over-50 women, work without pay—volunteer work—would not be attractive. The work ethic has played a most important part in our developmental years. Do you remember the saying: "Another day, another dollar?" And "He worked hard for every penny!"? Work has traditionally been rewarded with a regular paycheck—and a regular paycheck is still needed by many older people.

Rents increase. Medical bills can be staggering. Food costs rise. Extra income is desperately needed at a time in life when a job can be hard to get.

• *Other incentives for working after 50.*

"It's not only the woman who's already on Social Security who has problems," a woman reminded me. "It's women like me, too. Women in our middle years."

I asked her what she meant.

"I was just offered a good job," she said, "but I'm hesitating. The job pays close to ten thousand, but it's a new program, and there's no group health insurance available. When I was twenty, I wouldn't have cared. I *have* to care now. I can't afford individual medical coverage—I don't even know if I could get it, the shape I'm in—and one of my biggest incentives for working is a good group health insurance plan."

• *Feeling part of the world out there.*

"I like feeling part of the world out *there*," an over-50 woman told me, "and that's why I work. I was a wife for over thirty years and that's over. My husband passed away two years ago. My kids have their own families, their own lives. I stayed home for a year after my husband died, and that was *bad!* I felt like I was on the outside of everything. I didn't feel like I was part of anything *vital*. When I go downtown on the bus every morning, and I'm part of my office bunch that has to punch a time clock at eight-thirty, I don't feel as though I'm *any* particular age."

These are all valid reasons why the over-50 woman may want—indeed may *need*—to work. And these are all valid proof that employment opportunities must be made available to qualified women, regardless of their age.

Promises You'll Make to Yourself before Your First Day at Work

Before you go up on that elevator to be interviewed for your first venture back into the labor market in thirty-four years, promise yourself:

- "I won't take on the mother-role on the job. It's easy to slip into—I was a wife and mother for so many years—but a lot of people will resent it."
- "I won't be critical of the young girls in the office who gripe about working overtime and who spend a lot of time combing their hair. I won't get aggravated when they talk about their boyfriends instead of working. It's none of my business, and I'll make quick enemies if I do."
- "I won't run to the supervisor tattling on my coworkers. Even if I think that'll make her like me."
- "I won't constantly complain about the dirty ladies room and the cold office—especially when no one else does."
- "I won't keep talking about my grandchildren—even though they're the greatest grandchildren in the world."
- "I will not tell the truth when my co-workers ask, 'How are you this morning?' I will always say, 'fine!' "

- *The work world is different today!*

You're going back into the work world—and it's a different world from the one you may have left years ago. Workers *do* complain when they have to work overtime. People *do* stay home when they have colds. Secretaries are unionizing and saying things like "Don't give me roses. Give me raises!"

- *Catch up with the changes.*

Catch up with this new world, and try to understand it—even if you don't like it. Use the advantages of being over-50 on the job. Your years of living experience have given you extra insight and perception for problem-solving, and you can use your problem-solving strengths in the work world. Your years of living experience have made you more aware of differences in people (which means you can walk into an office on your first day at work and quickly discover who will help you and who won't). You're going to know (*because* of your years of living experience) how to work with the woman who's always complaining; how to talk to the man who never smiles; how to relate to a boss who's formal and distant.

• *Use the strengths you've gotten through getting older!*

Going back into the work world at the age of fifty-five, or entering it for the very first time at the age of fifty-two, can mean an exciting challenge. *Use* the strengths you've gotten through aging—through being a woman over-50—to also make this one of the most exciting experiences of your life.

CHAPTER 9

Strategies for the Career Woman (How to Get More Money and Power)

᠀

Making More Money

Are you being paid what you're worth? Dorothye and Loretta don't think they are . . . and in talking to them, we tried to work toward solutions.

"I had been on the job five years," Dorothye said, "and I found out this young man who had just been hired to do the same work I'm doing is getting sixteen hundred dollars more than I am."

"What did you do?"

"I asked for a raise—and my boss turned me down. No, I didn't quit. How can I? My husband's sick. He has emphysema. He'll never be able to work again."

"Are you looking for another job?"

Pause.

"I look in the Sunday ads. I'd like to get a job with the federal government. They pay more and it's more secure. I guess I should be looking harder."

Dorothye and her husband, both in their fifties, live on her salary (she's an executive secretary) and his dis-

ability benefits. They're putting a son through medical
school. Their income is tight. They've just about used up
all of their savings. She knows she can't quit her job until
she finds something better. She talked slowly and frequently sighed. She nervously pushed her hair back. It
would be hard for her to act aggressively.

- *Taking steps to get a raise.*

However, I suggested a small but definite step; that
she put a memo in her boss's mailbox: "Even though you
informed me that our budget does not allow any room for
an increase in my salary at this time, I would like to formally request that you consider a 10% increase built into
next year's budget for me. I am basing this request on
my work record, which you have reviewed and have
agreed is excellent." I also suggested that just before the
time when her employer begins to prepare next year's
budget, Dorothye send him a "reminder" note, attached
to a copy of this memo. Dorothye will have put into writing her exact expectations. And behaving in this assertive
way can make her *feel* more assertive, and then later *act*
more assertive.

Loretta said to me, "How can I ask for a raise when
our company's doing so poorly? My boss said the economy
hit us hard this year—."

- *A pitfall: identifying with the boss.*

Loretta is identifying with this company. She's been
with them for twenty-five years as head bookkeeper. Why
is she, like many saleswomen who work in "good" stores,
identifying with her place of employment? The man she
works for owns the company. She doesn't. He makes the
profits. She doesn't. He takes home a hundred thousand
dollars a year. She takes home less than eleven thousand
a year, after taxes. Does identifying with the company
make her feel closer to success and power? The reality
is that over-50 women who are making less than eleven
thousand dollars a year have no job power. Has she made
her work so large a part of her life that the company has
become an extension of herself? It's easy to fall into that
trap when you're alone, and work has become your total
life. Once Loretta understands that she is *not* part of her

boss's world, and that he (and what he represents) is not an extension of herself, she'll be able to view her situation from a critical distance and acknowledge to herself that an extra ten dollars a week in her pay envelope will not affect her boss's life style or the health of the business. As Letty Cottin Pogrebin, the author who writes about working women, said, ". . . even in this slumping economy, *some*body is making money; it might as well be you." Loretta's boss is delighted that she identifies with the company because he knows it makes her hesitant to be demanding.

- *Learning to be assertive.*

Also, Loretta finds it hard to be assertive because she's so used to saying "yes" to bosses (especially male ones). As women, we're taught to be agreeable to male authority figures—doctors, fathers, bosses. We see them as having power over us. They often do. But sometimes we invest more symbolic power in them than they actually have. *Can* we learn to say "no"? We can—once we're made aware of why we say "yes." Practice helps. Saying "no" the the first time makes it easier the next time.

- *How much to ask for.*

How much of a raise should you ask for? Read the want ads to compare what you're making with what other similar jobs are offering. Contact the personnel offices of government agencies to inquire about their pay scales. If you're a professional worker, subscribe to your professional journals (they frequently list job openings with salaries). The Los Angeles *Times* Sunday edition and the New York *Times* Sunday edition list professional and top and middle management jobs in their classified sections, and this is where you can get a good idea of how much comptrollers and social workers and hospital administrators and nurses and librarians and public relations specialists and advertising copywriters and college deans make as well as teachers and recreation workers and sales managers. Each newspaper reflects the salaries paid in different parts of the country—and you'll notice that salary differences often exist in various geographic areas for the same kind of work. You'll also quickly notice that industry is where the money usually is, rather than in social service and teaching jobs. This might mean that you would want a job as a public relations specialist with a financial organization rather than a hospital.

- *Using the "grapevine."*

Does your kind of work have a "grapevine"? In-group kinds of important gossip spreads where there's a grapevine; you'll find out about salaries, and who-got-a-raise-and-who-didn't, and who's leaving a job and who's being hired. That means you'll want to attend the conferences and meetings where you can hear what's happening. Join all the professional organizations connected with your kind of work, so you're *invited* to these meetings and conferences. Get to know your colleagues at these conferences and meetings, so as you're filling your coffee cup before the meeting starts, standing next to the woman who has a parallel job to yours at another agency, you'll be included in the conversation she's having with someone about salaries. Let your boss know you want to go to these meetings. Some employers balk. "We're too busy, you have too much to do at the office," or *"I'll* probably go over. I'll let you know what happened when I get back, though." What some of these bosses are really saying is, *"I* want to be the one who is visible." But press the issue. Tell your boss that these meetings and conferences will allow you to be more valuable in your work (and they will!). Try to work out a schedule where you go at least *some* of the time ("Can we alternate?"). If you're assertive and persistent in a non-hostile way, it's going to be very hard for your boss to keep saying no.

Attending these conferences and meetings and speaking up when you're there will pay off in other ways: It will let people in your field know how competent you are; it will give the director of another agency a chance to get to know you—so when a great job opens up, he (or she) will think, "Ah! *She* would be perfect for this spot—"

- *Ask people what they're making.*

Ask your fellow workers what they're making. What do you have to lose? All they can say (if they don't want to tell you) is, "I prefer not to discuss it." If you do ask, you'll also offer to tell them what *you're* making—fair is fair. I remember a woman who did ask, and was told, and was so angry when she found out what her co-worker was making (she was angry at her boss, *not* the co-worker), that she immediately began to look for another job, and she's now making two thousand dollars a year more. Sometimes we need that *push*.

· *Role-play approaching the boss.*

How do you ask for a raise? First, make a list of reasons why you deserve more money. Objective reasons are always better than subjective reasons. An objective reason: "86% of private-school teachers in this area, with my kind of background, are making $1,500 more a year than I am." A subjective reason: "I need the money!" Using your objective reasons as a base, ask your husband or sister or friend to role-play the asking-for-a-raise situation with you. First, you be the employer and have the other person be you. Then reverse the roles. Have the "boss" in the role-play present all kinds of probable objections. Grapple with these objections. After at least six role-plays (space them out over a couple of days so you'll have time to evaluate them in between), you'll be much more in command of yourself when you finally do go into your boss's office. You'll know what to say, what to ask, what to answer, and what to anticipate. You'll feel more self-confident.

"The role-play method worked beautifully for me," one woman said. "My boss constantly uses the 'attack' as a way of getting people off his back. This scares the people who work for him, so they either seldom make any demands, or when they do, they get so afraid when he 'attacks' that they're like a limp rag when he's finished with them—and there goes their demand. In the role-play I had deliberately incorporated the 'attack' I expected and I used all kinds of ways to avoid it *or* confront it, and then I would doggedly continue talking about the raise. I think my sister and I dreamed up at least twenty ways to handle him. We *worked*. But it was worth it. When I finally got in his office, I was amazingly calm. I was *ready*. How did I act? When the 'attack' began, I sat there, not saying a word. When he ran out of steam, I just picked up where I had left off. I kept talking about the *issue*—the raise—and I ignored his outbursts. I waited it out and in *ignoring* his attacks, I discounted them!"

I was intrigued. "Did you get the raise?"

She smiled. "Yes. And months later, he was walking down the hall with me after a meeting, and out of the blue he told me how much he had admired my 'cool' during that conference. In fact, he said that's what got me the raise. He said he liked my guts." Games? Yes, and games are distasteful—but know the rules!

- *What to do if you're turned down.*

If your request for a raise is turned down, you already know you can get mad and quit or get mad and stay— but what are your other options? One woman planned ahead immediately after her boss said no. Her job title was accounting supervisor. She knew she was going to begin looking for another job, so she decided to attempt to get her job title changed to accounting director. Wouldn't that look much more impressive on a résumé? While her boss was still feeling guilty about saying no to her, she presented her request. Being a person who saw himself as fair *and* generous, he hardly hesitated. Changing her job title didn't cost *money*. Within one week the maintenance man was changing her job title sign outside her office. Within one year she had a new job making much more money, based on that important job title she was able to list on her résumé.

- *Bargaining.*

A public-relations job opened up and a fifty-year-old woman applied for it. She was offered less money than she knew she deserved, but she didn't turn it down. Instead she bargained on the vacation leave benefit. She didn't settle for the twelve days a year that the agency offered. She asked for twenty-four days. And she got it—because, in dollars and cents, on paper, the agency could deal with that in their budget. "That made the lower salary worth it to me," she said, "because it's a high-pressure job, and I need more time off to unwind."

- *A union can bargain for you.*

Asking for more money is emotionally easier if you belong to a union. The union does collective bargaining for you. An employer feels much more pressure from a large group of organized workers than from one woman, sitting anxiously across the desk from him.

• *Coalition of Labor Union Women.*

If you are a union member, see if your city has a chapter of Coalition of Labor Union Women. CLUW is a national group made up only of women—a union-within-a-union. They make their needs heard as *women workers.* Why? Blacks and women workers have not always gotten the same benefits as other union members. Unions haven't always pushed as hard for them. CLUW recently held their first constitutional convention in Detroit, and 1,004 women from 60 unions registered as voting delegates. Women within unions, pressing for issues that affect women, can have a lot of clout—when the women are *organized.*

Reentering the Job Market As a Professional

You were a social worker or a teacher or a librarian many years ago, and then you stopped working to bring up your children, and now you want to go back to work. Adjust your thinking so you're ready to go into *allied* kinds of work, because you just might find your former field all tied up. You might find, because of the depressed economy, that there's a job freeze on teaching and social work jobs in your community. You might find all the jobs in the library field have been snapped up by recent college graduates.

• *Adjusting to the economy.*

What do you do? One former teacher who had taught elementary school in the 1940's found she couldn't return to her field because there were no job openings. She called all the community colleges in her area and asked to speak to the deans of continuing education. She let each dean know she had a master's degree in education, and that she could sew and lead discussion groups. She's now teaching thirteen hours a week in various senior centers for two of these community colleges. Her salary comes from government funds the schools have received to place outreach continuing education in Senior Centers.

"Tell your readers," she said, "this is being done throughout the country, and that they should apply for these jobs before each semester begins—including summer sessions. And tell them to start working on their master's degree if they want to keep teaching for community colleges. What should they major in? It doesn't matter. It's that piece of paper that matters." This woman was flexible enough to attempt teaching a whole different group from what she was used to; she had been imaginative enough to explore other avenues for teaching. "The payoff," she added, "is that I'm finding older people are easier to teach than a classroom of small children. They're not a captive audience. They *want* to learn."

Another former teacher approached the manager of a local department store and asked if she could set up a sewing school for teen-agers. She's been working there for two years now, and the school is in operation every afternoon and evening, and all day Saturdays. She administers the entire operation, and she supervises three sewing teachers. This brings the store a nice bonus income. The students buy their patterns and their fabrics and even their sewing machines there, as well as pay for the sewing lessons. And it encourages the students to buy *other items* in the store, as well.

Checking the Job Out

In looking for a job, find out as much as possible about the company to which you're applying. It's always effective to let the company or agency or school know that you've gone out of your way to find out who they are and what they've done· Be specific when you refer to what you've learned about them.

· *Ways to find out facts about the place.*

How do you find out these facts (besides looking them up in reference books in the library)? Businesses can be looked up in *Bradford's Directory of Market Research* and *The Occupational Thesaurus*. Publishing houses and advertising agencies can be looked up in *Madison Avenue* and *The Literary Marketplace*.

- *The value of contacting the umbrella funding agency.*

Perhaps there is an umbrella funding agency. *How* do you find out who the umbrella funding agency is? By asking the comptroller of the agency, who deals with funding. Call her cold, if you don't know her. If you're asked why you're inquiring, tell her you're writing a research paper or tell the truth—you want the information before you come in to be interviewed. Umbrella funding organizations always have large amounts of printed up-to-date statistics on hand, and it's good public-relations for them to give out the facts that give their agencies a good image (also, it helps when they have fund-raising drives). Ask the person in charge of public relations to send you their newsletter. This can be an excellent source of information on the function and philosophy and goals of their agencies—and it tells you who the important people in the agency are.

- *How to use your information.*

In your letter of application, *use* the information you've gotten. Example: "I would be proud to identify myself with an agency that has relocated over two hundred Russian-Jewish immigrants in the past two years." The woman who wrote this had first called the Associated Jewish Charities before writing her letter of application. She was applying for a job with her local Jewish Family & Children's Society agency, and she found out that the Associated Jewish Charities is their funding umbrella. Ninety-six applicants were interviewed for the job and this woman, who had done her homework, got it! She was older than any other applicant—and she got the job because she was the *only* applicant who came into the interview armed with hard, concrete facts. She told me that at strategic points during the job interview she would interject a fact she had researched, and she could actually see the pleasure on the director's face.

In order to employ this technique you have to be sure you space your initial call for an interview with the date of the interview so you have enough time to get these facts.

- *Payoffs to having the information.*

There are other payoffs to this technique. Once you've

found out all you need to know about the place of hiring, you may find you don't want the job after all, and save yourself later time and heartaches. Mia answered an ad for a job as a director of a large community organization. She had been active in the civil rights movement in the 1960's, and then later in the peace movement. More recently, she had been leading a more private kind of life, and she missed the excitement of collectively working for social change. She became even more interested in the job during her initial interview with the search committee. The office walls were covered with posters and there was an air of purpose and vitality to the people. After this successful interview, she agreed to a second interview with the board of directors, and she went home feeling elated. And then a friend who had an ear close to the workings in the city asked if she had heard about the conflicts in the organization. Conflicts? The rational part of Mia immediately took over and she made inquiries. She discovered the organization had hired three directors in one year—and all three had quit. She called the ex-directors and introduced herself—and asked them why they had resigned. They were open and frank and their stories were identical. It was a community neighborhood organization torn apart by unresolved differences in goals and philosophy. Half the members (neighborhood groups) wanted to focus primarily on community development; finding funding sources to build new businesses in the neighborhood to create new jobs. The other neighborhood groups wanted to continue as they had been since the 1960's, organizing around grass-roots neighborhood issues such as rat control and tenant-landlord relations. The organization had been greatly weakened by the conflict, and expected the director to solve the problems and restore the organization to its former position of strength —single-handedly. The director was also expected to attend meetings almost every night, as well as work eight hours each day. A sixty-hour work week! Disillusioned, Mia withdrew her application. If she hadn't investigated the situation, she would have given up the job she had (which wasn't a bad job), taken this precarious position, and then found herself with no choice other than resignation and no income.

Finding out facts in advance and having time to mull over them can have the opposite effect. It can help you realize that you *are* the person for the job. Sharon, a black public health nurse, was considering a job where, after inquiry, she found she would be the only black person on the professional staff. Three questions came to her mind: "Why didn't they hire any black professionals before?", "Will I be accepted by the rest of the staff?" and "Will I feel comfortable as the *only* black staff person?" She investigated further. She discovered that the new director, an ethical person, out of strong personal convictions, planned to change the image of this conservative southern agency, and because of funding reasons (the agency received community money) the board of directors realized they had better go along with this. The director told Sharon he planned to fully integrate the staff, and she wouldn't be the *only* black person on the board; she would be the *first* black person hired. When she thought long and hard about the situation, she came to the conclusion that if anyone could adapt to being the first black person in a white agency, where institutional racism was no doubt rampant—she could (she had been an officer in the army for many years, working with an integrated staff, and she had led a social life where her friends and associates were black and white). Sharon weighed the question, "Is the hassle worth it to me?" She decided it was—because of the excellent salary and the interesting work. And she knew she could always resign if it proved too tension-provoking, because she was already receiving a handsome army pension. Taking the job turned out to be a good decision. Sharon was able to wait it out, dispassionately and without panic, when she did meet resistance, and even to confront it when she felt it was necessary. She had come to the job with enough ego-strength *and* a sense of historical perspective to use all of her energy and intelligence doing the job, rather than becoming immobilized with fear and rage when conflicts came up. All of her positive strengths were ready, because she *had* investigated the work situation ahead of time.

Using Your Strengths—and Weighing
Advantages and Disadvantages

In applying for a certain job, changing your job from a
line worker to that of a supervisor, switching to a different
career when you're over-50, or asking for a raise, you
want to look critically at all the advantages and disadvantages, and evaluate your own particular strengths and
vulnerabilities, before deciding whether to do it.

• *Make a list!*

Making a list helps. Seeing your strengths listed on
paper makes you *feel* stronger. It also makes you feel
more objective when you see your vulnerabilities listed
(less afraid!). When you write down all the advantages
and disadvantages of taking that job, it gives you the
necessary distance to make a judgment. And you'll have
to juggle. You probably can't get everything you want
at that moment in a job, so you'll have to decide what
you're willing to give up in order to *get* more. That means
you'll have to be very aware of how much you'll lose
when you decide to give up something. Or how much
you'll gain. You will want to be honest with yourself
about what you need. You'll have to be very aware of
what is available—and what isn't.

• *Be realistic about what you want.*

"I didn't assess my real needs," an attractive over-50
woman confided, "and it made my life very confused for
a while. I had been in social work for years—I have my
Master of Social Work degree. Well, you know it's not
the highest-paying field in the world, so five years ago I
switched careers in order to make more money. I took a
job as sales manager with a cosmetics company. I became sales manager of the entire East Coast, and I really
made some fantastic money. I bought a condominium. I
went to Europe a couple of times a year. But when people asked me what I did for a living, and I said I'm a
sales manager—well, I felt embarrassed. All my friends
were professionals. So when a job came along as an assistant director of a social agency, I gave up my job as
sales manager—that was just six months ago—and went

back to social work. But the pay—I can't keep up the same life style. I had to give up my full-time housekeeper. I can't buy the same designer clothes I used to. I can't entertain the same way. I've just begun to realize that I might want the prestige of social work—but I want a high income *more!* I'm finally allowing myself to look at what I *really* want. Even if it upsets my long-established self-image. So now I'm getting in touch with the company again—."

"*And* getting in touch with your feelings," I said. She smiled.

Free Yourself from Ageism!

I met a woman at a dinner party whom I instantly liked. We sat in a corner talking about work. "I had always been considered aggressive and tough," she said, "even when I was young. I was—and am—one of the best editors around. I know it. And yet there I was, at a job interview, finding myself apologizing for being older. I wanted the job. I knew I could do it. Yet I heard myself saying, 'I know I'm not exactly young, *but*—.' I couldn't stop thinking about it afterwards. Why did I say that?"

· *Internalizing society's attitudes.*

We talked about it some more, and we both agreed that it's easy for women to begin internalizing how society feels about "women-getting-older." Over-50 women start acting apologetic. Feeling invisible. Pleading. Forgetting how much they've achieved because they feel so overwhelmed. Feeling insecure and without identity. "Here's one for you," the editor said. "A friend of mine—a woman who has her doctorate in philosophy—found herself name-dropping her *children's* names at a job interview! 'My son is Jay Conner, the district attorney,' she said . . . and 'my daughter just had a show at the Museum of Modern Art, have you read about it?' When I found out what she was doing, and I talked to her about it, she couldn't face it. 'Did I really do that?' she asked. I thought, here's a gal who's sharp and witty and who used to be dean of a prestigious women's college—and she

feels so insecure because of her age that she's reduced to
this! *Selling* herself through her family!"

• *How we're victimized by ageism.*

It's easy to feel insecure when society often sees the
over-50 woman as nonproductive and unimportant. It
can and *should* be said that older people are victims of
institutional and individual ageism in the work world. A
Department of Labor study found that physical incapa-
bility was the most common reason mentioned by employers for not hiring older people—despite the fact that
70 per cent of those employers had no factual basis for
their attitude. As automation and technology lessen society's need for human labor, and as jobs get scarcer
because of the economy, pressures mount for earlier retirement and keeping the older worker out of the labor
market. Employers often feel, "She's had her turn. She
worked for thirty years. I'll give the job to a younger
worker." Instead of looking at the economic reasons for
rejecting the older worker, and trying to examine viable
economic alternatives to the present system, people don't
want to see themselves as treating older people as dead-
wood, and they'll rationalize, saying, "She won't be able
to keep up the pace in the store," or "She gets a Social
Security check each month. She doesn't need the money."
Even easier is not *seeing* the over-50 person. You don't
have to be concerned about what you can't see!

Another technique is viewing the older person as a
child (a child doesn't have adult needs; a child doesn't
need to work). Treating the over-50 woman as though
she's frail and "over the hill" (how can she hold a job if
she's frail?) Saying how "cute" she is when she says
something witty (reinforcing the child image). And
then it's so easy for the over-50 woman to begin *acting*
helpless (like a child). This former dean of a women's
college had started *feeling* invisible—and that's why she
tried selling her children's credentials instead of her own;
unconsciously, she hoped their visibility would rub off on
her. A friend of mine, aged sixty, who was turned down
for the fourth time on jobs because of her age, started
having accidents. She cut her wrist last month, and then
she tripped over a corner of her living room rug last week,
hurting her back. "I don't think it's accidental," she told

me (she's a perceptive woman), "it's as though I'm acting-out these employers' feelings about me. A self-fulfilling prophecy. They're saying I'm not capable, and that I'm old—and I'm acting that way!"

• *Working together to make change.*

People are living longer, but their incomes are cut off long before they die. Jobs are getting scarcer and the competition for jobs is getting keener. Women forty to sixty-five face age discrimination in the work world. It's important to recognize all of this, and begin demanding that the already-existing legislation against age discrimination be enforced—that more funds be made available for enforcement. We can make these demands better collectively. The Grey Panthers and the National Council of Senior Citizens and the National Caucus on the Black Aged and the National Retired Teachers Association and the American Association for Retired Persons are working toward this goal. Joining one of these groups means you'll feel *support* when you go into a job interview. If you're turned down because of your age, you'll get angry and you'll turn that anger into collective social action—*with* your group. Individually, learn to appreciate yourself as an older woman who *does* have a great deal to offer. The living experience you had during the Depression made you tougher than many younger people. The countless every-day emergencies you coped with for forty years has made you more resourceful than many younger people. The griefs that came through losses have made you more compassionate than many younger people. That doesn't mean there aren't a great many very worthwhile younger people around. There are. But it does mean you have a lot of advantages that will make you a superior worker. You've *learned* more (you've had more *time* to learn).

• *Myths about the older worker.*

And don't swallow the myths you've heard about the older worker. Here are some that the Department of Labor has exploded:

Myth: "Older workers can't meet the physical demands of jobs."

Fact: Only fourteen percent of today's jobs require great strength and heavy lifting. Labor-saving machinery makes it possible for older workers to handle eighty-six per cent of modern jobs without difficulty.

Myth: "Older workers are absent from work too often."

Fact: The attendance record of workers over sixty-five compares favorably with that of other age groups.

Myth: "Older workers are too slow. They can't meet production requirements."

Fact: There is no significant drop in work performance and productivity in older workers. Many older workers exceed the average input of younger workers.

Surprised?
Encouraged?

The Job Interview

Walk into that job interview knowing that the interviewer may be prejudiced because you are older and have full confidence that you're going to act like the capable person that you certainly are.

• *Show pride in YOUR accomplishments.*

You won't sit there and talk about your children—coming off as "the mother." You're not going to act like the "wife of"—rambling on about the achievements of your husband. You're not going to apologize for being older—seeming helpless and frail. You *are* going to be proud of your accomplishments as a person in your own right, and you're going to list your accomplishments. You are not going to diminish the importance of the impressive things you've done in your life by saying, "But that was a long time ago." So what if it was? What you did was still important, wasn't it? You still learned from the experience, didn't you? You can still apply that knowledge to the job you're applying for, can't you?

- *Sit closer to the interviewer.*

On the job interview, offer to shake hands with the interviewer—before the interview, and when you're ready to leave. This makes you look and feel more in control of your environment. When you walk in, if you're vaguely waved to a chair across a big desk, choose the chair closest to the interviewer and *pull* the chair closer. Better yet, sit down on a *sofa* (if there is one near the desk). The closer you are to the interviewer, the better. Distance increases tension and formality on a job interview. Closeness makes you seen more accessible, and the interviewer *acts* more accessible. Don't ask to smoke. This is distasteful to many people. Lean back. You'll look and feel more relaxed.

- *How to dress.*

Dress like an executive when you go on that job interview. It will make you *feel* secure. It will make you *act* self-confident. And if the job interviewer sees you as an executive, it will be harder for her to offer you less money. How does an executive dress? In quiet, classic, and ageless clothes that don't have a dated or too-dressy look. In other words, as if you're going to an elegant, expensive restaurant for lunch. A layered look gives importance. Wear dark clothes in the summer. No-wrinkle fabrics—so you'll look fresh even though it's your third job interview that day. Wear classic jewelry. Gloves (but not the little white ones women wore in the 1940's). If you do wear a hat, take a good look at it: is it the fussy kind? You'll look rural and church-y in it—which may be fine for Sunday services, but not for a job. Once you're sitting across from that employer, take off any coat you might be wearing. Take off your sunglasses. You can't look self-confident hunched up in a coat, or hidden behind sunglasses (also, employers get very uptight when they can't look into your *eyes*).

- *Go easy on the perfume.*

Do you wear perfume? Be very careful about how much you put on before you go to an interview. As we grow older, our sense of smell can slowly decrease. It may be harder for us to detect the strength of odors as sharply as we once did—. To be on the safe side, press that nozzle even more delicately than you think is necessary—and only once.

* *How do you look? Dated?*

It may be necessary to make big changes, so check yourself out: Are you wearing eyeglasses that hang on a chain? Black "nurse" shoes because your feet hurt? Too-dark or too-bright lipstick? Is your hair dyed jet-black (that shoe polish look)? Do you have a caked-powder look? Are you wearing dry rouge that leaves spots of high color on your cheeks? Is your hair stiffly lacquered? Does your corset or girdle make swishing noises when you walk? Are you wearing ornate jewelry during the daytime (like gold earrings with pearl clusters)? All of these things make us look older.

"I feel angry," a woman told me. "I don't want to color my hair! I like the gray. And yet I feel I have to if I want to get a job in my field!"

"How badly do you need to work?" I asked.

She gave me a droll look. "Badly."

Coloring her hair (which she eventually did) was, in a sense, a political act. She decided she was willing to give up a tiny part of her identity (her gray hair) in order to get what she wanted. She acquiesced to the glorification of youth and the devaluing of age in order to make a big paycheck. A knowing act.

Color your hair, with subtle mixtures of shadings that look natural. Avoid a harsh, one-tone blonde. Stay away from gray streaking. And while you're at your hairdresser's, tell her to go easy on the teasing. A natural, casual look is younger. Your hair should look soft and shiny, not teased and lacquered. Invest in a good haircut. The shape of your hair will look great. Also, lift your hair a little at the temples, to take away years.

* *Your cosmetics.*

Take a look at all your lipsticks and foundations and powders and eye makeups. Have you been wearing the same shades and brands and *kinds* of makeup for the past five or ten years? If you have—the textures are probably too heavy and the lipsticks are the wrong colors and too dry. Are you applying your cosmetics the same ways you did ten years ago? You're giving out a 1965 image. Visit a good cosmetic counter in an affluent neighborhood (where the saleswoman will be aware of how to achieve an expensive, up-to-date look) and ask her to show you a light moisturizer. Choose liquid makeup to go over the moisturizer that is so sheer that some of your own skin shows through. Select a glowing translucent cheek gel. Now ask the saleswoman to show you how to apply all of this while you look in the mirror. When she's finished, notice how much younger your skin looks. How *dewy* it looks. Buy lip gloss or creamy lipstick to minimize any pucker marks above your upper lip (dry lipstick accentuates those marks). Has your face and throat skin gotten just a little like crepe paper? Avoid buying pearlized, frosted makeup and face powder (they give you a hard and caked look). And if your eyelids are wrinkled, stay away from powdered eyeshadow (use the creamy kind). Avoid drawing a hard, definite line with your eyebrow pencil; it will make you look older. Your goal is to try for a soft, glowing, translucent, dewy look, with rosy colors; a fresh look. No hard lines. It's a good idea to buy your new makeup a couple of weeks before your job interview. (And you can buy the same *kind* of cosmetics that she's shown you in a less expensive store, now that you know the kind of makeup you'll need.) Purchase a mirror with a magnifying glass and practice over and over again at home.

Do you see a wisp of hair growing from your chin? Bleach it if you have many or have them removed by electrolysis before your job interviews. It's safe and painless.

· *Disguise your figure faults.*

Now your body and your clothes. If your upper arms have become heavy and saggy, cover them with sleeves for your interview. If your jowls droop or if your throat's lined, wear a pretty scarf (these are *instant* ways of subtracting years). Do you have a "rubber-tire" above your waist? Wear a long-line bra.

· *Ask someone to look you over before the interview.*

One woman told me, "I'll have my married daughter look me over before I go on the job interview," (she was trying to get back into the publishing world after twenty-

five years at home). A daughter, however, may be uncomfortable with her "new" mother. The change might
make her feel displaced. If you suspect this is the situation in your case, who else can give you a once-over?
Choose someone who can be objective, perhaps a neighbor, or a fashion-conscious cousin . . .

Should You Lie about Your Age?

I feel there's no should or shouldn't. Do whatever you
are comfortable doing. However, don't just lie halfway
by coyly saying things like, "Must I tell you?" or "Let's
just say I'm over thirty!"

- *A realistic view.*

One astute woman shared her philosophy:

"Of course I lie, and I consider it an absolute necessity.
I call it 'surviving the system.' If I'm going to be rendered helpless by age-discrimination, if I'm going to be
turned down for a job only because I was born in a certain year, I'm going to have to protect myself—at least
enough to have money to pay my rent. I lie cheerfully,
disarmingly, and without any guilty conscience. If and
when society changes and begins considering me for jobs
solely because of my *qualifications* and realizes my chron-
ological age is meaningless as far as my head is concerned, then I'll be happy to be honest again."

"How old do you tell them you are?" I asked.

"Well," she said, "some employers start stereotyping
you as soon as they hear that number fifty. So I tell them
I'm forty-eight. Now later, I'll have to move that up. It
will depend on how I look. At this point I'm considering
a face-lift. As an investment."

"An investment in years of living comfortably," she
added.

- *Age has nothing to do with your ability!*

Another woman told me, "I just got a job as coordina-
tor of a food co-op pilot program, and I know they
wouldn't have hired me if they had known my real age.
And that's ironic, because if this job had come along
when I was younger, I wouldn't have known a thing about

food co-ops. You see, I joined one in my neighborhood a little over a year ago and I've been involved in the buying and the storage problems. What do they think—that people stop learning and doing after a magic age?"

- *Are there risks in lying?*

Can lying about your age get you into trouble? Your boss could fire you *if* she ever finds out the truth—or she might laugh with you. She might be so impressed by your work performance by then that she'd shrug off your deception. But she can't take you to court. You've done nothing illegal.

Personnel officers of businesses have told me that lying about one's age is done frequently. If you have lied, and are still working there when you're ready to retire, go to the personnel office and confess. They'll just change the records.

Should You Lie about Your Education?

Again, do whatever you're comfortable doing. What would the risks be? It's probable very few employers will check to see if you're really a high-school graduate—not when you're already over-50—and many private firms don't bother checking to see if you really graduated college.

- *Institutions that DO check.*

However, count on school boards and all city, state, and federal government agencies asking that your transcript be sent to them directly from the college where you graduated.

The Time to Bargain and Make Demands

The job interview is the place—and time—to dicker and to bargain, once you're offered the job. Not a month after you take the position. Not even after you sign the contract.

• *An approach to bargaining.*

A friend of mine is presently in the middle of negotiating. She was offered a salary that she felt was too low, and since it is a new program, she asked to see a copy of the grant proposal, so she could check how much money is really available; this way she'd know how much—if any —leeway she has in bargaining. She took a copy of the grant proposal home, and after a careful reading (which she couldn't have had the time for at the job interview) she realized that there was one lump sum written-in for four people's salaries. And she will be one of those four employees. This means that the salary breakdown for each of the employees is open for negotiation. My friend realizes that they want her—they're acting eager. So she knows that now is the time to drive a hard bargain, and she'll ask for more than she really expects to get, so she can name a lower salary or agree to less money, without any real loss. The problem is that if *she* gets more money, the other three people will get less. The real solution is to be able to work together, *collectively*, to get decent salaries for everyone.

Use Contacts

Do you know anyone influential who knows the top person at the place of hiring? This is the time—just before your job interview—to use these contacts.

• *What can your contact do for you?*

Ask your friend or acquaintance to call that top person a couple of days before you go in for your interview to put in a good word for you. You don't want her merely to say, "Mrs. Frank is a good person"; you want a plug that is specific and striking. You've already figured out what's wanted on the job, so when you call your contact, feed that particular information to her. Give your contact the words to use, without cramming them down her throat. Does the job call for a person who has a lot of contacts in the community? Ask your contact to tell the job interviewer how effective you were when you served on two boards with her—and in which ways you were effective; how you were able to relate to many broad layers in the community; how many people grew to know and respect your work.

• *Who are your contacts?*

You're fortunate, being over 50. You've had more years to cultivate contacts. Your contact could be the woman who was chairwoman of the PTA when your children were little—and who now is head of an important organization. Your contact could be a woman who was in the garden club with you—and who now is on the board of directors of the agency you want to work for. Ideally, of course, your contact should be someone who knows you in the capacity that relates directly to the job you're seeking.

• *Be aware of the politics.*

The politics of the times could affect your choice of a contact. For instance, if you're white and middle-class, and you're applying for a job with an inner-city poverty program, you surely don't want to pick a white middle-class politician to intervene on your behalf. That would be insensitive. You'll want to call a black politician (if you know one) to call the black director of the agency. And you'll also want to be sure this politician is known for his or her support of legislation that *positively* affects the lives of inner-city residents. You'll also want to be absolutely sure this politician respects and likes you—and would feel you're right for the job.

Age Discrimination Legislation

Suppose you do suspect (or know) that you're not being hired because of your age? Suppose you're already on the job and you're being fired because of your age? If this is the case, look for a pattern. If you're being "let go," are other older workers being fired, too? This is the kind of question an attorney would ask you, if you were going to attempt to file a lawsuit.

• *The Age-Discrimination in Employment Act.*

The Age-Discrimination in Employment Act (ADEA) covers you if you're forty to sixty-five years of age, and if you work for a company who employs twenty or more people, a labor union, employment agency, or a government agency. ADEA was passed in 1967, and in 1974 their funding went up from 3 million to 5 million dollars, to enable more implementation of the legislation (because of prior inadequate funding, there was a huge backlog of cases). This law prohibits age discrimination in finding and keeping jobs, in wages, and in other "terms, conditions, and privileges of employment."

• *When to use it.*

You can sue to seek reinstatement to a former position if you were let go because of your age. You can sue to get retroactive pay and to recover lost pension benefits. You can even sue to recover counsel fees, and to collect damages if you can prove mental duress during and after the time you were fired. Also, you're entitled to a jury trial. Some activist groups are pushing to see the legislation expanded to cover workers who are over sixty-five, since there is ample documentation that the over-sixty-five person often is as effective on the job as the younger person—and certainly, many over-sixty-five people need extra income.

• *Filing suit.*

How do you go about filing suit? If you have the money, (and it can be expensive!) find the best labor lawyer available in your area. If your income is very low, contact your local Legal Aid office. The Woman's Equity Action League (WEAL), 719 National Press Bldg., Washington, D. C. 20004, feminist groups of attorneys and law students, and Women's Law Centers can refer you to a knowledgeable lawyer. Why do you want to be so selective in choosing your lawyer? Because knowing what kind of defense to use, and what kind of lawsuit to file, is very complicated. Some labor lawyers file suit for an age discrimination case under more than one piece of legislation. The laws are complicated, and there are exemptions and even exceptions to the exemptions for each piece of legislation.

Your lawyer will have to notify the federal government that you're filing suit, under the Age-Discrimination in Employment Act, within 180 days after the firing. She will have to send this letter of notification, with return receipt, to the Secretary of Labor. Your attorney will also have to file notice of suit with the Human Relations Commission of your particular state. (In your state, the human relations commission may have another name). If investigators find violations, the Labor Department tries to persuade the employer to reverse the company's decision. If that's not successful, the department can resort to legal action.

Groups that assist in lawsuits are the Black Women's Employment Project, NAACP Legal Defense & Educational Fund, 10 Columbus Circle, New York, N. Y. 10019, and NOW Legal Defense & Education Fund, 641 Lexington Ave., New York, N. Y. 10022.

Equal Pay Legislation

Are you making less money than the man sitting next to you on the job—who's doing exactly the same work you are and has the same background as you?

• *The Equal Pay Act.*

Under the Equal Pay Act of 1963, women have to be paid the same salaries as men who are doing substantially the same work. Companies occasionally try to get around this by giving the man a different job title. Sometimes other tactics are used. For instance, a few years ago a department store in Boston was paying saleswomen less than salesmen, and their "justification" was that men's clothes are more difficult to sell than women's! A group of saleswomen anonymously reported this to the U.S. Department of Labor—and the women won. Since 1963, when this legislation was passed, about $48 million dollars has been found owing to more than one hundred twelve thousand workers. You're covered under this law, no matter whether you're a saleswoman, secretary, executive, or a professional or administrative worker.

• *How to file a complaint.*

Again, if you can afford it, use the services of a good labor lawyer. If you want to file a complaint anonymously—without the help of a lawyer—call or write your local office of the Wage and Hour Division of the U.S. Department (it's listed in your phone book). Or mail a complaint to the Wage and Hour Division, Labor Department, Washington, D. C., 20210. Your name, *if* you choose to give it, will be held in confidence.

When you file a complaint, investigators and attorneys will ask you, as in the Age-Discrimination in Employment Act, if there is a pattern of discrimination throughout the company. Try to get that information ahead of time—*before* you file suit.

The large majority of cases have been settled through negotiation, but if the company is resistant, the government can take the case to court.

The Equal Rights Amendment: How Does It Affect You?

At this time of writing, the Equal Rights Amendment has been ratified by thirty-five states three more states need to ratify by March, 1979, or the fight for ERA will die—and have to be started all over again. To show the slow progress of the ERA movement, only 1 state—Indiana—has ratified since 1975. There have been a string of defeats, where states have voted "no." National polls show a large majority of people in favor of ratification and legislators apparently have not listened to their constituencies.

- *How it affects your working life.*

What is it and how can it affect your working life? It is a constitutional amendment that states: "Equality of rights under the law shall not be denied or abridged by the United States or any state on account of sex."

The fight for ERA grew out of the woman's suffrage movement. Alice Paul, an active suffrage fighter during the early 1900's, changed the focus of the suffrage movement from waging state-by-state battles for the right to vote to working for passage of a *federal* amendment that would guarantee all women the right to vote. In 1916 she organized the Women's Party. Faced with the huge task of passing hundreds of bills to counter sex discrimination in each individual state, the Women's Party drafted the Equal Rights Amendment, and when it was introduced in Congress in 1923, it was promptly voted down. It has been reintroduced almost every year after that. Hearings on the amendment were held, and riders and clauses were proposed. The ERA was debated until 1972, when it was finally passed by Congress. A Gallup poll, taken in March, 1975, showed 58 per cent support for the passage of the ERA, and 24 per cent opposition. Supporters say that the ERA is a working woman's issue; an issue of equal pay, increased job opportunities, and fair, medical, sick leave provisions. Anti-ERA groups feel that the ERA would erase all the "protective legislation" that already exists for women. Most of the protective laws were passed in the late 1800's and early 1900's as a result of labor's struggles for shorter workdays, higher pay, and other demands. These laws *were* needed. But employers have since used this protective legislation as a tool for discriminating against women workers. The laws are used as an excuse for failing to protect women in low-paying jobs and not hiring them in higher-paying jobs. Examples? Women are kept from jobs as hotel clerks at night—and at the same time (this stemmed from a 1910 "protective law"), are allowed to work at the lower-paying jobs of scrubbing floors all night in the *same hotel!* "Protective legislation" means women aren't hired as miners and bartenders and express drivers—jobs that often pay more; jobs that some women want and can not apply for. The president of the International Cigarmakers Union summed it up in 1879: "We cannot drive the females out of the trade, but we can restrict this daily quota of labor through factory laws." The point is—women should have a choice in their applications for jobs. The woman who doesn't want to be a miner doesn't *have* to be one.

In 1969, the Equal Employment Opportunity Commission (EEOC) established guidelines that declared most protective laws in violation of Title VII of the 1964 Civil Rights Act. That's the law that included a prohibition against sex discrimination in employment. By 1972, one-third of the states had totally or substantially repealed their protective laws . . . and some of these laws have been changed to extend provisions to cover men as well as women. These have included weight-lifting limitations and overtime-wage laws. The Senate Judiciary Commit-

tee, which made recommendations on the ERA, felt the
pressure of women on the question of *extending* rather
than erasing the positive aspects of protective legislation,
and their majority report on the ERA says: ". . . such
restrictive discriminatory labor laws as those which bar
women entirely from certain occupations will be invalid.
But those laws which confer a special benefit, which offer
real protection, will, it is expected, be extended to protect both men and women. Examples of laws which may
be expanded include laws providing for rest periods or
minimum wage benefits or health and safety protections."
The ERA is multi-issued; if it is passed, it will affect the
lives of younger as well as older women. And, if it is
passed, it means that you (if you want to) can break into
what have been "all-male" jobs; you'll be able to be a
truck driver or an electrician or a mechanic, and no union
or employer will be able to refuse to hire you because
you're a *woman*.

• *Who supports the ERA?*
  Supporters of the ERA include the AFL-CIO, Ameri-
can Bar Association, the American Jewish Congress, the
League of Women Voters, the NAACP, the National
Council of Churches, the YWCA . . .

Knowing Your Job Rights—and Organizing

If you know your job rights while your job is (or seems)
secure, you won't get as frightened when and if your boss
tries to fire you. If you're part of collective action to stop
inequities in the work world, you won't feel so isolated if
you become the target of a pay cut.

• *Informing yourself.*
  For one dollar, you can order an informational packet,
Age Discrimination in Employment, from the National
Organization of Women (NOW) Task Force on Older
Women. Address: 3800 Harrison St., Oakland, California
94611. This is a group that is concerned about the needs
of older women, and they support and push the ongoing
enforcement of existing legislation protecting older women
workers. They support the ERA, and they're also working

to include barriers against age discrimination in other legislation designed to provide equal opportunity for all persons.

Other demands they're making: more government-funded programs providing jobs for older women (they feel volunteer work is an exploitation of women); further pension reform beyond the recent pension legislation that was passed; and they're particularly working toward legislation that allows women to accumulate Social Security credits under their own names for unpaid labor done in their homes while they're bringing up their children, so they'll have more financial security in their older years (which might eventually benefit your daughter!)

A Working Woman's Guide to Her Job Rights is available for sixty cents from the Superintendent of Documents, U.S. Government Printing Office, Washington, D. C. 20402—and this is full of information.

Secretaries are now uniting around common employment demands and unionizing. Traditionally, office workers didn't organize. They didn't think it was necessary and many of them thought it was illegal, even though the National Labor Relations Act guarantees most workers the right—*including* office workers—to unionize and engage in collective bargaining. This "right to unite" on the job is explained in detail by a secretary who helped organize her office into a union. Margie Albert, an older woman, has written two articles, "Taking Care of Business" and "Organizing Your Office" and you can get both of them by writing directly to her, c/o District 65, 13 Astor Place, New York, N. Y. 10003.

• *Working collectively for benefits.*

Organizing and uniting and unionizing is often frightening to an older worker. If you're afraid of getting fired, it's harder to make demands. Risk-taking might not seem worth it because there's the fear of not being able to get another job if you *are* fired. In a non-unionized office, there's the division between the older workers and the younger workers. When there is inequity in salaries, workers have a tendency to blame the higher-paid worker instead of the boss. There is often a rivalry between workers to see who can woo the boss better. The one who wins gets more favors. All these factors make organizing difficult. And then, when employers further divide the workers by labeling one group "professional" and the other "clerical" and the other "maintenance," it's even harder for each worker to see how uniting can make working conditions better for *all* of them.

Without unions, workers have no grievance procedure to deal with unfair dismissal or any kind of unjust treatment. Ironically, white-collar workers, who often consider themselves "elite," now often earn less than factory workers, the very group they feel superior to. And this is because it was the factory workers—the blue collar workers—who long ago unionized. The white-collar workers unfortunately saw themselves as "above all that" and their smaller paychecks are a reflection of that attitude. However, this is changing. Caseworkers in city social service agencies are unionized. Teachers are unionized. And now secretaries are unionizing. These groups are realizing that bureaucrats may reign in unions; but getting in the union and trying to change conditions from within while you're engaged in collective action to better your working conditions is far better than standing alone. If you're fired, and you know there are no just reasons, it's good to know you have a legitimate grievance procedure where you can go to your shop steward and he or she can put the wheels in action to reinstate you. Without a union, all you can do is slink out—defeated.

Women *are* getting their heads together despite their fears. Not too long ago six hundred women, black and white, met at the Martin Luther King Center in New York City to share their problems. They were blue-collar and white-collar workers, and they looked at questions that affect all working women: Is the Equal Rights Amendment a good thing? How can existing affirmative action programs improve women's working conditions? How can women be organized when they're afraid?

In the past couple of years, women have been getting together all over the country to examine questions like this—and to find common solutions. The National Black Feminist Organization (NBFO) and the National Caucus on Black Aged have called conferences to find solutions to the problems of the black working woman. Women reporters and editors are organizing. They're learning to file sex discrimination suits and they're drawing up affirmative action guidelines for equal job opportunities to present to employers. Dr. Donna Allen, 3306 Ross Place, N.W., Washington, D. C. 20008, is the editor of the monthly *Media Report To Women*. She's a dynamic over-50 woman who has long been active in mobilizing women to help themselves. Women artists are organizing. Women writers are organizing. Women filmmakers are organizing. There was a "Rosie the Riveter" conference recently, where women who had worked in factories during the Second World War devised strategies to put pressure on all government agencies responsible for enforcement of laws against employment discrimination.

- *The common interests of older and younger women.*

Older women are finding that their problems are very similar to the problems of younger women, and in a short number of years younger women will face the same income problems that their older sisters now have. Coalitions have grown between women of all ages and colors to change conditions. Middle-class women and working-class women are beginning to find common ground in the work world. New questions are being raised: "Is volunteerism a way of using women for cheap labor?" and "Is it true that at least half the people covered by pensions will never collect a penny?" Women's consciousness about their powerlessness and the potential of their powerfulness is being raised. And as their consciousness is being raised, women are finding new strength to *deal* with their problems in the work world.

Pension Plan Legislation

- *The Employees Retirement Income Security Act.*

Private pension plans began in really large numbers during the Second World War, when employers used them as a way to hang on to workers at a time when wages were controlled and labor was scarce. ("We can't give you a raise but we have a beautiful pension plan"). The Employees Retirement Income Security Act, signed by President Gerald Ford, places these private pension plans under comprehensive federal legislation for the first time. The law's provisions are being implemented in a staggered fashion. January 1, 1981, is the cut-off date for implementation.

• *How does this legislation affect you?*

If your company goes bankrupt or merges or falls by the wayside because of mismanagement, you'll still get your pension. And you have a right, after one year on a job, to join any existing pension plan where you work. Also, employers are now required to give you a certain amount of vesting protection.

What does "vesting" mean? It means that the company's pension contribution for you, the worker, cannot be taken away from you after you leave the job—if you've worked there a certain length of time. Specifically, under the new legislation, full vesting must be provided by the end of the tenth year of participation in a plan; 25 per cent vesting protection is provided after five years of participation in a plan, increasing by 5 per cent for the next five years, and then by 10 per cent per year until full vesting is reached in fifteen years. Workers with at least five years of service would have their pensions 50 per cent vested when their age and years of service equal forty-five—with 10 per cent added each year until full vesting is reached.

Unfortunately and ironically this last part could affect you adversely. This "rule of 45" could establish a new barrier to the employment prospects of the older worker. Will many employers want to hire the over-50 woman as readily, knowing that she's protected by this "rule of 45"? That she'll be able to collect on her pension plan?

This legislation has far-reaching effects. Previously an employer didn't have to pay off so many people after they retired or left his place of business. Very few people ever collected on the pension promise. The employer said "if you will give up all or part of a wage increase, I will put aside some money in a fund for when you retire, and you will get this in addition to your Social Security benefits." In reality, the employer often made money on the funds he did set aside, because his contribution was tax exempt, and he could invest that money in the stock of his own company or turn it over to his favorite bank to invest. The employees for whom the money was in trust had no say in its use. Since the majority of workers found they couldn't collect on the pension fund, this money, obviously, stayed in the pocket of the employer—and doubled and tripled or more.

Why couldn't many of the workers collect on their pensions? Because they had been laid off at different times by the same company—always before reaching the minimum time for becoming eligible for the pension. Or because the company went bankrupt. Or because a worker had to change her union local various times during her employment with a company (an example is the worker who is transferred from one branch of a company to another) and found she wasn't eligible for the pension because she didn't have enough time in with any particular union local. Or because a person changed jobs. Because a worker quit before a particular age at a place of employment where, "the plan is not designed to provide benefits for those who leave the service of the company while still employable." Because the company closed down. Because the union wouldn't pay a pension unless there was a continuous work period—without any breaks of unemployment—in the same company. Since labor lawyers are expensive, the employer could pretty well count on the worker not suing if she lost her pension—and this is indeed what frequently happened.

Even with the new legislation there isn't a portability provision; workers still can't transfer pension benefit credits from one employer to another. This makes for situations that are sometimes almost unbearable. A woman said to me, "I'm hanging on for another five years, even though I hate the job and I have a bleeding ulcer. I'll be damned if I'll lose my pension, not when I retire in a few years. That's right, I can't take my pension with me to any other job!"

Under this new pension legislation, companies and unions who have not had pension plans are *not required* to establish any. However, if they've already had a pension plan, they must purchase pension insurance from a Pension Benefit Guarantee Corporation, set up within the Department of Labor, to insure the pension benefits if the plan is terminated. This is what protects already-retired workers and those with vested benefits. Under this insurance plan, up to $750 a month can be paid to workers whose pension plans terminate.

As a worker, this new legislation entitles you to have a joint and survivor's annuity provision, and the survivor benefit cannot be less than half of the benefit that would have been payable to you.

If you're working for a company or union that doesn't have a pension plan, part of this new legislation allows you pension benefits out of your own pocket—if you wish. You can contribute up to 15 per cent of your annual income or $1,500 a year, whatever is less, in a special account. Income taxes on these contributions and the earnings of the account are deferred until the money is withdrawn on retirement.

Employers are finding with this new legislation, that it's getting very expensive to set up pension plans. Too many workers will now have to be paid off with the new vesting laws and since the employer does not have to set up a plan, it is possible that a growing number will not. A close look at the Employee Retirement Income Security Act of 1974 will reveal that even though it may prevent some of the worst excesses that occurred before the law was passed, the legislation still hasn't touched many of the problems that exist! Since some provisions of the law won't go into effect until 1981; what will happen to the countless older workers who are supposed to retire before that time? You or your husband may be one of them.

• *Further pension reform is needed.*

Meanwhile, if you or your husband is employed in a company that does have a pension plan, get a copy of your benefits. An employer is bound, by law, to give you a copy. Show it to a labor lawyer. The investment of the dollars you put out for that one-time-only consultation with the attorney, will be well worth it; she can explain the fine print to you. The lawyer can relate your pension plan to the new legislation and tell you exactly what you will get and what you won't get—so you'll be able to plan better for your retirement years.

Until You Retire—

If you're 50 you might be working for another twenty years. If you're fifty-five you might work for another fifteen years. Even if you're only going to be in the work force for another *five* years you want to know how to get every penny you're entitled to and how to get all the psychic rewards that are possible. So ask yourself these questions—

- "What do I want from work and am I getting what I want?"
- "Do I know *how* to get what I'm not getting?"
- "Do I realistically assess job risks and my strengths and vulnerabilities before I jump into a change? Before I decide *not* to change—?"
- "Do I know how to forget work, once I go home in the evenings?"
- "Do I make other areas of my life as important— or more important—than my work?"
- "Am I financially and emotionally getting ready for my retirement—*while* I'm working?

- *Your goals.*
Cash. Contentment. Which is most important in your work life? Strive for both of these goals. Make the rest of your work years the best of your work years!

CHAPTER 10

Returning to School

≈§ ह≈

Reasons for Going Back to School

Older women all over the country are asking themselves whether they should return to school . . . and many of them are *doing* it.

- *Every woman may have a different reason.*

Going back to school *can* mean a new job, a change in careers, a new career, or a ladder to a more prestigious position. It can mean just plain fun—if you love to learn. It can mean showing someone (your husband, your mother, your children) that you *can* do it—get a degree, that is. For some women, going back to school is the way to sharpen a skill, even though they have no intention of using the skill for money.

How about you?

- *Feelings about it—and fears.*

Returning to school. Older women do it for all kinds of reasons. Some are frightened at the idea—and do it anyway. Other women find it a great adventure.

"I *am* scared," Jo told me. She's slim and young-looking and was wearing a camelhair skirt. "Will I make it? I never had science or math in high school. I took a commercial course. We all did. It was in the 1930's and we knew we had to go out and get office or sales jobs when we graduated. No one had money for college."

"Why are you thinking of starting school now?" I asked.

"I work at the City Department of Social Services, and if I get a work-related degree I can become a service worker. I would like that. I'm an income maintenance worker now, and all I do is fill out forms——."

"What are you afraid of?"

"Tests! I haven't cracked a textbook in years. I looked at my son's college textbook the other night—it was on sociology—and I couldn't understand anything the first time I tried to read the page. It was all gobbledegook. I had to read the same page four times before anything made sense. And I'm known as a reader! I finish at least two books of fiction a week."

We sat silently for a few minutes.

"—I'll be over fifty-six when I graduate."

"Well," I said, "that's four years from now. Did you have anything else as interesting planned for the next four years?"

Jo is rather a special case: her investment in college could well pay off. Her agency *does* promote workers from income maintenance jobs to service jobs when and if they get work-related degrees. She's already experienced in the field at large. She already knows she would enjoy the work.

But what about the woman who has never worked—and at the age of 50, decides to go to college to become an art historian? Will college pay off for her in terms of a *new* career? Jobs are hard to get. Young recent college graduates can't find work in their fields, and they settle for less—or can't find *any* employment. Wouldn't it be harder for an older woman, in our age-discriminatory society, to crack a field when she has never worked in it?

Jo's fear of doing schoolwork again is realistic, but it's possible she could work through it and conquer it. She could take steps to prepare herself for tackling textbooks (admittedly, harder to read than fiction). She could try to choose the kind of college where tests are minimized and papers, instead, are expected (Jo is good at writing). She could choose a school that pays special attention to the needs of the older student and with some small successes the first year, she would no doubt become more self-confident.

Zenia's fifty-five. She's gone back to school for pleasure. She started a ceramics class at the local art school one night a week, and fell in love with using the wheel. She made three pots this semester.

"Are you going to take another ceramics class next semester?" I asked.

"Nope," she said, "I'll take a drawing class. And then, if I'm still well and about, I'm going to spend the next ten years taking life classes and sculpture classes and portrait classes—."

"—for a degree?" I asked.

She gave me a withering look. "I'm not interested in degrees. That's for people who think they're still living in the 1950's—when a degree could get you a professional job, pronto! They're not aware we're in another Depression. Me? I'll stick to my secretarial job and go to school for fun. So I don't turn into one of those old women who grab their granddaughter every time she visits and says, "Why don't you come more often? I'm so *lonely!*" Me—I won't be lonely. When I'm making a pot, I lose all sense of time, that's how absorbed I am. The day flies by!"

She picked up a pot she had just finished and held it up to the light. "Nice glaze, huh? Listen, we can decide to live for work or work to live. This is the time to work to live. Do you want to see my school catalogue? There might be a course you'd like—."

"I went back to get my high school diploma to show my children and grandchildren that I could do it," a grandmotherly looking woman said, "and I did it!"

"What are you going to do now—try to get a job?" I asked.

She smiled, "Oh, no. I like being home, my husband's retired, and we do a lot of things together during the day.

I did it because I wanted to *prove* something—that I *could* do it. Is there anything wrong with that?"

No. There certainly isn't.

Why Many Older Women Are Late-Bloomers

• *How we grew up: The material conditions.*

The 1920's and 1930's were a time when college women were mostly well-to-do. They came from comfortable middle- and upper-middle class families, or they were actually rich. Tuition wasn't readily within the reach of the mill worker's daughter, or the garment worker's child, or the migrant farmer's daughter. We didn't have inexpensive community colleges, and no-cost city colleges were a new concept. Student loans were non-existent. Scholarships weren't that plentiful. Times were so hard in the 1930's for many families that after a woman graduated from high school (if she didn't drop out sooner because of finances), she usually lived at home with her parents and paid room-and-board to help out until she got married.

• *The economics shaped the values.*

Women were expected to stay home after they were married and keep house. Because jobs were so scarce, if a woman went out to work, it was often thought that she was "taking the food out of another family's mouth." Many women spent lonely evenings while their ambitious husbands tried to better themselves; they went to law school and accounting school at night, after working all day. Hard times continued until jobs opened during the Second World War; defense plants opened and when the men went off to war, they left jobs behind for women— in factories and in offices. That's when many women went to work for the first time in their lives. Then, after the war, these same women quit or lost their office and factory jobs, making room on jobs for the returning soldiers. The same ideology existed as before (probably because of the economy): women were expected to be homemakers and mothers, not paid workers. They spent the long years ahead bringing up children, and when they did work, it was usually in clerical and sales jobs (sometimes seasonal) and factory work to help out while their husbands were getting settled and established.

They lived *through* their husbands and families.

Their husbands were considered to be doing the *real* work.

• *And how times changed!*

Then in the late 60's when the woman's movement began urging women to develop and examine their own needs (and the community college movement expanded, making low-cost education possible, as well as more accessible loans), a growing number of over-50 women began to ask themselves, "Why not *me?*" Many wanted to return to school—and some were terrified.

"How do I know I'll be able to understand the work?"

"I never had any science—."

"I'm afraid I won't be able to concentrate."

"My son says I'm crazy. 'What do you need it for,' he says."

• *What happens to women when they do
return to school?*

And when they did go back, they found they did very very well! Professors and school administrators and the women themselves found that they were self-disciplined, they got their papers in before anyone else, and they never missed a class and they lived up to their own high expectations with good grades on tests. Why? Perhaps because they felt this was their last chance . . . or because they were paying for it with hard-earned money . . . or because they felt they had to prove themselves to their husbands and their children—and to themselves. Sometimes other women—their peers with whom they had coffee klatches and played bridge—spurred them on, having started in school a year before. Sometimes their children and husbands encouraged them. Often, if they were already working, they were tired of being cheap labor (the 50-year-old women in the social work department who were making two thousand dollars less a year then the twenty-five-year-old women who were doing the same work and had a degree!).

Frequently the old resentment and angers (maybe never uttered before) spurred them on: These women had never forgotten or forgiven how the hard times had victimized them.

• *Four women talk about themselves.*

Beth said, "It was a question of whether my brother or I would be sent to college, and it wasn't a very big question. Where I come from the boys were always the ones to go. Parents figured that girls get married so what do they need college for. And they didn't have enough money to send each child. So in my family, Marcus went and today he's a certified public accountant making good money, and I'm a divorced grandmother who works in a crummy department store selling budget dresses. I still feel bitter about that. I was just as smart as Marcus—maybe smarter."

Selethia said, "I really wanted an education—I wanted it so much I could taste it. My parents were tenant farmers. I couldn't even go on to high school."

The woman who was with Selethia said, "Well, I finished high school and then I worked for a year and put some money away to pay for night school the next semester. But after working all day in a factory and going to school at night I was exhausted. And then I met my future husband and I quit school. . . ."

Myrna said, "I drew from the time I was little. All I wanted to do was go to art school when I grew up. When I finished high school it was the peak of the Depression, and I went to the art institute during the day and was a waitress at night. But the art supplies were so expensive I couldn't keep up, and the other students in my class were well-off. They dressed differently than I did—. My clothes —what I had—were really shabby. I quit after the first year. . . ."

"Do you draw any more?" I asked.

She smiled apologetically. "No."

All of these women are in their first year at a local community college. All of them are going at night, so they can keep their daytime jobs. All of them love it—and

are doing well (although two of them need some special
tutoring, which was easily arranged).

"Do you expect to graduate and go on to a four-year
college—and do you feel you'll make more money when
you graduate and get better jobs?" I asked them. They
were silent for a moment, then one of them defiantly
said, "How do we know?! We can't give you—or ourselves—any guarantees! But we're in there punching—and
I feel *good* about myself. If anybody had told me, three
years ago, that I'd be studying *psychology* this year and
getting good grades—I wouldn't have believed her!"

And Some Women Are Afraid to Try

And there are the women, like Jo, who are afraid to
try . . . and who *don't* try.

"I had two years of college before I got married," one
woman told me, "and I managed that by going to night
school every year and taking one or two courses, while I
worked in an office during the day. I didn't get married
till I was thirty, see, so I had more time on my hands to
go to school. I don't know whether I could even get any
credits for the courses I took, it was so long ago. Who
knows, the school I went to might not even be around
anymore."

Her daughter was sitting at the other end of the kitchen
table, combing her son's hair. "Ma, come on," she said,
"those are just excuses. You know it." She gave her
mother who was sitting in a housedress, chain-smoking,
a baleful look. "I know," the mother said, "and I guess if
I really wasn't so scared to go—I would go."

"College!" A woman looked at me incredulously, "I
didn't even finish high school! I'd love to go to college, but
that doesn't even seem real. Now if I could finish high
school, *that* would be something. But I'm not going to sit
in a classroom with a bunch of kids, I can tell you that—."

"There are ways you can do it without going to class
with kids," I said.

She looked away. "It's too late—."

But perhaps these women will feel different later.

Be Realistic about Your Needs

Is going back to school for YOU? It is if you're already in a work-related job where you know that a degree will mean a promotion or more money; if you NEED a high school diploma to get into a job-training program for older women; if you're a college graduate and KNOW that job openings exist if you get that graduate degree; if you have skills that would lend themselves to non-traditional jobs for women (carpentering, etc.) and need to polish those skills. IF YOU KNOW THAT, DESPITE THE ECONOMY, THERE WILL PROBABLY BE JOB OPENINGS FOR AN OLDER WOMAN IF YOU GET THAT DEGREE.

Or going back to school may be for you if, like Zenia, you're doing it for pure pleasure—without the hopes of a job payoff. Or if you're back at school to prove to yourself (and others) that you *can* do it. Going back to school may be very valid if you're going *not* to get a job—but to learn more about *yourself*.

- *Look honestly at your motives.*

Try to be honest about your motives. And try to assess your *motivation* (how much do you really want to go?). And, certainly, try to be very knowledgeable and realistic about what school can and can't do for you. Thousands of bright, capable and ambitious kids graduate from college each year—and they have a hard time getting jobs. If you are realistic about what you want from school, and what you can get—and how much you really want to go—then, it might be time for you to decide what *kind* of school you want and how you can fit classes into your schedule.

Budgeting Your Time

Some older women hesitate starting school because of time problems; they may be working at forty-hour-a-week jobs; they may have husbands who expect dinner on the table at a certain time every evening, and who do not want *their* lives disrupted, they may be reluctant to give up a weekly bowling group, or a bridge game.

• *Shortcuts.*

Here are some tips on how to budget your time if you are considering returning to school:

• do *all* your cooking over the weekend, and freeze already prepared dinners so all you have to do, each weekday night, is take a frozen dinner and pop it into the oven.
• see if you can easily get up an hour earlier every morning, before you go to work, and use that time to do your homework or study.
• if you can afford it, hire some part-time help to clean your house, freeing you for schoolwork and studying.

But you really have to be motivated to give up your bridge game or your bowling group. And if you *know* you want to return to school you'll accept the fact that you're giving up some short-term pleasures for a valuable long-term gratification.

Also, hopefully, as your husband sees you doing well and gaining a larger sense of identity through your accomplishments, he'll respect the "new" you enough to help with the cooking and cleaning—freeing you so you'll have more time to study.

Adult Degree Programs

A lot of learning is done through just plain living—and that's the idea behind adult degree programs.

• *What it is.*

Usually, this is a college program where you have to be over twenty-five years of age to enroll; where you receive "life experience" credits for significant learning gained through particular experiences—on the job, in your marriage, through bringing up your children, through traveling, and through volunteer work. This can cut your class time down considerably, allowing you to graduate sooner.

• *How it works.*

The usual procedure in acquiring life experience credits is that you and your school advisor go over your background together, choosing from the many significant life experiences you've had (and being an over-50 woman, you've had many) the ones you want to document as having taught you the most. You might feel there was something unique in the way you brought up your children. For instance, yours might have been a one-parent family, and you could document (write a paper, perhaps) how you coped, and what you learned through the experience. One adventurous woman brought her children up in an intentional community (a community formed by and for people who have common goals and a communal lifestyle and philosophy—such as a kibbutz), where organic farming and the extended family were valued, and she wrote a paper on how this had affected her children and their lives, and how, in turn, this had affected *their* children. She received ten credits for this paper. What can *you* document? The summer you and the children and your husband packed everything in the car, headed to Guanajuato, Mexico, and took Spanish language courses at the local university? Your years as a volunteer in the state mental hospital? Your experience as a volunteer fund-raiser for the Catholic Charities? Credits are often negotiable, and if you're a hard bargainer with a good case, your advisor might give you more credits than she had expected to.

"I can't imagine anything I could use as life experience credits," an over-50 woman told me. "My life has been so ordinary. I was married, kept house, brought up the children, and that was that."

As we talked further, I learned that she and her husband had started their own small business after the Second World War. He had gone to school under the GI Bill and learned upholstering skills and they opened their own shop where she was an active partner in the business, keeping the books, soliciting business, and even writing the ads to place in their local newspapers. The business enabled them to buy a home and put their children through college. Why not document what she learned through those work years? Certainly she had learned a great deal, putting into practice what business majors learn in college, without ever having taken a business course. The report was a snap for her to put together—and she earned ten credits.

A woman told me, "My advisor asked me what my most significant life experience had been, and I immediately got all choked up. I *knew*. I have a retarded child, and when she was five, we finally had to put her into an institution. We saw her regularly, and I can't tell you how much she has affected my life. I tried taking her home to stay last year—my husband died—but she's so big I couldn't take care of her. I couldn't lift her to put her in the bathtub and I couldn't dress her, my arthritis in my arms hurt so. And she cried a lot, she missed the girls there. I had to take her back to the place. This broke my heart. I felt so guilty. I still feel guilty. I wasn't going to write this up, even though it was—*and is*—the most important thing I've ever gone through. But I did write about it. I'm glad now I did. I learned so much more about myself and my feelings through writing that paper. It was a—a profound experience."

Of course you don't have to have had traumatic experiences like this in order to document your life. You might have had a significant *job* experience that taught you a great deal. One woman made a videotape to document the group work she was doing with adolescent pregnant unmarrieds. She asked a video major in the school to do the actual shooting and production work, while she did the directing. Another woman, who worked with the aged in the Appalachian mountains, documented her work life by getting together an oral history of the members in her program; she taped their voices while they spoke of their backgrounds—what they had been doing in the days of the First World War; what their values and life styles had been during their teen years. She wrote a short paper with it, an historical treatment of mountain folk, and came up with a really valuable piece of work.

Frequently schools allow you to accumulate up to thirty

or more life experience credits, and students sometimes
do it in segments of ten credits each.

• *Who offers adult degree programs?*

Private innovative colleges are more apt to give life
experience credits, usually through adult degree programs. Some public colleges are also offering this, but on
a more limited scale. The problem is that private colleges
are more expensive than public ones, so you might want
to explore, through the private school's financial aid office,
the possibility of paying your tuition by the month. This
is particularly good for the woman who works and can
draw on her salary. Antioch College, in some of its various centers throughout the country, offers this arrangement, and their classes take place mostly at night—
making it possible for the working woman to attend. Look
into other private schools that have reputations for progressive experimental programs, like Goddard College,
Plainfield, Vermont 05667 (where you can be a full-time
student in your own town, staying on campus—which
may be thousands of miles away—only six weeks a year)
to see if they include life experience credits in their catalogues. Generally, all schools that are under the umbrella
of the Union of Experimental Colleges offer this kind of
program. Go to your nearest large library and ask the
librarian to see a list of schools in this category.

The Weekend College

Now this is an exciting trend! And it's a growing trend
—programs where the student spends time on campus
only during weekends. One prestigious woman's college
arranges that the student spend every third weekend on
campus, taking classes from Friday evening through Sunday morning. The student eats and sleeps in the dorms.

• *Excellent for the working woman and*
the woman who lives alone.

This can be a great idea for the woman who is working
full-time *and* for the woman who lives alone. The working woman is often too tired to attend class at night, and
the woman who lives alone finds the weekend campus

relieving her possible loneliness. What better way to build a social life than to pack your suitcase every third week and spend the weekend with women your own age, in stimulating classes as well as in the intimate life of the dormitory? It's instant camaraderie. You're all there for the same reason: an education, a vacation, and companionship. Many women have developed close relationships out of this arrangement.

Call your local colleges to see if this kind of program is offered in *your* area.

Residential Mini-Courses

• *What they offer.*

The University of Oklahoma has been a pioneer in the residential mini-course idea, where you live on the campus a certain number of weeks a year and study independently at home the rest of the year. This school even encourages students to bring their families to stay with them during the time they're in residence.

• *Be sure you're self-disciplined.*

This can be a great way to earn a degree—*if* you're very self-disciplined. You also have to be aggressive and independent, because what happens is you chart your own learning for the time you're at home with your school advisor—and then it's up to you to see that you *do* study. For many people this is too difficult; they need that authority figure standing over their shoulder, day-to-day. KNOW YOURSELF before you enroll in this kind of program. Are you this independent and self-disciplined?

The Non-Traditional School: Pitfalls . . . Advantages

All of these programs we've talked about can be exciting and challenging—but be sure that if they're offered in a non-traditional school, you know what is expected of you.

• *A loose structure.*

Non-traditional schools can be very loosely structured, and it takes a special kind of personality to be able to accept this. They often don't have the curriculum ready until the week before the semester begins. They expect YOU to do most of the work—the teacher is more a facilitator than a directive instructor. They're *very* informal—a traditional kind of student might get pretty upset when she sees other students perching on the arms of broken down couches eating, smoking, and petting the large dogs that they've brought along—all during class time.

- *No Tests . . . No Grades.*

Some students *want* tests—to show themselves that they have learned, to show others that they've done well. They feel cheated when they find the non-traditional school does not test students—and often doesn't grade them either (it's usually a "pass-fail" after the end of the semester). How do *you* feel about this?

Some students who have completed the non-traditional college have found that the graduate school they're applying to will not accept pass-fail grading. And they find it out too late . . . which means *ask* before you hand over your money. (Call the graduate schools directly to inquire.)

Many non-traditional schools have you write an "evaluation" of what you've learned at the end of the semester— and the teacher writes an "evaluation" of your work. This is in lieu of a grade. Would you be comfortable with this?

- *Double check: Is the school accredited?*

Particularly, be sure the non-traditional school you're applying to is accredited. A distraught women said, "The program I enrolled in was on the campus of a traditional well-known college—it was an adult degree program— and I assumed it was accredited! After all, the college had excellent accreditation. Then, after I graduated, I applied for a job with the school board, and they turned me down —saying the *program* wasn't fully accredited! I should have checked it out."

In this case, the program was sponsored by the Union of Experimental Colleges, and hadn't yet achieved full accreditation (they were working toward it). The *college* was fully accredited—but the program merely rented space from the college; it wasn't part of the college. And no one had explained this to her. Why hadn't they? They were probably hungry for students, and took the chance that they would be accredited by the time she graduated. But they weren't—. What she should have done was call the accrediting agency *before* she registered (as *you'll* do!)

• *Who benefits from the non-traditional school?*

Non-traditional colleges can be the perfect answer for the student who is skeptical enough to check all information out; who is aggressive enough to ask questions and demand answers; who can study independently enough to write papers without the help of a teacher—and who has enough sense of self that she will scream and holler if she doesn't get what she was promised from the school. This is the student who will demand and expect that all the things promised will be *put in writing, ahead-of-time* —signed by the dean.

I'm not putting a downer on non-traditional schools: They can be an excellent choice because the classes are usually small and seminar-style—allowing feedback and maximum participation from the student; their class time schedule is usually very flexible—giving the woman who works full-time an opportunity to get her degree while keeping her job; they frequently hire teachers who question the values of our society—forcing the student (often for the first time in her life) to do the same; they attract older as well as younger students—so you won't feel isolated as an over-50 woman; they attract bright students —so the classes tend to be stimulating and exciting. It can be a fantastic choice for you if you're independent and critical and tough and smart. If you're all these things you probably wouldn't be too happy anyway on the campus of many traditional colleges (where you might feel part of a herd—faceless, nameless, and where you might find a lack of intellectual stimulation).

The Traditional Four-Year College

• *Who's comfortable there?*

The state or private *traditional,* 4-year college might be a good answer for:

- the woman who is uncomfortable in non-traditional schools
- the over-50 woman who took enough math and science and languages during her high school days to be eligible for admission to this kind of college (remember, many Depression-era women took "commercial"—business-related—courses instead of an academic major, so they could get jobs after graduation; they were intent on being practical, seeing no other choice)
- the woman who has amassed enough credits in her earlier years, so she just has another three to nine credits to get before receiving her degree

- *More rigid requirements.*

Are you getting the feeling that the usual traditional, four-year college has definite requirements for entrance and graduation? You're right! And no matter how smart you are, it's possible you can't enter this kind of school without the academic requirements.

This kind of institution usually gives regular written tests in their classes. Will you be comfortable with this?

It *is* an option—but understand it's limitations and requirements.

CLEP Tests—a Way to Get College Credits
Outside of Class

If you're just starting in a non-traditional or traditional college or community college and want to graduate faster, or if you're returning to school after just one semester or so of college "way back then"—consider taking as many of the College Level Examination Program (CLEP) tests as you can.

- *It's based on how much you know.*

These are tests given *outside* of the classroom where your grade depends on how much you've informally learned outside of a college course. For instance, you might have always been interested in social problems and people, and through your reading and life experience, you might have picked up enough information and knowledge to pass a wirtten test in sociology. If you pass the test, you get a certain number of college credits that you can apply toward your undergraduate degree. This is *not* the same as an Advanced Placement Test. The tests are administered by Princeton University and they're given regularly, on an on-going basis at sites all through the country. Each tests costs about $12.50—putting them in a price range that makes it possible for a large number of women to have access to them.

• *Where can you take these tests?*

For specific information on where to take the tests, and what areas they cover (Math? English Composition? Social Studies?), call your local colleges. They'll also give you specific time schedules as to when they're given. This can be an efficient and excellent way to cut down on your time spent in college and your tuition costs.

Credits Through TV and Radio

It's not a brand-new idea—and it works. Get up early in the morning, catch a show on astronomy, watch that same TV program every morning for several months, and then go in for a college exam related to what you saw on TV. Or relax in your own living room and listen to a philosophy course presented on the radio every day for a certain length of time—and then take the college exam.

• *What your responsibilities are.*

Actually, there are a few more things you must do: Before the radio or TV course begins, you have to register at one of the colleges that is either sponsoring the course or participating in it; you must purchase some textbooks (they give you a list); and you must really *study* during the course—both what you're hearing and/or seeing and what is in your textbooks. But what a fun way to earn college credits!

• *When are these programs scheduled?*

These courses are usually on public broadcasting stations, and often they're presented Saturdays and weekday evenings as well as in the early mornings and during the weekdays. For information on whether this kind of learning program exists in your area, call your local colleges. Sometimes the curriculum is listed in the TV and radio section of your newspaper. The college exams are given right in the college classroom. Tuition? Usually considerably lower than if you were to take the course in the classroom.

· *Who it can particularly help.*

This can be an excellent way to earn college credits if you're homebound (disabled); if you want to get a head start before you begin formal classes; or if you're working full-time and want to spend a minimum amount of time in the classroom.

Community Colleges—a Boon for the Older Woman

The community college can be exactly the right place for you if you're just beginning college and want to *ease* into the experience; if you have limited money for tuition; if you're just a little scared about how you'll make out (fearful about how well you'll do in certain subjects); and if you want to be sure there will be other older students in the classroom.

· *The community college may answer all your needs.*

Community colleges have come a long way, and in many areas now, they're way ahead of the four-year college. They're sensitive to the needs of the student who has been deprived of a good secondary education; they're very aware of the economy—and they show this awareness through low tuition and by offering course work to prepare the para-professional and the non-professional (they know that firemen and dental technicians and secretaries are always needed); they frequently group together the older women who are starting their freshman year—to identify and meet their unique needs. If they find, after talking to you, that you need help in a particular subject, they'll try to get you that help so you can comfortably go on from there. Sometimes they're accused of lowering their standards to meet the needs of the average or under-average student, but there has been many an older woman who has found this useful. She has started her college career in a community college—and then, after the two years, having gained self-confidence and found she *is* smarter than she thought she was, she finds she can go into her third year at a four-year college relatively easily.

• *It can be the answer for the working woman.*

One community college offers an industrial technology curriculum that allows a manufacturing plant worker to get college credits toward an Associate in Arts degree through her on-the-job experience and employer-training programs. This particular program developed through cooperative efforts between the college, local workers, and manufacturers. Students tailor the program to meet their needs. All that is required is that the student be employed in a manufacturing plant at least twenty hours a week while attending classes in the technology practicum seminars (which are scheduled so they don't conflict with working hours). This is typical of how the community college realistically meets needs of the working woman.

Scholarships and Grants and Loans for the Older Woman

• *Free tuition if you're sixty-plus.*

If you're over sixty, you might find that some of your local colleges will give you *free* tuition. This is particularly true of community colleges. Call and ask.

And under fifty or sixty, you'll want to know about financial aid. There are a surprising number of aid programs specifically for older-woman students.

• *A list of scholarships and grants and loans.*

Clairol, Inc., has a $50,000 *Loving Care Scholarship Program,* providing grants of $1,000 to fifty four-year colleges and universities throughout the country. These funds are awarded to women thirty-five years and older who are enrolled full-time or part-time in undergraduate degree programs, and the money awards are based on need and merit. Call the financial aid office of the school you're interested in to see if they're participants.

Altrusa International Foundation provides awards to women only, for training or retraining to qualify for employment. Stipends usually average $350 a year for each woman awarded, and they favor vocational education, such as nursing courses, x-ray technology courses, and bookkeeping courses (rather than more "academic" degrees). For further information, write The Chairman, Founders Fund Vocation Aid Committee, Altrusa International Foundation, Inc., 332 South Michigan Avenue, Chicago, Ill. 60604.

Another group that gives annual awards to women interested in training or retraining in vocational or technical studies (rather than an academic degree program) is the *Soroptimist International of the Americas*. Each year $2,000 each is given to fifteen women through their local clubs in fifteen regions. Write Soroptimist International of the Americas, 1616 Walnut Street, Philadelphia, Pa. 19103, for more details.

Business and Professional Women's Foundation Awards are given annually to women twenty-five years and older who are returning to school for undergraduate, graduate or vocational training after a break in their studies. Scholarships average $260 a person. Contact Business and Professional Women's Foundation, 2012 Massachusetts Avenue, N.W., Washington, D. C. 20036 if you think you qualify.

The Danforth Foundation offers a national graduate fellowship program to women with undergraduate degrees who want to pursue full- or part-time graduate study that would lead to secondary or college teaching. Preference is given to women who have completed their undergraduate work by age 50. Grants may be up to $4,000 a year plus tuition and fees. Write to the Director, Graduate Fellowships for Women, Danforth Foundation, 222 South Central Avenue, St. Louis, Mo. 63105.

The American Association of University Women awards dissertation fellowships to women who have completed all course work and qualifying examinations in a doctoral program. Contact the Director, AAUW Fellowships Program, 2401 Virginia Avenue, N.W., Washington, D. C. 20037.

Are you a college graduate who is interested in attending a graduate school of business? *The Sears Roebuck Foundation* is making $300,000 available in loan funds to "women only" of any age attending graduate schools of business. You can apply for loans up to $2,000. Write to the Business and Professional Women's Foundation (the organization that is administering the program), 2012 Massachusetts Avenue, N.W., Washington, D. C. 20037.

Diuguid Fellowship offers stipends of $3,600 to $6,000, and they're available to "mature women" in the southern section of the United States for retraining and study—if their career goals had to be deferred. Apply to The Executive Director, Southern Fellowship Fund, 795 Peachtree Street, N.E., Atlanta, Ga. 30318.

• *How to get more information.*
And this is only a partial list! You can get more information on awards and loans and funds for older women students through the financial aid offices of colleges and universities and community colleges; through college catalogues; and through asking the librarian at your public library to refer you to reference books and catalogues that have listings.

Don't confine yourself just to financial help for older women students; look for awards and loans and funds available to *any* qualified student (even though investigating scholarships and loans for older women *first* may pay off). And don't forget to constantly scan the bulletin boards in your local colleges. Scholarship and loan information is frequently posted.

The clever student or prospective student will want to apply to several places at one time for financial aid.

Vocational and Technical Training

Now that society is giving "permission" to women to be as clever with their hands as men supposedly are, countless women are finding that they're good at building and repairing and constructing. And some are attempting to find niches for themselves in the work world, using these skills.

• *Be realistic about what you can physically do.*

Before you decide to tackle a strenuous kind of job or job-training, however, assess your physical strength and your health. If you get dizzy easily, you won't want to climb ladders as part of your work; if your arthritis is in your hands, you'll find working an industrial sewing machine too painful. As in every other area of your life, be realistic in your assessment of your vulnerabilities *and* your strengths.

• *Where to get inexpensive training and apprenticeships.*

Where do you get training for vocational and technical kinds of work? The adult and community education divisions of your city or county schools may work in cooperation with local contractors, where opportunities for persons interested in apprenticeships are available. Requirements are usually that you have graduated from at least the ninth grade. You get half the starting salary of the journeyman's rate with your on-the-job training. You must also attend instructional classes. This way you can train to work as a carpenter, an electrician, a maintenance mechanic, a plumber, a sheet metal worker, or an asbestos-insulation installer. This same adult and community education division of your school system offers adult vocational courses, apart from the apprentice program. Hours for class are flexible, and the tuition is very low. The classrooms have modern equipment and industrially competent instructors. What kind of courses are offered? Blueprint reading, auto shop, air-conditioning and refrigeration, cabinetmaking, drafting, electronics, tailoring, welding, linotype, printing, and radio and TV repair. (Why shouldn't a woman open her own little TV repair shop? Plenty of older men do.) You can learn how to be a practical nurse; you can learn cosmetology and dressmaking and sewing. In fact, some adult centers in public school systems offer industrial sewing courses where you can learn to use high speed commercial sewing machines, to prepare you for factory work. Also offered in many centers are cashier-checker courses where you can learn the operation of a supermarket in a simulated supermarket atmosphere, using new modern cash registers and checkout counters. After completion of the course, you're ready to apply to your nearest grocery chain store for a job!

And there are typing courses for the woman who wants to work in an office—and shorthand and bookkeeping courses so you can get an office job or advance in your office job.

Counseling and placement services are also provided in these centers. You'll find adult and community education classes located in every city in the country, as well as in the suburbs and the counties (and then it would be under the sponsorship of the county board of education). Write your board of education (the adult and community education division) to have them send you information—or call them directly. They will tell you how and when and where to register for classes, and what the low fees are. Tuition is lower than private trade school.

• *Manpower on-the-job training programs.*

Cities throughout the nation are also offering low-paying, vocational, on-the-job training through the Manpower Training Skills Centers, originally established under the Manpower Development and Training Act of 1968 (MDTA) and now under the Comprehensive Employment and Training Acts of 1973 (CETA). What skills do you learn while you're getting paid to work? Keypunching, bookkeeping, typing . . . acetylene welding and burning . . . practical nursing . . . machine tool operating . . . and more. Call your mayor's office of Manpower Resources for information about programs in your area.

How to Graduate from High School with Other Adults

The school system *does* appreciate the fact that you would feel foolish sitting in a classroom with fifteen-year-old kids—and they don't expect you to.

• *If you want to finish ninth grade only.*

To finish the ninth grade (if that's what you're aiming for—maybe to qualify for an on-the-job training program), the division of adult and community education of your school system offers a special Ninth Grade Certificate testing program. The tests are given every week at adult centers of the adult and community education division of the schools, and there might be a small registration fee—perhaps $6. They can suggest ways to prepare yourself for the test (and these tests are given throughout the entire country).

· *Earning a high school diploma.*

If you want to earn a high school diploma, you can take a General Education Development Examination (GED), which is a battery of five comprehensive tests—and this is also given by the school board. They even have adult classes—attended only by adults—that can get you ready for the tests. These courses are always low cost and sometimes no-cost. The school system will also refer you to books you can read at home in preparation. Call—they'll tell you where and when you can take the five tests (they're given regularly and often). There is no charge, and visually-handicapped and Spanish-speaking adults are not left out of this opportunity: special GED tests are prepared for their easy understanding.

· *The public school system vs. private schools.*

Adult and community education has become very sophisticated. A lot is now being done for adults. People and programs are there to help you learn *and* earn, for no money or very little money. For this reason, I would suggest you prepare for your GED through the school system, with the low-cost or no-cost courses, rather than take preparation courses at the more expensive private business colleges.

Whatever We Do from Choice Is Usually Better Done

School. To have fun. To make new friends. To learn new skills. To show you can do it. To get a job. To keep a job. To advance in a career. To develop a passion. To learn.

Minnie just completed a cabinetmaking course at a local vocational school. She put homemade flyers under neighbors' doors, advertising her skills. She tells me, "As long as we're in a recession, or a Depression, or whatever you want to call it, people will need someone to fix things. No one in my neighborhood is going to throw away a good piece of furniture these days—they'll call me first. Three widows on this street had me do some cabinetmaking for them this year. They know me from church—they know I do good work and I don't charge a whole lot. They live alone, and they'd rather have me working in their house than some strange man."

You might be like the tall, willowy blonde I met last week. "I'm fifty—and I'm looking around for a school of social work that has evening classes and lets you do your field work in your own agency, so I can keep working."

You might be like that grandmotherly woman I told you about who said, "I went back to get my high school diploma to show my children and grandchildren that I could do it."

And that's the great thing about going back to school when you're over-50: You know why you're doing it; you know what the problems are; you know what the payoffs are—and if you finally get to the point of returning to school, it's because *YOU* want to. It is *YOUR* choice. And what we do from choice is usually much better done!

CHAPTER 11

Retirement: Make It the BEST Time

❧ ❧

Retirement: A Nasty Word? A Good Feeling?

A woman with bangs and big, round glasses said, "Honey, how you feel about retirement depends on how much money you've got. Don't let anybody kid you!" "No," a woman sitting with her said quietly, "it depends on whether you've got your health." And a woman listening to both of them said (as if she knew the truth), "You're both right. You need both. One's no good without the other." The woman who had been sitting outside the circle leaned forward, "You're *all* wrong," she said, "retirement doesn't depend on any of those things! If you're alone when you're old—retirement is like death. What good is it to retire if you have no one? If you're alone all the time?" Who is right?

Certainly money is important. Sometimes it can buy good health. A woman I met who wore glittery things in her hair and drank three martinis in a row told me it can also buy companionship. I'm looking at a new thought (for me): The woman who is not averse to taking risks may find retirement more enjoyable. Why? She's more "now" oriented. Even in her sixties, she's less worried about what's-going-to-happen-later. The woman who always expects *something* to happen to her (because she always *makes* something happen for her) likes her retirement more—even though she may be short on money and health and a ready companion. Maybe the dread of retirement can come from feeling that *nothing* will happen to you again. Nothing exciting. A woman can be afraid she'll never have any important decisions to make again. That there will be no more risks. That the life and verve and anticipation will go out of her daily life.

But I think all four women are saying something important, because to each of them it is money or health or companionship that has made the difference in *their* lives.

• *It depends on your living situation.*

I also think retirement is different (not better or worse) for the woman who's living alone; she has different problems and payoffs from the woman who is married to a husband who's retired—and both of these women have different lives from the couple who retires together (they both have been working), or the woman who retires while her husband is still working.

Retirement is certainly not the same for everyone. But are there some common denominators? And in which ways is life different for these women who are in different kinds of situations. What are the problems? What are the pleasures?

If Your Husband Retires While You're Still Working

Because a large number of husbands are older than their wives, it's quite likely that many husbands retire while their wives are still in the 9-to-5 world. This may present no problems at all—or it may present a lot of them, as the following stories demonstrate.

• *The wife who's a perfectionist.*

A woman said bitterly, "I was two years away from my own retirement—I was a teacher—and my husband retired. I can honestly say that it made me leave my job earlier than I had planned. It knocked apart our financial future!"

"What do you mean?" I asked.

"He's a slob!" she blurted out, "Look—you can see I like everything to look nice." I looked around. It was a spic-and-span living room with everything in its place. No newspapers lying around, no books open on tables. It could have been a decorator showroom, rigid and perfect,

"I could control everything while we were both working," she continued. "I'd make the bed in the morning and I'd wash the breakfast dishes before I left for school, and I'd get home an hour or so before he did in the afternoons. I'd be right there to see he didn't just drop his clothes on the floor after he came home from work. He'd read his evening paper before supper—and I'd fold it afterwards. But after he retired—! He'd still be in bed when I'd leave for work, and he'd make the bed later, but I had to do it all over again each afternoon—it was such a mess. I'd come home and find his socks on the bathroom floor and his shirt hanging on the back of the dining room chair. I'd go to make supper and find his breakfast *and* lunch dishes in the sink! 'Oh, I forgot,' he'd say. My spastic colon started acting up, we had one fight after another. Finally I decided to hell with it, I'll quit work now, even though it means a big cut in income—."

Could she have handled it differently? Possibly not. A perfectionist, it would have been very difficult for her to change. And her husband? I couldn't see him changing easily, either. Her choice of an early retirement means more control over her environment—which is very important to her (more important than the money). For her, it probably was the best choice.

• *The wife who resents her husband's freedom.*

"Before my husband retired," another woman said, "I felt so glad for him; glad he'd finally be able to take it easy and do the things he always wanted to do. And now—and believe me, I'm ashamed of myself for feeling this way—now that he's home and *I* still have to go to work, I'm jealous! I'm resentful, having to get up early every morning while he's lying there, sleeping like a baby. I look outside my office window and see that beautiful

sunshine and I know he's out having fun, while I still
have a whole day in that dreary office."

It's good she's acknowledging her feelings. It will help
her work through them. She can now do two things:
consciously and constantly remind herself that her husband started working when he was seventeen and that he
worked hard for almost forty years; that he *deserves* this
leisure time. And she can make herself feel better by doing one nice thing for herself every day—from buying herself a luxurious lunch and stopping at the library on the
way home for an indulgent browse, to getting a facial on a
long lunch hour. She needs to feel pampered these
days.

• *The couple who has to adjust its time clocks.*

"We're having trouble with our time clocks," another
woman wryly told me. "When we were both working, we
were morning people. We both got up at six o'clock, full
of energy, sang through our showers, ate a hearty breakfast while we watched the morning news, and sprinted
out of the house. By ten every night we were pooped, and
we were asleep by eleven (at least on weeknights). Now?
Well, my husband—he retired six months ago—he sleeps
late and when I'm tired at night after a long day at work
he's ready to make love! What do you do about *that?*"

I laughed with her. "You adjust your time clocks."

Because they have a good relationship, they were willing to look at the problem and try to find solutions. After
they talked it over, they decided that since she has less
flexibility than he, still operating in the demanding work
world, her husband would adjust his schedule to hers. He
respects her need to go to sleep early Monday through
Thursday. If he wants to stay up late on Tuesday night
—he watches the late late show alone. On weekends,
their time clocks mesh.

• *The role-defined couple.*

A woman posed a question: "Is it fair to ask my husband to start doing housework, now that he's retired and
I'm still working? I feel so guilty when I do—."

Does she feel guilty because deep inside she feels it's
the woman's job to do the housework? Does she feel that
it's demeaning for a man to scrub the floor or clean the

oven or run the vacuum? Perhaps she has been role-
defined all these years, and it *is* very hard for her to break
out of this—even though she knows that men often *do*
share household burdens in retired households. Well,
she could start by asking him to take over just one or
two tasks, and then see how she feels. Because if she
doesn't, it's probable she's going to end up feeling resentful, seeing him home all day while she's working, knowing she is carrying an outside workload *and* the
housework. If it is too difficult for her (and him?) to
make this adjustment, maybe they should think of having
a household worker come once every couple of weeks to
take over the heavy chores. If your husband does begin
doing any of the housework, be flexible: He will have his
own style of cleaning (isn't your style different from
your mother's?). He may have a different housework
schedule from you (and what's really wrong with doing
the laundry on Thursdays instead of Mondays?). He may
not be quite as thorough as you are (but how many people are going to look behind the dry sink to see if there's
dust?).

On the other hand, how do you handle a situation like
Nell's?

• *The husband who becomes rigid.*

"My husband's turned into a 'crazy-clean' since he
retired!" she said indignantly, "'Take your shoes off!' he
yells when I get home from work, 'my floor has just been
scrubbed!' He hovers over me when I make dinner to see
that I don't mess up his kitchen. It's *his* kitchen and *his*
floor since he's taken over the cleaning. And every evening when I get home from work he insists on taking me
on the 'grand tour' to see everything he's cleaned till I'm
bored to tears. I never imposed this police state on him
when *I* took care of the housework!"

Ride with it, Nell, and see if he'll make some compro-
mises. Like not taking you on the daily "grand tours"
(but be sure you do look around and tell him what a
great job he did that day!). Also, ask yourself: Is your
husband finding enough pleasurable and meaningful activity for himself? Is this plunge into housework an escape
from boredom or a way of telling himself that his life *is*
meaningful? A way to give order to his days? Perhaps

you can help him find important activites outside of the
house, such as volunteer work (yes, many men do volunteer work) or a daily chess game with a rediscovered
friend or a swimming class at the community center.

• *Pre-retirement planning helps.*

I think it is particularly difficult for the man who retires
before his wife if he has always been *dependent* on her
for companionship. If he has no other close friends (and
this is true of many men), and she isn't available during
his new leisure hours (which she isn't), he's apt to feel
anchorless, and lost, unless he has a hobby or passion he
can participate in alone. Pre-retirement planning, where
you anticipate what might happen, helps. Sit down together and help him seek new interests—so he'll ease into
them *before* he retires. He's always had an urge to take
pictures? Buy the camera *before* he retires. Suggest he
enroll in a photography class *before* he retires. By the
time he does retire, chances are he'll already be settling
into the darkroom he built in the basement.

When Your Husband Retires—While You've Always Been Home

• *"I married him for better or worse—but not for lunch!"*

Did you ever hear that saying? That means you've been
used to grabbing a quick sandwich between household
chores or meeting your sister or friend for lunch or going
without lunch because you're on a diet—and the day after
your husband retires he's saying to you, "What's for
lunch?" (expecting you to make it for him and eat it with
him). And then he's saying it to you *every* day! But it
means more.

It can mean that after he retires he also hangs around,
following you from room to room, standing there while
you're making a telephone call, waiting. What's happening? He's feeling lost and lonely. He hasn't made the
emotional transition to retirement. Be patient. Understand this is a difficult time for him.

It's not easy, changing your time clock and your routine and your priorities after forty years on the job. Usually, what happens is a person experiences a "high"

feeling right after retirement—and that euphoric feeling can last a couple of weeks or a couple of months. Your husband can now do everything he always wanted to do: sleep late every morning, go fishing every day, not shave at all (except when you force him), and watch the late show every night. Then suddenly it all goes stale. The party's over. What's next?

• *Help him plan his time.*

If he hasn't planned for what's next, he may zoom down low. There's nothing to look forward to in the mornings. The days last so long! He doesn't feel useful anymore. He's lost the role of worker—and he hasn't replaced it.

There are many ways to combat this depression and steps to take to avoid it. If, for instance, you've planned a big trip for after retirement, hold off for six months. Time that trip to take place just as the "low" is setting in—so he avoids the "low." Also, start making retirement plans long before retirement actually begins (so the low doesn't happen *after* the big trip, either). Things you will want to discuss include: how to plan leisure time, what time to spend together, how to divide up the chores. If you *haven't* done this pre-retirement planning, it's not too late. Sit down together and plan your husband's new leisure time *now* so the rest of his life is the best of his life. If he's known nothing but work all of his life—he'll really need your help.

• *Together, make a list.*

Get out two pencils and some paper and, together, make a list of the interests he *used* to have (go way back, to his teen years and start from there). Consider *everything* (yes, taking walks and playing poker *are* interests). Now, together, make a list of all his friends and relatives who are also free during part of the week (the ones he likes). Who? Perhaps a brother-in-law. A friend he hasn't seen in five years. A buddy in the American Legion. Match his interests with these people. Who can he do what with? Perhaps he'd enjoy visiting the veteran's hospital once a week to see an old friend who doesn't get many visitors. Maybe he'd like to call a couple of the guys he used to play cards with to see if they want to have a

once-a-week game (one determined wife called the local
senior center to ask the director if any of the members
had a card group going . . . and could her husband join.
That's where he now is, every weekday morning!).

• *One man's reaction.*

"Ah!" one irritated man exploded when his wife attempted to help him plan his retirement, "Leave me
alone, will you, babe? All I know is the garage business.
Whaddya want to do—make a different man out of me?"
Yes, she did. She knew that if she didn't intervene, he'd
hang around the house, getting more and more depressed.
Knowing he was a crackerjack automobile mechanic
(that's how he had made his living all those years), she
finally got him to agree to teach five of her friends how
to repair their own cars. At first he was amused
("Women!") but when he saw their enthusiasm, his interest quickened and he soon gained respect for their ability. Today he's teaching an automobile repair class for
women at a local community college and he has another
group of women coming over to his house once a week
for a regular class. He uses his home garage for the classroom, and an old car for them to practice on. He enjoys
the added income, and as his wife says, "He's Mr. Big
Shot to those women—and that's fine!"

• *Be willing to change YOUR routine.*

Be prepared, during your husband's transition into the
world of retirement, to change your routine somewhat.
Instead of spending two afternoons a week shopping with
your friends, how about spending one of those afternoons
with him? How about taking a drive in the country together or browsing through junk shops with him in the
older sections of town? Visiting friends together? One
couple got so involved with browsing through second-
hand shops (it became a perennial treasure hunt) that
they now load up their station wagon every weekend with
bargains they've bought and rent space in outdoor flea
markets and sell from the back of their station wagon.
Yes, more money—and particularly, a shared passion!
If your husband loves sleeping late (now that he finally
can), stop yourself from doing the noisy housework early
in the morning—running the vacuum cleaner and the

dishwasher. The rugs and the dirty dishes can be done after he gets up—perhaps by him.

"But I have a *routine!*" a woman protested. What is more important, the routine or your relationship? It turns out that that woman felt angry. It aggravated her that her husband could sleep while she had to get up and do the housework (or at least she felt that she had to get up and do the housework!). When she realized she was being punitive, she gladly handed those chores over to him and she had more time in the mornings to give to her church.

Remember, this is a period when your husband has the hardest adjustment to make. You still have the same role you've had all these years, that of homemaker. He has lost his role. Give, and then give some more. Make the rest of his time the best of his time.

You're Alone—and You're Retiring

In many ways you're fortunate—retirement may be easier for you. You've already become accustomed to large blocks of time alone, and it'll be easier to slip into retirement because you've learned how to be by yourself. You may even *like* being by yourself. You don't have to adjust a changed schedule to anyone else's needs but your own. You have to answer to no one *but* yourself about how to handle your changed income. You can give priorities to spending in the ways *you* prefer. *You* can decide for yourself whether to buy a new car or take a trip. It's *your* decision where to live. How to live.

• *What if you become ill?*

I think the unique fear of the woman living alone is: "Who will take care of me if I become ill? If I become disabled?" A real fear—because who *do* you have (if you're in this situation), especially if you have no children, or if your children have lost touch or live too far away? There may be no easy answer to this question. If you're on a low fixed income, you know you wouldn't be able to afford a private nurse or companion to live in, and the cost would be too high in one of those retirement hotels that provide medical services.

- *Where should you live?*

Some older women have tried collective living while they're *well*. They pool resources, rent a house together, cut down expenses, have company and solace. If one becomes ill, and is ambulatory, she can still cook, dress herself, get around somewhat, and contribute to the group. She knows there is someone there, if anything suddenly happens.

Perhaps moving alone into an apartment house for the older person (while you're *well*), may be for you. And if you're partially disabled you're eligible for sheltered housing.

In sheltered housing you can live independently in your own apartment, and know that you just ring a bell for help if you need it. There are prepared group meals each day, (which can be very important if you're no longer able to cook for yourself. There may be a social worker on the premises to be alert to any of your changing needs. There generally is a recreation program available in case you can't get out easily. Transportation to and from stores is often a service provided or shopping is done *for* you. In this type of setting, you can be as autonomous as you want to be and as you're able to be. Depend or *not* depend on any of these built-in resources. Come and go as you please and as you can. And just because you're living in age-segregated housing does not mean you have to spend your time only with older people. You can still remain active in the community! What does "partially disabled" mean? Arthritic, painful conditions, impaired eyesight, a chronic illness. Call your social service agency for information on sheltered housing.

- *The advantages of being alone.*

As a woman living alone, and getting ready for retirement—plan slowly and carefully. Planning will be reassuring in itself; it will give you a feeling of more control over your life. Even if your options are very limited, you'll at least know what they are, so you can choose carefully and begin *accepting* your choices. And don't lose sight of the advantages of being alone: you can stay up as late as you want to, watching television, without someone growling "When are you coming to bed?"; you can buy a new dress and not have to discuss it first; you can truly be *AN INDEPENDENT WOMAN.* Learn to *USE* that freedom by not being afraid of making the wrong choices. What's the worst that can happen if you *do* make a wrong choice? You'll regret it—but you can reverse your decision, because you *do* have only yourself to answer to!

If YOU Retire While Your Husband Is Still Working

This doesn't happen too often, because usually a wife is younger than her husband. However, I remember talking to a woman who had just retired from her job, while her husband, who is in his late sixties, refused to retire: he's a physician and loves his work. And, being self-employed, he has no mandatory retirement thrust on him!

"Did you feel lost, once you retired?" I asked her.

"No," she replied, "because I always had outside interests—even while I was working. I have more time to garden now, and I've gone back to painting—something I love doing but had stopped while I was working, because I was too tired in the evenings—and I'm taking a cooking class."

• *Start new projects.*

That's the key to successful retirement while your husband is still in the work world: pick up old interests and passions and renew them; begin completely new projects.

• *Don't expect more time from your children.*

What you *won't* want to do is expect your children, grown and with families of their own, to give you more time than they had before. They still have the same family responsibilities and they have their own routines (*and* friends).

But this is the time to call old friends who you didn't have enough time for when you were working. This is the time to join a daytime organization that interests you (a lecture group? a ceramics class?).

• *Pamper yourself.*

And this is the time to pamper yourself. Why *not* sleep until ten every morning? Why not rest in bed, reading, every afternoon when you're home?

• *You may have more energy than your working husband.*
And you'll find you have more energy for entertaining, if that's for you. And more energy for a fuller sex life with your husband. And more time to cater to him, the way you both like. However, remember—he's still working and his energy level has *not* changed. Adapt your expectations to that.

Money: Making It Work for Your Retirement Years

Alone, or living with a friend, relative, or husband— you want to be sure you spend and use your money wisely because you're no longer able to depend on a salary.

• *Credit.*
First, let's talk about credit. You might want to cut out all charge accounts, because they do invite impulse buying at a time when your income may be reduced. On the other hand, if you do want to use charge accounts, here's some good news: As of October 1975 through the Equal Credit Opportunity Act, a married woman gained the right to put an account in her own name. It also became possible to open an account in your maiden name, even if you're married. Since November 1, 1976, all new credit accounts opened and used jointly by husbands and wives must be carried in the files of the creditor and the credit bureaus in the names of *both* spouses (before, credit bureaus generally filed transactions under the husband's name only. After February 1, 1977, creditors became obliged to notify holders of older accounts that these may be changed on request to include both names (in case you've been using credit cards that are in your husband's name only. These changes are important—because many women have found themselves with no credit standing when they're widowed or divorced, since the joint account showed only their husband's name. Before these changes, a woman in her sixties, suddenly widowed, went into her favorite department store and found the charge account she had been using for thirty years now closed to her. She could only feel indignant and helpless.

• *Assets.*

It is important to know about your assets if you're retiring. At this time, federal tax law assumes that all jointly
owned property belongs to the first owner to die. Since
many husbands die before their wives, the full value of the
property is most likely to be taxed in the husband's estate. If the wife has joint ownership of assets with her
husband and then she is widowed, she has to have persuasive evidence that she contributed to the purchase of
these assets to fend off the tax collectors. Yes, joint ownership does mean lower executor's fees and quicker access
to the property—but if you have assets worth more than
$60,000 (and that's the point where a federal inheritance
tax begins), you might want to think about buying assets in your own name. There are ways to do this: If
your husband gives you a gift of up to $66,000 (to buy
those assets in your name), there's no tax. But he can
only do this once in a lifetime. He can also give you
gifts of up to $5,000 annually, without paying an imposed
gift tax.

• *Investments.*

Are you sitting on investments that may no longer be
right for you—and you don't want to part with them because your husband chose them for you years ago. For
instance, if you inherited a block of stock that your late
husband bought you, are sentimental or superstitious reasons preventing you from taking a look at its current
value?

Perhaps you should take advantage of the special financial services now available for women only. Banks
now have women's divisions and women's credit unions
and brokerage firms have departments serving women.
Banks have also been established *by* women. As a retired
woman, if you are alone, they may have good financial
advice and service for you. The First Woman's Bank in
New York City offers seminars for investments and insurance for women. The First National Bank of Montgomery, Alabama, advises women on qualifying for loans
and setting up investment programs, and helps women
plan estates. There is a woman's banking department at
the Fifth Avenue Bank in New York City. The La Salle
National Bank and the First National Bank, both in Chi-

cago, offers women's divisions for advice and services. The Feminist Federal Credit Union in Detroit serves women only—and was a forerunner in the woman's credit union movement. A widow without much of a credit history may stand a better chance of getting a car loan at one of these credit unions, even though she was turned down at a bank. Investigate institutions like these in *your* city.

• *Earnings.*

In pre-retirement planning, realize that your earning years between the ages of 50 and 65 have certain advantages: You'll have surplus money because you're probably finished supporting your children. Use these years to invest and save for your retirement. Consider investing in annuities. They provide you with protection as long as you live—and their rates are based on what your age will be when you begin receiving payments back from the company. In exchange for your investment, the company agrees to make regular payments to you, either for life, or for some specified time. Annuities, however, do not allow for the shrinking purchasing power of the money you get back. An annuity policy can't be cancelled. You can't borrow against it. Some annuity policies don't provide for survivors.

During your working years (as part of your retirement planning) you may want to use some of your surplus money to invest in ventures which may greatly increase the amount of capital you'll later have. A reliable broker can explain all the various available programs. Dividends are paid at different times by companies, so, if you wish, you can plan your portfolio so that your bond interests and dividends come due at various times of the year, giving you a regular on-going source of income to cushion the difference between your retirement income and your retirement expenses.

• *Mortgages.*

Are you selling your large home and purchasing a smaller one, now that you or your husband are retiring? Consider using your own money to pay cash for your new home instead of borrowing money for a mortgage. It's probable that in borrowing money for mortgage pay-

ments you'll pay an approximate 9 per cent interest rate
—and if you put your own money in a savings account
while you are borrowing the money for the mortgage, your
money in the savings account will only earn around 5
per cent interest. Save yourself about 4 per cent by "lend-
ing" yourself your own money. And if an emergency
comes up, you can always borrow against the house which
belongs to you.

Make a Will

Plan your estate! You might live longer than your
spouse—and you'll need to decide to whom you want to
leave your property.

• *"But I have nothing to leave."*

"But I have nothing to leave!" is a refrain heard often,
especially from widows or women living alone. Is that
really true? How about your cherished diamond ring and
the lovely Persian rug in your hallway, and your good set
of crystal and china? Wouldn't you like to leave the crewel
pillows you made to someone special . . . and the rare
books your husband collected to someone you love? So
you see, it's not just the wealthy woman who has property
to leave.

• *Be aware of the laws.*

Also, if you're married, you may want to *put in writing*
that if you should die first, your belongings would go to
your husband: If there is no will, the estate may be dis-
posed of according to the laws of descent of the state
where the property is located. If you leave no will, even
if you and your husband jointly owned property, your
husband may have to wait many months before gaining
possession. And what does "property" mean? Assets from
life insurance, savings bank and savings and loan association monies, Social Security money, stocks, bonds, pensions and profit-sharing plan monies, stock options, real
estate, inheritances, investments, business and professional
interests, furniture, jewelry, paintings, and books. Your
husband should also make a will. He should be sure you're
protected if he were to die first. If you both neglect draw-

ing up this important piece of paper, your heirs won't be able to sell or handle or distribute your property without the expense of asking the court for authority; your inheritance taxes or estate taxes may be more than they legally need to be, and the person who administers your will will have the extra expense of posting a bond. If you do make a will, you can leisurely choose the person you want to handle your estate.

* *Don't procrastinate.*

Why do some people keep putting off making a will? Superstition often gets in the way ("If I make a will, I'll die"). Making a will also means facing the fact of death. This is often difficult, I know, but making a will also means being good to the people you love!

* *Review your will periodically.*

Once you do make your will, review it periodically. Has there been a change in your financial condition? Your family situation? Are there changes in the *needs* of the people you're leaving your estate to? Consult a lawyer when you make up your will: There are taxes on some estates and in certain cases, deductions are allowed by law. The attorney can possibly help you save some money in state and federal death taxes. And tell a responsible person *where* you keep your will.

Social Security Benefits

* *Application procedure.*

Visit your Social Security office at least three months before you retire to find out just what your benefits will be; to get a complete breakdown as to your Medicare benefits (you're not eligible before the age of sixty-five); to find out when and how to apply for benefits. Take proof of your age with you to the Social Security office. Find out how much less your monthly checks will be if you apply for early benefits, at the age of sixty-two.

* *Facts.*

Facts about your Social Security benefits:

- They're tax free.
- If you get retirement benefits before sixty-five, the the payment amount is reduced. At sixty-five, you get the full wife's benefits, which is 50 per cent of the amount your husband is entitled to at sixty-five years of age.
- They don't *automatically* begin. You have to make an application.
- As of this time of writing, the maximum amount of Social Security a beneficiary can earn without any loss of cash benefits is $3,000 a year (it went up from the year before). If you earn more, you'll have your benefits reduced one dollar for every two dollars you earn above the earning limitation.
- You can get benefits when your ex-husband starts collecting retirement or disability payments if you are sixty-two or older *and* were married to him at least twenty years!
- You may also get payments if your ex-husband dies, provided you're sixty or older (50, if you're disabled) and you were married twenty years or more.
- At the age of seventy-two, you no longer have a ceiling on how much you can earn. Nothing will be deducted from your Social Security checks.
- Even if you don't have dependent children when your husband dies, you can get widow's benefits if you are sixty or older.
- The amount of your monthly payment depends on your age when you start getting benefits and the amount your deceased husband would have been entitled to or was receiving when he died.
- Widow's benefits range from 71-1/2 per cent of the deceased husband's benefit amount at age sixty to 100 per cent at sixty-five. So, if you start getting benefits at age sixty-five, you'll get 100 per cent of the amount your husband would be receiving if he were still living.
- If you're disabled, you can get widow's benefits as early as age 50, but your payment will be less.
- If you and your husband divorce before completion of twenty years of marriage, you lose all rights to Social Security benefits as his *dependent* (and if you aren't eligible for *primary* benefits).

• Ordinarily, a widow loses her Social Security rights when she remarries. But, if you remarry at sixty or older, your widow's benefits might continue. The amount you would get would be 50 per cent of the retirement benefits your deceased former husband was entitled to. If your new husband gets Social Security checks, however, you can take a wife's benefits on his record if it would be larger than your widow's benefit.

• *Check your Social Security account.*

How can you be sure your account is in order when you're ready to retire? To get a record of the annual wages (or self-employed income) credited to your account for the last four years of work, and to find out the *total earnings* credited to your account since January 1, 1937, request form OAR-7004 from your local Social Security Office (it's listed in the phone book under "United States Government, Department of Health Education and Welfare"). Complete the form, and send it to Box 57, Baltimore, Md. 21203. This information can be particularly helpful to you if you work seasonally, or if you changed your name through marriage, or if you were in the job market off-and-on. You may have felt insecure, wondering if your Social Security credits were being properly recorded.

• *Social Security reform needed for women.*

Many people feel important reform is needed in Social Security legislation to give women security. Several legislators are proposing that women receive Social Security credit for their non-paying, child-rearing years, and that the arbitrary twenty-year rule for divorced women be cut considerably; that old age *and* disability *and* widow's benefits be simultaneously available to the older woman (you can only receive benefits under one category); that widow's benefits be available when a woman hits forty—because that's when making a living becomes harder; age discrimination starts playing a part in her work life. *There are 2.2 million women in their middle years who are too young for Social Security benefits—but who are alone and who can't find work!* Bills have been passed in some states that would provide these women with multipurpose centers called Centers for Displaced Homemakers to train and retrain them for employment . . . and The Alliance for Displaced Homemakers, a national group recommends these women be eligible for unemployment compensation.

As I write this, California's Center for Displaced Homemakers is at Mills College in Oakland. Baltimore, Maryland, has a Center for Displaced Homemakers. How about other states? Florida has passed a bill without appropriation; they'll go before their state legislature in the winter of 1977 to seek funding. Minnesota, New York, Pennsylvania, Ohio, and Massachusetts have pending legislation to establish Centers. The following states have legislation to be filed in the 1977 session: Georgia, Mississippi, Louisiana, S. Dakota, N. Dakota, Montana, Illinois, Idaho, Oregon, Texas, Missouri, and Washington.

States that are still drafting legislation are Arkansas, Oklahoma, New Mexico, and New Jersey. The national bill (HR 7003/10272) will be re-introduced January, 1977, asking that the federal government fund 90 per cent and the states fund 10 per cent for these multi-purpose Centers.

Centers for Displaced Homemakers serve men, also. However, as the Director of the Baltimore Center pointed out—there are few men in our society who *are* displaced homemakers. Women, mainly, comprise this disadvantaged group.

Social Security benefits lag way behind cost-of-living increases. Wage earners who make salaries of over $32,-000 pay less than 2 percent of their income on Social Security taxes—while those who earn under $10,000 pay almost 6 per cent! We shouldn't get rid of Social Security under our present economic system—it's all we have— but we can march behind those who are fighting for reform of Social Security legislation.

• *How to get your Social Security checks mailed directly to your bank.*

Having your checks mailed directly to your home invites theft from your mailbox. There is now a direct deposit program available. More than three million recipients are now voluntarily participating in this program at banks and financial institutions throughout the

nation. You are permitted to have your monthly Social
Security and Supplementary Security Income checks mailed
directly to your account in your bank, or to your
savings-and-loan institution. No matter where you live, it
eliminates the need to travel to the bank to cash or deposit
your Social Security check. How do you go about having
your check mailed directly to your bank and deposited in
your personal checking account? Ask your bank to send
you form SF 1100, which you must complete and sign. If
you need help in completing the form, the bank will assist
you. You—or the bank—must send the completed form
to your local Social Security office. The Social Security
Administration will then authorize the Treasury Department to send your payment to the specified bank each
month. It takes about ninety days to process your form.

* *Can you get other retirement benefits
  sent to your bank?*

Recipients of railroad retirement benefits, civil service
annuities, and veteran's benefits also have a direct deposit program available, according to the U.S. Treasury
Department. The program for civil service retirees began
in April 1976; the program for rail retirees began in
November 1976; for Veterans Administration beneficiaries
the program began in January, 1976.

Supplementary Security Income (SSI) at the Age of Sixty-five

* *What it is.*

At the age of sixty-five, if your Social Security benefits
are under $167.80 a month, you are eligible for govern-
mental assistance—a monthly Supplementary Security Income check. A married couple must make no more than
$251.80 to be eligible. Before January 1974, this supple-
mentary income was called Old Age Assistance, and was
rendered through local departments of social service. This
adult program of assistance was taken over by the federal
Supplemental Security Income program, and is now administered through Social Security offices. Many recipients
have found this is much better; they no longer feel "ex-

posed" sitting in the waiting room of their local department of social service.

Supplementary Security Income is also available to people in need, regardless of age, who are blind or disabled.

• *Are you eligible?*

Perhaps you're eligible for this income. If so, call your Social Security Administration office and ask how to apply. You paid a lot of taxes all your life (or your husband did) and this is *not* charity: It is your due.

Thirty-eight Budget Tips

1. *Before you buy a new car,* determine what kind you'll need for the next two years and how much you can afford for monthly payments (if you're buying on time) and stick to that decision—no matter how persuasive the salesperson is in that glossy showroom. Your monthly car payments over a three-year period shouldn't be more than half of your housing costs (rent or mortgage). If you're trading in your old car, stop at your bank or a bank that makes auto loans and ask to see the latest Official Used Car Guide of the National Automobile Dealers Association, or the Kelley Blue Book. For financing, use a bank or credit union rather than having the dealer finance the car for you (too high an interest rate).

2. *Buy clothes only during sales,* and look for "irregulars" in lingerie; buy clothes in thrift shops in good neighborhoods; check special outlet and discount stores where factories wholesale their clothes and bedspreads and shoes (but don't buy at one where the discount price is higher than you would ordinarily pay in a retail store). Now that you have time, make your own clothes (much less expensive) and take advantage of fabric sales, buying inexpensive remnants with which you can make blouses and skirts.

3. *Get your teeth fixed at dental clinics* (you now have the free time to sit in the waiting room for long periods). The work is high-level and the price is cheap.

4. *Take advantage of free health screenings* at churches and community centers and senior centers—to be

checked regularly for heart disease, diabetes, glaucoma, cancer, high-blood pressure, impaired hearing, impaired vision and lung ailments.

5. *You can now save a lot of money on food,* because, being retired, you have the extra time for comparison-shopping and cooking (no more fast convenience foods that are expensive because you're tired from a day at work; no more shopping at *one* store because of lack of time).

6. *Grocery shop in two or three stores each week,* instead of one, to get value, price and quality.

7. *Arrange your shopping time so your grandchildren are not with you;* the cookies and candies are too tempting for them, and you'll find it hard to say no. You'll spend much more money than you had planned.

8. *Shop at discount food stores when you can,* instead of chain supermarkets. There's less variety, a more spartan look, and few or no specials—but most items are cheaper.

9. *Read the daily newspapers thoroughly for food specials;* especially look for weekend specials.

10. *Plan the week's menu around that week's special* at two or three nearby stores; be sure the stores are not so far away that you're making up the difference in the price of gas and oil if you're driving; know the regular food prices so you know what you're saving.

11. *Make a shopping list and stick to it.* A non-negotiable list eliminates impulse buying.

12. *Don't buy already-prepared meat items,* such as meat loaf. Prices are much higher (and you now have the time to do leisurely cooking).

13. *Buy low-cost cuts of meat,* which are just as high in nutrition. It may take longer to cook because the meat is tougher—but you now have the time. Tenderize the meat by stewing in a sauce or by simmering.

14. *Extend meat dishes* with rice or noodles or macaroni or spaghetti.

15. *Buy fresh, frozen, or canned fish. It's sometimes cheaper than meat.*

16. *Buy large birds* (they're cheaper than smaller ones).

Cut the bird up yourself to save money. "Self-basting" turkeys are more expensive.

17. *Brown eggs are often cheaper than white eggs,* and just as nutritious.

18. *A large-size egg gives you the most money value.*

19. *The grade of eggs have nothing to do with nutrition* (they're all nutritious); they only indicate how stiff or viscous the egg is.

20. *Non-fat, dry milk and evaporated milk are cheaper than whole milk.*

21. *Buy house brands in canned goods.* (It's cheaper. It's the store's private-label brand.)

22. *Buy large- or medium-size cans,* even if there are only two of you—or one person. You'll still be ahead on savings.

23. *Read labels:* Ingredients are listed in the order of predominance, starting with the greatest amount. For instance, a can of beef stew listing the gravy first contains more gravy than meat.

24. *Save money by learning label terminology:* Fruit juice contains only juice, a small amount of flesh of the fruit, and preservatives; a juice drink, punch, cocktail, or nectar has between 10 per cent and 50 per cent juice, plus water, sugar, vitamins, and artificial flavoring.

25. *The grade of meat and poultry doesn't relate to the food value.* It relates only to the tenderness, juiciness, and flavor. In the case of beef, also to the ratio and conformity of fat to lean.

26. *Frozen orange juice concentrate is cheaper than buying oranges* and squeezing the juice yourself, and you can store it for months.

27. *Instant coffee is about half as expensive as perked or drip coffee.* You'll find that it's easier to regulate how much to make with instant.

28. *If you live alone, see if your food market packages just one chop (at no extra cost).* That way, it's less tempting to make more for yourself at one sitting when you don't really need it.

29. *Cereal in individual serving boxes is more expensive than in large boxes.*

30. *Even cheaper—cook your own breakfast cereal!*

31. *Diet foods are more expensive* than their equivalents.

32. *Frozen french fries may be less expensive than making your own*—because of the price of the fat.
33. *Buying food you don't really like just because it's on sale is a waste of money*—because you probably won't eat it.
34. *Day-old bakeries are excellent sources for low-cost bread, cakes, and pies.* Many chain food stores feature a special basket where day-old baked items are always on display for sale.
35. *Food coupons (in the newspapers) can be really important cash savings.*
36. *Premiums offered with certain products are seldom good buys* because the value of the premium offered is usually inflated and the money you have to spend often pays the full cost of the premium, plus handling, packaging, *and* postage.
37. *The Federal Trade Commission says that supermarket games (sweepstakes, etc.) shouldn't lure you to buy in a particular store*—because your chances of winning are so low.
38. *Don't be persuaded to buy a freezer*—if the only ones left at home are you and your husband. The "freezer plans" (where you have to buy a certain amount of meat, etc., each month) are not worth it for the two of you.

When It's GOOD to Spend More Money on Food

· *For convenience.*

You might want to spend more money to get certain conveniences. For instance, if you're living alone, and you don't have transportation, and there's no one to take you food shopping, and you find it hard to carry heavy bags of groceries to your home from the store—you might want to consider shopping at the small food store on the ground floor of your apartment house. Yes, it's more expensive than the bigger chain food store, but you can order by telephone and have the order delivered right to your door (the delivery man might even be nice enough to bring the bags in and put them on your kitchen table). This service is particularly important to you if you're disabled or ill, or if you don't want to venture out in snow and ice. (Be sure you know who the delivery boy is before you let him enter your apartment.)

• *For the personal touch—when you live alone.*

"I prefer the small stores," a woman told me, "because shopping there is a social experience—even though it's more expensive. I live alone—I'm retired—and sometimes the only person I talk to all day is the store owner. He's friendly, we chat, he always asks me how I'm feeling (and he means it!). I pick up my daily newspaper, and I feel like he's made my day, bless him."

• *For fun!*

"I live in the Italian section of Boston," a woman said, "and shopping at the little grocery stores there is like shopping used to be in Europe, where I grew up. I go out after breakfast, I go from fruit store to fruit store and compare what they have. I argue a little with the storekeeper, I banter with another—. I pick out my fruit, then I go to my favorite bakery. Ah—a fresh loaf, just baked! Never can you get that in a chain food store! And when I go to my butcher's, he knows just what cuts I like. Before I retired, I didn't really have the time to have this kind of fun—. Yes, to me, the extra money is definitely worth it. It gives more *quality* to my life—."

So being retired can mean different things, even when determining your food shopping needs. Be sure to weigh all of these factors—economy, time, sociability, convenience, quality—when you decide how to shop. No two people have *identical* needs—even if they're both retired.

Making A Budget

• *Get out your pencil and paper—to pin down your expenses.*

The Bureau of Labor says that the "average" retired couple has a budget like this:

Medical Care: 7.3%
Housing: 33.6%
Food, Beverages: 37.7%

Goods, Services: 13.6%
Transportation: 8.9%
Clothing: 8.9%

How do *your* figures match?

If you're getting ready to retire, fill in the blank spaces in the chart below and figure out what your *expenses* will be:

Monthly Expenses	Present Cost	Anticipated Cost After Retirement
Housing		
Food		
Clothing		
Medical Care		
Transportation Costs		
Savings		
Taxes		
Personal & Miscellaneous		
Recreation		
Home Maintenance		

And in completing the "anticipated cost after retirement" column, keep the following in mind: You can cut down mortgage payments by having your house paid for *before* you retire; and since you're no longer working, you don't have to buy special clothing for your job, and you can cut down on how much you use your car (*and* take advantage of any lower bus rates for the sixty-five-and-over citizen). Is it possible that you are entitled to a tax cut on your property in your area, once you reach the age of sixty-five? No more money to put out for office gifts and office lunches; and take advantage of low-cost and free lunches and recreation in senior centers!

What Will Your Income Be?

Wait! Don't put your pencil away! Take a few minutes and fill this out:

Monthly Income Source	*Present*	*Anticipated*
Veteran's Compensations		
Salary		
Annuities		
Pension		
Social Security		
Interest On Savings Account		
Savings Account		
Bonds & Preferred Stocks		
Common Stocks & Investment Trusts		
Government & Corporate Bonds		
Life Insurance		
Interest from Loans & Mortgages		
Stock Dividends		
Other Sources		

• *Have you thought of ALL your sources?*

What are other sources? Sale of real estate, rents, royalties. Now compare how much of a gap there will be between your income and your expenses. Do you need to produce more income? Look at some possible assets (and fill this out):

Asset	Amount
Bank Balance	
Cash Value of Car	
Cash Value of Insurance	
Cash Value of Business	

Can you think of more?
And be sure you know what liabilities you have:

Liability	Amount
Accounts Due	
Notes Due	
Debts	
Unpaid Taxes	

Now subtract your liabilities from your assets to get your net worth.

- *Begin to live on your retirement income before retirement.*

It's a good idea to begin living on your retirement income six months *before* you or your husband retires. Easing into it this way, *before* you're under the strain of the other changes that go with retirement, lessens "retirement shock." It will also give you a little extra for your nest egg, because the money you save while still working those six months can go in the bank. And easing into your retirement budget before you retire is more like a challenging game than a necessity; if you slip here and there, and spend too much one week, you won't feel as grim as you would if you weren't working—and it'll give you the time and experience to really learn how to live on less before you actually have to.

Should You Move to Another Part of the Country?

You might consider moving to another state, for health and/or social reasons. Let's look at some areas that are popular with retirees, and see what they have to offer:

• *Southern California, coastal area.*

Experts say the climate is Mediterranean, one of the finest four-season climates in the world. The summers are made pleasant by sea breezes, and there's almost no rain for two to six months. The winters are not cold (you might wear a lightweight coat). Temperature? About 48 to 60 degrees F. during the winter months, and around 72 to 78 degrees F. during the daytime in the summer, with cooler evenings. The relative humidity in the winter, at noon, is about 45 to 56 per cent, and 52 to 60 per cent in the summer months. In the winter, the sun shines, during daylight hours, 68 to 71 per cent of the time!

San Diego has a large retired population in the surrounding communities. The area enjoys a dry subtropical climate, and many cultural activities.

La Jolla, a suburb of San Diego, is inhabited mainly by retirees. It's an area that was originally settled by artists, writers and people in the theater. It's located on a rocky and beautiful headland, fronted by many sandy coves.

Then there is Coronado and Escondido and Oceanside and Laguna Beach—all near San Diego, all within a short distance of Mexico. Other cities in the area that attract retirees are Pasadena, Long Beach, Oxnard, Santa Barbara, and Ojai. If you settle in any of these areas, you'll find the weather delightful, all year round.

• *Southern California, interior areas.*

The climate is generally warmer and drier than on the coast of southern California. The humidity is low, there's no fog or smog, and retirees who suffer from asthma, neuritis, sinus, and bronchial ailments frequently find relief from their symptoms. Riverside, Banning, Corona, Beaumont, and Palm Springs are popular retirement areas.

• *Central California, coastal region.*

There are mild temperatures all year round, and no clearly defined seasons. Fogs? Yes, but they usually disappear by midmorning. However, this does mean less sunshine. There is some spectacular scenery in this general area—the Monterey Peninsula area, the towns of Carmel and Monterey—and deep-sea fishing, clamming, and small-game hunting are popular sports. Other cities are Pacific Grove, Los Gatos, Palo Alto—all with large populations of retired people.

• *Florida.*

This is the state that attracts the largest numbers of retirees on the East Coast. California is the only state that competes with Florida as a retirement spot. Winters in Florida are usually nearly fifty degrees warmer than the northern states. Sunshine? Five to six hours a day in the winter. Florida has very hot days in the summer, but they're relieved by afternoon, semi-tropical showers. What particularly attracts countless retirees is the fact that Florida has no state income tax. Personal and property taxes are low. And you don't have to be wealthy to live in Florida; many older people, living only on their Social Security benefits, have settled in South Beach, a part of Miami Beach. The entire area of Miami (as well as other sections of Florida) offer many low-cost and no-cost attractions geared especially for over-sixty people. Coral Gables, Fort Lauderdale, Hollywood, Daytona Beach, and Ormond Beach all attract many retired persons. The well-to-do retiree will find plenty of manicured and fancy condominiums to her taste, and restaurants and beautiful shops along Worth Avenue in Palm Beach are well-known . . . so you can see there is a wide range of incomes among the vast numbers of retired men and women in Florida.

• *The Southwest.*

Stay away from the northern table lands that range from six thousand to twelve thousand feet. This kind of altitude is not easy on older folk. But the southern section of Arizona, and to some extent New Mexico, has a mild dry climate and a lot of sunshine. There is a mild winter temperature—as well as natural mineral springs. Tucson,

Arizona, attracts retirees who seek relief from sinus trouble, asthma, rheumatism, and arthritis. The area offers many cultural and educational opportunities, as well as a wide range of recreational activities, such as golf, horse-back riding, and swimming in municipal pools.

If you are considering moving to another state, check into the state and local tax situation *before* making major changes. (the only state that has *no* inheritance tax is Nevada!). Definitely consider the climate (climatologists and doctors feel that a mild, warm, year-round climate is best when you're over-sixty); choose areas that have *less* pollen, smoke, and acids that pollute the atmosphere (for your health!); consider areas that do not have sudden or severe changes in the weather, because your body has to adjust to meet these changes. Be sure you find out what the living expenses are in the area—and then decide if you can meet those expenses.

And the best way to really make a wise decision is to take your time—visit the area you're interested in moving to as frequently as possible *ahead* of time. Talk to people who have retired there. Get their opinions. Feel the place out.

Should you sell your home?

• *Advantages*

Are you thinking of moving to an apartment or a smaller home? Advantages could be less upkeep, lower costs (no mortgage payments or taxes or home insurance), and a more convenient living arrangement (no steps!).

• *Turn your home into more income.*

On the other hand, keeping your home could mean extra income: renting out a room to a student or renting out the third floor to a couple can supplement your Social Security checks. Staying in your big house can mean more room when the family visits, and you can continue to putter in the garden (which you may love). Staying in your home means having the same neighbors (you may value their friendship), and being close to the stores and

doctors you've dealt with for years, and having the same
space and shapes around you that have grown to be
familiar and important—the bay window that overlooks
your hollyhock bushes, the nook in the corner of the den
where you do your sewing, and the crazily put together
kitchen where everything's so disorganized but where
you've loved to cook and bake for thirty years.

If you are thinking of selling, make a list of advantages
and disadvantages—as *you* see it.

A Retirement Community?

If you do decide to move, what about a retirement
community? Different people feel different about this kind
of living.

• *Some people love it.*

Some retirees value the planned activities designed
especially for older people and the medical facilities that
some of these retirement villages offer.

• *Others hate the idea.*

Others hate the age-segregation. They miss young
voices and young faces. "Besides," one over-sixty-five
woman said to me, "did you ever see those old people
riding those big tricycles? They're all over those retirement villages—and they look *nutty!*"

Nutty or not, it's to many retired people's liking. Some
people are very happy in retirement villages. They *like*
the daily cocktail hour, when they get together at the
communal clubhouse, and the structured classes where
everything is taught from ceramics to Swedish Walking.
(Free college extension courses are now offered at Retirement Village, Sun City, in Arizona).

• *If you're left alone after the move.*

However, I think it can be difficult to *stay* in some retirement villages if you're suddenly left alone; if your husband dies after you've already settled in. Many retirement
villages are couple-oriented, but some aren't. Be sure you
find this out before moving. You can feel pretty lonely living there by yourself.

An Apartment House for Older People?

• *What kind of people live in them?*

Will you feel a sense of community in one of these apartment houses?

Marcella, whom I hadn't seen in two years, was at a conference I was attending a few weeks ago. When I had last seen her, she was sixty-three years old—and very busy teaching sociology at a college twelve hours a week. She is a small vibrant woman, given to quick movements and witty comments. Her idea of a good time is to talk for hours with close friends over wine and cheese . . . to beat a colleague at a game of chess . . . to argue over what's happening in Angola. When I saw her at the conference, she told me she was retiring (*"Made* to," she said dryly. "I turn 65 this year."). She looked tired and she sounded desperate.

"I'm thinking of moving into one of those retirement apartment houses," she said.

I was startled. "Why?"

"Well, I'm looking for people I can relate to—feel good with. I want to replace the camaraderie I have with the people I work with. You know, people to go to concerts with, and to art galleries with—."

"Marcella," I wanted to help her understand what I already knew, but I didn't want her to feel she was left with nothing, "an apartment house for older people is not an academic community. It's not a community of—intellectuals. Oh, there are some very bright people living in them, but there are a lot of average people, too. People who like to talk about clothes and television shows and— are they *your* kind of person?"

We looked at each other, silent.

"Maybe," I continued, "you want to find people like yourself—form your own intentional community. Marcella, you know you hate small talk. You were never good at it. You *need* intellectuals in your life!"

Well . . . we got busy, and right now Marcella is calling her local National Organization of Women (NOW) office, and the People's Free Clinic in her town, and everyone she knows, to see if someone *like* herself is looking for a roommate. She's discovering that it *is* harder for a woman like herself to find a group that meets her needs—but isn't it hard for the intellectual of any age to find kinship outside of particular *kinds* of communities? If she can't find a roommate or an already established intentional community (she got a list of the ones in her area), she'll run some ads in magazines and newspapers that attract readers like herself: *Ms.* magazine, *Prime Time* (a newsletter for the older woman that her NOW office referred her to), The *Village Voice*, the *Saturday Review* . . .

• *Be selective in your housing arrangements*.

There's no reason for a woman like Marcella to be less selective than she was in her pre-retirement years. Or for *any* of us to be less selective as we grow older, no matter what our tastes and values—. We know that everyone has equal worth, and we also know with whom we're most comfortable (we've been around long enough to know that!), so we want our life to have as much texture and flavor as possible. Remember, where you live has a lot to do with whom you'll be spending time.

A Mobile Home?

Seven million people live in mobile homes—and 25 per cent of them are retired. Right this minute, on a super-highway, a graying man, driving a car, is saying to his wife sitting beside him, "Look at that! Now *that's* the way to live!" A large mobile home has just whizzed by, obviously headed for warmer climes.

• *Mobile home living . . . the advantages*.

It does have its payoffs: economy (cheaper than buying a house), camaraderie (some mobile home owners travel in groups across the country), and mobility (a great way to satisfy your sense of wanderlust). These are the kinds of payoffs that appeal to many retired persons.

• *The problems*.

If you are thinking of purchasing a mobile home, take some precautions. Be sure it will stand up to the weather conditions in the areas where you want to take it. For instance, will you be *planting* it in Florida? Hurricane season in that state means you'll want to be sure your home won't tip over—which happened to hundreds of mobile homes on the east coast of Florida, not too long ago. Why did this happen? Most of those homes had no anchoring whatever to the concrete foundation. You need parts and equipment to take care of that—which doesn't normally come with the purchase of the home. And check: How is the insulation? The wiring? The heating and cooling facilities? Adequate for where you're going? Does the home have enough electrical outlets? How's the plumbing? Look for a certificate on the mobile home wall (provided by the manufacturer), stating the geographical zones for which the home has been designed. The certificate also tells you the lowest outdoor temperature at which the furnace will hold a 70-degree indoor temperature. Is there enough natural light in the home? How's the ventilation? And be sure the home doesn't have hinge-hung doors and walk-in closets or conventional freestanding furniture (you want built-ins).

• *Performance standards.*

If the mobile home manufacturer you're dealing with (through the distributor) belongs to the Mobile Home Manufacturers Association, they subscribe to a code of production standards (known as the A119.1 code) that not only specifies the use of certain materials and supplies, but also sets performance standards. Want to see a copy of the code? Request it from the Publications Division, MHMA, 6650 Northwest Highway, Chicago, Ill. 60631.

• *Get references about the dealer.*

Also, have your banker investigate the dealer you expect to buy the mobile home from. Ask the dealer for names and addresses of people who have bought his homes. Get in touch with them—and be sure he gives you at least ten names.

• *Is this the kind of home for you?*

Particularly, look at your own personality and living needs before finally deciding on a mobile home. Is privacy very important to you? You love your husband or

your sister or your friend (or whomever you're planning to share the home with), but that's awfully close
quarters to live in. Do you need a lot of space for certain
belongings (like darkroom equipment or art supplies)?
Will you have enough space in the average mobile home,
which is about sixty feet long and twelve feet wide? Is
the move from a spacious home to a mobile home going
to be an emotional shock—too sudden a change? If you're
going to plant it permanently in a different state, have
you tried visiting that area enough times and for long
periods so you *know* you'll like it there? If you're *not*
going to plant it and you're going to do a lot of traveling
—do you like being on the road that much?

One woman I spoke to ended up hating her mobile
home. She is an avid antique collector, had lived in a
twelve-room house for thirty-five years, loved to give
lavish dinner parties, and had a close set of friends. Her
husband, who retired from his dental practice a year ago,
talked her into their purchasing a mobile home so they
could satisfy his frustrated desire to travel throughout the
year. Biting her tongue with fury, she sold her antiques.
They move around too often for her to replace the
friends she lost. Even if she could make a new social life,
she knows she'd never have enough room to really entertain the way she likes. She's beginning to hate her husband almost as much as her mobile home (well, not really
—but she's always angry at him).

But another woman I know loves her mobile home.
She and her husband owned a modest, tract house—
small, unpretentious—for many years. She's adaptable,
gregarious, and loves meeting new people. She likes doing
things on the spur-of-the-moment (cooking up a pot of
stew for guests; dropping her housework to take a walk
with her husband). She isn't a "possession" person; she's
more of an "experience" person. This couple has been on
the road for three years now (since her husband retired)
and she's not tired of it yet. She proudly showed me
through the small living room, pointing out how the furniture takes up so little room. "Easy to clean," she said,
"and nothing to it. It only takes me an hour to clean the
place!"

• *Rent one first.*

Before you definitely decide on the purchase of a mobile home—rent one. Yes, that's right, rent one during a vacation (*before* you or your husband retire) and see how you feel after the two or three weeks are up. Try doing this during several vacations because you'll notice things the second and third time around you weren't aware of during the first trip. A mobile home can open a wide, new world for you—or make your life miserable. Like any other large change in your life—try it first.

Moving to Another Country

Are you considering moving to another country for your retirement? Perhaps you and your husband came here from Greece or Italy, and want to spend the years ahead there. Israel may represent your "homeland" to you, and like many Jewish-Americans, you may have purchased an apartment there in anticipation of your retirement years (you can't rent apartments in Israel). You might want to retire to Mexico, drawn by the beauty, the culture, and the possible low-costs.

• *Facts to consider.*

What do you want to consider if you're thinking of moving to a different country? Well, unless your finances are in unusually good shape, you won't be able to travel back-and-forth to the United States that often to see your children and grandchildren—and a visit every couple of years may not seem enough to you, now that you're getting older. Also, will your health (and your husband's health) *permit* you to make more frequent visits? Can your children afford to visit *you* often?

How about your relationship with old friends? Will it be hard or easy to pull up roots and leave them? Are you going to a country where you already know people? If you aren't, is there an English-speaking community? Will it be easy to build a new social life?

• *Visit as many times as you can—before you move!*

The ideal way to determine whether you really want to move to a particular country is to visit the place as many times as possible, before you make the final move, and visit as a prospective resident—*not* as a tourist.

• A woman retires to Israel!

"By the time I moved to Israel," a woman said, "I had gone there about ten times. I never stayed at hotels. I'd either stay at a friend's apartment or I'd rent a room for the four weeks. Once I stayed in Natanya, and I knew afterwards I didn't want to settle there, and a few other times I stayed in Jerusalem. After I stayed in Tel Aviv five times I decided that's for me! I bought my apartment six months before my move. I have my Social Security checks sent to me. The exchange rate is very good. My dollar stretches farther there. Of course I had a hefty savings account before I left the States. I wouldn't have dared go without that cushion——."

Retirees may be less eager to settle in Israel these days because of the tensions in the country, the apprehensions about another war.

• A woman retires to Mexico.

A woman who retired to Oaxaca, a small city in southern Mexico, said, "I rent a tiny house in the hills outside of town, and it's a gem of a house. Designed by an architect. It's only one hundred and ten dollars a month! And there's a trailer park where other retirees live. A few others rent or buy houses, like I do."

"What made you decide on Mexico?" I asked.

"I was a commercial artist for thirty years—a fashion illustrator—and my dream was to retire and paint somewhere. So here I am! I chose southern Mexico because it's cheaper than some of the other areas in this country. I like the Indian street life. I'm not too happy about being so careful about what I eat all the time—you have to be in this country—but everything else makes it worth it to me. The medical care is much less expensive than in the States. There's nothing plastic about this culture. It's just a beautiful country!"

• What about your health?

Consider your health when you're deciding whether to move to another country. Altitude can affect your physical and mental condition. A friend moved to Mexico City and found she suffered from indigestion every night. She visited Cuernavaca, a town not too far from Mexico City, and her symptoms disappeared! The doctor later told her that, very often, the thin air of Mexico City (perched seven thousand feet up) often affects people's digestive systems. Cuernavaca, around five thousand feet high, is considered a perfect altitude. Extensive research by the Instituto Nacional de Cardiologia in Mexico City found that people who do not suffer from heart disease can be comfortable up to ten thousand feet. However, if you or your husband suffer from a serious heart ailment or a degenerative disease or arthritis or if you're very nervous, you'll be more comfortable and stay healthier at an altitude no higher than sixty-five hundred feet. If you or your husband suffer from sinusitis or kidney trouble, talk to your doctor before moving to an altitude above five thousand feet.

You're in *good* health—and you are moving to an altitude of over five thousand feet? Don't be frightened or surprised if you experience some digestive upsets the first few days, or feel tired and breathless. Within a week the hemoglobin content of your blood should change and your respiration rate will pick up and you'll feel acclimatized. Of course, if you don't feel better, consult a doctor.

Climate can affect your health, too (as I mentioned before). Extreme cold weather might make life difficult for you if you suffer from diabetes, chronic nephritis, or arteriosclerosis. Generally, as we grow older, cold weather bothers us more.

• *How about costs.*

Climate can also affect our *pocketbook*. Moving to a warmer climate means only one set of clothing a year (no special clothes for winter), and it certainly means less fuel costs—if we're paying for that ourselves. Climate affects our mobility. It's harder to get around in an area where there are a lot of snowstorms.

Have you thoroughly checked out the cost of living in the country where you're considering moving? Have you investigated the moving costs? Have you looked into the exchange rate? If you are considering opening a retirement business, better find out if that country's government allows non-citizens to operate a business!

• *It is a big step.*

Moving from one country to another *is* a big step. If you're married, you'll want to ask yourself a crucial question: If I'm suddenly left alone in that new place, will I be able to cope? But don't worry: If you do make a mistake by moving, it is not irreversible. Sure, it will take money and effort to *again* change your living conditions; but people do it all the time. If you are enough of a risk-taker to move in the first place—you'll probably have enough emotional stamina to make the move back. The worst that can happen? You'll feel and be temporarily uncomfortable. Is that so terrible?

Your Relationship with Your Grandchildren

A lot of newsletters and literature pass my desk, and I particularly liked this anonymous article written by an eight-year-old, somewhere:

WHAT A GRANDMOTHER IS
By a Third Grader

"A grandmother is a lady who has no children of her own so she likes other people's little girls. A grandfather is a man grandmother. He goes for walks with boys and they talk about fishing and tractors, and things like that.

"Grandmothers don't have to do anything except be there. They're old, so they shouldn't play hard or run. It is enough if they drive us to the market where the pretend horse is and have lots of dimes ready. Or, if they take us for walks, they should slow down past things like pretty leaves and caterpillars. They should never say "hurry up." Usually they are fat, but not too fat to tie kids' shoes. They wear glasses and funny underwear. They can take their teeth and gums off. It is better if they don't typewrite or play cards except with us. They don't have to be smart, only answer questions like why dogs hate cats and how come God isn't married. They don't talk baby-talk like visitors do, because it is hard to understand.

When they read to us they don't skip, or mind if it is the same story again.

"Everybody should try to have one, especially if you don't have television, because grandmas are the only grown-ups who got time."

• *What kind of a grandmother are you?*

Are you that kind of grandma? Bet you're not! Bet you *are!* Because when you look at your ash-blonde hair and size ten dress in the mirror you know you aren't the grandma with the funny underwear. Because you *don't* talk baby-talk to your grandchildren. Because you *can* take your teeth off (or at least some of them). Grandmothers come in all shapes and sizes and colors and kinds. What kind are you? What kind do you *want* to be? What kind do your children want you to be?

• *The critical grandmother.*

Hannah is one grandmother of my acquaintance. "Whenever I go over to my daughter's," she said, "I see another new expensive toy from her in-laws. They're wealthy—they own a dress factory—and my granddaughter's bedroom is *stuffed* with things they bought her: a television set (and she's only five!), clothes, toys! It's a crime, they spoil her to death—"

I said, "I never heard you complain before."

She glared at me.

She never *had* complained before. She had been too busy working. She just retired two months ago and she hasn't yet replaced her lost role as "worker"—so she's caught up in jealousy of her daughter's in-laws. As she finds meaningful activities to replace that lost role, she'll again realize that the *time* she spends with her granddaughter is as important as the *money* they spend. It's just that right now she's feeling inadequate . . . as many of us do during a period of transition in our lives.

• *The grandmother with unrealistic expectations.*

Elinor's another grandmother. Her husband retired this year, and they're now able to spend the entire summer at their house on the lake. Elinor's very upset because Jeff, her fourteen-year-old grandson, doesn't want to spend the summer with them.

"He came with us for two weeks every summer since he's been seven! He loved it—fishing with my husband, swimming—and now that we can finally stay up there the whole summer, he doesn't want to go!"

"Honey," her husband said patiently, "he's fourteen. He doesn't want to leave his friends."

"But I counted on it!" she wailed. "And this is the first year we can all be together the whole summer. He could at least come with us and *see* if he likes it—!"

Elinor was refusing to give up her unrealistic dream: that Jeff would stay the same; that for now and the years ahead (at least the next few years) he would run through the woods and call "Grandma! Can I have some cake?" and proudly catch fish with his grandfather. She (because of her needs) was forgetting that grandchildren grow and change—sometimes suddenly—and develop different *kinds* of relationships with their grandparents.

Relationships with Grown Children

• *Expectations.*

Are you being realistic about what to expect from your *children* once you've retired?

"I thought my daughter would be happy that we could finally spend more time together," a despondent woman told me, "and after I retired I'd drive over to see her and the baby every other afternoon. Then, after a couple of weeks, she said, 'Mom, call me first, will you?' I said, 'What do you mean, don't you want to see me, now that I'm finally free after working all these years?' This is my only grandchild. I should call my daughter first? Since when are families so formal? And then when I did call first, half the time she was too busy to see me—." This grandmother was caught up with her *own* needs. She wasn't looking at her daughter's need for time alone, or to be with her friends.

"I'm retiring in two weeks," another woman said, "and I have reservations right after that to fly to Chicago to spend some time with my son and his family."

"How long will you stay?" I asked.

She gave me a coy look.

"Oh, who knows? I bought a one-way ticket. I might stay for a month or more—"

Did she talk it over with them? Do they know her intentions? Did their invitation imply a time limit? This "visit" has the makings of a potentially explosive situation.

• *Are you being sensitive about their need for privacy?*

Before retirement (yours or your husband's), you may have been too busy to invest large amounts of your time and energy in your children and grandchildren. Now you may be eagerly saying to your husband, "Let's stop over after breakfast and see how everyone is! I'll take some of the pot roast from last night—." A bribe? So they will welcome you? Because deep down, you know they need their private time? And they do! They need the privacy and time to scream at each other and to make love and to lie in bed and rest in the afternoon and to gossip on the phone with their friends and to do the housework. Bringing up a family is hard work. It is demanding (remember?). As much as they love you and like you, your more-frequent phone calls and knock-at-the-door means disrupting their routine; it means *change.* "But I can babysit more often now!" a woman said indignantly. Yes, but do you expect anything in return? More attention? More time? Let your children give you clues as to how often they can and want to see you.

And your children may have very different expectations regarding you now that you retired.

• *The unrealistic adult child.*

"Since my mother was a career woman," James said, "she never had much time for the grandchildren. Well, my wife and I sort of expected that once she retired, she'd pay more attention to them. Take them to the zoo, call them every day, you know —. But she's still busy at her own things, dashing around, going to meetings instead of work, and if they hear from her every two weeks, they're lucky." He looked angry, and his wife, sitting next to him, looked self-righteous. "*My* parents are more caring," she said. She pulled their two-year-old, who was leaning against her, closer, and whispered to him, "Grandma and Grandpa love you, don't they?"

I remembered James when *he* was little, angry because his mother was too busy to go to PTA meetings. During spring carnivals, when the other mothers would be behind bake tables on the school playground, *his* mother was at a conference table in New York or at her desk in her office. What he didn't want to accept was the fact that his mother just isn't a "children" person. She never was. And now that she's retired, she still isn't. Maybe what James needs help in realizing is that his children can (and *do*) get nurturing from *other* important people in their lives: their parents and their mother's parents. They'll do all right. It's *James*—not his children—who needs help. He was an only child (his parents had divorced when he was two), and he has never forgiven his mother for not giving him the kind of attention he wanted and needed when he was little. Why did he expect her to change, now that she was retired? "Well," he said bitterly, "I thought she'd mellow. She's older." I think perhaps James has a stereotype of how people—women—are supposed to behave when they're "older." How grandmothers are supposed to feel and act. But grandmothers are as varied as younger women. Many younger women find it hard to relate to small children—even their own—and so do many grandmothers. Maybe James's mother will feel closer to the children when they're teen-agers (James is forgetting how much pleasure his mother got from introducing him to Europe during the tour they took together when he was fifteen and how they read plays aloud, to each other, when he was fourteen).

- *The overprotective grown child.*

"This might sound strange to you," a forty-year-old man said, "but I want my mother to slow down. She's worked hard all her life. Now that she's retired, she's still killing herself. There are five of us, and she runs around buying our children clothes on sale, and she is in her kitchen every day baking and cooking so she can bring food over to our houses—like we're starving!—and when she hears anyone is sick, she comes right over to cook and clean and take care of things. We love her—but she has high blood pressure and she's pushing sixty-seven, and we wish she'd take it easy. She worked hard all her life in the business with Dad—he died two years ago—and it's time she slowed down."

What this loving and concerned son doesn't realize is that his mother might fall apart if she *did* slow down. She feels useful and needed as long as she can run around the way she does, administering to the needs of her big family. She's a warm and likable woman who is sensitive to her children's needs: Even though she's right there when they need her, she backs away quietly (leaves their house) when a husband and wife quarrel or when she senses they want to be alone. She never offers advice and she never criticizes. The family pattern is rather like the old days when extended families were the fashion (grandma living in the same house as the grown children, cooking and baking and baby sitting), only, in this case, grandma goes back to her own home after fussing over everyone. It works beautifully. Her daughters-in-law are grateful for her help when a child is sick. If her daughter can't use the beef stew grandma brings over that day, the daughter just puts it in the freezer for another time. Grandma is needed, grandma is useful . . . *so let her be!*

Your Relationship With Your Ex-Daughter-In-Law (Or Ex-Son-In-Law)

Divorce is not an unusual phenomenon in our society. And it usually is traumatic to everyone involved. When there are children involved, all kinds of questions and problems and conflicts can arise. I sat and talked to one young woman who was very upset.

She was attractive. She was about thirty. She smoked one cigarette after another, anger on her face, "My ex-in-laws both just retired, and I know they spend a *lot* of time at their children's homes, but do they call *my* child and take her out? No! So I *am* divorced from their darling son—does that mean my daughter should be an outcast? How do they think *she* feels? *She* knows they're taking her cousins out to lunch every week!"

• *Put your grandchild first.*

Divorce is difficult for grandparents, too. What role should they play with the ex-daughter-in-law or ex-son-in-law? With the grandchild who lives with the ex-daughter-in-law? No rules of etiquette for that! You make up your own rules. And if you're confused (and it's easy to be confused with no rules) just try to follow *one* rule *you* set-up: Be kind. That means you will want to continue to be as loving with your grandchild as before the divorce. You used to call her every few days? Why not now? Okay, the first few times on the phone with your ex-daughter-in-law might be stiff and self-conscious, but you're grown-up enough to shrug that off. You feel awkward picking up your grandchild at your ex-son-in-laws's house? Especially since he remarried? All right, try to see your grandchild when she's with your daughter. And if you can't, and you must pick your grandchild up at your ex-son-in-laws's—don't back out. Realize that your grandchild is going through a very difficult time (the child always hurts the most from a divorce), and she or he needs your love. With an older grandchild, perhaps he or she can meet you at a favorite restaurant, or take a bus to *your* home.

- *Don't be critical or prying.*

And, of course, you will *never* be critical of *any* of your grandchild's parents or stepparents when you're with your grandchild. Or ask any prying questions—no matter how casually.

Get Ready for the UNEXPECTED!

Family relationships are different as you grow older . . . different when you retire—more time on your hands. The grandchildren grow up, with different needs as they get older. Times have changed. The family network is not just you and your children and your grandchildren: There's another set of grandparents in the picture, too. Your children may divorce, may remarry. Then you have to start all over, form new relationships, decide what to do about the discarded ones.

- *Different times, different values.*

"You don't understand!" a woman said urgently. "My son—he's a widower—wants me to come to his house to see the children, and he's *living* with a woman! I told him I could never accept that, and he says if I want to see my grandchildren, I have to accept his way of life. I could never do that!"

I do understand. This sixty-year-old woman finds it too difficult to accept a value system so different than the one she has lived with, and her son insists on her accepting it—and accepting the relationship he has with this woman. I hope they find a compromise. The children are caught in the middle. Time sometimes works this kind of conflict out.

• *Illness . . . How much do you tell a grandchild?*

"Life can be *very* different from what you expect," a woman said, staring into her coffee cup. "Take my husband. He didn't expect to retire. He's sixty-two, and was a very successful psychotherapist. All right, so now he has a chronic disease and he can't practice anymore. Between operations and being in the hospital, he's home biting his nails. How much reading can he do? The kids come over with our grandchildren, and the children discover that their grandfather can't roughhouse anymore. What do you tell a thirteen-year-old who used to go mountain climbing and skiing with his grandfather? Do you tell him Grandpa is going to die soon?

Well, perhaps you do. A thirteen-year-old suspects. If you do tell him (and whether to tell or not should be a decision his *parents* make with his grandfather and you), tell him gently, slowly. The younger grandchildren? They may be too young to understand, and you just have to remind them that Grandpa gets very tired and he can't play as hard as he used to. Find distractions for them when they visit. Make their visits short.

Expectations. Needs. What are *yours?*

Your New Leisure Time

Does a meaningful retirement mean leisure time? Must one learn to enjoy leisure, with no guilt feelings, if one is going to enjoy retirement? Leisure is uncommitted time, when you can do whatever you want to do.

For the Woman Over 50

• *Work . . . How important is it to you?*

To most of us who grew up with the work ethic, a meaningful life means—work. Duke University's Center on Aging found that among 200 men and 200 women, 52 per cent of the men and 55 per cent of the women stated they got more satisfaction from work than they did from leisure. Only 12 per cent and 16 per cent, respectively, preferred leisure.

• *Leisure . . . attitudes toward it.*

Maggie Kuhn, who founded the Grey Panthers, scorns the "playpen" activities of some senior centers. Is she scorning leisure? George Bernard Shaw said, "A perpetual holiday is a good working definition of hell." Dr. Edward J. Stieglitz, the author of *The Second Forty Years,* wrote, "Success or failure in the second forty years, measured in terms of happiness, is determined more by how we use or abuse our leisure than by any other factor . . . a superabundance of leisure, or the abuse thereof, has marked and initiated the decadence of cultures throughout history."

I think George Bernard Shaw and Dr. Stieglitz grew up learning the work ethic, too. It's hard to unlearn it.

I met a retired film editor who enjoys her leisure, so she enjoys her retirement. "It's great being able to just *sit,*" she said. "It's so nice not having to race up from the breakfast table, to go to work. I just sit . . . and I daydream . . . and I look at the patterns the morning light makes on the leaves outside the window. I never had time to really watch the light before! It's wondrous to see. . . ."

My head says, "One must learn how to enjoy leisure—without any guilt feelings." But will I be able to do this when I retire, as this film editor has?

• *Some people continue with the same negative attitudes.*

How do you feel about *your* new leisure time? Probably how you felt about leisure when you were younger. The compulsive homemaker who couldn't sit down after supper and relax when she was forty (she had to do some ironing and sewing, maybe some more cleaning) will, no doubt, still feel too guilty to do much sitting down when she's sixty-five.

- *And some can adapt to leisure.*

"I had to *learn* not to work," a woman told me, "and that meant I had to learn I had the right to enjoy not working."

"Did you learn?" I asked her.

She nodded. "I developed a plan for leisure—like I had a plan for work all those years. I broke down my new leisure time, after retirement, the same way I broke down my work week—by the day, by blocks of time—by 'tasks.'"

"Tasks?" I asked, "that *really* sounds like *work.*"

"What I did was neatly package 'leisure tasks' each day," she continued. "On Mondays I attend a lecture series, on Tuesdays I take a crafts class, on Wednesdays I go to my health club, I spend Thursdays with my daughter, and on Fridays I swim at the 'Y' and have lunch and play cards with some friends. I never deviate. I don't dare yet."

I must have looked skeptical. "Do you *enjoy* everything you're doing?"

"Love it!"

We looked at each other, she amused and I questioning.

"Look," she continued, "this is like when I was younger and wanted to lose some weight. I couldn't seem to stick to a diet. Then a doctor said to me '*use* your compulsiveness—the same compulsiveness that makes you eat—to diet.' And it worked. I ate the same diet food everyday—compulsively. The same amounts. I'm now carrying out a *plan* for leisure, sticking to the plan—just like work. But it's not work! I enjoy it—because I 'worked hard' planning it. It makes it *seem* like work!"

She looked at me challengingly, "So don't laugh."

Another woman: "I found myself visiting the place where I had worked almost every day after I retired—like I couldn't let go. They'd make jokes and say things like 'Hey, do you want us to clear a desk for you?' After a few weeks, I began to notice that people seemed to have less time for me. The same women I had worked

with for thirty-five years would rush by and hardly look
at me and mutter 'oh, hello.' That's when the reality hit
me. I *had* to find something to do. For a while it was bad.
I felt like I was coming apart. I never had learned how to
use whole days of spare time. There was no one to spend
time *with*—my children live in another city, my friends
are still working, and my husband passed away a few
years ago. So I went to the pastor of my church and said,
'Look, do you know of anything I can do?' 'You type,
don't you,' he asked. 'I type *and* take shorthand,' I told
him. 'That's how I always made my living.' He grabbed
me! The church could afford a secretary only half a day
—and he had work piled up. His secretary just couldn't
get to everything. So now I go over every afternoon for
two or three hours and take up where she leaves off. You
see, this is more like *work*—even though you call it leisure."

• *Playing without guilt.*

It's "more like work." This is what both women were
saying. This is the way they "play" without guilt.

"My husband and I were both teachers," another recently retired woman said, "and we both retired the
same year. We're both 'do-ers'—know what I mean? So
we immediately got involved in the senior citizen program
at the 'Y' and each of us voluntarily leads a group. He
leads a weekly discussion group. I teach a creative writing class. We both joined a social club in the program.
Now we visit our children in Florida three times a year
instead of once a year—and we're joining a ballroom
dancing class in a couple of weeks. I guess leisure (to us)
means working hard at creative *fun* things—. Doing
them with as much determination as our jobs took. Planning for them as carefully as we planned for our jobs. We
want to be able to look at what we do and say 'here now,
wasn't that a good job!' Or—'wasn't that worthwhile!'
We can't just sit around—." Another interpretation of
leisure. Another way of accepting it. All of these women
are "enjoying." And isn't this what matters?

- *A woman who's alone—how she uses her leisure.*

Another woman said, "My husband and I planned an active life for after he retired, and then suddenly he died . . . a couple of months before he was supposed to retire. Some retirement!"

I asked her what she's doing.

She looked startled for a second. "Me? Well, I'm trying to get myself together. I'm trying to set priorities, to use my daughter's phrase. To find out what's most important to me. I'm trying to look at the whole picture: How would I like to spend the next three years? What would I do right now if I knew I would die next year? That question makes me *focus*. I had always planned my retirement years to coincide with his. I hadn't looked at myself as an independent *alone* person. I had to begin looking at the question: Do I now want to spend my retirement years doing what we had planned to do together? Well, I know I do want to go to Europe (we had planned that for right after his retirement). I've never been there. So maybe I'll go with a group, on a tour. I'll pick a group of people like myself—maybe a group that's made up of women my age."

She had never used the word "leisure." But she *is* planning her leisure time.

- *A retired couple looks at leisure.*

"At first," a woman told me, "my husband and I fought over how to spend our leisure time. Then we realized we didn't have to do everything *together*. He enjoys certain things, I enjoy other things . . . so now he goes his way, I go my way, and at other times there are certain things we do together." Coping with guilt feelings. Defining "leisure." Learning how to use it. Different tasks for different retirees.

- *How do you feel about YOUR new free time?*

I've heard it said that we spend less time and care in choosing a leisure activity than we do in buying a car. Is this true of you? Don't let it be!

Volunteer Work

• *Different views.*

There is quite a heated debate in progress regarding
volunteer work. Some people, especially feminist groups,
feel it is exploitatively "using" people, because people
who are not paid for meaningful work they are doing become cheap labor that profits someone else. Others feel
it is taking jobs—paid jobs—away from workers. And
others feel volunteer work is honorable: that there is a
keen and valid satisfaction in giving a part of oneself to
community service, without pay.

• *Is it for you?*

How YOU feel is up to you. How YOU feel is all right,
no matter what your opinion—because there is no such
thing as an absolutely "correct" position; it is a matter of
perspective. Volunteer work can be very broad—so you
may feel comfortable and right getting involved in political work with a candidate for public office (not feeling
this is taking work away from someone), when you might
not feel good about volunteering your time in a hospital.

• *The right kind of volunteer work . . .*
  Questions to ask yourself.

If you decide to be a volunteer, choose the kind of unpaid labor that gives you an opportunity to contribute to
what you consider a worthwhile goal, to belong to a group
that gives you the company of congenial people; and that
perhaps gives you a chance for recognition—because recognition is important to all of us. How can you choose the
best kind of volunteer work for *YOU?* Ask yourself:

• Does it require a skill I already have?
• Will my health allow me to do this kind of volun-
  teer work?
• Do I have the time to give it that it needs?
• Is it something about which I care a great deal?
• Is it something that will hold my attention for a
  long period of time?

- Are the people involved the kind of people I like?
- Can I easily get to the place where I volunteer?

Also consider whether you want to work with people or things. "People" work encompasses: children who have reading problems, political candidates, performing personal services for the elderly—taking them shopping or to a clinic—visiting patients in mental hospitals. "Things" work can mean: typing for a community center two mornings a week, volunteering in a library, making scrapbooks for children's hospitals, recording books for the blind by reading aloud. You know by now if you're a "people" or "thing" person. So be selective.

- *How to find the right volunteer job.*

How can you find meaningful volunteer work? Where can you look? Call your Community Chest, your community centers, your local hospitals. Check with the civic and religious and social groups in your community. Contact the League of Women Voters. Call your local political party representatives. Call your local Girl Scouts' or Camp Fire Girls' Office. Get in touch with a People's Free Clinic or a Woman's Growth Center. Call your local Urban League or National Association of Colored People (NAACP) office. Contact the National Organization of Women's (NOW) office. Call libraries, universities, community colleges and social service agencies. Get out your Yellow Pages (your telephone book) and see if there's a central bureau that acts as a clearing house for nonprofit agencies in need of volunteer help (it might be listed under "Volunteer," or "Extension Service"). Would you like to be a Meals-on-Wheels volunteer? They need people to drive and take the food to the housebound recipient. Nursing homes are always looking for dedicated volunteers. Do you want to make phone calls for the Red Cross—perhaps call the same person every day at the same time, to let them know someone cares? Would you like to serve a daily hot meal to a group of older people in a senior center? Perhaps you'd like to present book reviews to special groups, or assist with fund-raising drives? As you can see, volunteerism is very broad—and no matter what your interests and skills and personality, there is something for *you.*

But be sure you care terribly about what you volunteer to do, or you'll be bored.

• *Choose a meaningful task.*

Having a prior commitment to an issue can keep your interest level high. Pollution? Peace? People who become involved in issues usually were interested in that issue *before* they gave their time. So their interest continues. Volunteer guides in art museums come to that volunteer work with an already-established interest in art. If you volunteer to raise money for the local opera company, chances are that you're already an opera buff. If you volunteer to work in a public school, no doubt you've already been interested in children and education.

When you call the place where you're applying to volunteer—to whom do you ask to speak? The director of volunteers. Or the person in charge of the office of volunteer services.

One city has a "hot line" for women, where women voluntarily answer telephone calls from troubled women in crisis. They refer them to agencies and give them advice and counseling. These volunteers are ex-social workers, who now have retired. Would you enjoy that?

• *Government-sponsored volunteer work . . .*
  with a stipend.

If you want to do volunteer work for the federal government for a small stipend, with a commitment as firm from you and the government as a paid job, consider applying for one of the following programs:

VISTA (Volunteers in Service to America): work in an inner-city school or an Indian reservation, or in a mental hospital, giving service. Or work in an impressive VISTA program such as the Chicago Senior Ethnic Find Program, which has spread to other cities that have large ethnic populations. Sixty-three VISTA volunteers serve thirty-five ethnic communities in four cities helping confused people (who have trouble understanding the larger culture) interpret letters they receive from Social Security and the departments of social service. The people served are German, Italian, Serbian, Ukranian, Polish, Korean, Jewish, Cuban, Puerto Rican, Mexican, Arabic . . . any older person who is confused by the language and red-tape and bureaucracy of the institutions that send them checks and demand documentation of needs. If you, as a member of an ethnic group who can speak and read and write the language of that group, are interested in helping with the problems of the non-English speaking elderly American, you can give valuable service in this area. Write to VISTA, Washington, D. C. 20506.

IESC (International Executive Service Corps): Were you working, all these years, in financial management or administration or product-designing or marketing? This private group which is organized by leading corporation executives working with the U.S. State Department, may be able to use your skills. Write to Executive Service Corps, 545 Madison Avenue, New York, N. Y. 10022.

THE PEACE CORPS: You didn't know they recruit older people? Send for the pamphlet, *Older Americans in the Peace Corps,* Senior Manpower Recruitment, The Peace Corps, Washington, D. C. 20025, and they'll tell you how much you're needed (as you probably already know, the Peace Corps is an overseas service organization of the government).

SCORE (The Service Corps of Retired Executives): have you had years of work experience in sales, advertising, marketing, finance, production control, engineering, or personnel relations? SCORE may be able to use your skills in assisting small business people. To apply, request SBA Form #610 from the Small Business Administration, Washington, D. C. 20416

FOSTER GRANDPARENTS: Are you over sixty and on a low income? Work up to twenty hours weekly with children in institutions, holding them—rocking them—giving them love. Write the Administration on Aging, Health, Education and Welfare for information on this program in *your* area. They pay a stipend of $1.60 an hour and provide transportation and a daily lunch.

PROJECT GREEN THUMB: For low-income farmers (or retired farmers). The work? Beautifying public areas. Apply to the Department of Labor, Washington, D. C. 20506.

RSVP (Retired Senior Volunteer Program): another funded program that exists through the nation. Your local

Commission On Aging office can tell you if this program exists in your city. There's a very small stipend (covering your transportation money—maybe your lunch, too), and you serve in meaningful ways: perhaps serving a daily hot meal to a group of aged in a senior center, or volunteering time in a nursing home.

- *Volunteer work to match your personality.*

You'll find some kinds of volunteer work attracting the very fashionable kind of woman: working as an art gallery guide, serving on committees to plan benefit dances. You'll find other kinds of volunteer work attracting other kinds of women. For instance, you might find a dedicated homemaker working in the kitchen of a community center, getting the buns and coffee ready to serve after a lecture. You'll want to be *comfortable* with the people you serve with—because meaningful, rewarding volunteer work should also be a good social experience (wasn't it important to enjoy the people you worked with in the job world—before you retired?), so carefully choose the *kind* of volunteer work you'll be doing. You can afford to be choosy: They need *you*.

Mandatory Retirement

For many of us, there's no choice: We have to retire. "Mandatory retirement"—at the age of sixty-five or seventy we're called into the personnel office and told what our retirement benefits are; we're later given the retirement dinner with the gift; and the next day our whole life has radically changed. We're home for good.

"Retirement shock." That's when in response to this forced retirement our body and our psyche starts to hurt and react in unexpected unpleasant ways.

- *Retirement should not be mandatory.*

Why should determining when to retire be any different from determining whom to hire and whom to promote and whom to transfer and whom to terminate? Why shouldn't it be an *individual* decision, rather than an arbitrary age? Some people need to retire when they're 50, because their health is bad and they feel unable to work. Don't we all know a vigorous eighty-year-old woman who could turn the world around—and easily hold a challenging nine-to-five, five-day-a-week job? Why shouldn't the decision of retirement be based on *qualifications*—whether you can hold the job? Also, whether you *want* to continue working?

• *What one firm does instead.*

The De Havilland Aircraft Corporation in Canada has abandoned aged-based mandatory retirement. Instead, they test their employees on an on-going basis to see if they can still function on the job, and then keep them indefinitely as long as they can work and want to work.

• *Do you have recourse if you're being forced to retire?*

What can you do if you're being forced to retire? Well, you can fight it in court. In the past few years the Supreme Court has dealt with at least two major mandatory retirement cases. But that's expensive. You can join collective action groups that try to change the system to end mandatory retirement. Change may not come about in time to affect *your* situation—but your input might make it possible for your granddaughter to stay on her job as long as she's able and willing. You can also try to get ready for your retirement, by attending the pre-retirement classes that are offered free of charge in a growing number of companies and by local Commission On Aging offices and by community centers and senior centers. You can organize your friends who are going to be retired, to meet once a week in your living room to choose a different aspect of retirement each week and discuss it (budgeting, use of leisure time, changing family relationships). If you do meet in a living room, use this chapter as your guide. Discuss a section of it each week. The earlier you begin planning your retirement, the easier it'll be to feel and be more in control of your changing life when it happens.

Make the Rest of Your Years the Best of Your Years

Retire. The dictionary presents various definitions. "To withdraw from action or danger"; "To fall back"; "To march away from the enemy"; "To withdraw from circulation or from the market"; "To withdraw from usual use or service"; "To withdraw especially for privacy."

I suggest another definition: "TO *GO FORWARD* into years of *Pleasure!*"

CHAPTER 12

"What Shall I Be?"
"Where Shall I Go?"
"Who Shall I Be?"

I listened to hundreds of over-50 women in the four years before I began this book, and during the two years that I spent writing it. Thank you—all of you—for teaching me so much. You spoke to me on the jobs I held, at pre-retirement panels, as my friends, and forgive me, I eavesdropped on you in so many restaurants. You taught me how hard and exciting it is to live, and how women can be so adaptive when we have to survive, and how good our anger can be when when we have to change—and you taught me how smart we are. How strong we are. When you ask yourself, "What shall I do?" and "Where shall I go?" and "Who shall I be?" I ask myself those questions, too. . . .

What are the answers? Will we in the years ahead, be what the researchers call the "Re-Organizers"—women who begin *new* activities and make *new* friends and start *new* projects in our older years? Will we be "Holding-on" people: continuing to drive ourselves hard in the same ways we did; tenaciously clinging to our jobs and our families and our old pleasures? Or will we be "disengaged" —moving away from role commitments? What happens to our lives will somewhat affect our choices, don't you think? If we're left with inadequate incomes and poor health and no meaningful relationships, we may become "disengaged" through defeat. But our personalities have some continuity—even through old age.

I met a young woman in a brick, suburban house who is cautious and avoids taking risks. She was waiting for her husband to come home from work. She loves her husband. She has her health. She will probably be cautious and avoid taking risks when she is old.

A sixty-year-old woman who has been in the hospital three times this year with coronaries sat and talked to me, recalling her earlier days, bumming on freight trains from city to city. The radio blared and a cat sat on her lap and people kept coming in from other rooms to say hello. A zestful lady. Pain and fear hadn't changed her personality.

It is very hard to grow old: everyone's fascinated by extreme old age and afraid of ordinary old age. In Peru, they put a picture of a 145-year-old man on a postage stamp—because he lived so long. In New York, some old women live in welfare hotels—because they've out-lived their "productivity." Gerontologists gathered to view a 168-year-old man in Soviet Georgia. Grown children avoid seeing their aging mother in a nursing home.

You can try to protect yourself by denying you are old (my great-aunts, in their nineties, called themselves "the girls"). You can label other old people "them." Since women outlive men by about six years and four months, and only 5 per cent of all aged people are in institutions, and women's life expectancy is about seventy-five years of age (if you're sixty-five, you can expect to live another seventeen years), you'll probably be around for a while, out among people, and you might be tired of denying that you're old. Since 9 million people live to be over seventy-five, it's very possible you'll be one of them—so what kind of an old lady do you think you'll be?

I think you can learn to deal with your aging and changing body. You can ignore external messages saying you're invisible. You can thumb your nose when people imply you're "over the hill." You can still dance the hora at your granddaughter's wedding (and outdance all the others). You may find it hard to *see*, so you can *feel* the sculpture when you visit a museum. You can still yell

"Bingo!" when you win a game—any game. You can *use* your existing strengths. If you've always been well-groomed, and now you can't bend down to tie your own shoes (and this can happen to some of us when we get older), you can buy shoes that don't have to be tied. You can take out your dentures at night and reflect, "I'm glad I can *hear.*" You can hold up your arthritic fingers and say, "I'm glad I can *walk.*" You can touch your great-grandchild's face and think, "Thank God I can *love.*" People will try to tell you what to do and you will decide for *yourself* what's best for yourself. And you will know —because you will be alive and smart and tough and soft through years of living and loving. You will have *SURVIVED.*

"What shall I do?" Whatever you want. You can be autonomous.

"Where shall I go?" Hundreds of places to choose from —if you let yourself.

"Who shall I be?" *YOU.* The you who learned to cope and deal with all the questions and betrayals of getting older. The you who knows how to yell and shout and scream, because that means you're alive.

You WILL become that kind of tough-outside, soft-inside old woman because you will be very much intact, even though you may be worn and torn around the edges. Sometimes you'll be soft-outside and tough-inside. You will have made it. You will make it (maybe you have already) because you acquired a lot of wisdom through living and watching and listening and reflecting. You'll be a great old lady . . . just like you were (or are) a pretty fantastic, middle-aged woman. Your SELF is big and strong. No more worry about your image and what people think. Your SELF is shaped—monumental, and an example to fretful younger women. Your SELF is powerful. Your SELF speaks for itself—now and later.

Let it!

Further Reading

❧ ❧ ❧

WHO WE WERE; WHO WE ARE

Elder, Glen H. Jr. *Children of the Great Depression.*
Chicago: University of Chicago Press, 1974.

The school experiences of 167 individuals born in the
years 1920 and 1921, and how these experiences shaped
their feelings and their values. To order the book, write
the University of Chicago Press, 11030 S. Langley Avenue, Chicago, Ill. 60628.

Kramer, Sydelle and Masur, Jenny. *Jewish Grandmothers.*
Boston: Beacon Press, 1976.

Ten immigrant experiences of women now over-50 . . .
who came here as "greenhorns."

Baum, Charlotte and Hyman, Paula and Michel, Sonya.
The Jewish Woman in America. New York: Dial, 1976.

The Jewish woman from the *shtetls* of Eastern Europe
and the cities of nineteenth-century Germany until now;
historical figures; oral histories; relationships of the woman
to their sons and their husbands and their daughters and
to each other. Their resistance and their willingness to

assimilate into the larger culture—and the price they paid for the decisions they made.

Kahn, Kathy. *Hillbilly Women.* New York: Doubleday, 1975. Available in paper from Avon Books.

Nineteen portraits of southern mountaineer women: daughters, wives and mothers.

Jackson, Jacquelyne, ed. *Aging Black Women (Selected Readings For the National Caucus on the Black Aged).* Washington, D. C.: College & University Press, 1975.

Dr. Jackson, a well-known, black gerontologist, has put together writings by black authors about older, black women that reflect the social, economic, emotional and political history and conditions of the rural and urban black woman.

Tovar, Frederico Ribes. *The Puerto Rican Woman.* New York: Ultra Educational Publishers, Inc., 1972.

A slim book that explores her history in Puerto Rico and her life as an immigrant in this country, with a few glimpses at Puerto Rican women who have "made it."

Ladner, Joyce. *Tomorrow's Tomorrow: The Black Woman.* New York: Doubleday, 1972.

This is Dr. Ladner's dissertation—it examines younger black women in a particular setting; and this reflects their mother's and grandmother's values and life styles.

Howard, Jane. *A Different Woman.* New York: E. P. Dutton and Co., Inc., 1973. Available in paper from Avon Books.

A documentary-style piece of writing. Howard has interviews with women of different ages in different parts of the country; women of different socioeconomic backgrounds.

Reed, Evelyn. *Woman's Evolution.* New York: Pathfinder Press, 1974.

A writer-anthropologist who is political and over 50 writes a scholarly, yet readable, book about evolution as it relates to women . . . from matriarchal clan to patriarchal family.

WIDOWHOOD, SEPARATION, AND DIVORCE

Langer, Marion. *Learning To Live As A Widow*. New York: Julian Messner, 1957.

Timeless, because it deals with grief and loneliness, and how to cope with the everyday, small emergencies by yourself.

Champagne, Marian, M. *Facing Life Alone*. Indianapolis: The Bobbs-Merrill Co., Inc., 1964.

The author believes that if you're alone, you're alone —whether you're widowed or separated; and the problems are similar in many cases. She also talks about her own coping.

Woman's Survival Manual (A Feminist Handbook on Separation and Divorce). Philadelphia: Women in Transition, 1974.

Very practical—and hopeful. What to do and how to do it when you're no longer someone's wife.

WORK

Bird, Caroline. *Everything a Woman Needs to Know to Get Paid What She's Worth*. New York: David McKay, 1973.

Read this selectively—because Bird is not writing it only for the older woman who has more trouble getting a job or getting a raise, but for working women in general. She's good with tactics and strategy, and some of her ideas may apply to you.

Shelley, Florence D. and Offen, Jane. *When Your Parents Grow Old*. New York: Funk & Wagnall, 1976.

A concrete guide for the middle-aged caring children of the aged. A directory. A concerned book.

YOUR AGED PARENT

Poe, William D. *The Old Person In Your Home*. New York: Charles Scribner's Sons, 1969.

Dr. Poe is particularly good at answering medical questions.

VOLUNTEERISM

Loeser, Herta. *Women, Work and Volunteerism*. Boston: Beacon Press, 1974.

Good experience or a free-labor rip-off? Loeser explores this.

HEALTH

The Boston Women's Health Book Collective. *Our Bodies, Ourselves, a Book By and for Women*. New York: Simon & Schuster, 1973.

Menopause is discussed, and so is our sexuality, and our daughters' attitudes, and the kind of health care we need and don't get too easily. Not technical, with illustrations.

Samuels, Michael and Bennett, Harold. *The Well Body Book*. New York: Random House, Inc.; Berkeley: The Bookworks, 1975.

One of the authors is a physician, and it's a reassuring book . . . it de-mystifies the practice of medicine and the drugs used by doctors, and tells you how to listen to your own body and respect your own judgment. A little mystical, too, but some readers will like that (the authors talk about how colors affect our health).

Frankfort, Ellen. *Vaginal Politics*. New York: Quadrangle Books, 1972.

Knowledge is power: the importance of knowing about your body and doctors, and how male doctors can unwittingly (?) abuse us.

Weideger, Paula. *Menstruation & Menopause*. New York: Alfred Knopf, 1976.

The author interviewed 558 women to see how they feel about their own menstruation and menopause. She's a member of the staff of the Women's Health Forum in New York City, and de-mystifies the female physiological processes.

Lupton, Mary Jane, Delaney, Janice and Toth, Emily. *The Curse. The Cultural History of Menstruation.* New York: E. P. Dutton, 1976.

"I have the curse." *I* used to say, "I fell off the roof!" These three feminist authors examine the roots of our attitudes. They also take a look at menopause.

Llewellyn-Jones, Derek. *Everywoman And Her Body.* New York: Taplinger Publishing Co., Inc., 1971.

Oriented toward helping us become better health consumers and learning more about our own gynecological needs.

Chessler, Phyllis. *Women and Madness.* New York: Doubleday, 1972. Available in paper from Avon Books.

Ms. Chessler is a psychologist, and she sees society as the culprit in women becoming mentally ill, and in how they're medically treated.

BASIC BOOKS

Friedan, Betty. *The Feminine Mystique.* New York: W. W. Norton & Co., Inc., 1963.

One of the earlier feminist books in this wave of feminism . . . more gentle than militant . . . examines the suburban housewife's feelings . . . the "empty nest" syndrome . . . the middle-aged woman's options.

Millett, Kate. *Sexual Politics.* New York: Doubleday, 1971.

Millett shows how authors, past and present, have viewed women and their roles in their writings; how they have seen women as passive and vulnerable.

Greer, Germaine. *The Female Eunuch.* New York: McGraw-Hill, 1971.

How women feel about their sexuality, their bodies, and men, relative to their psychological and cultural history.

MIDDLE AGE & AGING: HOW IT'S VIEWED

De Beauvoir, Simone. *The Coming of Age*. New York: G. P. Putnam's Sons, 1972.

De Beauvoir, now in her sixties, gives us a historical and global view of aging, seeing capitalism as responsible for the aged person's hunger and feelings of alienation.

LeShan, Eda. *The Wonderful Crisis of Middle Age*. New York: David McKay Co., 1973.

Another perspective! LeShan is optimistic (she also does not have the class perspective that de Beauvoir has) and she shares her self-actualization philosophy with us . . . as well as her own life as a middle-aged woman.

Curtin, Sharon R. *Nobody Ever Died of Old Age*. New York: Little Publishing Co., 1972.

A very young author, concerned and curious, gets into the lives of real people who are old, and writes "in praise of old people, in outrage at their loneliness." Honest and indignant and full of sensitive feeling.

Jonas, Doris and David. *Young Till We Die*. New York: Coward, McCann & Geoghegan, Inc., 1973.

A retired (older) social-scientist couple explore the biological, behavorial, and psychological impact of aging —and the writing is chatty yet authoritative.

Simon, Anne W. *The New Years: A New Middle Age*. New York: Alfred Knopf, 1968.

A psychiatric social worker (and an over-50 woman) examines the options of the older person.

Harris, Janet. *The Prime of Ms. America*. New York: G. P. Putnam's Sons, 1975.

A multi-issue book for the middle-aged woman, geared mainly toward the middle-class woman.

Comfort, Dr. Alex. *A Good Age*. New York: Crown Publishers, Inc., 1976.

An uplifting book about the many accomplishments of

people in their later years by the famous gerontologist
who wrote *The Joy of Sex*.

RETIREMENT INFORMATION

Musson, Noverre. *The National Directory of Retirement
Residences: Best Places to Live When You Retire*.
New York: Frederick Fell, Inc., 1973.
   If you plan to move . . . after you've analyzed what
you really want in the way of resources and neighbor-
hoods, and how much money you'll have.

Holter, Paul. *Guide To Retirement Living*. Chicago:
Rand-McNally & Co., 1973.
   A directory, with descriptions of trailer parks, retire-
ment homes, and retirement hotels. Very specific.

Otto, Elmer. *Rehearse Before You Retire*. Appleton,
Wisconsin: Retirement Research, 1972.
   A step by step method to plan your retirement.

SEX

Felstein, Ivor. *Sex in Later Life*. New York: Penguin
Books, 1973.
   Planned Parenthood agencies consider this one of the
better books on how to adjust your thinking and behavior to your changing sexual needs.

Masters & Johnson: *The Pleasure Bond*. Boston: Little,
Brown & Co., 1975.
   Popular-style rather than academic. "A new look at
sexuality and commitment."

Chartham, Robert. *Sex and the Over-Fifties*. Chatsworth,
Calif.: Brandon Books, 1969.
   Very specific, without expecting you to be a sexual
acrobat.

Butler, Robert N., M.D. and Lewis, Myrna I. *Sex after
Sixty*. New York: Harper & Row, 1976.

Factual, dealing with common medical problems (such as heart disease) and sex very effectively, lay-people's language; easy-to-understand.

DEATH & DYING

Kübler-Ross, Elisabeth. *On Death and Dying*. New York: Macmillan Publishing Co., 1969.
Very valuable for families who live with a terminally ill patient. Written by the best-known expert in the field, who believes that the dying person goes through definite steps and stages in preparing to die; through denial and acceptance; through anger and grief; through final acceptance. Ross tells us how to feel less frightened by the situation and how to meet some of the needs of the patient.

MEDIA & WOMEN

Haskell, Molly. *From Reverence to Rape: The Treatment of Women In The Movies*. New York: Holt, Rinehart & Winston, 1974.
Haskell feels that filmmakers show us the way society views women, and she gives us illustrations.

Rosen, Marjorie. *Popcorn Venus: Women, Movies, and the American Dream*. New York: Coward, McCann, 1973.
A noted film critic analyzes how movies define as well as reflect us—past and present.

LESBIANISM

Martin, Del and Lyon, Phyllis. *Lesbian/Woman*. San Francisco: Glide Publications, 1972.
Informative, whether you're a lesbian or not.

HANDBOOKS & DIRECTORIES & MANUALS

Gager, Nancy, ed. *Woman Rights Almanac*. Bethesda, Md.: Elizabeth Cady Stanton Publishing Company, 1974.
  On legal rights, employment, politics, women's organizations.

Rennie, Susan and Grimstad, Kirsten, ed. *The New Woman's Survival Source Book*. New York: Alfred Knopf, 1975.
  A national directory listing places and groups women can go to for all kinds of help . . . with a special section written for the older woman.

NEWSLETTERS, AND PAMPHLETS

Collins, Marjorie, ed. *Prime Time*. 168 W. 86th St., New York, N.Y. 10024
  An excellent feminist newsletter for older women, edited by an older woman. It examines work, sex, relationships, and it tells the reader where groups of older women are meeting throughout the country, so you can join them in consciousness-raising sessions. $7 a year for 11 issues and $4 for 6 issues—but only $3.50 a year or $2 for six issues if you're living on a fixed Social Security income and/or if you're unemployed.

Jackson, Jacqueline, ed. *Black Aging*. P.O. Box 3003, Duke University Medical Center, Durham, N.C. 27710
  A newsletter for non-professionals and professionals with the major emphasis on new and pending legislation, research, training of people to work with the black aging, services for the black aging, and resources.

Health Right News (HRN). Medical Committee for Human Rights. 1520 Naudain St., Philadelphia, Pa. 19146
  Written and edited by a counter-AMA national group of medical professionals

Tax Benefits for Older Americans (frequently revised). Bureau of Internal Revenue from Superintendent of Documents, U.S. Government Printing Office, Washington, D.C. 20036. (25¢)

Fact Sheet—Employment and Volunteer Opportunities for Older People (frequently revised). Public Information Office, Administration on Aging, U.S. Department of Health, Education and Welfare, Washington, D.C. 20201. (Free.)

Protecting Older Americans Against Overpayment of Income Taxes (frequently revised). Superintendent of Documents, U. S. Government Printing Office, Washington D. C. 20402 (35¢)

Continuing Education Programs and Services for Women. Superintendent of Documents, U.S. Government Printing Office, Washington, D.C. 20402. (70¢)
 A state-by-state report for women who want to return to school after years out of the classroom.

You and the Law. Administration on Aging, available from Superintendent of Documents, Government Printing Office, Washington, D.C. 20402. (25¢)
 Emphasis on retirement problems . . . a basic legal reference (how, why and when to see a lawyer).

Guide to Home and Personal Security. Action for Independent Maturity, 1909 K St. N.W., Washington, D.C 20006. Free. How to reduce the risks of burglary and how to prevent home accidents, and what to do about fire prevention.

DIRECTORY

State Agencies on Aging
&
Regional Offices

෴

Need information-and-referral help? Need direct service help? Call or write any of the following agencies and they will refer you to the proper source of help nearest you.

These are state and area agencies on aging, established under Title III of the Older Americans Act of 1965 (as amended). These agencies serve as advocates for the older person and coordinate activities on their behalf. They also provide information about services and programs. Consider this listing your hotline!

Alabama:
Commission on Aging
740 Madison Ave.,
Montgomery, Ala. 36104
Tel. (205) 269-8171

Alaska:
Office on Aging
Department of Health &
  Social Services
Pouch H
Juneau, Alaska 99801
Tel. (907) 586-6153

American Samoa:
Government of
  American Samoa
Office of the Government
Pago Pago, Samoa 96920

Arizona:
Bureau on Aging
Department of
  Economic Security
Suite 800, South Tower
2721 North Central
Phoenix, Ariz. 85004
Tel. (602) 271-4446

Arkansas:
Office on Aging
P. O. Box 2179
Hendrix Hall
4313 West Markham
Little Rock, Ark. 72203
Tel. (501) 371-2441

California:
Office on Aging
Health & Welfare Agency
455 Capitol Mall, Suite 500
Sacramento, Calif. 95814
Tel. (916) 322-3887

Colorado:
Division of Services
  for the Aging
Department of
  Social Services,
1575 Sherman St.
Denver, Colo. 80203
Tel. (303) 892-2651

Connecticut:
Department of Aging
90 Washington St., Rm. 312
Hartford, Conn. 06115
Tel. (203) 566-2480

Delaware:
Division of Aging
Department of Health &
Social Services
2407 Lancaster Avenue,
Wilmington, Del. 19805
Tel. (302) 571-3480

District of Columbia:
Office of Services
  to the Aged
Department of
  Human Resources
1329 E. St., N.W.
  (Munsey Bldg.)
Washington, D.C. 20004
Tel. (202) 638-2406

Florida:
Division on Aging
Department of Health &
Rehabilitation Services
1317 Winewood Blvd.,
  Bldg. 3
Tallahassee, Fla. 32301
Tel. (904) 488-4797

Georgia:
Office on Aging
Department of
  Human Resources
618 Ponce de Leon Ave.
Atlanta, Ga. 30308
Tel. (404) 894-5333

Guam:
Office of Aging
Social Services
  Administration
Government of Guam
P.O. Box 2816
Agana, Guam 96910

Hawaii:
Commission on Aging
1149 Bethel St., Room 311
Honolulu, Hawaii 96813

Idaho:
Office on Aging
Department of
  Special Services
Capitol Annex No. 7
509 N. 5th St., Room 100
Boise, Idaho 83720
Tel. (208) 384-3833

Illinois:
Department on Aging
2401 W. Jefferson St.
Springfield, Ill. 62706
Tel. (217) 782-5773

Indiana:
Commission on the
  Aging & the Aged
Graphic Arts Bldg.
215 North Senate Ave.
Indianapolis, Ind. 46202
Tel. (317) 633-5948

Iowa:
Commission on
  the Aging
415 West 10th
  (Jewett Bldg.)
Des Moines, Iowa 50319
Tel. (515) 281-5187

Kansas:
Services for the
  Aging Section
Division of Social Services
Social & Rehabilitation
  Services Department
State Office Building,
Topeka, Kan. 66612
Tel. (913) 296-3465

Kentucky:
Aging Program Unit
Department for
  Human Resources
403 Wapping St.
Frankfort, Ky. 40601
Tel. (502) 564-4238

Louisiana:
Bureau of Aging Service
Division of
  Human Resources
Health & Social
  Rehabilitation
Services Administration,
P.O. Box 44282,
  Capital Station,
Baton Rouge, La. 70804
Tel. (504) 389-6713

Maine:
Bureau of Maine's Elderly
Department of
  Health & Welfare,
State House
Augusta, Me. 04330
Tel. (207) 622-6171;
  ask for 289-2561.

Maryland:
Office on Aging
1004 State Office Building
301 W. Preston St.
Baltimore, Md. 21201
Tel. (301) 383-5064

Massachusetts:
Executive Office of
  Elder Affairs
State Office Building
18 Tremont St.
Boston, Mass. 02109
Tel. (617) 727-7751

Michigan:
Offices of Services
   to the Aging
1026 East Michigan
Lansing, Mich. 48912
Tel. (517) 373-8230

Minnesota:
Governor's Citizens
   Council on Aging
Suite 204,
   Metro Square Bldg.
7th & Robert Sts.
St. Paul, Minn. 55101
Tel. (612) 296-2544

Mississippi:
Council on Aging
P.O. Box 5136,
   Fondren Station
2906 N. State St.
Jackson, Miss. 39216
Tel. (601) 354-6590

Missouri:
Office of Aging
Division of
   Special Services,
Department of
   Social Services
The Broadway State
   Office Bldg.
Jefferson City, Mo. 65101
Tel. (314) 751-2075

Montana:
Aging Services Bureau
Department of Social &
   Rehabilitative Services,
P.O. Box 1723
Helena, Mont. 59601
Tel. (406) 449-3124

Nebraska:
Commission on Aging
State House Station 94784
300 S. 17th Street
Lincoln, Neb. 68509
Tel. (402) 471-2307

Nevada:
Division of Aging
Department of
   Human Resources
Room 300, Nye Bldg.
201 S. Fall St.
Carson City, Nev. 89701
Tel. (702) 882-7855

New Hampshire:
Council on Aging
P.O. Box 786
14 Depot St.
Concord, N.H. 03301
Tel. (603) 271-2751

New Jersey:
Office on Aging
Department of
   Community Affairs
P.O. Box 2768
363 West State St.
Trenton, N.J. 08625
Tel. (609) 292-3765

New Mexico:
State Commission on Aging
Villagra Bldg.
408 Galisteo Street
Santa Fe, N. Mex. 87501
Tel. (505) 827-5258

New York:
Office for the Aging
N.Y. State
    Executive Department
855 Central Avenue
Albany, N. Y. 12206
Tel. (518) 457-7321

New York City:
Office for the Aging
Room 5036
2 World Trade Center
New York, N.Y. 10047
Tel. (212) 488-6405

North Carolina:
Governor's Coordinating
    Council on Aging,
Administration Building
213 Hillsborough St.
Raleigh, N.C. 27603
Tel. (919) 829-3983

North Dakota:
Aging Services
Social Services Board
State Capitol Building
Bismarck, N. D. 58501
Tel. (701) 224-2577

Ohio:
Commission on Aging
34 North High St.,
    3rd floor
Columbus, Ohio 43215
Tel. (614) 466-5500

Oklahoma:
Special Unit of Aging
Department of Institutions,
    Soc. and Rehab. Serv.
Box 25352, Capitol Station
Sequoyah Memorial Bldg.
Oklahoma City,
    Okla. 73125
Tel. (405) 521-2281

Oregon:
Program on Aging
Human Resources
    Department
315 Public Service Building
Salem, Oreg. 97310
Tel. (503) 378-4728

Pennsylvania:
Office for the Aging
Department of
    Public Welfare
Capital Associates Building
7th & Forster Sts.
Harrisburg, Pa. 17120
Tel. (717) 787-5350

Puerto Rico:
Gericulture Commission
Department of
    Social Services
Apartado 11697
Santurce, Puerto Rico
    00910
Tel. (809) 725-8015
(Overseas Operator)

Rhode Island:
Division on Aging
Department of
  Community Affairs
150 Washington St.
Providence, R.I. 02903
Tel. (401) 528-1000
Ask for 277-2858

Trust Terr. of the Pacific:
Office of Aging
Community
  Development Div.
Gov. of the Trust Territory
  of the Pacific Islands
Saipan, Mariana Islands
  96950

South Carolina:
Commission on Aging
915 Main St.
Columbia, S.C. 29201
Tel. (803) 758-2576

Utah:
Division of Aging
Department of
  Social Services
345 South 6th East
Salt Lake City, Utah 84102
Tel. (801) 328-6422

South Dakota:
Program on Aging
Department of
  Social Services
St. Charles Hotel
Pierre, S. D. 57501
Tel. (605) 224-3656

Vermont:
Office on Aging
Department of
  Human Services
56 State St.
Montpelier, Vt. 05602
Tel. (802) 828-3471

Tennessee:
Commission on Aging
S & P Bldg., Room 102
306 Gay St.
Nashville, Tenn. 37201
Tel. (615) 741-2056

Virginia:
Office on Aging
Division of State Planning
  and Community Affairs
9 North 12th Street
Richmond, Va. 23219
Tel. (804) 770-7894

Texas:
Governor's Committee
  on Aging
Southwest Tower, 8th Floor
211 East 7th Street
Austin, Tex. 78711
Tel. (512) 475-2717

Virgin Islands:
Commission on Aging
P.O. Box 539,
  Charlotte Amalie
St. Thomas,
  Virgin Islands 00801
Tel. (809) 774-5884

Washington:
Office on Aging
Department of Social
    and Health Services,
P.O. Box 1788—
M.S. 45-2
410 W. Fifth
Olympia, Wash. 98504
Tel. (206) 753-2502

West Virginia:
Commission on Aging
State Capitol,
    Room 420-26
1800 Washington St.,
    Charleston, W. Va.
    25305
Tel. (304) 348-3317

Wisconsin:
Division on Aging
Department of Health &
    Social Services
State Office Building,
    Room 686
1 West Wilson St.
Madison, Wis. 53702
Tel. (608) 266-2536

Wyoming:
Aging Services
Department of Health &
    Social Services
Division of
    Public Assistance &
    Social Services
State Office Building
Cheyenne, Wyo. 82002
Tel. (307) 777-7561

REGION I (Conn.,
    Maine, Mass., N.H.,
    R.I., Vt.)
J.F. Kennedy
    Federal Bldg.
Government Center,
    Room 2007
Boston. Mass. 02203
Tel. (617) 223-6885

REGION II (N.J., N.Y.,
    Puerto Rico,
    Virgin Islands)
26 Federal Plaza,
    Rm. 4106
Broadway & North Sts.
New York, N.Y. 10007
Tel. (212) 264-4592

REGION III (Del., D.C.,
    Md., Pa., Va., W. Va.)
P.O. Box 13716
36th & Market Sts., 5th Fl.
Philadelphia, Pa. 19101
Tel. (215) 597-6891

REGION IV (Ala., Fla.,
    Ga., Ky., Miss., N.C.,
    S.C., Tenn.)
50 Seventh St. N.E.
    Rm. 326
Atlanta, Ga. 30323
Tel. (404) 526-3482

REGION V (Ill., Ind.,
    Mich., Minn., Ohio,
    Wis.)
29th Floor
300 S. Wacker Drive
Chicago, Ill. 60606
Tel. (312) 353-4695

REGION VI (Ark., La.,
   N. Mex., Okla., Tex.)
Fidelity Union
   Tower Bldg.
Room 500
1507 Pacific Avenue
Dallas, Tex. 75201
Tel. (214) 749-7286

REGION VII (Iowa,
   Kans., Mo., Nebr.)
12 Grand Building, 5th Fl.
12th & Grand
Kansas City, Mo. 64106
Tel. (816) 374-2955

REGION VIII (Colo.,
   Mont., N. Dak., S. Dak.,
   Utah, Wyo.)
19th and Stout Sts.,
   Rm. 7027
Federal Office Building
Denver, Colo. 80202
Tel. (303) 837-2951

REGION IX (Ariz.,
   Calif., Hawaii, Nev.,
   Samoa, Guam, T.T.)
50 Fulton St., Room 204
406 Federal
   Office Building
San Francisco, Calif. 94102
Tel. (415) 556-6003

REGION X (Alaska,
   Idaho, Oreg., Wash.)
Dexter Horton Building,
   Room 1490
710 2nd Avenue
Seattle, Wash. 98104
Tel. (206) 442-5341

Index

Abortion, 9

Adult degree programs, 334-37

Age discrimination laws, and lawsuits, 313-15

Aged parents, 164-219; alternate solution for, 206-8; black, 216-17; body changes in, 180; chronic brain syndrome, 184-91; chore services for, 192; community mental health center for, 209; differences among homes for, 210-14; effect on marriage of grown children, 204-5; escort services, 191; family responsibility for, 169-70; fathers, 172-79; feelings, 217-18; food stamps, 194; geriatric services, 213; grown children and, 172-79; help for, 191-98; homemakers, 191, 199; hospitalization, 191, 211, 212; hot lunches, 193-94; independent, 202, 211; Information-and-Referral services, 192; losses faced by, 165-66; Meals-on-Wheels, 191; mentally ill, 208-10; money help, 194; mother-daughter relationship, 170-72; nursing homes, 212-17; in own home, 198-200; private services, 210-11; role reversal and, 165; sense changes in, 180-81; strength from experience, 218-19; telephone reassurance programs, 193; visiting nurse for, 192-93; and woman over 50, 166-74, 200-4; world of, 181-82

Aging, physical changes in, 180-82

Ageism, 304-5, 310-11

Anti-depressants, 20-22

Anxiety, 24-26; 76-77; drugs for, 25-26

Apartments, 383-84

Appearance, 70-83

Assets, 363

Bachelors, gay, 108; perennial, 106-8

Benefits, Social Security, 366-70; working collectively for, 319-23

Body, changing, 30-32; feelings about, 110-11. *See also* Men.

Breast cancer, 13-14; self-examination, 13, 41

Budgets, food, 372-75; making up, 375-76; retirement, 371-74; widows', 239

Cancer patient, 160

Career woman, advantages and disadvantages, 302-3; benefits, 319-33; black, 301; checking job out beforehand, 298-301; effect on ERA, 316-18; equal pay legislation, 315-16; free-pay legislation, 315-16; freedom from ageism, 303-6; job interview, 306-19; job rights, 318-21; lying about age, 310-11, or education, 311; making more money, 291-97; myths about, 305-6; pension plan legislation, 321-24; professional, reentering job market, 297-98; strategies for, 291-325; time to bargain and make demands, 311-12; victimization by ageism, 304-5

Cars, 237-39, 371

Cataracts, 28

Cell-therapy, 75

Classes, 96

Clergy, 44

Clinical psychologists, 43-44

Clothes, 74, 371; for job interviews, 307-9; for overweight, 78-79

College, community, 343-44; credits, through CLEP, 341-42; through TV and radio, 342-43; non-traditional, 338-40; residential mini-courses, 338; scholarships and grants, 344-46; traditional four-year, 340-41; weekend, 337-38

College Level Examination Program, 341

Community Health Services, 68-69; mental health, for aged, 208-10

Con men, 241

Corman-Kennedy Bill, 54-55

Couples, 401; role-defined, 354-55; and widows, 247-48

Credit, 362

Cruises, 94

Cystitis, 12

Daughters-in-law, 157-58; ex-, 395-96

Day care, for aged parents, 197-98

Dental care, 32, 54, 66

Depression, 14-24; coping with, 17-20; in husbands, 143-47

Divorce, 105-6; after 50, 119-21; Social Security benefits and, 367

Doctors, 129-30; family, 36-38, choosing, 38-40; general practitioner, 38; gynecologist, 40-42; man or woman, 48-50

Douches, 11-12

Down's Syndrome, 9

Drinking, 27

Drugs, 20-22, 65, 160; anxiety-relieving, 25-26; saving money on, 52-54, 160

Earnings, 364. *See also* Finances; Money.

Elder Artisans, 276

Employees Retirement Income Security Act, 321-22

Employment agencies, 271; free, 271; government, 271; for older worker, 271-72; private, 272-73; temporary, 273

Energy, 31-32

Equal Employment Opportunity Commission, 317

Equal Pay Act, 315

Equal Rights Amendment, 316-18

Estrogen replacement, 4-8, 41; maturation index, 5-6; new developments in, 7-8; safety, 6

Eyes, 27-29, 66, 70; diseases, 28-29; lift, 70-74

Face-lifts, 70

Family care homes, 214

Family doctor. *See* Doctors.

Fathers, dependent, 172-79

Feminist therapist, 47

Finances, retirement, 375-78; for widows, 239-43

Food, 74, 80; anti-aging, 74; budget for, 372-75; hoarded by aging parents, 187-88; stamps, 194

Foster Grandparents, 276

Foundations, grants for older women, 344-46

Gerovital KH3 Treatment, 77-78

Glaucoma, 28-29

Grandparents, expectations of, 153-57; relationships with grown children, 390-92

Grey Panthers, 19, 20, 305

Grown children, demanding, 177-79; objections to remarriage from, 123-25; relationships with, 392-95

Gynecologists, 40-42

Hair, 80, 81, 82, 83; coloring, 308

Health clubs, 79

Health insurance plans, 60-62, 159-60; dental and vision care, 66; group, at job, 64-65; major medical, 65; private, 66-67; proposed national, 54-56; by retirement organizations, 60-62

Health organizations and services, 67-68, 68-69, 371

Hearing, 31; impaired, 182-84

Help, 158; for aged parents, 191-98; from clergy, 44; during husband's affair with younger woman, 150; for ill husband, 158-59; from other women, 23

Herbs, 77

High school, for adults, 348-49

Home, sale of, 381-82

Homes for aged, 214

Hospitals, choosing, 50-52; 211; services for aged, 191, 212

Household worker, 280-83

Husbands, 361-62; depression in, 143-47; freedom resented by wife, 353-54; ill, 158-62; over 50, sex changes in, 128-32; retirement, planning for, 356-59; wife still working, 352-56; rigid, 355-56; terminally ill, 161-62; womanizing, 151-53; and younger women, 147-51

Hysterectomy, 8, 10-11

Impotence, 130, 133-36, 139

Information-and-Referral Service for the Aging, 274

Intercourse, painful, 8

Internist, 36-37

Intimacy, avoiding, 97-99

Investments, 363-64

Job, group health insurance through, 64-65; See also Career woman; Working.

Labor unions, 297

Late pregnancy, 8-9

Lay therapists, 43-44

Leisure, in retirement, 397-400

Living together, 113-14

Makeup, 81, 82; for job interview, 308-9

Marriage, changing, 127-63; good, 127-28; long-term, 162-63

Maturation Index Test, 5-6

Mature Temps, Inc., 272

Medicaid, 39, 55, 59-60, 68

Medical care, 35-69; for aged parent, 189; choice of man or woman doctor, 48-50

Medicare, 39, 55, 56-59, 68; not covered, 58; part A and part B, 57-58; plan to supplement, 62-64

Men, aging bodies, 111; married, affairs with, 99-101; multiple marriers, 106; older sperm of, 9. *See also* Husbands.

Menopause, 1-3, 41; effects, 3; symptoms, 4

Mental health, 42-47; directories, 47

Mobile homes, 384-87

Money, 239-43; making more, 291-97; saving, on drugs, 52-54

Mortgages, 364

Moving, after retirement, 387-90

National Health Insurance program, 54-56

National Organization of Women, 315

Operation Mainstream, 274

Orgasm, 142-43

Plastic surgery, 70-74

Psychiatrists, 42-43

Psychotherapy, 22, 23, 25, 27, 42-47, 189-90; choosing a therapist, 45-47

Relationships, 88-90; with bachelors, 106-8; being physically accessible, 90-91; with divorced man, 105-6; emotional accessibility, 96-99; ending, 108-10; intimacy, 96-99; with in-laws, 157-58; involvement, 88-90, 93-94, 95-96; with married man, 99-101; meeting

men, 90-93; out of the neighborhood, 93-94; with a younger man, 101-3
Remarriage, 103-4; different aspects of, 121-26; for widowers, 103-4
Résumés, 263-71
Rest homes, 214
Retina, separation of, 29
Retirement, 351-408; apartments for older people, 383-84; benefits of, 366-70; budget tips for, 371-74; income, 377-78; making last years best years, 407-8; making will, 365-66; mandatory, 406-7; money for, 362-65; mobile homes, 384-87; moving after, 379-81; new leisure time and, 397-99; preplanning for, 400; readiness for the unexpected, 396-97; retirement communities, 382; selling home, 381-82; relationships, with grandchildren, 390-92, with grown children, 392-95; *See also* Social Security.

Scholarships, for older woman, 344-46
Schools, 326-50; adult degree programs, 334-37; budgeting time for, 333-34; high school, 348-49; late bloomers, 329-34; realism about, 333; reasons for going back, 321-29; return to, 326-50; vocational and technical training, 346-48. *See also* College.
Senior Aides Program, 273-74
Senior centers, 194-96
Senior Community Aides Program, 274
Senior Companion Program, 277
Senses, 30-32
Sex, 41-42; changes in patterns, 130-32; differences in, 116-17; for over-50, 84-88; myths about, 132-33; organs, changes in, 138-39; pleasing yourself, 111-12; quality of, 110-13; changes after 50, 137-40; taking responsibility for, 114-15;

turn-ons, 140-43; where to make love, 112-13
Single woman, 117-18; money for retirement, 362-65
Singles bars and clubs, 91-93
Skin, changes in, 29-30; facial, 30
Small business from home, 283-86
Smoking, stopping, 26-27
Social Security, 55; checking an account, 368; benefits, 46, 366-70; direct mailing of checks, 369-70; reform needed, 368-69
Son-in-law, 157-58; ex-, 395-96
Supplementary Security Income, 370-71
Surgery, 41; plastic, 70-74

Testosterone replacement, 136-37
Teeth and dentures, 32. *See also* Dental care.
Travel-study programs, 95-96

Umbrella funding agencies, 299
Urinary infections, 11-12

Vaginal infections, 112-13
Vocational rehabilitation, 279
Vocational and technical training, 346-48
Volunteer work, 402-6; finding right kind, 403-4; government sponsored, 404-6

Weight, 32, 78, 81, 82
Widowers, 103-4
Widows over 50, 220-52; alone, in couple-oriented society, 247-48; and car, 237-39; changes in life-style, 226-27; coping with feelings, 220-22; dating, 245-46; eating habits, 227-28; finances, 239-43; grieving, 223; holidays, Saturdays, and Sundays, 233-34; identity, 224-26; living again, 250-52; loneliness, 230-34; loss of sex-relationship, 228-30; moving in with children, 234-36; new men in life, 243-46; relatives'

expectations, 248-50; Social Security benefits, 367-68

Wills, 365-66

Wives, understanding sex changes, 131

Woman over 50, alone, at retirement, 359-61; job counseling, 279-80; older and better, 32-34; reasons for working, 286-88; retired, with husband still working, 361-62; sex and, 84-88; sex changes in, 137-40; and younger men, 101-3. *See also* Single woman.

Working, for non-career woman, 253-90; contacting employers, 261-62; employment agencies, 271-72; employment especially for, 273-77; entering and reentering work world, 256-58; first day at work, 288-90; follow-up letter for interview, 270-77; job counseling, 279-80; job locations, 260-61; lists of strengths and talents for jobs, 258-60; programs for older workers, 277-78; realism about, 257-58; reasons for working, 286-88; résumés, 263-69; 286-88, covering letter for, 269-71; small businesses, 283-86; telling it as it is, 253-56; using contacts, 262; vocational rehabilitation, 279; volunteer work, 370; want ads, 262-63. *See also* Career woman.